Value-Based Management of the Rising Sun

Monden Institute of Management: Japanese Management and International Studies **(ISSN: 1793-2874)**

Editor-in-Chief: Yasuhiro Monden *(Meijiro University, Japan)*

Published

Vol. 1 Value-Based Management of the Rising Sun
edited by Yasuhiro Monden, Kanji Miyamoto, Kazuki Hamada, Gunyung Lee & Takayuki Asada

Monden Institute of Management
Japanese Management and International Studies – Vol. 1

Value-Based Management of the Rising Sun

editors

Yasuhiro Monden
Mejiro University, Japan

Kanji Miyamoto
Osaka Gakuin University, Japan

Kazuki Hamada
Seinan Gakuin University, Japan

Gunyung Lee
Niigata University, Japan

Takayuki Asada
Osaka University, Japan

World Scientific

NEW JERSEY • LONDON • SINGAPORE • BEIJING • SHANGHAI • HONG KONG • TAIPEI • CHENNAI

Published by

World Scientific Publishing Co. Pte. Ltd.
5 Toh Tuck Link, Singapore 596224
USA office: 27 Warren Street, Suite 401-402, Hackensack, NJ 07601
UK office: 57 Shelton Street, Covent Garden, London WC2H 9HE

Library of Congress Cataloging-in-Publication Data
Value-based management of the Rising Sun / edited by Yasuhiro Monden ... [et al.]
p. cm. -- (Monden Institute of Management : Japanese management and international studies, ISSN 1793-2874 ; vol. 1)
Includes bibliographical references and index.
ISBN 981-256-683-X
1. Industrial management--Japan. 2. Corporations--Japan. 3. Cost control. 4. Value.
I. Monden, Yasuhiro, 1940– II. Monden Institute of Management (Series) ; vol. 1

HD70.J3V34 2006
658.15'52--dc22

2006040500

British Library Cataloguing-in-Publication Data
A catalogue record for this book is available from the British Library.

Typeset by Stallion Press
Email: enquiries@stallionpress.com

Printed by FuIsland Offset Printing (S) Pte Ltd, Singapore

Monden Institute of Management

Mission of the Institute and Editorial Information

For the purpose of making a contribution to the business and academic communities, Monden Institute of Management is committed to publishing this book series, a kind of book-length journal with a referee system, worldwide and continuously.

Focusing on Japan and Japan-related issues, the series is designed to inform the world about research outcomes of the new "Japanese-style management system" developed in Japan. It also includes the Japanese version of management systems developed abroad. In addition, it publishes research by foreign scholars and concerning foreign systems that constitute significant points of comparison with the Japanese system.

Research topics included in this series are management of organization in a broad sense (including the business group) and the accounting that supports the organization. More specifically, topics include business strategy, organizational restructuring, corporate finance, M&A, environmental management, business models, operations management, managerial accounting, financial accounting for organizational restructuring, manager performance evaluation, remuneration systems, and management of revenues and costs.

The research approach is interdisciplinary, which includes case studies, theoretical studies, normative studies and empirical studies.

Each volume will contain the series title and a book title which reflect the special theme of each volume.

An editorial board of international standing is being established by the board of directors of the Institute. In each volume, guest editors who are experts in the volume's special theme will serve as the volume editors.

Preface

Japanese companies have struggled for revival for more than ten years, in the aftermath of the stock and land price bubble burst of 1991. Under this long-term, severe recession, Japanese firms have made every effort to recover, and are now just beginning to revive. Their aim is to materialize the *Japanese concept of business value*, to restructure their businesses, redesign their organizations and construct new business models.

In this book, we compiled *cases and theories that support these innovations and reforms*, in the hope that they may be of some benefit to those companies who wish to revive their businesses.

The overall structure of our book is as depicted in the following scheme:

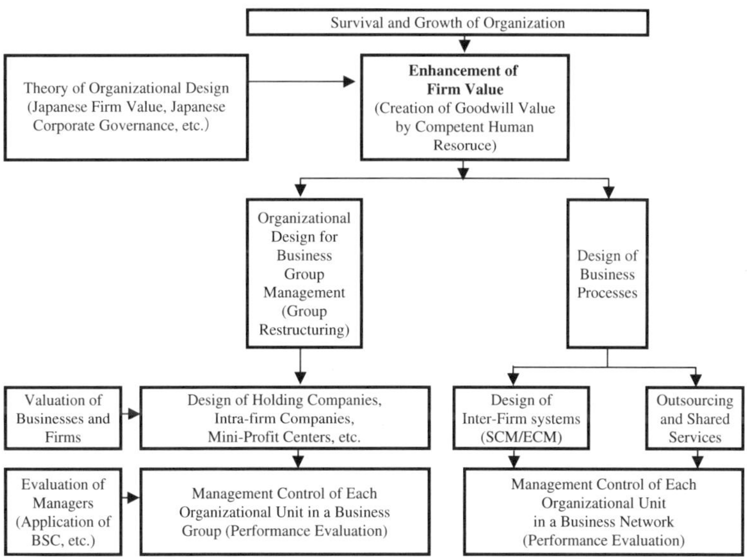

Scheme of Firm Value and Organizational Design

First, we focus on how business and organizational restructuring should be carried out to improve the value of a business group or an individual firm; we also discuss *how managers should be evaluated* in restructured organizations.

Japanese companies may adopt a system of corporate governance through stockholder power, since it is the stockholders who ultimately drive business or organizational restructuring, but the created value added is the "goodwill" (or corporate brand) of the company, which originates in the efforts of competent human resources and in customer relationships formed over a long period of time. This means that the company value is actually created by the employees, customers and all other stakeholders, and thus the company must be a tool for use by all stakeholders.

Therefore, under the *Japanese corporate governance* system, top management seeks to implement not only management for the sake of the stockholders, but also *management in view of sustaining the company itself*, thus achieving positive extra-return or residual earnings. This extra-return should later be allocated to all stakeholders and not merely to the stockholders.

Because the goodwill or corporate brand of a firm is created by the human resources or core competence (based on human capabilities and assets) of the firm, as mentioned above, top management should select those businesses which evince such core competence, and should reorganize those businesses through integration or division to increase their value. Otherwise, top management ends up merely reshuffling these businesses among various organizational units or abolishing some of them altogether. Furthermore, it is possible to carry out a mega-merger that goes beyond the group of consolidated firms in question and covers industry-level restructuring by establishing a *holding company*. Uniquely Japanese systems, such as the *global company*, the *intra-firm company*, the *division using a balance sheet* and the *mini-profit center*, are also discussed in this book.

Such organizational reforms can be supported by various accounting procedures and financing techniques.

In order to enhance the profitability and business value of the business group as a whole, *efficient ways of handling business operations and processes* must be introduced in addition to the selection of prospective business. In other words, it may improve the value of the group if each of the companies specifies its core business and makes an alliance with the other companies to form a better *supply chain*, rather than the group vertically integrating and merging all functions of the business. Also, cases of *shared services and outsourcing* are introduced and discussed in this book.

Finally, the editors include some of Japan's unique ideas on financial and managerial accounting theories in Part 5, which may be of some comparative reference to other countries.

Thus, this book is composed of the following five parts:

Part 1. Theories of Organizational Design — Corporate Value and Organizational Boundaries
Part 2. Planning and Control of Business Strategy — Valuation of Firms and Evaluation of Managers
Part 3. Design and Control of Decentralized Business Units in the Business Group: — Holding Company, Intra-Firm Company, Division, Mini-Profit Center and Global Company
Part 4. Design and Control of Business Processes — Process Reengineering, Supply Chain, Shared Services and Outsourcing
Part 5. Basic Theory on the Nature of Accounting for Organization Management

This book will not try to include any paper that merely introduces or summarizes American models and standards or their techniques, as seen in most American college textbooks; rather it comprises original Japanese ideas, as follows. Actually, the "Rising Sun" in the book title is a literal translation of "Japan."

1. Most chapters describe some *characteristics typical of Japanese firms.*
2. The book includes *concepts or techniques originally developed in Japan.*
3. The book describes *unique ways in which methods developed in the US have been applied at Japanese firms.*
4. The book discusses systems developed in countries other than Japan, but they will provide a backdrop for comparisons with the Japanese system.

The editors are very grateful to Ms. Juliet Lee Ley Chin, Social Sciences commissioning editor of the World Scientific Publishing Company for her various invaluable efforts to make our book contract a reality. Further, Ms. Chean Chian Cheong, the book editor, is also much appreciated for her handling of our manuscripts. Finally, the co-editors and contributors of this book will be amply rewarded if it contributes new ideas or knowledge to the literature on business management and managerial accounting, thereby being of some use to people around the world.

This book is the inaugural issue of the book series, *Japanese Management and International Studies* published by the Monden Institute of Management (http://mondeninst.hp.infoseek.co.jp/). The editors of this book are committed to publishing a good series continuously.

Editor-in-Chief
Yasuhiro Monden
17 April 2006

Contents

Part 5 Basic Theory on the Nature of Accounting for Organization Management

PART 1

THEORIES OF ORGANIZATIONAL DESIGN: CORPORATE VALUE AND ORGANIZATIONAL BOUNDARIES

CHAPTER

1

Business Value, Human Assets and Organizational Restructuring

Yasuhiro Monden

Professor, Faculty of Business Administration, Mejiro University

1.1 Introduction

Japanese companies have struggled for more than ten years since the bubble burst in the early 1990s, but now the rebirth of Japanese firms is underway through both business and organizational restructuring. This chapter will present a comprehensive theory of business performance improvement through organizational restructuring. The author will focus on how human resources or assets improve the business value of a company and how organizational restructuring should be carried out with a focus on human assets or core competence.

1.2 Business Value and Corporate Governance

1.2.1 *Shareholder value and human assets*

1.2.1.1 *Management based on shareholder value*

The value of the firm for the shareholders can be defined as having two aspects. The first aspect is the *total shareholder value* or the total number of stocks times the current stock price. The second is the *book value of the owner's capital* + the *market value added* (MVA), or the market value of the owner's capital; the MVA is the sum of the present value of each year's expected amount of future extra-return or the residual earnings that the company is expected to yield over an infinite long period of years.

Now, according to Ohlson's model (Ohlson, 1995), the extra-return stands for the accounting net profit minus the owner's capital costs. The summation of the expected extra-return for each year discounted by the owner's capital cost rate is the *accounting goodwill* or *corporate brand*.

The sum of the present value of the future estimated free cash flow is equivalent to the total shareholder value of a company composed of only the owner's capital. This thesis has been theoretically proven by Miller and Modigliani (1961). However, the total shareholder value is equal to the *book value of the owner's capital* + the *market value added*. In other words, for infinite long-term future periods, the difference between the extra-return and the free cash flow, under the assumption that the "clean surplus condition" (i.e., no additional net investment) is satisfied, is merely the difference in the recognition timing of revenue and expense, and thus the difference between the two methods has nothing to do with the shareholder value.

Therefore, the thesis that *the management style which improves the extra-return or the residual earnings will also improve the total shareholder value* can be derived from both Olson's model and the theory of Miller and Modigliani. From this viewpoint, it is often said that management based on shareholder value (value-based management) will improve the stock price and thus the shareholders' interest (i.e., the dividend and capital gain).

1.2.1.2 *Human assets as goodwill or corporate brand*

Now, since the value of a firm, as the total amount of the investments of all investors, equals the total amount of the current shareholder value + the total amount of the current creditor value, it follows that the value of the firm equals the book value of the owner's capital and the creditor's capital + the market value added, or, to use another expression, the value of the firm equals the book value of the total capital invested + the market value added.

This market value added is *accounting goodwill*, as stated above. While the book value of the total capital invested is composed of the "tangible" assets on the balance sheet, the goodwill is an "intangible" asset that does not appear on the balance sheet of the book value. In order to increase the value of goodwill, it is necessary to conduct business activities which boost residual earnings or extra-return. The causal factors that create goodwill are as follows (Nomura, 2000, pp. 15–18):

A: External causal factors: brand, company image, relationship between customer and supplier.

B: Internal causal factors: manuals, information systems, concepts, and value systems.
C: Causal factors pertaining to individuals: competence, know-how acquired through experience.

All of these factors are collectively called *human assets or intellectual assets*, and it is important to take good care of them, and implicitly of the employees embodying these assets, if the aim is to enhance shareholder value.

1.2.2 *Balance between human-asset-based management and shareholder-value-based management*

As stated above, the market value added is the value created by human intellectual assets existing within a firm. It is not an *individually identifiable* intangible asset like a patent of some engineering technology; rather, it is a value created by the *capability* owned by the company, and it is the fruit of the *core competence* of the firm.

If a capital market behaves efficiently, the value of the intellectual assets of a firm will be properly reflected in the stock price. (However, since speculative factors enter the capital market and the stock price is constantly changing, the value of a firm's intellectual value cannot be correctly grasped by the stock price in practice.) Thus, theoretically, when the management of a company does its job excellently and continues to ensure extra-returns every year, the stock price will eventually increase and the shareholders' income in the form of dividends and capital gains will be enhanced. It is very important to understand this causal relationship, because it should not be reversed; i.e., actions which are intended to increase the stock price itself, such as IR (investor relations) activities, should not be regarded as the primal objective.

In other words, the primal mission of management must be to improve the company's ability to offer goods or services of better quality to the customers, rather than to simply increase the stock price. *This mission-based management fosters and utilizes* <u>*human capital*</u>; *it is management based on* <u>*employee value*</u>. To put it another way, *in order to enhance the stockholder value, management must keep in mind that the employee value is a means of enhancing or constraining the stockholder value.* However, this does not necessarily require management to be nice or generous to the employee. The employee should be motivated by management to establish a higher professional standard, and to find it pleasurable to reach and maintain that standard. Also, each employee should seek to enhance his or her own competence or skill, so as to survive in the labor market.

1.2.3 Relationship between value-based management and corporate governance

Although the stockholders are given certain powers of corporate governance, this does not imply that their rights will have the highest priority among the rights of all stakeholders. The stockholders can demand to cover their minimum necessary rate of investment as cost of capital, and the management of a company can accept such a demand as a driver of corporate governance leading to the earning of a positive residual income.

However, top management must consider the survival and development of *the company itself* as its supreme goal, in order to achieve not only the shareholders' goal but also the goals of many other stakeholders simultaneously. The reason is that the top management represents the company as a *legal person* who must serve society as a whole rather than the stockholders only. This, in my opinion, is one of the important features of the Japanese company. In other words, a company is a social instrument to be *utilized* by all stakeholders for achieving their individual ends.

During economic depressions, the actual residual earnings might be smaller than the targeted residual earnings. Even in such situations, the allocated amount of the *value added* (note: the value added in this context is different from that in Section 1, and is composed of the net profit, wages, capital cost, etc.) must be reduced fairly for all stakeholders. According to the Japanese model, it is regarded as *unfair* if every portion of the value added allocated to each stakeholder *other than stockholder* is reduced so that the targeted amount of residual earnings can be realized for the stockholder's dividend payment. Rather, shareholders should undertake their stockholder's responsibility by accepting the consequences of governance failure, in the form of dividend cuts or the offsetting of the owner's capital with the accumulated loss.

However, it could be objected that this principle of *fair allocation* is impossible to uphold in practice, because the CEO (chief executive officer) will be fired by the stockholders in the general stockholder meeting if he or she is unable to achieve the target residual profit for the shareholders. Only the stockholders have a solid legal right to expel the CEO from his or her position. Nevertheless, such inappropriate enforcement of the stockholder's right should be prevented by a logical and persuasive explanation of top management strategy, namely that a reduction in the employees' salaries, retirement pensions, annuities, etc. may temporally lead to the achievement of the target profit, thus boosting the stock price, but the stock price will eventually fall due to the discouragement and low morale of the employees.

Thus, top management must concentrate on ensuring *positive* residual earnings by creating *additional* value added rather than by changing the allocation ratio of the value added among various stakeholders. If this is done, the stockholder value will increase steadily over a long period of time.

It should be emphasized that a business organization will not survive unless each stakeholder's interest is satisfied. A similar idea is expressed in Chester Bernard's *organizational equilibrium theory* (Bernard, 1938). According to Bernard, when each participant's contribution to the organization (stakeholder or member) is rewarded in the form of a side payment or incentive offered by the organization simultaneously to all participants, then the organization itself will survive. This equilibrium between contribution and side payment is called the "*efficient* condition." On the other hand, when the official goal or policy of the organization, be it a profit goal, ROE or total sales goal, is materialized through good management planning and control, then the organization is said to be under the "*effective* condition." Where there is *efficiency*, *effectiveness* is also present because of the enhanced morale of the organization members, and vice versa. My thesis, applied to Bernard's theory, is as follows: the activities which produce *effectiveness* are mainly intended to boost shareholder value; this goal is historically thought of as one of the important policy goals of *current* business enterprise, and is established through negotiations or fights among various parties (stakeholders).

The activities directed toward the attainment of the employees' personal goals are efforts to cultivate and manage human assets with care. This can be partially achieved through legal rules which guard various stakeholders' rights, just as the stockholder's interest is guarded by the corporate law of corporate governance. When the CEO tries to maximize the stockholder value using many constraints and severe requirements, then the CEO's capacity to create additional value added will be severely hampered and his managerial efforts will inevitably face more challenges. Thus, Japanese management operates in a severer environment than in any other around the world.

1.3 Strategy for Selecting the Core Competence When Restructuring an Organization

1.3.1 *The concept of "core competence"*

The expression "core competence" was first proposed by Prahalad and Hamel (1990), and is utilized as a basic conceptual tool for *business selection*, which is the reverse of *business diversification*. This concept seems to be useful as a link between the concept of human assets and that of organizational restructuring.

A core competence is a business *capability* that will contribute to the future development of new products and services, thereby boosting the competitiveness of the company on the market. This capability is a causal resource which produces company profit. Here are some examples of core competence:

1. The ability to create a value that can be accepted by a customer.
2. The ability to create a competitive organization.
3. The ability to enter new field, market or product line, etc.

Further, in order to generate a core competence, the company should have a main customer from whom it can derive a profit, as well as excellent strategic resources such as technology, patents, brands and a governing position in a business network.

In other words, the core competence is *the capacity of a company to infuse novelty into the market*; this is similar to the famous concepts of Schumpeter, "innovation" or "creative disruption," both of which are created by the entrepreneur. This strategic business resource or innovation capacity is equivalent to the human assets or intellectual assets discussed in the previous section. *A business that has a core competence or excellent human asset is called a "core business."*

1.3.2 *Selection of a core business*

There are three directions which diversification and divestiture can take, based on the concept of core competence:

1. A diversified company can create additional value that attracts investors when *synergy* is realized as a consequence of the integration of plural businesses in the same group. Such synergy will not appear unless each business in the group has some core competence. For instance, suppose

a company is manufacturing a copy printer. This company could reduce the manufacturing cost of the printer drastically if it can *acquire* a highly automated assembly plant for manufacturing printer cartridges. In this case, it should go ahead with M&A (merger and acquisition) to take over an automated printer-cartridge manufacturing business. Synergy may accrue not only between businesses of different kinds but also between businesses of the same kind. Thus, the same kind of business may be acquired through M&A from the market, in order to maximize the scale merit.
2. If no synergy occurs between the diverse businesses of a group, the CEO of that group may decide to extract the core business from the group and make a separate public offering for that core business on the stock market. This is a divestiture decision.
3. Rather than creating a *vertically integrated* company, the CEO may set up each business unit as an independent company, so that the companies can participate in the supply chain more effectively, mutually providing their core competence functions as part of the same chain.

1.4 Contingency Theory for the Selection of Diversification and Specialization Strategies

There are many Japanese companies that diversify their businesses, but business valuation is carried out with the aim of selecting a "good" business and then concentrating on that business. However, business group management in consolidated companies is much more popular in Japan than divestiture strategies, and the design of organizational structures under diversification is much more discussed than that under divestiture. It seems to me that either a diversification strategy or a specialization strategy must be adopted, contingent on the business environment.

1.4.1 *Various organizational structures*

When redesigning the organizational structure of a company through diversification, there are several organizational forms to choose from:

1. *Multi-divisional organization.*
2. An *intra-company*, which is not a legal entity but is a *big* division in a legal company and comprises several *smaller* business divisions.

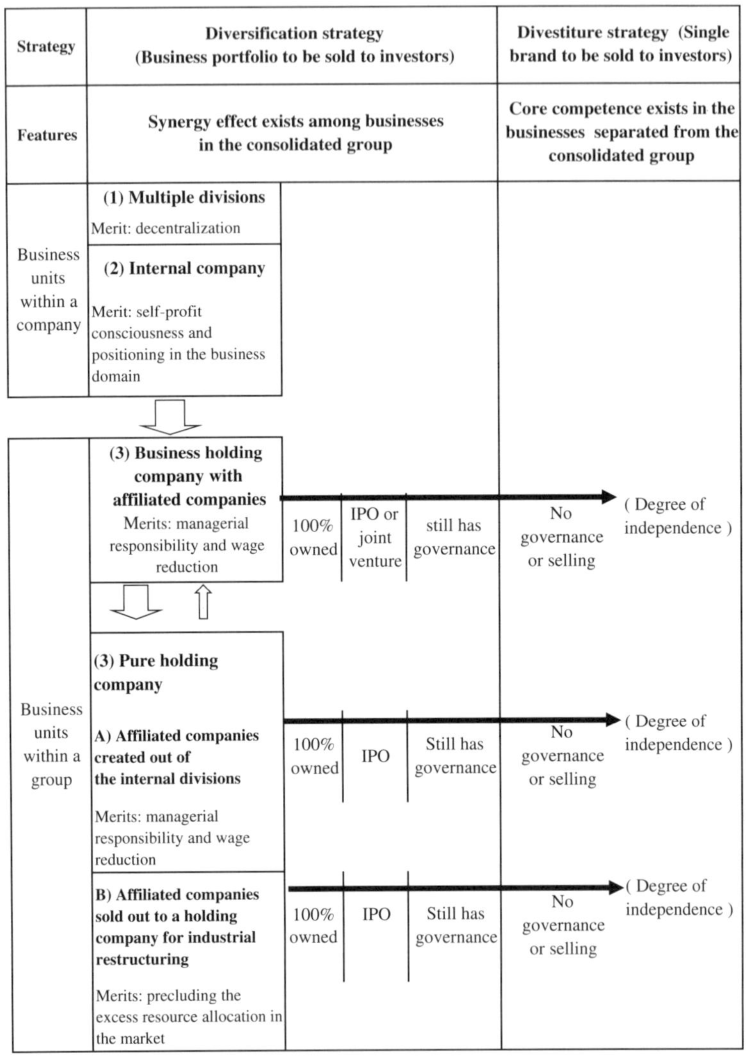

Fig. 1.1 Diversification strategy and separation strategy

3. A *business holding company*, which conducts some business activities.
4. A *pure holding company*, which conducts no business activities but is only holding the stocks of the subsidiary companies.

It is important to discuss the differences between these various organizational forms. Figure 1.1 provides a summary of my ideas on this problem.

1.4.2 *Selection of business consolidation and business divestiture strategies*

My opinion on the strategy selection problem is very simple, as summarized below:

1. A strategy of diversification through consolidation requires that the following conditions be met:
   First, some *synergy* must exist between several businesses in the same group. Second, an overlap of the same kind of business units must exist within the group, and they must be reshuffled by the CEO of the group so that only one business unit remains in its own business domain; the business units must be integrated and the structure made as *slim* as possible.

   Although in the US diversification might not be as popular as divestiture at this moment, the obvious merit of diversification is that if a business unit will be better off or will derive *some additional income* when it enters a *coalition* with some other business unit, then group management based on diversification makes sense. This is the case in which the "*core condition*" of the *theory of cooperative games* is satisfied.
2. A divestiture strategy requires that the following conditions be met:
   First, suppose that there is some ill-performing or *non-core-competent* business which has no synergy with any well-performing business. That business should be split off or spun off, or even sold. Second, even if the business in question is a *core-competent* one, the top management might decide to separate it from the existing company anyway, in order to make sure that its business value is valuated *fairly* on the stock market.

1.4.2.1 *Economic difference among various types of organizational units in a group*

In adopting a diversification strategy, there are many companies which split off their internal businesses, making them subsidiary companies. Then, from the viewpoint of the business group as a whole, what is the economic difference between subsidiary companies and internal divisions or intra-companies? It is my opinion that there is essentially no difference between subsidiary companies and intra-divisions or intra-companies, because all of these business units can be included in a consolidated business group and the top management of the central company must manage these various types of units *equally*, to enhance the value of the consolidated business group as a whole, even though each of the business units is located either within or outside the parent company.

Then why does a company *actually* split off or spin off its internal businesses in the form of subsidiary companies or as more independent companies on the stock market? In the case of Japanese companies, the merits of splitting a large company into several subsidiaries may be summarized as follows:

1. The responsibility of the manager will be clearer: Unlike internal divisions or intra-companies a subsidiary company has the legal obligation to report and pay taxes. When the financial performance of the subsidiary company worsens, it will immediately go bankrupt. The top manager of a subsidiary company holds the legal responsibility for contracts, suits and compliance to laws. From this judicial viewpoint, the manager of a subsidiary company will be much more motivated to perform well than any internal-division or intra-company manager.
2. Reductions in labor cost will be more feasible: Establishing a *smaller* company in a local district where many people can be hired would reduce the labor cost. Further, if a plant is established as a subsidiary company locally or in a developing country, it can employ much young labor. These are the merits in terms of geographical location.
3. M&A and divestiture will be much easier: Some of the businesses of a company are easier to fuse with those of another company if the partial businesses in question are spun off. Also, withdrawal of some business from a certain business domain would be much easier, because it can be done by merely selling the stock of the subsidiary company in question.

1.4.3 *Solving the conflict of interest between the business group and the affiliated companies*

In US and European companies, it seems that when a company splits off an excellent business unit as an affiliated company, it often has the affiliated company issue IPO (initial public offering) stocks, to make it more independent in the market, and the shareholders can valuate the performance of the business unit in question directly on the stock market because, as a legally independent entity, it must disclose its financial statements, thus precluding any *information asymmetry* between the company and the shareholders. As a result, the stock price can receive a fairly large boost.

However, when this policy is considered from the viewpoint of the consolidated business strategy of the business group as a whole, the policy often entails a *conflict of interest* between the parent company of the consolidated group and the minor stockholders of the affiliated company (i.e., the stockholders which do not own stocks of the parent company); let us call the affiliated company "Company A." This is a conflict between total optimization and sub-optimization. In other words, the problem is the lack of *goal congruence* within the group.

For example, the CEO of the whole group may think that the group profit would improve if he or she would shrink Company A's business, shifting a part of its business and its resources to another company belonging to the same business group. But if such reshuffling were to be implemented, Company A's profit may decrease as well as its stock price, and the business value of Company A would be reduced. This is a conflict of interest between the parent company (the group in this case) and the affiliated company.

On the other hand, if Company A were to be transformed into a subsidiary company *owned 100%* by the parent company through a stock exchange, then the minor stockholders of Company A would be the new additional shareholders of the parent company, and thus the formerly minor shareholders' interest would coincide with that of the group as a whole, and goal congruence would be achieved. Therefore, the *complete* (100%) holding of a subsidiary company's stock is very popular in Japanese companies which seek to restructure their businesses.

1.4.4 *Two steps in the process of business group restructuring*

The process of business group restructuring, which brings about an organizational change in the consolidated business group, proceeds *first* by the establishment of 100% ownership of the subsidiary companies; this entails the halting of the public offering of the subsidiary company; *second,* it reshuffles various businesses between the parent company and the subsidiary companies, so that each business can be transferred to its own business-domain company. This second stage, i.e., business reshuffling, is carried out through company split-off or divestiture.

1.5 Patterns of Organizational Restructuring from the Viewpoint of the Business Group

Let us now consider the patterns of various organizational restructuring processes from the viewpoint of group management. There are four fundamental types of restructuring patterns, and they are combinations of two criteria: (1) whether the restructuring is conducted inside or outside a certain consolidated group; and (2) whether it is conducted on the divisional level or the group level. The four patterns are as follows (this classification is partly based on Konuma (2002)):

Pattern 1: Organizational redesign on the *divisional level outside the consolidated group*.
Pattern 2: Organizational redesign on the *group level outside the consolidated group*.
Pattern 3: Organizational redesign on the *divisional level inside the consolidated group*.
Pattern 4: Organizational redesign on the *group level inside the consolidated group*.

Pattern 1 is further divided into the following two sub-types:

1-1. Integration type: joint venture, M&A on each business unit level, and new business investment
1-2. Divestiture type: subsidiary company, spin-off and business sales

Pattern 2 implements industry-level restructuring by merging large companies or by establishing a pure holding company.

Pattern 3 is further divided into the following two sub-types:

3-1. Business restructuring in an intra-company or subsidiary company.
3-2. Business reshuffling among various subsidiary companies, or between an intra-company and a subsidiary company.

Pattern 4 represents a transition to a pure holding company within the consolidated business group.

The most value-boosting restructuring patterns are Patterns 1 and 2. The other two restructuring patterns, especially Pattern 3, are often confined to the reshuffling of existing organizational units to avoid overlapping businesses within the group. Such reshuffling may contribute to the streamlining of the company through BPR (business process restructuring), but, unless they withdraw from non-profitable businesses, the business value of the group as a whole will not increase because the limited funds and human resources are still poured into ill-performing businesses. In Japan, Pattern 4 is increasingly implemented these days; mega-mergers of large companies through the establishment of pure holding companies reduce the total number of firms in the industry. These mega-mergers are seen especially in banking, raw materials, etc.

Further, *business process innovation* through the creation of an effective supply chain is another method of organizational restructuring. There are two forms: (1) internal BPR (business process restructuring) within an individual company; and (2) inter-company BPR. The reader should note that value creation can be achieved not only by selecting a good business, but also through an effective *operations management* of the businesses.

1.6 Conclusion and Summary

First, the purpose of organizational and business restructuring is to enhance the value of the company. Restructuring means redesigning the company in order to boost the value of the consolidated group as a whole, to which various business units belong. A major portion of the corporate value is the stockholder value, which is equivalent to the total number of stocks times the current stock price of the company. When this amount exceeds the book value of the owner's capital, the company is said to have created *goodwill.*

Shareholder-value-based management is aimed at enhancing the current stock price, but this must be achieved through human-resource-based management, because human assets or intangible assets are an important constituent of the shareholder value.

Corporate governance proceeds on two levels. First, the stockholders of a company exert corporate governance over the top management of that company, because the top management is appointed and expelled by the stockholders. Second, the top management then motivates the employees to adopt a positive and pleasant attitude to their work in order to ensure the generation of profit. The top management should also persuade the shareholders to think of the long-term maximization of profit rather than the short-term, because the ultimate purpose of the shareholders is *stable* profit maximization. Top management members should strive to ensure the company's survival and long-term growth, since they represent the company (as legal person), and must do so as loyally as possible.

Further, since the origin of goodwill is the human resources which constitute the specific business capability or core competence of a company, the top management should select a *good* business based on the existent core competence, and should proceed to business integration (or diversification) and divestiture. This paper has shown how such organizational restructuring should be conducted.

References

Bernard, C. I. (1938). *The Functions of the Executive*, Harvard University Press.

Konuma, Y. (2002). *Group Restructuring of Japanese Companies*, Diamond Pub. Co. (in Japanese)

Miller, M. and Modigliani, F. (1961). Dividend policy, growth, and the valuation of shares, *Journal of Business* 34-4, 411–433.

Nomura, K. (2000). *Consolidated Business Management and Restructuring*, Zeimukeiri-kyokai. (in Japanese)

Ohlson, J. A. (1995). Earnings, book values, and dividends in equity valuation, *Contemporary Accounting Research* 11-2, pp. 661–687.

Prahalad, C. K. and Hamel, G. (1990). The core competence of the corporation, *Harvard Business Review* 68-3, pp. 79–93.

Special Committee of Japan Accounting Association, chaired by Y. Monden (2004). *Research on Managerial Accounting for Business Value and Organizational Restructuring: Final Report*, Japan Accounting Association. (in Japanese)

CHAPTER

2

Organizational Boundaries and Firm Value: Japanese-Specific Management and Concepts

Noboru Harada

Professor, School of Management, Tokyo University of Science

2.1 Introduction

Managerial accounting is expected to play a new role in the presentation of information useful in facilitating strategic decision on the *boundaries of a firm*. In a complete and competitive market, a firm must correspond to its *product marketing positions* in industry structure and external environment. This view plays a central part in determining strategic activities in a limited sense. This is called "*equilibrium-based perspective*." But in an imperfect and competitive market, because a firm can have influence on its behavior and performance through *strategy* as a reflection of *manager's consciousness*, an effective strategy may add value to the firm.

The term boundaries here imply a field analogous to field of gravity or electromagnet in physics, meaning the *organization* as the cooperative system in which manager can consciously coordinate activities or forces, extended in a broader spatial and time-horizontal perspective. As a result, the object of managerial accounting has extended far beyond the formal and informal organization, including *interfirm organizations*.

Coase (1937) first advocated the notion of *transaction costs* to offer an explanation for *the existence and the boundaries of a firm* in the field of neoclassic economics. A multiagent game in its extension views firms as players, and focuses on competitive interactions between players through the market or mechanism for collective choice rather than particular plays and outcomes of individual players (Shapiro, 1989). This view has disregarded most aspects of strategy, and has not considered the strategic activities and performance in individual firms or the *evolution of dynamic capabilities* fueled by *organizational learning* and *innovation.*

The purposes of this chapter are to gain an economic insight into the activities and performance in individual firms under the restructuring of an organization as a coordination of specialized individuals, to analyze the mechanism to create dynamic capabilities for achieving a *sustainable competitive advantage*, and to find the *criteria of economies* on which it is useful for firms to decide their own boundaries. Finally, because the ways of deployment of capabilities and adoption of criteria differ among firms, they can drive Japanese-specific management and accounting, distinguishing them from those seen in Western firms.

2.2 Organizational Boundaries of a Firm

The emphasis on the boundaries of a firm has gradually shifted the sources of a sustainable competitive advantage from the traditional *transaction-cost perspective* to a *resource-based view.* Then strategy would have potential for affecting the boundaries of the firm.

2.2.1 *Existence and boundaries of a firm*

Holmstrom and Tirole (1989, p. 65) have posed criteria that should be satisfied for *the existence and the boundaries of the firm* as Coase (1937) suggested. They can improve so-called "*allocative efficiency*" through the allocation of resources for their better use in the market.

2.2.1.1 *Coase's theorem in transaction-cost perspective*

Coase (1937) and Langlois *et al.* (1995) defined differential costs ΔC to explain the existence of a firm as follows:

$$\Delta C = C_P - C_M, \tag{2.1}$$

where C_P is the production costs per unit of organized transaction, and C_M is the transaction costs per unit acquired in the market.

Let's array the activities in order of increasing costs of organized activities. If $\Delta C < 0$, the firm has a cost advantage to organized activities and will acquire dissimilar activities until $\Delta C = 0$. Activities in this range are within the *boundaries of a firm.* The rest is attributed to the *market.*

2.2.1.2 Sophisticated transaction-cost model

Williamson (1975, 1985) and Klein *et al.* (1978) enriched transaction costs economics by introducing the following new concepts:

1. Incomplete contracts under uncertainty: These imply that the collaboration of parties with *bounded rationality* that limits human capabilities in the formulation and solution of complex problems cannot specify a complete and conditional *ex ante* contract in detail about the distribution of common income under every condition that may arise in the future. If the unexpected and unstipulated events occur, their relative bargaining power determines this distribution.
2. Asset specificity: This implies that *firm-specific assets* bring higher value in use at intrafirm than on a spot market, but may cause *hold-up problem*, in that either party has incentive to hold back from the investment with inefficiency. The high possibility of *ex post* contractual hold-up determines *ex ante* investment decisions.
3. Sophisticated transaction-cost model: Williamson (1975) developed a transaction-cost model that extended transaction costs from traditional *ex ante* costs to *ex post* costs, such as opportunity costs and hidden costs.

Let's define *transaction costs* as a function of *uncertainty* u, the *frequency of transaction* q, and *asset specificity* s. And let's assume that $TC[u,\ q,\ s|a_1]$ is linear and monotone increasing, given the internally organized transaction $a_1 \in A$, and $TC[u,\ q,\ s|a_2]$ is convex and monotone increasing, given market used transaction $a_2 \in A$. The internal transaction $a_1 \in A$ is more efficient, as either u, q, or s increases. If $TC[u,\ q,\ s|a_1] < TC[u,\ q,\ a|a_2]$, the internal transaction with lock-in effect may save transaction costs, mitigate *opportunistic and selfish behavior*, and improve investment incentives rather than market transaction through outsourcing. Then *long-term contracting* is more desirable to firms than spot market.

2.2.2 Limits of organizational boundaries of a firm

Organizational boundaries can be given an explanation by the following *principles of economies* that are applied consciously to management. But these principles function well to some extent, but give rise to limits.

1. Economies of scale: These mean that the larger production quantities of a single kind of product are, the more reduction in average cost is

achieved through the centralized and specialized production or *common pool resources*. Thus the optimal firm size is determined by minimum average costs. But in an imperfect and competitive market, when the cost function $C(q)$ or revenue function $R(q)$ is nonlinear, quantity q^* that satisfies this equality $d/dqR(q) = d/dqC(q)$ maximizes income. The optimal size of boundaries of the firm may exist there.

2. Economies of speed: These create value for the firm by increasing *turnover of capital* in a given period, that is, shortening of business processes or lead time through a value chain, supply chain, and just-in-time system. Income π_t in period $(t-1,\ t)$ is defined as the integral of income function $\pi(t)$ as follows:

$$\pi_t = \int_{t-1}^{t} \pi(t)\, dt. \tag{2.2}$$

Ijiri (1990) called $\frac{d}{dt}\pi(t)$ "*momentum*" analogous to velocity in physics.

3. Economies of scope: Teece (1980), Panzar and Willig (1981), Hallwood (1994) gave an explanation for the *economies of scope* by cost savings resulting from producing several kinds of products in one firm rather than respective firms. Let $T = \{T_1, \ldots, T_l\}$ denotes partition of $S \subseteq N$, and $Y = \{y_1, \ldots, y_n\}$ is the vector of quantities. Here, $\cup_i T_i = S$, $T_i \cap T_j = \phi$ for $i \neq j$, $T \neq \phi$ and $l > 1$. $C(y_S,\ \omega)$ denotes the *multiproduct cost function* for producing only the products in the subset $S \subseteq N$ at Y and prices ω. $C(y_{T_i}, \omega)$ is the *individual production cost* of product i. There are *economies of scope* if the following inequality is satisfied:

$$\sum_{i=1}^{l} C(y_{T_i}, \omega) > C(y_S, \omega). \tag{2.3}$$

4. Economies of combination: These yield benefits for individual firms if interfirms construct *competitive and cooperative system* through supply chain, alliance and collaboration, etc. While each firm retains autonomy, it can gain a share of income earned by an interfirm organization. But this weak and loose linkage will be dissolved, if one firm selects opportunistic and selfish action. Commodities as *trust*, reputation or *commitment* have to be set in order for this linkage to work well.

2.3 Strategy and Organizational Boundaries of a Firm

Positive research found that the variance of return in intraindustry is larger than that in interindustry, and strongly suggests the relative importance of *firm-specific internal factors* in comparison with effects in industry and external factors (Rumelt, 1991; Grant, 1991, 1996).

2.3.1 *Strategy and uncertainty*

The insights of necessity and its conscious application to management have profound implications for the *creative formation* of a firm's strategy. The *strategy* plays a role to cope with the inherent *uncertainty* and to focus on economic rents as sources of a sustainable competitive advantage.

These uncertainties comprise *systematic* and *unsystematic* ones. The former stimulates manager's judgments for coping with an unknown future. The latter relates to market imperfection, including *bounded rationality* and the *opportunism* that implies the manipulation and concealment or distortion of information. While strategy is possible to cope with *unsystematic uncertainties* and to mitigate their effects, it is difficult to eliminate *systematic uncertainties* (Langlois *et al.*, 1995, p. 18).

In an imperfect and competitive market, each firm can influence its activities and performance through strategy adopted. Strategy focuses not on products and markets but on business processes. The capabilities in key processes may constitute a sustainable competitive advantage.

2.3.2 *Strategy and organizational boundaries of a firm*

Strategy is the most important variable that creates *economic rents*, and affects the boundaries of a firm. The formation and implementation of creative strategy require that a firm matches its existing capabilities with those that manager perceives necessary for the future. Manager must coordinate and learn capabilities. This is called "*adaptive efficiency.*"

If the firm generates them internally or acquires them through the market or seeks to exploit existing knowledge, it can improve its ability to deploy and develop it. *Organizational leaning* and *innovation* will create *opportunities* to extend the boundaries of a firm. The boundaries of specialized firms will tend to be smaller than those of diversified firms.

2.4 Resource and Knowledge as Strategic Capabilities

The *resource-based view* integrates a firm's resources and capabilities into sources of a sustainable competitive advantage if the resources are valuable, rare, inimitable, and nonsubstitutable. *Sustainability* implies that core competence has lower rate of obsolescence, lower availability of substitutes and difficulty of duplication by rival firms. But the *knowledge-based view* extends them to the comprehension of *organizational learning* and *heterogeneous profitability differences* across firms (Barney, 1991).

2.4.1 *Resource-based view of a firm*

Richardson (1972), Teece (1982), Nelson and Winter (1982) regarded a firm as *a set of tangible and intangible resources*, especially intangible resources. Richardson (1972) introduced capabilities as a useful concept. The mutual interactions between tangible and intangible resources generate *capabilities* through the integration of knowledge. *Capabilities* emphasize the firm's capacity to adapt, integrate, and reconfigure internal and external resources purposefully to achieve a sustained competitive advantage. They refer to experience, skills, knowledge, and functional competences to cope with a changing environment.

Langlois *et al.* (1995, p. 7) classifies *capabilities* into *intrinsic core* and *ancillary* ones. The former is so idiosyncratic, inimitable, and uncontestable that other firms cannot imitate capabilities in the short and medium term. Therefore it is valuable and distinctive. The latter is imitable and contestable in the short term and determines the boundaries of a firm. *Competitive advantage* lies upstream of mass production stage and rests on the firm's *intrinsic core capabilities* or *core competence*.

As a result, this view focuses on the economic rents accruing from firm-specific resources rather than from product market positioning. The boundaries of a firm are determined by the relative costs of developing capabilities internally or acquiring them.

2.4.2 *Knowledge-based view of a firm*

This view considers *knowledge* as the most strategically significant resource of a firm, which can be acquired, transferred, or integrated to achieve a sustainable competitive advantage (Grant, 1996). While the traditional view focused on explicit knowledge as "*justified true belief*," a new view is based on *explicit and tacit knowledge*, especially tacit knowledge. *Organizational capabilities* refer to the *routine* as the patterns of interactions among capabilities to solve specific problem successfully. If *tacit knowledge* is attributed to specialized members, it is the integration of individuals' specialist knowledge, and difficult to imitate it (Grant, 1996). When knowledge is assimilated, it is socially justified and *codified*. Message that is codified is a useful resource as information, but enhances the possibility for other firms to imitate it.

Organizational learning and *innovation* enhance the relative value of capabilities and can alter the behavior and performance in individual firms through either of acquiring new capabilities or of reconfiguring existing knowledge, called "*combinative capability*" (Kogut and Zander, 1992). If capabilities are *heterogeneously distributed* across firms, and the *profitability differences* are stable over time, the linkage between a firm's capabilities and sustainability of its competitive advantage becomes a key factor (Barney, 1991). Then a firm is regarded as *a bundle of heterogeneous resources* that creates exclusive *market positioning*.

A firm can earn excess return when its *core competencies* are acquired, combined, and leveraged by strategy (Prahalad and Hamel, 1990). As these capabilities can be duplicated by rival firms over time, eventually this excess return may disappear completely in the market (Decarolis and Deeds, 1999; Winter and Szulanski, 2000). The features of this thinking are *Ricardian rents* (return above opportunity costs) as the source of interfirm profitability differences, and a *dominant strategy* that holds that knowledge is the foundation for a sustainable competitive advantage (Winter, 1995; Grant, 1996; Kogut, 2000).

2.4.3 *Dynamic resource-based view of a firm*

While the resource-based view has been a relatively static approach to strategy, the nature of capabilities in a long-term strategy implies that *dynamic capabilities* are characterized as complicated *routines* that emerge from *path-dependent evolutionary processes* (Eisenhardt and Martin, 2000). *Knowledge transfer* and *learning* provide the mechanisms for driving the *evolution of dynamic capabilities*.

2.4.3.1 *Dynamic capabilities and path-dependent evolution*

This approach implies that a sustainable competitive advantage depends on *managerial processes* like alliance, product development, strategic decision, etc. Teece *et al.* (1997, p. 516) defined *dynamic capabilities* as the firm's ability to integrate, build, and reconfigure internal and external competences to address a rapidly changing environment. They only play a central part in the *value-drivers* to renew capabilities in key processes so as to achieve congruence with a rapidly changing environment.

All capabilities, however, change potentially with adapting, learning, and innovation. While dynamic capabilities may be idiosyncratic to a firm and *path-dependent* in its emergence, superior performance exists for particular dynamic capabilities across firms in dynamic environments. These may have *commonalities* that any firms may get the same results as when firms can develop them along *path dependencies* and *market positions*. In a hypercompetitive market, they rely extensively on new knowledge created for specific situations (Eisenhardt and Martin, 2000). As a result, *path dependencies* may form the *gene of organization* so as to explain the implications of the *cultures* and *constitution* in the firm.

Many firms do not necessarily own the ancillary capabilities for all their activities. If all firms must reply on *dissimilar capabilities* owned by other firms, firms must transfer them through acquisition, alliance, and joint ventures, or create and transfer them through internal R&D activities. One firm can extend existing ancillary capabilities to create new knowledge, and reconfigure existing knowledge to establish new capabilities through a pattern of reintegration. Other firms may develop and form *tacit knowledge* and *core capabilities*. If they would be costly for competitors to imitate, they create value for a firm but eventually diffuse in the market and cease to provide a competitive advantage in the near future.

2.4.3.2 *Dynamic capabilities and their lifecycle*

Helfat and Peteraf (2003, p. 999) classifies *capabilities* into those to perform individual tasks and those to coordinate the individual tasks as a team, and depict the *capability lifecycle* as the evolution of capabilities in each stage of founding, development, maturity, and decline.

Capability branching in lifecycle processes occurs when factors have a strong impact enough to alter the current positioning of the capabilities in any lifecycle stage. The key factors are *internal selection*, such as managerial decisions, and *external selection*, such as changes in demand, technology, and government policy, etc. A firm may renew the stage of dynamic capabilities as new techniques become available through R&D, or redeploys R&D capabilities between markets. Thus this theory gives an explanation for the emergence and sustainable heterogeneity of capabilities. Radical and *systematic innovations* restructure the already established value chain, and create new stages of it or even a whole chain from scratch, to eliminate coordination through vertical integration.

In contrast, the market may acquire more capabilities over time and narrow the boundaries of a firm. Techniques developed by one firm may be imitated by other firms. In the long term, the relative abilities of firm and market would determine the boundaries between them because all capabilities diffuse in the market, leading to vertical disintegration.

2.5 Decision of Organizational Boundaries and Firm Value

Firms create value by innovatively bundling and leveraging their resources and capabilities and exploiting core competence to achieve a competitive advantage. A manager can enhance either the possibility to earn more present income or the possibility to earn income in the future. The solution of this trade-off may become *long-term satisfactory income* and should bring value for the firm over the long term.

2.5.1 *Creation of firm value and capabilities*

The goal of a firm is to secure *long-term sustainable satisfactory income.* It is possible by focusing on *intrinsic core capabilities* and *tacit knowledge.* Especially, because tacit knowledge is idiosyncratically synergistic, inimitable, and uncontestable, it can create value for the firm.

The creation of value for the firm generates *residual income*, such as *excess income*, *abnormal earnings*, or EVA^{TM}. In any case, it comes from the core capabilities that are unlikely to change, and erode over time. But the boundaries of a firm may alter as rival firms gain the same *core capabilities*, diminishing the relative value of those capabilities. Thus a firm must achieve greater income than the *expected return* in the market.

2.5.2 *Firm value and Ohlson's firm's equity valuation model*

The alternative models of *firm valuation* are the discounting dividend model, discounted cash flow model, economic profit model, accounting income model, etc. *Firm's value* comprises creditors' value and share-holders' value. Share-holders' value also is called equity value. Firm's value and share-holders' value are formally different, but both have the same characteristics without the loss of generality. Of course this similarity must be proved. Thus we will focus on Ohlson (1995), Feltham and Ohlson (1995) which formulate *equity valuation* based on accounting income, and define the variables as follows:

P_t: net asset value, date t,
bv_t: firm book value, date t,
d_t: dividends, date t,
x_t: earnings for the period $(t-1, t)$,
fa_t: net financial assets, date t,
oa_t: net operating assets, date
ox_t: operating earnings for period,
i_t: net interest revenues for period,
R_F: one plus the risk-free rate that assumes investors' risk neutrality.

The equity value P_t is given by *discounting dividend model* as follows:

$$P_t = \sum_{\tau=1}^{\infty} R_F^{-\tau} E_t[d_{t+\tau}], \tag{2.4}$$

where $E_t[\cdot]$ is the expected value operator conditional on information available at date t. This is called the "*present value relation.*"

The equations of the "*clean surplus relation*" are given as follows:

$$bv_t = fa_t + oa_t, \quad x_t = i_t + ox_t, \quad bv_t = bv_{t-1} + x_t - d_t. \tag{2.5}$$

And the "*net interest relation*" is assumed as follows:

$$i_t = (R_F - 1)fa_{t-1}, \tag{2.6}$$

Abnormal earnings x_t^a is defined as follows:

$$x_t^a \equiv x_t - (R_F - 1)bv_{t-1}. \tag{2.7}$$

Combining Eq. (2.7) with clean surplus accounting gives the following:

$$d_t = x_t^a + R_F \cdot bv_{t-1} - bv_t. \tag{2.8}$$

Substituting Eq. (2.8) for Eq. (2.4) becomes as follows:

$$P_t = \sum_{\tau=1}^{\infty} R_F^{-\tau} E_t[x_{t+\tau}^a] + \sum_{\tau=1}^{\infty} R_F^{-\tau} E_t[-bv_{t+\tau} + R_F \cdot bv_{t+\tau-1}]. \tag{2.9}$$

When $\tau \to \infty$, $R_F^{-\infty} E_t[bv_{t+\infty}]$ converges to 0 because $R_F > 1$. The firm's equity value is given as follows:

$$P_t = bv_t + \sum_{\tau=1}^{\infty} R_F^{-\tau} E_t[x_{t+\tau}^a]. \tag{2.10}$$

And Eq. (2.7) is rewritten as follows:

$$x_t^a \equiv \left(\frac{x_t}{bv_{t-1}} - \frac{i \cdot bv_{t-1}}{bv_{t-1}} \right) bv_{t-1} \equiv (r - i)\, bv_{t-1} \tag{2.11}$$

where r is return on equity, and i is risk-free rate.

2.5.3 *Organizational boundaries and value added*

The decision criterion on the boundaries of a firm depends on the ordering of spread $(r - i)$. When $r = i$, this decision cannot create value for the firm. When $r < i$, it will decline value. When $r > i$, it will add value. But though $r > i$, it may not connect with value. This is because r may have a tendency to become smaller than i in the near future.

A firm must take into consideration the lifecycles of products or strategic business units and the introduction to new business and select "*centralization and selection of business*" through *product portfolio management* to improve "*diminishing returns to scale*" and diversify business risks. Because this strategy may have no rationality in the very short term, a firm will expect to earn residual income in the long term.

Therefore a firm estimates the stream of income from normal operating activities except abnormal and special items in the future by each scenario and calculates expected value weighted by probability of respective scenarios, taking into consideration a firm's capabilities. Equity value p_t rewrites Eq. (2.10) as follows:

$$P_t = bv_t + \sum_{\tau=1}^{\infty} \frac{E_t[x_{t+\tau}^a]}{(1 + i_R)^{\tau}}. \tag{2.12}$$

If this equation can be solved with respect to i_R, internal rate of return is gotten. When $i_R > i$, this strategy has value relevance in the long term.

2.6 Concluding Remarks

The nature of Japanese-specific management and accounting could be distilled from the view based on capabilities and knowledge, and is generally recognized as *horizontal and relation-specific long-term relationship* between intrafirm or interfirms through long-term contracts.

First, the *lifetime employment relationship* makes it more favorable for employees to nurture firm-specific and special skill, as well as tacit knowledge gained through experiences and on-the-job training, than through transaction at the spot market. Layoffs and firing will cause the firm to lose them. *Seniority system* can accumulate job-specific skills over time, and play an important role in *interactive communication* between superiors and subordinates on skills and routines.

Second, Japanese firms often adopt *rank-order tournament* by promotion and upgrading to introduce the internal labor market to a firm. This competition plays a part in *incentive system* and the *organizational learning* to develop capabilities and core competence. But promotion is slower than an efficient pace in order to maintain the *high-powered incentives.* This promotes *loyalty* or *team spirit.* But *merit-based reward* crowds out *intrinsic motivation.* Western firms promote higher-talent employees quickly and invest in their training. This quick promotion may stifle incentives for other employees to acquire new skills.

Third, Japanese firms determine the boundaries of a firm so that internal transactions have lower transaction costs than market transaction to acquire the requisite capabilities in the long-term viability. The decision on the boundaries requires *return over the costs of capital*, and yields good effects on business activities in the long term. Firms estimate the costs, revenues or cash flow in the future and select action that can create value for the firm, including *social* and *economic valuation.* Hereafter, a firm must emphasize social value as well as economic value.

This is because firms should cope fairly with *value claims* from various stake-holders, with the consequence that they will contribute to shareholders' value added in the long term. Modern firms, as social institutions, must coordinate fairly the *conflict of interest* among stake-holders. If the relationship among stack-holders lacks fair distribution of outcome, a firm may not continue to be going concern. The share-holders' value maximization model may create incentives for manager to earn income, to keep the stock price high in a short term, and to engage in the *discretionary action.* Therefore corporate governance problems may raise, and a firm must address this trade-off. But the *stake-holder model* has partially more important phases than *share-holder model.*

Fourth, complex *interactive communication*, with conversations at various levels of an organization in intrafirm and interfirm, is a *control lever* (Simons, 1994) for creative formation of strategy and enhances the probability of motivating organizational members to search for new business opportunities and new strategies through organizational learning. When hierarchical and horizontal communication has value for the firm, the conversation processes through accounting information can enhance *goal congruence* by sharing of value sense and its interpretation among members.

This is practiced in Japan as TQC/TQM, small group activities, decision by consensus, emphasis on upstream or downstream of product market, etc. These practices focused on firm-specific investments from various viewpoints to enhance quality of products.

Fifth, Japanese firms tend to exploit capabilities to coordinate individual tasks as a team or group rather than to perform individual task. Especially, when manager has to coordinate relationship between business operations to cope with changes of expected internal and external environments or unexpected changes, organizational members perform not only their own specialized task, but also multitask, including tasks without contract. This voluntary coordination system as a team is Japanese-specific in management, rooted in *integrated and context-specific capabilities* through organizational learning.

Finally, Japanese-specific and strategic management also has faced evolutional changes. But it may have aspects that make it more efficient and profitable than its Western counterparts. The hasty and uncritical introduction of Western-type management must be avoided, because it is not necessarily thought to be a desirable solution conductive to efficient operation. Japanese management must rooted in traditional cultures and develop a new management style suitable for the global environment.

Whether Japanese-type or Western-type management proves superior will be determined by competition in external markets, but Japanese firms must exhibit creative ingenuity. To provide a foundation for future research, we must develop not only theories which find their hypotheses in Japanese management, but also conduct *empirical research* that verify the hypotheses through field research (Winter and Szulanski, 2000; Jacobides and Winter, 2005) or positive research (Schroeder *et al.*, 2002; Ray *et al.*, 2004; Zaheer and Bell, 2005). Moreover, empirical research will have to upgrade predictive power in strategic management.

References

Barney, J. (1991). Firm resource and sustained competitive advantage, *Journal of Management* 17-1, pp. 99–120.

Bierly, P. E., Kessler, E. H., and Christensen, E. W. (2000). Organizational learning, knowledge and wisdom, *Journal of Organizational Change Management* 13-6, pp. 595–618.

Coase, R. H. (1937). The nature of the firm, *Economica* 4, pp. 386–405.

Decarolis, D. M. and Deeds, D. L. (1999). The impact of stocks and flows of organizational knowledge on firm performance: an empirical investigation of the biotechnology industry, *Strategic Management Journal* 20-10, pp. 953–968.

Eisenhardt, K. M. and Martin, J. A. (2000). Dynamic capabilities: what are they? *Strategic Management Journal* 21-11, pp. 1105–1121.

Feltham, G. A. and Ohlson, J. A. (1995). Valuation and clean surplus accounting for operating and financial activity, *Contemporary Accounting Research* 11-2, pp. 689–731.

Grant, R. M. (1991). The resource-based theory of competitive advantage: implications for strategy formulation, *California Management Review* Spring, pp. 114–135.

Grant, R. M. (1996). Prospering in dynamically-competitive environments: organizational capability as knowledge integration, *Organization Science* 7-4, pp. 375–387.

Hallwood, C. P. (1994). An observation on the transaction cost theory of the (multinational) firm, *Journal of Institutional and Theoretical Economics* 150-2, pp. 351–361.

Helfat, C. E. and Peteraf, M. A. (2003). The dynamic resource-based view: capability lifecycles, *Strategic Management Journal* 24-10, pp. 997–1010.

Holmstrom, B. R. and Tirole, J. (1989). The theory of the firm, in Schmalensee, R. and Willig, R. D. (eds.), *Handbook of Industrial Organization* 1, North-Holland, Amsterdam, pp. 63–133.

Ijiri, Y. (1990). *Introduction to Momentum Accounting: A New System of Performance Evaluation for the Growth of the Firm*, Nippon Keizai Shinbunsya.

Jacobides, M. G. and Winter, S. G. (2005). The co-evolution of capabilities and transaction costs: explaining the institutional structure of production, *Strategic Management Journal* 26-5, pp. 395–413.

Klein, B., Crawford, R. G., and Alchian, A. A. (1978). Vertical integration, appropriable rents, and the competitive contracting process, *Journal of Law and Economics* 2-2, pp. 207–326.

Kogut, B. and Zander, U. (1992). Knowledge of the firm, combinative capabilities, and the replication of technology, *Organization Science* 3-3, pp. 383–397.

Kogut, B. (2000), The network as knowledge: generative rules and the emergence of structure, *Strategic Management Journal* 21-3, pp. 405–425.

Langlois, R. N. and Robertson, P. L. (1995). *Firms, Markets and Economic Change: A Dynamic Theory of Business Institutions*, London and New York: Routledge.

Nelson, R. R. (1991). Why do firms differ, and how does it matter? *Strategic Management Journal* 12-1, pp. 61–74.

Nelson, R. R. and Winter, S. G. (1982). *An Evolutionary Theory of Economic Change*, Cambridge, Mass.: The Belknap Press of Harvard University Press.

Nonaka, I. (1994). A dynamic theory of organizational knowledge creation, *Organization Science* 5-1, pp. 14–37.

Nonaka, I. and Takeuchi, H. (1995). *The Knowledge-creating Company: How Japanese Companies Create the Dynamics of Innovation*, Oxford University Press.

Ohlson, J. A. (1995). Earnings, book values, and dividends in equity valuation, *Contemporary Accounting Research* 11-2, pp. 661–687.

Panzar, J. C. and Willig, R. D. (1981). Economies of scope, *The American Economic Review* 71-2, pp. 268–272.

Prahaland, C. K. and Hamel, G. (1990). The core competence of the corporation, *Harvard Business Review* 68-3, pp. 79–91.

Ray, G., Barney, J. B., and Muhanna, W. A. (2004). Capabilities, business progresses, and competitive advantage: choosing the dependent variable in empirical tests of the resource-based view, *Strategic Management Journal* 25-1, pp. 23–37.

Richardson, G. B. (1972). The organization of industry, *Economic Journal* 82, pp. 883–896.

Rumelt, R. P. (1991). How much does industry matter? *Strategic Management Journal* 12-4, pp. 167–185.

Schroeder, R. G., Bates, K. A., and Junttila, M. A. (2002). A resource-based view of manufacturing strategy and the relationship to manufacturing performance, *Strategic Management Journal* 23, pp. 105–117.

Shapiro, C. (1989). The theory of business strategy, *RAND Journal of Economics* 20-1, pp. 125–137.

Simons, R. (1995). *Levers of Control: How Managers Use Innovative Control Systems to Drive Strategic Renewal*, Harvard Business School Press.

Teece, D. J. (1980). Economies of scope and the scope of the enterprise, *Journal of Economic Behavior and Organization* 1, pp. 223–247.

Teece, D. J. (1982). Towards an economic theory of the multiproduct firm, *Journal of Economic Behavior and Organization* 3, pp. 39–63.

Teece, D. J., Pisano, G., and Shuen, A. (1997). Dynamic capabilities and strategic management. *Strategic Management Journal* 18-7, pp. 509–533.

Williamson, O. E. (1975). *Markets and Hierarchies: Analysis and Antitrust Implications*, The Free Press.

Williamson, O. E. (1985). *The Economic Institutions of Capitalism*, The Free Press.

Winter, S. G. (1985). Four Rs profitability: rents, resources, routines and replication, in Montgomery, C. A. (ed.) *Resource-based and Evolutionary Theories of the Firm: Towards a Synthesis*, Boston: Kluwer Academic Publisher, pp. 147–178.

Winter, S. G. and Szulanski, G. (2000). Replication of organizational routines: conceptualizing the exploitation of knowledge assets, Working Paper, The University of Pennsylvania.

Zaheer, A. and Bell, G. G. (2005). Benefiting from network position: firm capabilities, structural holes, and performance, *Strategic Management Journal* 26-9, pp. 809–825.

CHAPTER

3

Business Revitalization Based on the Financial Restructuring of Japanese Companies

Yasuto Monden

Director, Investment Banking Department
UBS Investment Bank

Yasuhiro Monden

Professor, Faculty of Business Administration
Mejiro University

3.1 Introduction

Japanese companies have been struggling for revival for more than ten years, after the bubble of stocks and land prices burst in 1991. Under this severe recession, the financial structure (i.e., the debt/equity ratio) of Japanese firms, as well as their profitability (i.e., the ROE or return on sales), has been unsound.

This chapter will explore the approach that would lead to the rebirth of Japanese companies. In other words, the authors will examine from the theoretical and policy viewpoints how the innovation of the financial structure should proceed and what has been done so far for the revitalization of Japanese companies. Section 2 will discuss the basic principles of financial restructuring, and Sections 3 through 5 will show how the owner's capital (equity) has been improved in the practices of Japanese firms.

3.2 Approaches to the Two Sources of Capital for the Revival of a Company

Bankruptcy of a firm occurs when the company has so much excess debt that it cannot pay it back. Usually, a company goes bankrupt when it has a so-called "overdebt," a situation where the total amount of debt far exceeds the total amount of assets. In accounting, the following formula describes the value of a company's total assets:

$$\text{Total assets} = \text{total debt (or the total amount of the creditor's capital)} + \text{total owner's capital}$$

When the total assets are smaller than the total debt, the owner's capital is *negative*. In order to restore *positive* capital to a company with excess debt, the following two approaches must be adopted for the debt and the equity capital, respectively:

1. Reduction of the debt capital.
2. Increase of the owner's capital.

The reduction of the debt capital (or liability) requires the implementation of the following measures:

1. Abolition of loans by the banks (i.e., direct reduction of the debt on the company side).
2. *Debt equity swapping*, in which the balance of the loans owned by the banks is purchased by a "rebirth fund" (or investment fund) or by other monetary institutions, and then changed into stocks. This is also called a *securitization of debt.*

For the reinforcement of the owner's capital, the "rebirth fund" (or buyout fund) firms, banks and/or other competitive companies and employees/managers will offer the funds necessary for purchasing the stocks and for undertaking the added equity of the company in question. The investment fund first responds to the equity increase and acquires the stocks existing on the market so that it can gain governance power, and then it begins to restructure the company. Thus, it eventually brings about the recovery of the company, whose value is enhanced.

This chapter will first focus on how *governmental* or *state-backed funds* can help restore companies through debt reduction or equity increase. In Japan, the government-backed restoration of companies has been carried out using the following institutions and frameworks:

1. Industrial Revitalization Corporation of Japan (IRCJ).
2. Industrial Revitalization Law.
3. The Resolution and Collection Corporation (RCC).
4. Injection of public funds into the banks.

The process of business value improvement and business recovery through these institutional means will be examined. This chapter will then examine how the *private equity fund* or private financial sponsor reinforces the owner's capital, and how it can be used to create business value and promote the revitalization of a company.

3.3 Restructuring through the Industrial Revitalization Corporation of Japan (IRCJ)

The Financial Services Agency of the Japanese government announced a *finance revitalization program* at the end of October 2002; the purpose of this program is to remove bad loans granted by major banks, and the Japanese government kick-started the program on November 11 of the same year. The IRCJ, which is a legal state-backed company, was established to implement this *finance revitalization program.*

The IRCJ was established as an institution belonging to the Deposit Insurance Corporation of Japan, along with the Resolution and Collection Corporation (RCC). The role of the IRCJ is as follows:

> The IRCJ will select a company that has an *excess debt* to the banks, if it satisfies two conditions: it is a *company in need of control*, and is judged as *restorable* by the IRCJ. Then, the IRCJ will purchase at a *reasonable* price the loans given to the ailing companies from those banks that are not the main bank of the company in question, and assist the revitalization of the company together with the main bank.

Therefore, the IRCJ stands on two foundations: the banks (that gave *bad loans* to the industrial companies) and the industrial companies (that owe *bad debts* to the banks). However, in this section, the authors are mainly interested in the rebirth of industrial firms, and so the restoration of ailing banks through governmental aid will be examined in Section 3.4.

The role of the IRCJ has not remained confined to the purchasing of bad loans from *non-main* banks; recently, the IRCJ has also been providing funds for purchasing new stocks in view of enlarging the owner's capital. This was done, for example, when the IRCJ began to assist the restoration of Kanebo (a cosmetics company) and Dai-ei (a large retail company) in 2004.

The function of the IRCJ can also be fulfilled by private banks and private investment funds, but the Japanese government has created a state-backed fund because the main banks lost their financial power during the 1990s.

Thus, the fund created by the Japanese government is used to rebuild a sound transaction relationship between Japanese banks and Japanese industrial firms. Traditionally, Japanese banks, especially the main banks, have kept a long-term transaction relationship with their client companies, and they have all of the available information related to those companies in order to better monitor the quality of management of those companies.

Traditionally, when a certain company goes through a rough period, the main bank of the company decides if the company can be restored or not. If the company has the potential to come back, the main bank will extend its full financial support. (This type of help is not popular in the US.) However, for the assistance offered by the main bank to be effective, the financial structure of the bank itself must be sound. The main banks in Japan after the bubble burst, however, were not able to bear the brunt of the financial assistance needed by the distressed companies, because they were already under a heavy burden due to the depreciation and abolishment of the bad loans; also the non-main banks were apt to ask for additional help from the main banks. Therefore, no agreement among banks and industrial firms regarding restoration plans was reached, time was wasted, and the dire financial condition of the companies was further aggravated. Thus, a governmen tal fund had to take over. If Japan had a market that can widely resell bank loans like in the US, the need for a governmental fund would be small.

Furthermore, even though the loans are sold and separated from the balance sheet of the bank in question, the bad debt continues to exist on the industrial company side, which must be financially assisted through some scheme on the capital market. The Japanese capital market does not provide a good environment for such a scheme. Thus, the IRCJ is again needed to assist the revitalization of the companies in debt.

Now, there are two problems which the IRCJ must solve in providing financial support. The first problem was pointed by Mr. Seijuro Shiokawa, former Minister of Finance, who metaphorically asked whether or not the

IRCJ has the capacity to act as *Yama, the Great Judge of the Court of Hell* in Buddhism. In effect, he asked whether the IRCJ really has the ability to distinguish between restorable and non-restorable companies; the main concern is that the public fund of the IRCJ should not be a mechanism for extending the life of non-profitable companies that should disappear in a competitive market. In other words, the IRCJ should not prevent the removal of *excess* firms in various industries.

Mr. Tei-ichi Tanigaki, the Minister of Industrial Revitalization, is of the opinion that *Yama the Great* is simply the market in which the industrial firms operate. This means that the IRCJ must play the role of coordinator for various sponsors in the market who assist the ailing industrial companies after the IRCJ has bought out the loans of the banks. The players in the market include not only the companies in need of revitalization, the non-main and the main banks, but also private equity funds, rival companies in the same industry and large high-performance companies which are able to *bid* an offer to buy the ailing business in an auction.

According to this model, the IRCJ carefully checks the financial *due diligence report* of the company in need of revitalization, participates in the bidding at the auction in order to introduce its fund, and plays the role of coordinator in the auction market by exercising its legally authorized right of coordination. The IRJC prepares a road map for the restoration of the company, and selects the most appropriate sponsor for each kind of business by coordinating the various players in the market, while also sending the *turn-around manager* (the re-builder) to the company to start the process of business restructuring.

There is another state-backed organization called the Resolution and Collection Corporation (RCC), which fulfills a function similar to that of the IRCJ. Why was an organization similar to the IRCJ established under the same parent organization, the Deposit Insurance Corporation of Japan (DICJ)? The RCC not only recovers loans instead of the banks, but it also helps revitalize the industrial companies. The RCC *purchases* and *recovers* (collects) bad loans, but its main job is to collect loans. This is based on the differences between various categories of loans in terms of soundness. The RCC handles bankrupt companies and those suspected of bankruptcy, while the IRCJ mainly handles companies in need of control whose debt interest is waived. Thus, the IRCJ handles only relatively sounder, restorable companies. Also, the IRCJ can provide public funds to boost the owner's capital of a company, but the RCC cannot. Figure 3.1 below shows the relationship between the IRCJ, RCC and DICJ.

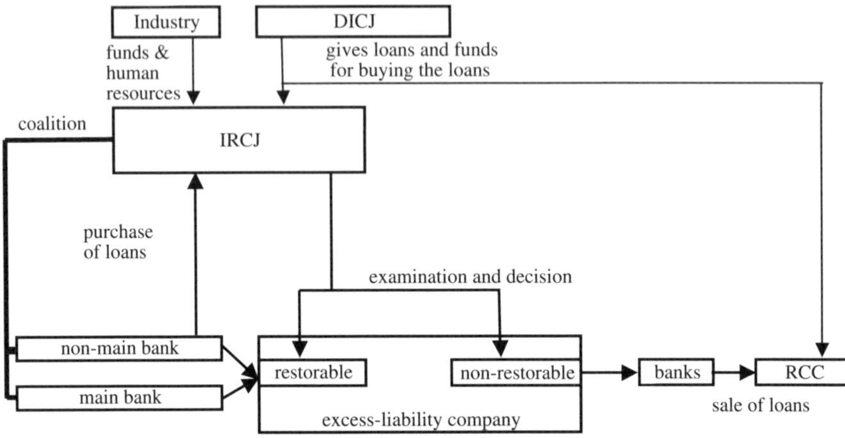

Fig. 3.1 Relationship between the IRCJ, RCC and DICJ

The second problem for the IRCJ is to figure out what incentives should be given to non-main banks for selling their claims (loans) to the IRJC. This is essentially a problem regarding the purchasing price for the claims. If the price is higher than the current price, the incentive is larger, but the acquired loans must be sold again on the market after three years, and the government may incur some loss then, thus burdening Japanese taxpayers. Eventually, the IRJC must buy the loans at a *fair* current price, and so there will be no price incentive for the banks. However, government monetary administration may provide another kind of incentive. When bad loans are bought out by the IRCJ from the non-main banks, the amount of depreciation of the bad loans may be reduced as well as the amount of accumulated allowances for the bad loans.

In the case of industrial firms assisted by the IRCJ, there is another incentive, tax waivers, offered to the main banks as follows:

1. The main bank can capitalize on the non-tax depreciation when it abolishes its loans to the ailing firm.
2. The industrial company can also offset the *capital gain of the liability waiver* extended by the main bank with the depreciation of its bad loans.

It should also be noted that substantial side benefits have been realized due to the appearance of the IRCJ. Business restructuring is now being vigorously promoted by the leaderships of banks, and the activity of the Resolution and Collection Corporation (RCC) has intensified. Especially important is the fact that the weaker or ailing businesses are being removed earlier from the market, while stronger or excellent businesses are retained and nurtured.

3.4 Revitalization of the Banks by Injection of Public Funds

In this section, the authors will examine how the injection of public funds into Japanese banks was carried out as a special part of the financial revitalization program prepared by the Financial Services Agency in October 2002. The case of the Risona holdings group, which received public funds (Special Aid no.1) on June 1, 2003, is discussed.

The Special Aid was given to the Risona holdings group in the form of a government purchase of new common stocks worth 396.4 billion yen at 52 yen per stock and new preferred stocks with votes worth 1,663.6 billion yen at 200 yen per stock, both issued by the Risona holdings group. Then, in August 7, 2003, the government acquired more than 70% of the vote of the Risona holding group, thus gaining the governance right. As a result, Risona became a state-owned bank. The government decided to receive *zero* dividends from the common stocks and *lower* dividends from the preferred stocks.

With this injection of public funds, the improvement of Risona's capital structure was achieved by decreasing and increasing the equity at the same time. First, the accumulated loss (negative figure) in the equity part of the balance sheet was offset by the positive figure of the paid-in capital (= capital and legal reserves). Then, the public funds injected into the company increased the equity capital. Although the book value of the gross equity was reduced in the first stage, the actual amount of the equity was enlarged afterward, and so the total number of stocks issued on the market increased and the stock price went down due to dilution. (In the case of the restructuring of the Ashikaga bank, the government compulsorily purchased all of the stocks at *zero* price in the first stage. As a result, the equity of the existing shareholders became null. But no such radical approach was adopted in Risona's case.)

It should be noted that the Risona group received public funds from the government twice previously, in 1998 and 1999, in the form of preferred stocks without votes and deferred stocks amounting to a total of 1,100 billion yen. At that time, the original members, Daiwa bank and Asahi bank, still existed. However, that aid did not succeed in launching Risona's actual business restructuring. The equity ratio of the Risona group as a whole was 3% and that of the Risona bank alone was 2%, while the minimum requirement as a domestic standard was 4%. However, with this third injection of public funds in 2002, Risona's equity ratio has gone up to more than 12%. The purpose of the public fund injection that amounts to almost 2,000 billion yen is definitely to enlarge the equity. Even though the bad loans must be depreciated, the equity ratio should not be worsened further.

The injected public funds are supposed to be recovered by the government after 15 years, when Risona has recovered its earning capability and the government can sell the stocks on the market. Unless the injected funds can be recovered, the rescue of Risona will turn out to be a tremendous tax burden on the Japanese population. To enable the recovery of the injected money and the increase of the stock price on the market, Risona has to carry out business restructuring. This is another type of shareholder-value-based management, where the shareholder is the state government.

3.5 Business Revitalization through Buyout Funds

3.5.1 *Basic function of equity funds or buyout firms*

In Japan, a *rebirth firm* is a firm managing a so-called "equity fund" or "financial sponsor" established by an investment company. An investment company establishes a *fund firm* by collecting investment money from various investors. Using this money, the fund firm buys a company undergoing restructuring; in other words, it purchases not only ill-performing companies but also well-performing companies.

Therefore, a rebirth firm is a kind of *buyout fund* firm. When an ailing company is acquired, the rebirth firm usually sends managers to the company to give advice on and supervise business revitalization, thereby enhancing the company value before the company is finally sold on the market. This means that the rebirth firm sells the stocks of the company in question after the completion of restructuring. Thus, if one only looks at the initial and final actions of a rebirth firm in relation to an ailing company, one only sees stocks being bought and the same stocks sold later, with a capital gain between the two stock prices.

It is expected that the role of the main banks which used to provide funds and restore ailing industrial companies when the banks were much stronger will eventually be replaced by the buyout funds. Such revitalization is very important for the rebirth of Japanese companies.

3.5.2 *Environmental difference in the buyout funds between Japan, Europe and the US: Management conventions unique to Japan*

There are various environmental differences in the buyout business between Japan, Europe and the US, and these differences will continue to exist in the foreseeable future. Therefore, the development of buyout fundy activities in Japan is also likely to maintain its entirely unique direction from now on.

Funds of smaller size

During the past few years, many new buyout firms have been established and have entered the Japanese market, but the interesting aspect is the scale of the funds. Most funds range from a few tens of billion yen to 70–80 billion yen, and deals in excess of 100 billion yen are very scarce. Within this fund size range, the best target deal is probably worth 10–20 billion yen. Deals of this size are classified as mid-market private equity deals or small- to mid-market private equity deals. Such deals are targeted by fund firms established by Japanese banks and security companies, as well as by foreign buyout funds. Thus, this market is highly competitive and governed by the seller.

Features of the companies targeted for buyout

Business companies which enter deals of this size usually have a few to several hundred employees and sales of 10–20 billion yen. Such firms are relatively easy to put on IPO, and it is also easier to find various *exit strategies* with regard to them. These are the typical Japanese middle-sized firms. Most of them depend on the main bank or the *Keiretsu* of the business group, and operate in a Japanese business environment characterized by life-long employment and wage hierarchies according to seniority. Therefore, this market is very tough for foreign funds to penetrate.

On the other hand, buyout funds in Europe and the US usually target *non-core* businesses about to be split off from a larger company. Such a non-core business is usually not purchased by another company, even though it is not in the red. Although it is not a business in distress and still yields a positive cash flow, it has no synergy with the *core* businesses of the parent company, and is the most desirable target of buyout firms. In Japan, however, such *sound* companies are very competitive targets of deals due to the size of the buyout funds and the scarcity of similar businesses.

Now, when it comes to large-sized deals exceeding 100 billion yen, the option to sell a business to a buyout fund is rarely adopted in Japan, since some formidable problem usually appears. Large deals usually conceal huge *excess debts* that even the main banks have given up on. Some examples are Nissan Motors just before Renault began to help, the retailer Daiei (DAIEI) currently controlled by the IRCJ, and the former Shinsei bank revived by the Japanese government and Ripplewood.

Incentives to the seller: A feature unique to Japan

As a result of the very severe competition among the many private equity funds, the market has become strongly seller-governed, and this tendency is observed especially in cases where a subsidiary firm of a large parent company is put on the market. The real difference between the Japanese and European/US buyout environments is that the Japanese market offers unique incentives to the seller. The seller is encouraged not to demand the highest price possible on the current market, but to offer as *nice an image of the company* as possible. This implies that the Japanese seller holds the interests of stakeholders other than the stockholders in very high regard. Here is a list of the conditions imposed by the Japanese seller:

1. Never incur any debt that exceeds the current level
   Although it may be hard to believe, there are many managers in Japan who think that an increase in liability would damage the social credibility of the company. This may be based partially on the idea of *zero-debt management*, put successfully into practice by high-performance, iconic Japanese companies such as Toyota and Matsushita; on the other hand, there may be an excessive sensitivity to the risk of bad loans (or bad debt on the company side). This traditional wariness of excess debt inclines the seller to insist upon D/E (debt/equity) ratios of less than 1.5. Especially middle-sized firms tend to impose this demand. Thus, since the buyout firm cannot offer sufficient funds due to the inability to muster the necessary leverage, the valuation of the deal made by the buyout firm will be *lower*. This seems rather strange, considering the historical fact that Japanese companies have enjoyed a high level of financial leverage in the post-war boom. One would think that this leverage would logically validate *higher* valuation!
2. Never restructure at the expense of employees
   The condition to "never fire the workers and never shutter the plants" is often insisted upon by the seller in Japan. This means that it is difficult

to improve the performance and cutting costs the easy way, i.e., by removing employees. *Yet performance can be improved by reengineering or creating efficient ways of operations and enhancing top-line sales. By announcing all employees of the company that there will be no employee restructuring, the top management can boost the morale of the people and encourage them to refine their job-related ideas and skills and implement improvements.* The value of the firm that the company has created for its own survival and growth is the creation not only of the shareholders but also of the employees.

3. Never replace the top management
   It is often said in the Japanese market that a buyout in the form of an MBO (management buyout) is quite acceptable even if the acquisition is made with the aid of a buyout fund. If a buyout company wants to replace the top management, it will not get a deal. Besides, if the buyout was offered as an MBO, especially when the deal concerns a subsidiary company of a large corporation whose former directors are now working as the top executives of the subsidiary, then the parent corporation can avoid the criticism that it has cut off its subsidiary and its former employees. Of course, the buyout fund can replace members of the top management after the deal is made since it holds the majority of votes at the general shareholder meeting, but if it does so, its reputation or brand will incur much damage in a fiercely competitive buyout market and will find it difficult to secure the next deal. *In the environment of "repetitive games," where the participants play repeatedly, a partner who betrays the counter-partner "today" to get a gain cannot have a cooperation of the counter-partner "tomorrow." Therefore, under the repetitive games the cooperation of all of the players will be always achieved.* Thus, when a change of top management is felt to be really necessary, then the buyout firm should propose the details of the turnover policy to the existing management before both parties enter the negotiation.

3.5.3 *Results of the concept of non-debt management*

Naturally, the reader may ask why buyout firms in Japan can invest in deals in which it is impossible to accrue any more debt on the one hand, and the IRR (internal rate of return) of 25% must not be reduced on the other hand, even though the financial leverage necessary for IRR enhancement cannot be mustered. This conflict, however, can be solved, through the reduction of the selling price on the seller's side. The result, though, is that the valuation offered by the buyout funds in Japan is relatively lower than that in Europe and the US. *After making the deal at a lower price, the buyout firm restores or improves the deal in question by applying a severe reform and sales plan, and finally selling it on the market or putting it on IPO. This is how the buyout fund can earn an IRR of 25% in the end.*

From the viewpoint of capital restructuring, one of the characteristics of the buyout funds in Japan is their inability to accrue debts, as already mentioned, and so they are inclined to pile up *higher* amounts of equity capital than the buyout funds in Europe and the US. However, the buyout firm sometimes carries out a *recapitalization* after making the deal; in other words, it introduces some of the debt capital after the buyout. But this amount of added liability is usually not large.

3.5.4 *Relationship between LBO (leveraged buy-out) and the size of the deal*

The fact that there are fewer large-sized deals in Japan implies that the chances for the buyout firms to earn a large profit are also fewer. Unfortunately, this situation will not change until the maximization of the selling price becomes the primal goal of the parties on the Japanese M&A market. On the other hand, in the European and US markets, the vendor (seller) firm hires CPA (certified public accountant) to prepare a very detailed report called the "vendor due diligence report" in exchange for a very substantial fee. This report is composed of a few thousand pages, and is used by the buyout firm to borrow as much debt as possible from the bank and to offer the highest price to the seller. Unless this report is provided, the banks and the major investors, as prospective providers of the debt capital, cannot determine with any degree of accuracy the necessity of the amount of funds demanded by the buyout firm, and thus the buyout firm cannot procure the highest possible amount of debt to achieve sufficient leverage. In Japan, however, the *vendor due diligence report* is not commonly used yet. Because large deals are not yet popular on the Japanese market, genuine LBOs have not occurred yet in Japan. This may be the old problem of the chicken (lack of large deals) and the egg (absence of LBOs).

For the buyout funds in Japan to acquire European or American characteristics, changes in the Japanese business environment must occur first. Until then, Japanese buyout firms are likely to develop along their unique path.

3.6 Conclusion

The authors have explained in this chapter how *balance sheet restructuring* is conducted in Japanese companies both through state-backed funds and the private equity funds in terms of excess liability reduction and enlargement of the owner's capital. However, financial restructuring aided by a third party is like a camphor injection administered to a weakened body. Real business restructuring must be carried out to *streamline* the companies with the potential to bring in positive profit continuously. This *streamlining* is in fact a *restructuring of the income statement*, to be achieved through business reengineering or restructuring. The restructuring road map must indicate various cost-cutting and revenue-boosting strategies along the way, and these must be promoted by a turn-around manager introduced by the fund provider or by the inside managers and general employees.

References

Ishiguro, N. (2003). *Strategy for Industrial Revitalization*, Toyo-keizai Shinposha. (in Japanese)

Gilson, S. C. (2001). *Creating Value through Corporate Restructuring*, New York: John Wiley & Sons, Inc.

Monden, Yasuhiro. (Ed) (2005). *Management Accounting for Value-based Organizational Restructuring*, Monden Institute of Management and Accounting. (in Japanese)

Monden, Yasuto. (2005). Weblog of 2005-03-27 and 2005-04-07; http: londonib. exblog.jp/

Rowley, I. (2005). Japan: Let's not make a deal — despite a few big transactions, private-equity buyouts by foreigners are scarce, *Business Week*, May 30.

CHAPTER

4

Corporate Social Responsibility Assumed by the Merchants of Japanese Yedo Period

Kozo Suzuki

Director of Land Use Planning
Assets Management and Contracting Division
Bureau of Waterworks, Tokyo Metropolitan Government

4.1 Background of CSR in Japan

Nowadays, interest in Corporate Social Responsibility (CSR) has risen in Japan. It is difficult, however, to consider recent CSR in Japan if one holds that CSR was born in Europe and America. Rather, it is important to understand the cultural and the historical background of corporate culture of this country when we discuss current CSR in Japan (Ko *et al.*, 2003). Especially, there are suggestions that Japanese companies in the Yedo Period (1590–1868) had been concerned with CSR (Okamoto, 2004), but it is an under-examined area.

The Western market system is the pre-eminent system in the world today. But, in fact, at a time when the U.S.A. was still an English colony, in the Yedo Period, a market economy system that was not so fundamentally different from today had developed in this country.

There existed fixed currency exchange rate systems, linking the settlement of international trade with China and Holland, and exchange businesses, and market interest rates. These economic systems helped make Yedo City (the current Tokyo), a metropolis of over a million people, one of the greatest cities in the world at that time.

In operation among the individuals and trade associations of commerce and industry of the time were systems of ethics and structures not dissimilar to those of CSR today. Considering the process of Japanese growth up to modernization in the Meiji Period and subsequent growth in economic power up to today, it could be said that that the experiences of a market economy cultivated over 400 years are "in the blood" of the Japanese, if you will, that it is second nature. This contains the relationship to Corporate Social Responsibility.

4.2 CSR and Business in the Yedo Period

For the businessmen of commerce and industry in the Yedo Period, continuation ("going concern" or "growth") of their business or enterprise was the most important objective. The systems to realize this growth were "codified articles" (*toiya-jouhou*) made by each merchant trade association or *kabunakama*. In addition, individual mercantile families made "office regulations" for their own enterprises. The difference between "articles" and "regulations" was a matter of scale. The former were setting standards and procedures for all members of the *kabunakama* association, the latter for individual enterprises.

In these codified articles, various items were elaborated for putting their corporate social responsibility into practice. For example, duty of observance of laws and ordinances, obedience to policies of the Shogunate (Bakufu Government), security for rights in business profit and interests of the same profession or merchant guild, conservation of clients and consumers, transaction rules between members of the *kabunakama*, penal regulations for violations, and processes of managing on disputes between members in the same *kabunakama* (guild).

As for the relation between these codified articles and individual enterprises, the articles were established by associations of private enterprises that were particularly active in promoting their businesses. On the other hand, there were the cases where newcomers, on entering an existing *kabunakama*, had already established codified articles of their own. In both cases, individual members of the same profession, the *kabunakama* trade associations, although autonomously managed, made the codified articles self-governing. These articles functioned as the rules and regulations for the all *kabunakama* members.

In the Yedo Period, codified articles made by each *kabunakama* had to be accepted and approved by three senior town officials (*cho-doshiyori*), the headquarters of citizens organization in the Yedo City. These hereditary *cho-doshiyori* posts were held by the Naraya, Taru, and Kitamura lineages. The approval of the articles by the *cho-doshiyori* meant that they had been recognized officially by city commissioners (*machi-bugyo*) of Yedo City and the Bakufu Government. The posts of city commissioners of Yedo were very high ranking in the Bakufu Government, acting as they did as the magistrates of jurisdiction, citizen administration and economics of Yedo City.

After the mid-Yedo Period, competition and the entry of new enterprises became vigorous and prosperous in various sectors of industries. Especially, among businesses in fields of particular promise or profitability, there was intense competition among established merchant houses, and between this group and new enterprises. In this atmosphere, the official recognition of trade associations (*kabunakama*) and setting of codified articles had the effect of securing the rights and interests of existing enterprises. But on the other hand, codified articles also worked to prevent confusion in the market place during this period of intense competition.

Accordingly, codified articles kept the balance of competition and cooperation.

4.3 CSR in Codified Articles Made by Kabunakama

The Kyoho Era (1716–1736) saw the first attempt by the Bakufu Government to take countermeasures against market circulation by using the *kabunakama*. Codified articles established in the time of the "Kyoho Reforms" will be introduced here.

It was the case among Stone Dealers that wholesaled stones for building were collected from each region in the country, and then supplied to the brokerages in Yedo City. The codified articles for Stone Dealers (Tokyo Metropolitan Archives, 1968a) were written in Kyoho 10 (1725). They included items in effect restraining the rising of prices of building stones in addition to the duty of observance of laws and ordinances.

On the other hand, some items were written for the protection of customers by stipulating that suppliers actually live in each region, for the security of profits of the members of the Stone Dealer, and for the rejection of inefficient brokerages. In those days, the Bakufu Government used the *kabunakama* as the executive organizations for economic policies, for instance reducing prices; so actually, they had acted to maximize profits of their members. And due to the progress and growth of economic power of commerce and industry, the *kabunakama* and their members exerted a strong influence on society.

In the Houreki Era (1751–1763), the Bakufu Government began to both officially recognize the *kabunakama* and to levy indirect taxes (*myoga-kin* and *unjou*) on them. In the codified articles of the *kabunakama*, new types of items appeared to address their profit gains and the levying of *myoga-kin*. For example, the Cotton Wholesale Dealers Trade Association of Shirako-Gumi established codified articles in 1763 (Tokyo Metropolitan Archives, 1968b). The articles included the following item, "in order to foster prosperity among the member enterprises and make their management carefully, we establish this article and each item." In other words, one of the important purposes was the realizing of future profits for the members of the Cotton Wholesale Dealers. Growth and continuity, the ongoing concern, were recognized as the most important objective in their business or enterprise.

In these articles much weight and gravity were given to the observance of laws and ordinances, obedience to the policies of the Bakufu Government, clarity in business dealings, and security for rights in business profit and interests of members.

In particular, to maintain and increase profits, one item was made giving a discount of 20 percent from the market price in dealings between the members, and prohibiting disposals by sale for less than market price to non-members. But, for consumer protection, items prohibited price boosting through putting up goods for auction, and statement of the official rate of commission had to be declared.

These articles were established through a process of competition and criminal suits between the Cotton Wholesale Dealer Trade Associations of Shirako-Gumi and Oodenmachou. The Shirako-Gumi *kabunakama* was a group of new, high-growth enterprises. The Oodenmachou *kabunakama* was an established traditional group on the decline. There had been frequent disputes between the two that had disturbed business practices of both member and non-member alike.

Typically detailed in the codified articles were items describing or detailing the "goodwill" transactions and issues between *kabunakama* members, items of the commercial registration (similar to today), and membership fees. This was why that the management of "goodwill" in trade had become important via the official recognition of the *kabunakama*.

4.4 Functions of the *Kabunakama*

Next, we will examine the structure of business and industry administration of the Shogunate that had given public character to the *kabunakama* (merchant guilds or trade associations), and the relation between the Bakufu Government and self-regulating *kabunakama*.

During the Kyoho Era (1724), the merchants who handled several essential items (such as rice, liquor, firewood, salt and cotton) were summoned to the office of the senior town official (the Naraya; one of the cho-doshiyori) in Yedo City. They were ordered to organize as *kabunakama* in order to restrain a significant rise of prices for daily necessities by price adjustment and mutual self-monitoring by members in the same profession.

These measures made a new political mechanism for commerce and industry, that of using the decision-making process or order: senior town officials (*cho-doshiyori*) → trade associations (*kabunakama*) → individuals in commerce and industry. This process was incorporated into the existing system of the governance of cities: Bakufu Government → city commissioners of Yedo (*machi-bugyo*) → senior town officials (*cho-doshiyori*) → town administrator (*cho-nanushi*) → citizens.

Most of the economic policies of the Bakufu Government were put into operation through this system. The business and industry administration of the Bakufu Government had depended on the autonomously functioning merchant associations (*kabunakama*), established by individuals in commerce and industry. In effect the *kabunakama* functioned as "grassroots" organizations for economic policies of the Bakufu Government.

On the other hand, *kabunakama* had a public character to put their demands to the policies of the government, and to adjust their conflicts in the groups, too. And codified articles were established by such function in the background, and they were given public power.

The mid-18th century saw a worsening of the Bakufu Government finances that depended on taxing rice (land tax). In response the government resisted increasing taxation on rice to focus on new sources of revenue from product circulation.

During the Tanuma Era (1759–1786), the Bakufu Government oversaw progressive economic policies. Tanuma Okitsugu, a member of the Council of Elders (*roju*), recognized the *kabunakama* and encouraged the increase of the Nagasaki trade, the increased production of marine products such as dried shark fin, and also the need of copper for the acquisition of foreign currency, and the use of surplus funds for financing and loans.

The official recognition of the *kabunakama* was undertaken as a part of the progressive overall policy. As part, the Bakufu Government guaranteed a monopoly and competition protection for the enterprises of *kabunakama* organized by those within the elite levels of commerce and industry. In return, the government required them to pay taxes (*myoga-kin*, *unjou*), the equivalent of the current "business tax," and also to maintain limits on *kabunakama* membership.

The *kabunakama* were managed autonomously, being permitted to allow their members to adjust profits of the industry as a whole, keep their codified articles, and settle disputes between their members. There were cases of infringement against the rights and interest of the *kabunakama* by a non-member or the other industries. The *kabunakama* brought the cases before the court of city commissioners for protection or intervention by the Bakufu Government.

In the case of a merchant house being a member of a *kabunakama*, it was still an individual, independent business enterprise. However, it was significantly handicapped if it was not joined to a *kabunakama*, and as the scale of business increased, this tendency was also increased.

Kabunakama varied according to the times, type of industry, and differences among districts. A fact in common was that an individual enterprise or merchant could not open their doors without first joining a *kabunakama*, and to do so, it was necessary to be granted "citizenship" or "membership" by all members in the industry or the *kabunakama*. As the selection was done among the members of *kabunakama*, they were, in effect, selecting the person who was deemed suitable for fulfilling the social responsibility as a president of a business in the same profession.

4.5 Importance of "Going Concern" as Seen in the Revival of the Miscellaneous Wholesale Dealers

The Bakufu Government also regarded "going concern," or viability and longevity of commerce, as most important in its policy making, it being one of the reasons for establishing the codified articles which include items equivalent to CSR. This is evident in the text of the "Report of the Revival of the Miscellaneous Wholesale Dealers" in Kaei 4 (1851).

This historical text recorded the Bakufu Government's decision to revive the Miscellaneous Wholesale Dealers Association (*Sho-tonnya*), which had been abolished 12 years previously. The document recorded the process of policy decision making by the city commissioners of Yedo City that had jurisdiction over this revival, the staff of the city commissioner (*yoriki*, *doshin*), and the senior town officials (*chou-doshiyori*), along with the achievements and the genealogies of each miscellaneous wholesale dealer.

Within these documents, there are many descriptions of efforts by merchants, wholesale dealers, *kabunakama*, and the Bakufu Government to realize economic viability and longevity.

In Tenpou 12 (1841) the Bakufu Government had abolished all *kabunakama* and various associations organized by commerce and industry, citing them as the reason for price increases of goods through a monopoly of distribution. It sought price reductions by the liberalization of new competition.

However, this act caused chaos in the economy. Primarily, since the concept of *kabunakama* was destroyed, so too was the ability to finance a business by borrowing money based on the merchant's "right of business," or *kabu*. And the entry of new enterprises was difficult in sectors of the "exchange" industry that required capital power and high levels of trust. As a result, the prices reduction by promotion of free competition failed. In addition, the flow of operational loans to small suppliers through wholesale dealers hierarchy was adversely affected, too. And, in the sectors relatively easy to enter, the smoothness of circulation was obstructed by excessive competition and destruction of the existing system of distribution (Suzuki, 2002).

To further compound the situation, due to a devastating flood in the Kanto region and a conflagration in Yedo the prices of all goods had skyrocketed. The Bakufu Government was under extreme pressure to establish social policies in order to prevent widespread acts of vandalism (*uchikowashi*) and rioting. In 1851, the Bakufu Government's hands were forced by these problems, and for a solution, it made the decision to revive the *kabunakama* it abolished a decade previously.

The person in charge of the revival of the *kabunakama* was Kagemoto Toyama, one of the city commissioners. Toyama sent a study to his superior official of the Shogun's Council of Elders. In it he suggested that, "If business rules are returned to pre-abolition conditions it will reinforce the enterprise power of the citizens (*cho-nin*) and return confidence and viability to small-scale businesses. This will ease social tension, so the public sentiment will stabilize." In the Yedo Period, the word of "citizen" meant a person who held considerable property, governing business and credit.

The major contents of the Order of the Revival of Various Wholesale Dealers followed in the Toyama document. These included, for example, the restrictions on licensing, exemptions from of *myoga-kin* (business) tax, roles in price reduction, prohibiting number limiting of members of *kabunakama* (abolition of entry barriers).

In the draft of the Order that was prepared by the city commissioner's office, it was evident a basic principle was that serious consideration be given to the "on going concern" of business (Historiographical Institute The University of Tokyo, 1959). The following description is to be found in this draft.

> "The citizens should not consider their position a luxury, but be thankful for the benevolence of the Shogun who had brought the peace, and they should endeavor to maintain the permanency of their businesses." They should be "thankful for living in Yedo City safely, consider the convenience of their situation in the four social classes (warriors, farmers, craftsmen, and merchants), and run their businesses steadily and honestly."

In the Yedo Period, the exchange dealers (*ryo-gae*), functioning much as banks of today, were typical of the enterprise in the market. In the text of the Revival, a description is given of the process of a dispute between existing exchange dealers and newly established enterprises. The existing exchange dealers had conducted business before the abolition of the *kabunakama* in 1841, while the new dealers had started the business after the revival.

In the dispute, the existing exchange dealers called for the rejection of new entries, appealing to one to the city commissioners. Their most important claim was that their "going concern" (viability) had suffered from the new entries. Conversely, one requirement for the new exchange dealers was recognition by the city commissioner of their ability to be viable, long-term business concerns. This confirms that both the Bakufu Government and citizens had regarded long-term viability or continuation, the going concern of business important.

4.6 Office Regulations of Merchantile Houses and Social Responsibility

Finally, we will examine the relationship between the office regulations of individual merchantile houses (as opposed to the codified articles of the *kabunakama*, see Section 4.2) and corporate social responsibility. One example is the office regulations that were set by the Cotton Wholesale Dealer of Hasegawa for its branch in Yedo City (*Yedo-dana*) in 1768 (Tokyo

Metropolitan Archives, 1978). The head office of Hasegawa was in Kishuu (contemporary Wakayama Prefecture), and its main profession was cotton and ginned cotton. The former regulations were revised for two reasons. Firstly, it was considered that the old regulations had become lax and out-of-date. Secondly, the executives of *Yedo-dana* had suffered financial losses by dealing with issues outside of their main profession.

The new regulations required the observance of laws, ordinances and policies of the Bakufu Government, and good business practices, especially emphasizing the strictly prohibition on expanding the scope of their business. There were, however, managers of *Yedo-dana* who violated this latter regulation. This resulted in the president of the head office ordering them to tender a written oath (Tokyo Metropolitan Archives, 1982), pledging diligence of their profession and cost reduction practices.

These regulations and the required oath had been based on business values of the day. The essence of the value was to not change the business form, and to continue the business in the long-term, so "going concern" was most important. Such office regulations were common in many enterprises and merchant houses.

In the governance of enterprises in the Yedo Period, concentrating on a main profession, observation of the laws and ordinances, restraint of extravagance, the reliable collecting of debts or bills, and prevention of inferior credits were considered very important. On the other hand, judging from the situation of the executives of enterprises, expanding the scope of their business was paramount to them, so it had been necessary to prohibit it repeatedly in office regulations. In the latter case this was because there had been opportunities for them to enter into other industries or profession sectors, after they accumulated trusts and funds in their main profession.

The evaluation of large-scale enterprises in discharging their social responsibility had been clearly demonstrated in times of natural disaster, famine, and cases of fire. When these enterprises had not held a high standing in public estimation for CSR, they became targets of vandalism (*uchikowashi*) by residents. Therefore, when famines, for example, occurred, large scale enterprises often offered food and financial aid to the tenants who lived in their tenement houses or to residents living in the town where the enterprises was located.

On one hand, it was enough for enterprises to observe the laws and ordinances of the Bakufu Government, follow the codified articles and traditional business practices of the *kabunakama* and take care of the relationship with their customers and the member of the *kabunakama*. But, in order to hold and enjoy their economic activities in the city, they had to make efforts to raise their social evaluation in the eyes of the people.

4.7 CSR that Links the Public and the Private

A characteristic of Japanese industry in the Yedo Period was the development of diverse industries, such as those devoted to the production of food by agriculture, for example intensive rice crops, the textile industry, including the production of cotton and silk, and the mining industry (gold, silver and copper etc.).

These industries had needed diverse social relationships, and as such required a different background from the "individualistic" structure of Western and American industry in those days. In Japan, the territorial management of feudal lords (*daimyo*) and the economic activities of commerce and industry were run by organization of households (*ie*) that were much like business firms. The households of samurai were pyramidal organizations for governing the country, and under this system, the economical activities of agriculture, manufacturing, and commerce were managed effectively, ensuring their longevity.

Furthermore, it was a typically Japanese characteristic that enterprises that maintained continuation from the ancient times had been respected, given that this was achieved with much difficulty. Therefore, both the government and the management respected the longevity and viability of such enterprises.

It was in this climate that many codified articles were established, containing items similar to today's CSR. Items made to respect not only the profits of management but also the various stakeholders such as those in the same profession, the suppliers, the customers, the government, and the local residents.

Accordingly, the evolution of corporate social responsibility as an element of Japanese economic activities and the development of the system are parallel with the early modern history of the Japanese economy itself. CSR had matured from "folk" customs both universal and general to established economic policy. Japanese people have attached importance to CSR, and used it to connect the public and private since early modern times.

However, this "social system" of management, based on the social agreement developed in Japan, has been increasingly eroded during the economic growth after the World War II and the collapse of the so-called "bubble" asset-inflated economy.

For persons of having some knowledge of the early modern economic history in Japan, it may seem quite ironic that corporate social responsibility is now a focus of interest in the European and American style of capitalism in the 21st century.

References

Historiographical Institute, The University of Tokyo (1959). Shotonnya-saiko-shirabe 2, *Tokyo Daigaku Shuppankai*, pp. 5–6. (in Japanese)

Ko, I., Tsuji, N., Scot, D., Seo, T. and Kubo, S. (2003). Kigyou no Shakaiteki-sekini, *Nihon Kikaku Kyokai*, pp. 10–15. (in Japanese)

Okamoto, K. (2004). CSR Nyumon, *Nihon Keizai Shinbun Sha*, pp. 28–33. (in Japanese)

Suzuki, K. (2002). Shihonshugi ha Yedo de Umareta, *Nihon Keizai Shinbun Sha*, pp. 268–270. (in Japanese)

Tokyo Metropolitan Archives (1968). Ishi Tonnya Nakama Shoyo Tamari, *Tokyo-shi-shi-ko Sangyohen* 12, pp. 519–522. (in Japanese)

Tokyo Metropolitan Archives (1968). Tokumi Nakama Hikae, *Tokyo-shi-shi-ko Sangyohen* 12, pp. 176–184. (in Japanese)

Tokyo Metropolitan Archives (1978). Okite Hou Ki, *Tokyo-shi-shi-ko Sangyohen* 22, pp. 523–530. (in Japanese)

Tokyo Metropolitan Archives (1982). Okite Hou Ki, *Tokyo-shi-shi-ko Sangyohen* 26, pp. 387–388. (in Japanese)

PART 2

PLANNING AND CONTROL OF BUSINESS STRATEGY: VALUATION OF FIRMS AND EVALUATION OF MANAGERS

CHAPTER

5

Valuation of Businesses and Evaluation of Managers: The Global Standard and Japanese Models

Yasuhiro Monden
Professor, Faculty of Business Administration, Mejiro University

5.1 Introduction

After the Japanese economy bubble burst in 1991, the mentality of Japanese top management changed dramatically, from employee- and/or customer-oriented to stockholder-oriented. Until 1991, top management did not need take shareholders into consideration, because the stock price continued to increase and the shareholders easily earned capital gains. However, because top management teams have become unable to steadily earn a sufficient profit, they have come back to the fundamental reality that the owners of the companies are in fact the stockholders, and so the stock price has become the principal evaluation criterion for them, opening the way for *shareholder-value-based management*.

However, since the strength of Japanese companies, in other words the value of their goodwill, lies in human capacity and team work, the author will discuss the ways in which the goals of various stakeholders may be compromised. From this discussion will hopefully arise a new Japanese model of management. This is the age of global standards for various systems of management. The author would like to propose Japanese models for business valuation and the evaluation of managers which are compatible with the global standard.

This paper will discuss the three stages of management, i.e., "plan, do, see," in a broad sense. The first step focuses on *strategy formulation*, the second step focuses on *strategy implementation* (or strategy control), and the final step deals with the *performance evaluation of managers and employees at all levels.*

For each of these three steps, *the author discusses how the concept of residual earnings should be applied to business valuation and the evaluation of manager performance.* Although there are many other methods of evaluating performance which can be used simultaneously with the above measure, the author focuses on residual earnings in this paper.

The first topic is the *valuation system used for business selection*, which is a theme of business strategic decision. There are uniquely Japanese ways of valuating a business in view of business selection and redesign of the organizational structure. The value of a business is measured in order to enable (1) M&A (mergers and acquisitions); and (2) the restructuring of intra-business units and subsidiary companies.

The second topic is *the system of evaluating the performance of managers of decentralized business units.* How can the Japanese evaluation system be applied to managers of decentralized units, such as divisional managers, intra-company managers and subsidiary company presidents? Also, all managers and employees in each of these units must be given their own evaluation tasks. How can these tasks be determined?

The above two mutually related topics will be explored from the viewpoint of residual earnings in the following sections one by one.

5.2 Valuation of a Firm in View of Business Selection: A Survey

Let us first conduct a basic survey of the current knowledge about the value of a firm. There are three accounting methods used as the basis of business valuation. These are: (1) future free cash flow (FCF); (2) future economic profit (residual income (RI) or residual earnings (RE) such as economic value added (EVA^{TM})), where RE = NOPAT (net operating profit after tax) – the total capital cost; and (3) Ohlson's RE (which is the *accounting* net profit after tax minus the owner's capital cost).

Using these indices, the value of a firm can be measured in the following two ways:

1. Value of the firm

   = sum of the present value of the future estimated FCF.

2. Value of the firm

$$= \text{sum of the present value of the future estimated RE} + \text{initial book value of the total assets.}$$

Here, the sum of present value of the future estimated RE is equivalent to the *corporate brand*, *goodwill* or *market value added*. If Company X wishes to buy Company Y, the Company X has to pay not only for the book value of the total assets minus the debt value of Company Y, but also for the goodwill of Company Y calculated using the above formula.

On the other hand, the value of the firm can be defined from the market side as follows:

$$\text{Value of the firm} = \text{shareholder value} + \text{creditor value.}$$

Here, the shareholder value is the total current value of the stock, whereas the creditor value is measured according to the book value in practice.

The above two definitions of the value of a firm are logically connected, as the theory of Miller and Modigliani (1961) shows. The valuation of a firm according to its FCF or RE is linked to the stock price as follows:

$$\text{Shareholder value} = \text{sum of the present value of the future estimated RE} + \text{initial book value of the owner's capital.}$$

Ohlson (1995), assuming the clean surplus condition, has developed the following formula:

$$\text{Shareholder value} = \text{sum of the present value of the future estimated Ohlson's RE} + \text{initial book value of the owner's capital.}$$

Thus, the selection of a business according to the larger FCF- or RE-based firm value will theoretically enhance the stock price.

The theory of Miller and Modigliani is logical, because the FCF is the maximum amount of money that the top management can *freely* allocate to the stockholders as dividends, and if the FCF increases, then the stock price will also increase because the shareholders will welcome the larger dividends. However, all variables in this theory are future estimated figures: the RE is the stockholder's estimated residual earning over a given future period and the stock price is also future-estimated. Thus, this theory cannot be empirically tested using *past* data. It is absurd to try to verify the correlation between the actual stock price and the actual RE figure over a short period, since the stock price fluctuates due to many other factors, including speculation. The theory also assumes that all other factors are constant and that the market is characterized by perfect competition, which is not possible in the real world.

Now, using the value of a business as calculated above, the business will be selected according to the following criteria:

* If the value of a business > the book value of its total assets, then the business is a value-creating one that should be continued.
* If the value of a business < the book value of its total assets, then the business is a value-destroying one that should be discontinued.

Then, how can we practically measure the value of a business that survives indefinitely as a going concern? There are two simplified methods of valuation, assuming that the FCF during any future period t is constant and the same as that during the initial period, $t = 1$, or supposing that the RE during any future period t is constant and the same as that during the initial period, $t = 1$. Under these assumptions, the simplest methods are:

$$\begin{aligned}\text{Value of the business} &= \text{FCF in period 1} \div \text{capital cost rate.}\\ \text{Value of the business} &= (\text{RE in period 1} \div \text{capital cost rate})\\ &\quad + \text{initial book value of the total assets.}\end{aligned}$$

The above methods are based on the formula of infinite geometric series. Further, the following methods are also used:

$$\begin{aligned}&\text{Value of the business}\\ &\quad = (\text{sum of the present values of each FCF for the coming 5 years})\\ &\qquad + \textit{present value} \text{ of } \{\text{the FCF in period 5} \div (\text{capital cost rate}\\ &\qquad - \text{growth rate})\}.\\ &\text{Value of the business}\\ &\quad = (\text{sum of the present values of each RE for the coming 5 years})\\ &\qquad + \textit{present value} \text{ of } \{\text{the RE in period 5} \div (\text{capital cost rate}\\ &\qquad - \text{growth rate})\} + \text{initial book value of the total assets.}\end{aligned}$$

5.3 Determination of Target Residual Earnings

How can we incorporate the requirements of stakeholders other than investors into the handling of the residual earnings? If this is possible, then the global standard emphasizing the shareholder's goal can be reconciled with the Japanese management style emphasizing the employee's goal.

In setting the target NOPAT, which constitutes the residual earnings, the various goals of stakeholders such as the employees, customers, local residents, etc., must all be taken into account. That is, profitability measures coordinated with various goals other than the investor's goal should be considered, or, in other words, the *residual earnings must be maximized under the constraints of many other goal requirements*. Therefore, top management should coordinate the goals of various stakeholders when it makes decisions regarding fund allocation.

Decisions regarding fund utilization in this context include (1) the planning of cash flows; and (2) the planning of periodical allocations of revenues and expenses. Examples of (1) are cash-outlay (expenditure) plans for facility investments, R&D and pensions. Examples of (2) are allocation plans for depreciations of R&D expenditures, goodwill, facilities, etc., to stimulate the profit motive of investors.

For this purpose, the necessary cash payments to each stakeholder can be planned using a *balanced scorecard*. Here, it should be emphasized that the origin of the balanced scorecard lies in Japanese TQM. In the preface of the book by Kaplan and Norton (1996), it is said that they got the idea of the balanced scorecard from the *corporate scorecard* of Analog Devices, Inc., which was in turn adopted from Yokogawa Hewlett Packard, a company that had introduced Japanese TQM. Another similar tool has also been reported: the *tableau du bord* developed in France (Bouquin, 1997). It should be noted that similar ideas appear independently in various countries throughout the world.

Now, the balanced scorecard described by Kaplan and Norton consisted of the following four viewpoints:

1. Finance viewpoint (goal of the stockholder).
2. Customer viewpoint (goal of the customer).
3. Learning and growth viewpoint (goal of the employee).
4. Internal business process viewpoint (goal of the customer).

Examples of the learning and growth viewpoint (goal of the employee) are (1) the planning of employee training costs to facilitate the professional development of employees; (2) the planning of R&D costs for acquiring knowledge assets; and (3) the planning of retirement pensions, etc.

Let us examine in more detail the planning of *retirement pensions*. The following is a formula describing the pension expenses:

Annual pension expenses
= (the total pension expense based on labor costs and interest costs for the year)
– (the revenues accrued from the application of the pension asset).

This amount of annual pension expenses will also be added to the *allowances for the retirement wages*. Now, the revenue from the applied fund will be smaller and the yearly pension expenses will be *larger* if a *lower* return ratio is estimated, and as a result the allowances for the retirement wages will be greater. (Japanese companies are applying *higher* expected return ratios when measuring the annual pension expenses. However, *lower* return ratios were more realistic in the 90s Japanese economic climate.)

If the yearly pension expense is *larger*, then an *excess debt* due to the enlarged allowances for the retirement wages may appear on balance sheet and a net deficit on the income statement, such that the stock price of the company will fall and fund procurement will be difficult. Eventually, the company may go bankrupt.

Therefore, at least the *minimum* amount of pension and reserve for the retirement allowance which the employees find satisfactory must be considered in planning the target NOPAT, and the *minimum* amount of capital cost for the investors will be deducted from this target NOPAT. In order to clear these minimum requirements or constraints imposed by various stakeholders, top management must ensure *positive* residual earnings (= target NOPAT – total capital cost).

Because the investors' funds come from global capital markets, the minimum capital cost must be covered, while the employees' labor costs are changeable due to their domestic feature. But both groups of stakeholders *must* be treated fairly.

5.3.1 Income sharing and stockholder value in the long term

The RE is considered to belong to the investors, but the author proposes that they should belong to the company itself rather than the investors only. That is, the survival of the company is the supreme goal of any business, and the purpose of creating and enhancing the business value of a company is to ensure business survival and growth, because all stakeholders are using the company as a means to their own personal goals, i.e., salaries, dividends, etc. Thus, the RE should be maximized and allocated to (or shared by) various stakeholders under the constraints imposed by the capital and labor markets on the capital and labor costs, etc. If the RE is *negative*, then the stockholders must also take responsibility for their failure to control the top management team properly, in the form of dividend cuts and capital losses. This is what the author calls *the Japanese model of RE*.

The CEO of a company may attribute his or her unwillingness to cut the dividends to the possibility that he or she might be fired by the stockholders in the annual shareholder meeting. And the right to fire the CEO does indeed belong to the stockholders. However, the CEO should try to convince the shareholders that merely cutting the labor costs will eventually damage the stockholder value and implicitly the stock price of the company, since a massive reduction of labor costs will damage the RE in the long run, as it will undermine the human capital that creates the company's *corporate brand* or *goodwill*, which constitutes the higher value of the firm. Unless human resources are highly valued and human-resource-based management is applied, no corporate brand can be created and maintained, and so a reduction in human capital will damage the stockholder value in the long run. From this perspective, the current legal scheme of capitalism is imperfect and should be reformed as soon as possible.

5.3.2 *Capital sharing*

Above, a concept of income sharing among shareholders, employees and many other stakeholders was proposed. This idea may be extended to the concept of capital sharing. Essentially, the capital invested by the stockholders will not be redeemed to them again, whereas the bond capital invested by bond holders must be refunded at a given moment in time. This means that part of the stockholders funds (legal capital reserve) is used to stabilize the financial conditions of the business. That amount should be utilized for paying back the company debt, etc., when a financial crisis strikes. Corresponding to the magnitude of this liability, the stockholders are endowed with substantial voting rights in the stockholder meeting. Therefore, their excessive claim to as much dividend as possible on the basis of their capital ownership, must be forcibly limited.

Also, the concepts of expense and revenue should be considered. An expense is essentially a fund that should be deducted from the capital, whereas a revenue is a fund that should be added to the capital. Thus, if the employees are told that the capital belongs only to the shareholders, they will not be motivated to save their excess spending money or their excess assets in their workplaces.

Further, under the life-long employment system and the wage hierarchy according to seniority, two traditional features of Japanese companies, the salaries of younger employees have to be kept at lower levels and the shortage in payment is given to them as they age. (It should not be considered that the amount of shortage is given to the existing elder employees.) This means that the amount of shortage in payment for younger employees should be regarded as an employee *retained income* kept within the current company capital.

Therefore, the capital on the balance sheet of a company should be considered as a common wealth of the stockholders and the employees. Or, to put it differently, the capital should be considered to belong to the company itself, because all stakeholders are using the company and they all contribute to the enhancement or maintenance of the current capital.

5.4 Method of Measuring of the Business Value of an Internal Company or Division

Japan has a unique way of keeping track of the performance of internal companies or divisions: each internal company or division has its own *artificial balance sheet*, which shows the divisional debts, divisional owners' capital and divisional total assets. (The internal company is usually a business unit which has aggregated several internal divisions.) In Western countries, companies do not normally use such *divisional balance sheets*. The divisional owner's capital is set based on the internal capital system. There are several of methods of setting the divisional internal capital. The first method is to calculate the divisional owner's capital as the divisional total assets minus the divisional debt endowed by the central HQ. The second is to designate a portion of the company's legal capital allocated to the division as the divisional capital, based on the divisional total assets or fixed assets. The third is to calculate the divisional capital depending on (1) the necessary amount of working capital for the divisional sales plus; and (2) the amount of fixed assets of the division. The third method is described in detail in Monden (1985).

The divisional FCF and RE are easy to measure using the divisional balance sheet, the divisional income statement and the headquarters' capital cost rate.

5.5 Tools for Controlling the Selected Business

There is a tool called "business process mapping analysis" developed by American consulting firms for implementing and controlling selected businesses; it is also very similar to the *policy deployment system* of Japan's TQM. This technique comprises the following four steps:

1. The *target RE* is broken down into various major revenue items, cost items and asset items. These items will further be traced to each operating process in the value-chain of the business in question (Figure 5.1).
2. The *value drivers* (major factors) that influence the major costs, revenues and asset items of each process are then identified.
3. The *key value drivers* (KVDs) are selected from the value drivers, in terms of sensitivity and feasibility with regard to the improvement of the business value.
4. The KPI (key performance index) and KPM (key performance measure) are derived from the KVD. Examples of KPI are manufacturing lead time, inventory turnover, development lead time, etc.

The target residual earning of the business consists of (1) and (2):

(1) The NOPAT consists of:

Operating revenues --------- Sales revenues ----- *Sales process*

Operating expenses *Processes of value-chain functions:*

- R&D cost ------------- *R&D process*
- Manufacturing cost -- *Manufacturing process*
- Marketing cost ------ *Marketing process*
- Sales cost ----------- *Sales process*
- Logistics cost ------- *Logistics process*

(2) The CAPITAL COST consists of:

Owner's capital cost

Creditor's capital cost

Assets ------------------------

- Monetary assets
- Inventory assets
- Fixed assets

Fig. 5.1 Policy deployment

5.6 Criteria for Evaluating the Managers of Divisions, Internal Companies and Subsidiary Companies

It is well known that the ROI (return on investment), ROA (return on assets) and ROE (return on equity) have some disadvantage when used for evaluating divisional managers. That is, they may induce sub-unit managers to make *sub-optimal* decisions. On the other hand, the RI or RE can always induce the corporate *total-optimal* decisions. Concretely, if the ROI of a new investment project is greater than the capital cost rate, then the total RI of the division which adopted this new project will always improve.

Thus, the RE (for examples, EVA^{TM} and its relatives) will induce the following responses when used for evaluating a manager's performance: (1) total-optimum behavior; and (2) value-based management. The second advantage implies stockholder-value-oriented management, in that if a divisional manager improves the RE figure, the stock price of the company also improves.

5.6.1 *Evaluation methods for employees at all levels*

MBO (management by objectives), which is based on the *policy deployment* of TQM or *process mapping analysis* described in the previous section, determines the target amounts of various evaluation measures for the tasks of the managers and employees at all levels of the organization.

5.6.2 *Japanese model of residual income: Intra-company interest system under the intra-company capital system*

There are numerous variations on the RE measure, which include:

1. RI, traditionally used in the US multi-divisional companies.
2. EVA^{TM}, based on the theory behind the CAPM (capital asset pricing model).
3. Ohlson's residual earning, which is the *accounting* net profit after tax – the owner's capital cost.
4. Intra-company interest system under the intra-company capital system used in Japanese multi-divisional companies or intra-company (business unit) systems (These systems were initially developed in 1944 by the Matsushita Electric Company, Ltd.).

The details of the Japanese intra-company interest system under the intra-company capital system were first introduced by Monden (1985) and discussed by Kaplan and Atkinson (1998) and others As a kind of the RE systems.

Let us compare the capital cost of the typically American RI with the unique Japanese capital cost system. First, the capital cost of the American RE = weighted average capital cost rate × the *total assets* on the balance sheet. On the other hand, the capital cost of an intra-company capital system = $\sum$ capital cost rate $the_{the}\times$ capital the_{the} on the balance sheet, where capital the_{the} is the source the_{the} of the capital funds introduced into the division. Examples of capital cost the_{the} are (1) the short-term interest rate for a short-term debt; and (2) the long-term interest rate for a long-term debt and for the internal capital. Both the short-term and the long-term interest rates are usually the *prime rate* offered by banks to excellent companies. (The internal capital system of a division was explained in Section 5.4).

In other words, the Western system charges the capital cost to the asset side (or the debtor's side) of the balance sheet, while the Japanese system charges the capital cost to the capital sources side (or the creditor's side) of the balance sheet. The reader may think that the two are the same because the weighted average cost of the capital was initially measured based on the owner's cost and the creditor's cost separately. However, since Western countries use no balance sheets for the divisions or intra-companies within a firm, they cannot identify the sources of the various capital funds introduced into each division or internal company.

Further, regarding the objects of interest charge, there are three types of intra-company interest systems:

Type 1: Interest is charged only on short- and long-term debts.
Type 2: Interest is charged on (1) short- and long-term debts; and (2) the intra-company (divisional) capital.
Type 3: Interest is charged on (1) short- and long-term debts; (2) the intra-company (divisional) capital; and (3) the retained income.

Among these, the third type is essentially equivalent to the RE system of $\mathrm{EVA}^{\mathrm{TM}}$ and the like.

There are various advantages to charging interest on the capital sources side of the balance sheet, which are not seen in Western systems, as follows:

1. It will *directly* motivate the divisional managers to pay back the division's debt. It is true that, on the balance sheet, the total amount on debtor side is equivalent to the total amount on the creditor side, and when the debtor side is decreased, the creditor side also decreases automatically; nevertheless, the Japanese system directly motivates managers to reduce the debt itself.
2. It will not motivate managers to make only R&D expenditures that will be *quickly* depreciated, and it does not discourage them to invest in the *long-term* projects.
3. The capital (debt capital) invested into assets which are almost depreciated will also be apt to be paid back to the creditors.
4. The *accumulated deficit* or *retained deficit* will be explicitly shown on the division's balance sheet.

Additionally, it should be mentioned that the American RE, such as EVA™, is a more sophisticated concept which takes the risks involved in the capital market into account, thanks to the CAPM theory, but the internal capital system does not take the market risk into account explicitly even though it would be more feasible. However, American-RE advocates also emphasize the importance of capital-cost consciousness of the managers over the theoretical aspect of the risks involved in the security market. This capital-cost consciousness of the managers is also the most important aspect of the Japanese internal interest system. Further, the internal capital system is not used to evaluate legally independent firms. Thanks to the American RE concept, Japanese companies are now evaluating their subsidiary companies as well as their own companies according to the American RE concept.

5.7 Conclusion and Summary

There are three main Japanese models of business valuation proposed by the author. The first is *the Japanese model of residual earnings*. The residual earnings are usually believed to belong to the investors, but they should belong to the company itself rather than the investors alone. Thus, a firm should be valuated according to new criteria, using the concept of residual earnings. The RE should be maximized and allocated to various stakeholders under the various constraints imposed by the capital market, the labor market, the consumer market, etc.

The second is *the Japanese method of measuring the business value of internal companies or divisions and the divisional managers' performances.* Each internal company or division has its own *artificial divisional balance sheet*, which shows the debts, owners' capital, retained income and total assets of the internal company or division in question. The divisional FCF and RE are easy to measure using the internal balance sheet, the income statement and the headquarters' capital cost rates. In other words, there is a unique Japanese way of measuring the divisional residual income using *the intra-company interest system under the intra-company capital system*, whose original merits have been demonstrated in this paper.

Third, the tools for controlling the selected business, which are the *balanced scorecard* and *business process mapping analysis*, are similar to the *policy deployment system* of Japan's TQM. These techniques are also used when determining the target amounts of measures for evaluating all employees of a company. MBO (management by objectives) based on the *policy deployment* of TQM relies on balanced scorecards and business process mapping analyses.

In conclusion, the author believes that combining the tools of the East (the Japanese concept of residual earnings, the internal interest system under the internal capital system, the policy deployment system, etc.) with the tools of the West (the balanced scorecard, the CAPM theory, EVA^{TM}, the residual income, Ohlson's residual earnings, etc.) will promote the development of a superior management system. Although Western tools are sometimes believed to be the best in the world, constituting a global standard, eventually no company will be able to compete when all companies in the world use the same global standard. Therefore, we have to continuously develop tools and concepts that surpass the current best ones.

References

Grant, J. L. (1997). *Foundations of Economic Value Added*, Frank J. Fabozzi Associates New Hope.

Bouquin, H. (1997). *La Comtabilite de Gestion*, Presses Universitaires de France.

Hiki, F. (1996). Purposes and functions of internal capital system, *Cost Accounting Research* 20-2, pp. 43–45. (in Japanese)

Kaplan, R. V. and Atkinson, A. A. (1998). *Advanced Management Accounting*, 3rd ed, Prentice Hall.

Kaplan, R. V. and Norton, D. (1996). *The Balanced Scorecard — Translating Strategy into Action*, Harvard Business School Press.

Kaplan, R. V. and Norton, D. (2001). *The Strategy-Focused Organization*, Harvard Business School Press.

Miller, M. and Modigliani, F. (1961). Dividend policy, growth, and the valuation of shares, *Journal of Business* 34-4, pp. 411–433.

Monden, Y. (1985). Japanese management control systems, in Monden *et al.* (ed.) *Innovations in Management: The Japanese Corporation*, Engineering and Management Press.

Ohlson, J. (1995). Earnings, book values, and dividends in equity valuation, *Contemporary Accounting Research* 11-2, pp. 394–409.

Ogura, N. (1995). Functions and limitation of divisional balance sheet from the viewpoint of capital cost management, *Cost Accounting Research* 19-1, pp. 55–66. (in Japanese)

Penman, S. H. (2002). Tying valuation to performance with financial analysis, *The Journal of Management Accounting, Japan* 10-2, pp. 3–12.

Prince, T. A. (1964). The motivational assumption for accounting theory, *The Accounting Review*, July, pp. 553–562.

Solomons, D. (1965). *Divisional Performance: Measurement and Control*, Richard D. Irwin.

Stewart, G. B. III. (1991). *The Quest for Value — The EVA^{TM} Management Guide*, HarperCollins Publishers.

CHAPTER

6

Valuation of Business Based on EVA-Type Metrics in Japanese Companies

Shufuku Hiraoka

Professor, Faculty of Business Administration
Soka University

6.1 Introduction

Japanese managers have been interested in management methods that create corporate value through capital efficiency since the latter half of 1990s. They have focused on the cost of capital, which is the return expected by the stockholders.

Stern Stewart & Co. in the US developed EVA^{TM} (economic value added), whereas many Japanese managers have independently create EVA-type metrics to measure and create corporate value. Such metrics have been used for the valuation of business, for instance.

In this chapter, we will present three EVA-type metrics that have been discussed to date by researchers. Then, we will explain how EVA-type metrics are used in Japanese companies for business valuation. Finally, we will re-examine the validity of EVA-type metrics for business valuation.

6.2 Three EVA-type Metrics

Traditionally, EVA-type metrics are certain kinds of economic profit (Marshall, 1890; Copeland, 1994; Peterson and Peterson, 1996).

The next 3 metrics are representative examples.

6.2.1 *The abnormal earnings included in the Ohlson model*

The Ohlson model of economic profit is a well-known metric. It calculates stockholder value as the stockholder capital book value at the beginning of a given period plus the present value of the abnormal earnings expected in the future (Ohlson, 1995). The abnormal earnings are defined as follows:

$$\text{Abnormal earnings} = \text{net income} - \text{equity book value at the beginning of a period} \times \text{risk-free rate.}$$

When an enterprise is being valuated, the net income in the above formula can be with the equity book value at the beginning of a period for financial reports. However, those values are based on financial accounting standards. Therefore, they are merely values influenced by the accounting policies rather than values influenced by the strategies for increasing corporate value. Nevertheless, because it is easy for investors to obtain these values, some studies (Inoue, 1998; Fujii and Yamamoto, 1999) have demonstrated that in Japan the Ohlson model can explain the market value to some extent.

Moreover, if only the risk-free rate is used, the capital assets pricing model (CAPM) need never be to calculate the cost of capital. We should pay attention to the fact that the equity of a business unit needs to be clarified in order to valuate that business unit with the Ohlson model. Therefore, if an enterprise consists of a certain number of business units, we should distribute the whole equity among the business units. Alternately, since it is easy to grasp the assets of a business unit separately, it is possible to substitute the equity of the business with the net assets of the business, if the debt of the business unit is clarified first.

Yet, even in such a case, we must pay attention to the following:

1. The total net assets of all business units do not equal the whole equity in many cases.
2. The risk-free rate does not reflect the risk of a business unit.

6.2.2 *Residual income*

The residual income (RI) is another well-known metric. It was first introduced at General Electric to manage the business divisions (Horngren *et al.*,

1996; Aoki, 1998). The RI is calculated as follows:

$$\text{RI} = \text{profit before interest} - \text{imputed interest.}$$

Because the profit before interest is based on accounting, it is similar to the net income in the Ohlson model. However, it is not the net income but the profit before interest-charged division. For example, the controllable profit, contribution margin, operating profit on the income statement, the business profit-added financial return on the operating profit, etc., are used. There are several variations of RI, and this is where it differs from the Ohlson model most markedly. On the other hand, the imputed interest is the cost of capital. When considering the cost of equity, we should apply the weighted average cost of capital (WACC), which is the reflected the ratio between the liability with interest and the equity, when we determine it. In the US, it is very difficult to find cases in which the liability with interest and the equity are distributed among business divisions (Ogura, 1995, 1996); instead of the capital of the business division, the total assets of a business division are used to calculate the cost of capital. There are Japanese enterprises that calculate the RI using the cost of capital determined by this method. Even if we call it an EVA-type metric, it differs clearly from the EVA developed by Stern Stewart & Co., and should simply be called RI. There are the two types of WACC used for calculating the RI, as follows:

1. Only the rate of the cost of capital is applied to all business divisions as a whole.
2. The rate reflects the risk of each business division.

As stated above, this concept of RI differs from that used in the Ohlson model in both the profit before the cost of capital and the profit after the cost of capital. Also, the cost of capital-charged division is deducted from the profit before interest, because the RI has been adopted for the purpose of evaluating the performance of a division from the beginning. Furthermore, not only the profit but also the assets are based on accounting in RI, another point of difference from EVA. Also notable is the fact that the CAPM is not necessarily useful for calculating the cost of equity in RI. For instance, the cost rate of equity could be thought of as the expected dividend plus the capital gain divided by the stock price at the beginning of the given period, which is the total shareholder return. In calculating the cost of equity, although we may always be forced to utilize the CAPM in calculating the EVA, we do not always make use of the CAPM in calculating the RI.

6.2.3 EVA, an invention of Stern Stewart & Co

EVA is a trademark of Stern Stewart & Co. It is a metric used for valuating a corporation. It was used as a financial indicator in the beginning (Stewart, 1991). At present, it is also used as an internal management system (Ogura, 2000).

The EVA is defined as follows:

$$\text{EVA} = \text{net operating profits after tax} - \text{WACC} \times \text{capital}.$$

The net operating profit after tax (NOPAT) is not simply the value of the operating profits after the tax has been deducted in accounting. By the same token, the capital is not simply the value-added liability with interest on the equity in accounting. Stewart (1994) has demonstrated that the EVA is a type of RI with peculiar characteristics. Biddle *et al.* (1997) have emphasized that the differences between the RI and the EVA lie in the adjustment items for the profit and the capital. According to Aoki (1998), the RI is merely a metric used for evaluating the performance of a division, while the EVA is not only related to the market value added (MVA) but also to the bonus system. The values of the profit and the capital are not used in accounting but modified in accordance with the manager's purposes. The MVA is defined as follows:

$$\text{MVA} = \text{market value} - \text{capital after adjustments}.$$

If the book value of the liabilities is equivalent to the current price of the liabilities, the MVA can also be defined as follows:

$$\begin{aligned}\text{MVA} &= \text{stock price} \times \text{outstanding capital of stock}\\ &\quad - \text{capital with some adjustments}.\end{aligned}$$

Including some of the specifications mentioned above, the differences between the EVA and the traditional RI can be summarized as follows (Hiraoka, 2002, 2003):

1. The profit and capital of the RI are based on accounting, while those of the EVA undergo some adjustments that seem to be important for implementing business strategies.
2. The CAPM is used to calculate the cost of equity.
3. The advanced EVA system includes the bonus system.
4. Since the EVA is related to the MVA or the stock price, management is emphasized as the creator of stockholder value.

The adjustments applied to the EVA are customized in accordance with the individual needs of the enterprises that receive consultancy from Stern Stewart & Co. Some of the adjustments are described below (Stewart, 1991; Matsui, 1999; Tsumori, 1999, 2001; Hiraoka, 2002, 2003):

1. Add the present value of the non-capitalized leases to the net property, the plant and the equipment.
2. Capitalize the R&D and marketing expenses.
3. Change the method of appraising inventories from LIFO to FIFO.
4. Do not depreciate intangible assets (especially goodwill and trademarks).
5. Convert provisions into cash flow.
6. Cumulate unusual losses (or gains) after taxes (for example, restructuring expenses).
7. Adjust some items of the consolidated financial statements (minority interest, equity method, goodwill, foreign currency adjustment).
8. Subtract marketable securities and constructions in progress.
9. Include non-interest-bearing long-term liabilities (for example, retirement and pension allowance).

Are some of the EVA-type metrics used in Japanese enterprises genuine EVA metrics or traditional RI metrics? What peculiar characteristics do these metrics have? These issues will be discussed later.

6.3 EVA-type Metrics Adopted by Japanese Enterprises

In this section, we would like to present the EVA-type metrics adopted by Japanese enterprises.

6.3.1 *EVA at Kao*

The EVA was first introduced at Kao via the Andrew Jergens Company (the Kao Brands Company at present) in the US in 1997. After that, it was introduced as a whole. In fiscal 2005, it will to be introduced in all subsidiary companies and foreign companies of the Kao Group. Needless to say, Kao has received consultancy from Stern Stewart & Co. It has been one of the most important aims of the people at Kao to increase the EVA, because this metric is intertwined with the compensation (bonus) system affecting everyone, from top management to clerks. It is the first attempt in Japan at engaging all employees in the boosting of the EVA.

The main adjustments that brought to the profit and the capital are the following (Ito, 2001):

1. Unusual losses (or gains) for restructuring businesses.
2. Goodwill resulting from M&A.
3. Purchased right of brand marks.

The EVA and the capital after adjustment are calculated as follows:

$$\text{EVA} = \text{sales} - \text{taxes} \pm \text{adjustments} - (\text{capital} \pm \text{adjustments}) \times \text{WACC}.$$

$$\text{Capital after adjustments} = \text{net working capital} + \text{fixed assets} \pm 1, 2 \text{ and } 3.$$

It is possible for the manager of each business unit to grasp the EVA as it is calculated above. The main purpose of the EVA adopted by Kao seems to be to enhance performance management. However, if the manager pays attention only to the EVA of one fiscal year, he or she may be misled in the decision making process concerning investment and business. Concentrating on the short-term EVA may result in a decrease in the long-term EVA. When a business is valuated, the long-term EVA is relevant, and the business value is equivalent to the present expected value of all future EVA created by the business plus the initial capital after adjustment. If the business value is positive, the business is continued. If the business value is negative, the business is terminated. Because Kao wants to concentrate management resources on the important and new businesses, the EVA is utilized to valuate the businesses in view of long-term success.

6.3.2 *SVA at HOYA*

In 1998, HOYA adopted a metric called the "stockholder value added (SVA)" for valuating its businesses and managers. Stern Stewart & Co. did not provide consultancy to HOYA on this matter; the SVA was independently introduced, because the EVA was deemed to be too complicated. The SVA differs from the EVA in that it makes use of assets instead of capital. The assets of the businesses are used as well. Therefore, the weighted average cost of assets (WACA) is used instead of the weighted average cost of capital (WACC), as follows:

$$\text{WACA} = (\text{interest expenses for interest-bearing liability} + \text{cost of equity}) \div \text{total assets}.$$

The cost of equity is independently calculated as follows:

$$\text{Cost of equity} = \text{rate of expected return} \times \text{equity}$$
$$= (\text{The long-term interest} + \text{risk premium}) \times \text{equity}.$$

As for the rate of expected return, it is not certain whether or not the CAPM is used. HOYA has stipulated the rate of expected return at 8%. The net operating profit after tax (NOPAT) is calculated as follows:

$$\text{NOPAT} = (\text{operating profit} + \text{financial income}) \times (1 - \text{effective tax rate}).$$

Here, the NOPAT is generally called the "business profit after tax" in financial analysis. The SVA is defined as follows:

$$\text{SVA} = \text{Total assets} \times (\text{NOPAT}/\text{Total assets} - \text{WACA})$$
$$= \text{Total assets} \times (\text{ROA} - \text{WACA}),$$

Where ROA is the return on assets, the return is NOPAT, and the assets are the total assets.

There are never complicated adjustments to be made in the SVA. In this, it is similar to the RI. The profitability is controlled through the ROA at HOYA, because it is easy for managers and their subordinates to understand the assets included in the ROA. Japanese management traditionally respect voluntary actions and opinions, since they are connected to continuous improvement. The SVA has some characteristics typical of Japanese value-based management, fusing Japanese management with EVA-based management. Furthermore, the SVA has been utilized not only to evaluate the managers of business divisions and subsidiary companies, but also to allocate management resources to them. It is the total management (including business restructuring, budgeting and managing value drivers) that creates the corporate value of the HOYA group as a whole.

6.3.3 *NEP at the Nippon Paper Group*

An EVA-tape metric was introduced at the Nippon Paper Group in fiscal 2000. At first, it was used to measure the performance of the businesses and factories of the Nippon Paper Co. The Nippon Paper Group did not receive consultancy from Stern Stewart & Co. on this matter, and this original metric has been called the "NEP" (Nippon Paper Economic Profit). It was introduced in the subsidiary companies and in the Daishowa Paper Co. in fiscal 2001. The managers of the Nippon Paper Group have utilized the

NEP in order to improve the capital efficiency of the group as a whole. They thought that a metric should be simple and create concrete profit. Therefore, they designed the NEP so that it could be easily and effectively calculated, as follows (Ichige, 2001):

$$\text{NEP} = \text{recurring profit} - \text{cost of equity.}$$

Later, they started to deduce the capital invested in the business from the balance sheet in order to calculate the WACC. If the WACC is used, the profit before the cost of capital is the profit before interest. It is similar to the business profit as defined in financial analysis. At the Nippon Paper Group, the profit after taxes is used to valuate the company as a whole, and the profit before taxes is used to evaluate each business. The latter method prevents the return of taxes to the businesses that raise deficits, in order to maintain overall adjustability If they use the profit before taxes after the cost of capital for evaluating the businesses, they would simply be using the RI. Furthermore, the return on investment (ROI) has been used to see the spread with WACC. The NEP is calculated as follows:

$$\begin{aligned}\text{NEP} &= \text{business profit before taxes} - \text{WACC} \times \text{capital}\\ &= (\text{business profit before taxes/capital} - \text{WACC}) \times \text{capital}\\ &= (\text{ROI} - \text{WACC}) \times \text{capital.}\end{aligned}$$

The WACC before taxes was set at 6.64–7.1% (cost of equity, 12%; interest, 2%). If the WACC is applied to the companies in the group, the intended capital structure is as follows:

$$\text{Equity} : \text{Liabilities} = 50 : 50.$$

In the Nippon Paper Group, the use of the NEP has brought about a shift in management resources from businesses with a lower capital efficiency to others business with a higher capital efficiency, raising the overall capital efficiency; it has also induced employees to effectively utilize the assets and decrease useless inventories in the work place. However, if the Nippon Paper Group intends to further promote EVA-type metrics for management, they should clarify the meaning of economic value once more, consider some new adjustments, and find new ways of linking the metrics with the compensation system.

6.3.4 *CCM and MEP at the Matsushita group*

Matsushita Electric Industrial and Matsushita Electric Works both belong to the Matsushita group. The former took possession of 51% of the equity of the latter as a result of a take-over bid in fiscal 2004. Before this, the Matsushita group had valuated the businesses separately. The EVA-type metric adopted by Matsushita Electric Industrial is called the "CCM (capital cost management)," and is an original method. Needless to say, the Matsushita group has not received consultancy from Stern Stewart & Co. in this matter. The CCM is calculated as follows:

$$\begin{aligned}\text{CCM} &= (\text{operating profit} + \text{dividend received})\\ &\quad - \text{cost rate of invested assets} \times (\text{total asset} - \text{financial assets}).\end{aligned}$$

The cost rate of invested assets is as follows (the concept of TSR is partially integrated):

$$\begin{aligned}&\text{Cost rate of invested assets}\\ &\quad = (\text{interest} + \text{dividend} + \text{capital gain})\\ &\qquad \div (\text{total assets} - \text{financial assets}).\end{aligned}$$

The actual cost rate of invested assets was uniform, about 8% (the rate of the national bond plus the risk premium) overall. At that time, the CCM was utilized to valuate and evaluate 16 main affiliate companies and 7 imitative companies as separate business units (consolidated subsidiary companies which are related) of Matsushita Electric Industrial, as a new management tool for boosting the stockholder value. The differences between the CCM and the EVA are as follows.

The NOPAT in the EVA becomes the operating profit plus the dividend received in the CCM. However, it does not involve complicated adjustments. It is the business profit before tax in financial analysis, if there is no interest received. It is the profit before the cost of capital, which is also used to calculate the RI. It includes the dividend received, because the stocks of the subsidiary companies are appropriated on the balance sheets of the business divisions as imitative companies. On the other hand, it does not include the interest received, because the invested assets do not include the financial assets that produce the interest received, and this is done in order to avoid the contradiction which occurs when the fund balance and the asset efficiency are estimated (Tomo, 1999; Monden, 2001).

The ROA was introduced at Matsushita Electric Industrial in 1998, to estimate the capital efficiency of the business. However, the ROA fell when the fund balance increased, because the cash flow had been estimated beforehand. Therefore, the CCM was introduced in 1999. The financial assets, including the fund balance, are deducted from the invested assets, thereby eliminating the negative influence of the fund balance on the capital efficiency. The increase in the fund balance does not directly influence the CCM in the same fiscal year. The CCM and the cash flow may be concomitantly used, because the deterioration of the cash flow influences both economic safety (solvency) and business value. Theoretically, the business value based on the CCM equals the business value based on the cash flow. The concomitant use of the CCM and the cash flow confines itself to the estimation of stockholder value. This is also the advantage of the EVA.

Matsushita has used the invested assets for the same reason as HOYA. If managers use the CCM, they can direct their subordinates to downsize the inventories and equipment in order to boost stockholder value. Since it does not involve complicated adjustments inherent in the EVA, it is actually the RI. The weight of the CCM was raised in April 2000 to 30% for the evaluation of the presidents of business companies.

Matsushita Electric Works introduced a system of 5 imitative companies in November 1998, and has adopted the MEP (Matsushita Electric Works Economic Profit), which is an original EVA-type metric. The MEP is calculated as follows:

$$\text{MEP} = (\text{return before interest on capital} - \text{cost rate of capital}) \times \text{capital}.$$

The MEP evaluates the imitative companies belonging to Matsushita Electric Works. However, it includes the subsidiary companies which belong to each business. They are consolidated in accordance with the purpose of management accounting. A 5% cost rate of capital is applied to all business units as the rate of the expected return to the stockholder. [Refer to Hiraoka (2004) regarding the attempt to calculate the WACC based on the CAPM using the consolidated statements and stock prices of Matsushita Electric Works.] The weight of the evaluating managers is 15%, lower than at Matsushita Electric Industrial. Nonetheless, a link with the salary of the executive employees is clearly present.

At Matsushita Electric Works, the MEP seems to be useful for business restructuring, because it highlights the businesses that destroy corporate value and those which create it. One business was even terminated based on the MEP (Hiraoka, 2003).

When Matsushita Electric Works became a subsidiary of Matsushita Electric Industrial in fiscal 2004, the Matsushita group's brands were unified. Some businesses may be restructured in the future, and the CCM and MEP may be unified as well.

6.3.5 *EVA-type metrics adopted by other companies*

The EVA-type metrics adopted by other companies are listed in Figure 6.1. They seem to be nothing more than portions of the EVA-type metrics used in Japan. Actually, the number of Japanese companies that have already

Name of company	Method of calculation
Advantest	operating profit after tax ÷ business assets – WACC (5.6%) – market rate of expected interest (2.4%)
All Nippon Airways	recurring profit – net interest expense – bonus-related machine – capital charge (2–4%)
Asahi Glass	operating profit after tax ÷ (operating capital × WACC (6%))
Asahi Chemical Industry	operating profit after tax – cost of capital
Casio	operating profit on sales × capital turnover – WACC (5%)
Daikin	operating profit after tax – (total assets – money in hand) × cost rate of capital (6%)
Dainippon Ink & Chemicals	operating profit after tax of business division – cost of capital
Fuji Electric	profit after tax – cost of equity (7%)
Japan Tobacco	operating profit after tax – interest of liabilities – cost of capital
Kansai Electric Power	operating profit + interest and dividend received – corporation tax – cost of assets* (4%)
Mitsubishi	division profit – cost of capital – business risk
Nissan Chemical Industries	operating profit after tax + interest received – cost of capital
Oki Electric Industry	recurring profit + interest expense – tax – cost of capital (5.5%)
Orix	business division profit before tax – capital after risk adjustment × expected return to stockholder (5%)
Osaka Gas	operating profit after tax – cost of capital
Sanwa Shutter	operating profit after tax – capital × cost rate of capital (6%)
Takeda Chemical Industries	profit before interest after tax – interest expense – tax – dividend
TDK	profit before interest after tax – (equity + borrowing) × cost rate of total capital (8%)
Toshiba	profit before interest after tax – (equity + borrowing) × cost rate of capital (6–18%)

Refer to Hiraoka (2002).
The percentages show the actual cost rate of capital.
Cost of assets* = total assets of the business divisions × WACC (4%) × (equity + interest bearing liabilities) ÷ total assets.

Fig. 6.1 EVA-type metrics adopted by other Japanese companies

adopted EVA-type metrics or are studying the possibility exceeds the number of companies listed in Figure 6.1 (Hiraoka, 2002).

6.4 Conclusion: Re-examining the Validity of EVA-type Metrics

As has been noted, we can confirm the validity of EVA-type metrics by observing their widely diffused expressions in Japanese practices.

However, we need to re-examine why enterprises tend to adopt original metrics, and whether the adopted metric matches the purpose of the enterprise in question.

It is important for the CEOs to find a metric that reflects the needs of the capital market. Furthermore, they must promote decentralized business-value management, so that they can use the metric for valuating business units and functional units.

It is necessary to link management systems such as the BSC (balanced scorecard) to EVA-type metrics, in order to create concrete business value.

The BSC links certain value drivers to those performance parameters on which operational managers focus. We expect EVA-type metrics to be continuously reviewed and improved, so that we can easily link between them and systems such as the BSC.

References

Aoki, S. (1998). The nature of EVA (economic value added) and various problems in it, *JICPA Journal* 512-March, pp. 60–64. (in Japanese)

Biddle, G. C., Bowen, R. M., and Wallance, J. S. (1997). Does EVA beat earning? Evidence on association with stock returns and firm values, *Journal of Accounting and Economics* 24, pp. 301–336.

Copeland, T., Koller, T., and Murrin, J. (1994). *Valuation*, 2nd ed., Willey.

Fujii, H. and Yamamoto, T. (1999). The comparative study regarding the stock prices explanation power of accounting information and cash flow information: the attempt of the application and improvement of Ohlson Model, *Kaikei* 156-2, pp. 14–29. (in Japanese)

Fukazawa, M. and Kawauichi, S. (1999). "RAPM" interweaving risk and restructuring business, *Diamond Harvard Business*, Oct–Nov, pp. 64–72. (in Japanese)

Hiraoka, S. (2001). The study of financial valuation models: focusing EVA, *The Japan Industrial Management & Accounting* 61-1, pp. 68–76. (in Japanese)

Hiraoka, S. (2002). Boundary between EVA and other economic profit measurements in Japan, *The Journal of Management Analysis Research* 18, pp. 24–32. (in Japanese)

Hiraoka, S. (2003). Business valuation based on EVA for management accounting, in Monden, Y. (ed.) *Organization Structure and Management Accounting*, Zeim-keiri-kyokai, pp. 19–37. (in Japanese)

Hiraoka, S. (2005). Valuation and goal growth rate of business segments: The case study of Matsushita Electric Works, Ltd., in Monden, Y. (ed.) *Organization Design and Management Accounting for Corporate Value*, Zeim-Keiri-Kyokai, pp. 89–99. (in Japanese)

Horngren, C. T., Sundem, G. L., and Stratton, W. O. (1996). *Introduction to Management Accounting*, 10th ed., Prentice Hall.

Inoue, T. (1998). The empirical study of corporate value based on accounting numerical value, *Kaikei* 153-6, pp. 44–66. (in Japanese)

Ichige, J. (2001). Inside control measurement for investigating capital efficiency, *Kigyokaikei* 53-5, pp. 102–103. (in Japanese)

Ito, K. (2001). The development of the EVA management in Kao Co., Ltd., *Kigyokaikei* 53-2, pp. 35–41. (in Japanese)

Matsui, K. (1999). Investment strategy: EVA guide, *Goldman Sachs Japan Research* 10-25, pp. 1–6. (in Japanese)

Marshall, A. (1890). *Principle of Economic*, Vol. 1, New York: Macmillan&Co.

Michael, C. E. (1994). *The Search for Value*, Harvard Business School Press.

Monden, Y. (2001). Theory and practice regarding corporate value management: the assertion of the best of east to the best of west, *Kigyokaikei* 53-1, pp. 134–143. (in Japanese)

Ogura, N. (1995). The function and limit of business division balance sheet from the view point of cost of capital management, *The Journal of Cost Accounting Research* 19-1, pp. 55–66. (in Japanese)

Ogura, N. (1996). The new tide of business division system as management accounting, *JICPA Journal* 486-Jan, pp. 69–75. (in Japanese)

Ogura, N. (2000). Economic value added as management accounting in Japan companies, *Kaikei* 157-5, pp. 14–30. (in Japanese)

Ohlson, J. A. (1995). Earnings, book values, dividends in equity valuation, *Contemporary Accounting Research* 11-2, pp. 661–687.

Peterson, P. P. and Peterson, D. R. (1995). *Company Performance and Measures of Value Added*, The Research Foundation of The ICFA.

Stewart, G. B. III (1991). *The Quest for Value: The EVA^{TM} Management Guide*, Harper Business.

Stewart, G. B. III (1994). EVA™: fact and fantasy, *Journal of Applied Corporate Finance* 7-2, pp. 71–84.

Tomo, M. (1999). Does CCM of Matsushita surpass EVA?: new management method for stockholder value, *Junkan-keirijyoho* 8.20/9.1, pp. 4–7. (in Japanese)

Tsumori, S. (1998). *Economic Profit*: EVA^{TM} *Management Guide*, Chuo-keizai-sya. (in Japanese)

Tsumori, S. (2001). EVA^{TM} *Value Creation Management*, Chuo-keizai-sya. (in Japanese)

CHAPTER

7

Value of Firms and Performance Evaluation

Noboru Ogura

Professor, Graduate School of Business Sciences
University of Tsukuba

7.1 Introduction

Stewart (1991) stated that the discounted present value of a set of expected economic value added (EVA^{TM}) acquirable in the future period represents the market value added (MVA) exceeding the book value of its equity. Also, Ohlson (1995) asserted that the discounted present value of a set of expected residual incomes resulting from the subtraction of capital charges from accounting profits can explain the stock price of an enterprise just like the dividend discount model used in corporate finance.

Accounting profits have been criticized by researchers of corporate finance on two points, because they contain revenue and cost items not accompanied by cash flow, such as the periodic allocation of costs, including depreciation and the amortization of goodwill, the reservations for future cash-outflows and the profits or losses on asset valuation. One point on which accounting profits were criticized is that they are not apt for discount calculation using the cost of capital; that is, long-term economic calculation which takes into consideration the time value of money is impossible with accounting profits. The other point is that it is difficult to obtain reliable figures because enterprises may intervene arbitrarily in the selection of the methods of cost allocation or the methods of asset valuation.

The EVA model proposed by Stewart (1991) and the residual income model presented by Ohlson (1995) suggested the possibility that accounting figures in the form of residual income as a result of subtracting the capital charge from the accounting profit can also conform to the calculation as per the discounted present value method using a cost of capital, provided that a certain rule governs the relationship between the profit-and-loss calculation and the calculation of assets and liabilities. These models provided a basis for challenging the criticisms by the theorists and practitioners of corporate finance and have come to be highly regarded among researchers on accounting in recent years.

In the following section, the mathematical conditions in which the EVA model and the residual income model become equivalent to the enterprise value model based on cash flows are reconfirmed. Based on the result, it is shown in Section 3 that the residual income model in the broad sense (including the EVA model) is immune only to the first point of the criticism from the view point of corporate finance. However, in Section 4 we would like to demonstrate, regarding the second point, that the cash-flow information is not conspicuously superior to the accounting information, and that the same criticism would be applicable to the cash-flow information.

7.2 The Conditions on which the FCF Model Agrees with the Residual Income Model

Stewart (1991) showed in Chapter 4 of his book, *Quest for Value*, that the discounted present value of EVAs acquirable in the future and the book value of the current equity expresses the theoretical market value of a firm which is equal to the one based on the future free cash flows (FCFs). As described in textbooks on corporate finance, assuming that the future FCFs is entirely applied to the payment (interest expense and principal repayment) to the lenders of liabilities and the payment of dividends to the shareholders, the expected economic value of an enterprise for shareholders can be considered to be the discounted present value of the future FCFs after deducting the present value of the liabilities.

Furthermore, assuming that all shareholders make rational investment decisions so as to maximize their expected economic value, the stock price can be considered to come into balance at the value of the expected economic value, which can be determined by deducting the present value of the liabilities from the discounted present value of the future FCFs, divided by the issued number of shares. Accordingly, if it is assumed that the shareholder value (SV) of an enterprise can be expressed by the product of the present stock price by the issued number of shares, the shareholder value can be expressed by a formula which uses the future FCF,[1] as follows:

$$SV_0 = \sum_{i=1}^{\infty} PV(FCF_i) - PV(LB_0), \tag{7.1}$$

where

SV_t: shareholder value at time t ($t = 0$ expresses the present moment),
$PV(\cdot)$: present value,
FCF_i: free cash flow during period i,
LB_t: liabilities at time t.

Stewart (1991) set forth the possibility to replace the discounted present value of the FCFs in formula (7.1) with the discounted present value of EVAs and the book value of the equity.[2] However, Stewart (1991) only showed numerical examples, that the calculation result of the FCF model equals that of the EVA model; he did not demonstrate any mathematical condition for this agreement.[3] We will show in this paper by defining the mathematical conditions, that the FCFs can be replaced by the discounted present value of any form of residual incomes as well as the EVAs, as long as a certain relationship is maintained between the profit or loss and the assets/liabilities. For the sake of simplification, we will consider that the EVA is also a form of residual income. We use four exogenous variables, five endogenous variables and some conditions defining the relationship between the investment (payment for fixed assets) and the cost allocation, all of which corroborate the above analysis, as presented below.

[1] In the case where the payment to the creditors of liabilities and shareholders is to come from current monetary assets as well as future FCF as sources of payment, those monetary assets (M_0) also should be taken into consideration in formula (7.1).

[2] In the calculation of the economic value added, Stewart (1991) referred to the sum of the equity and the interest-bearing liabilities as "capital," and he determined the capital charge by multiplying the capital by weighted average cost of capital. Therefore, this verification also shows that, to put it more precisely, the discounted present value of EVAs and the book value of the capital is equal to the discounted present value of FCFs.

[3] Watanabe (1999) also tried the same verification, but he did not show any mathematical condition.

7.2.1 Exogenous variables

$$\begin{aligned} \text{Investment: } & I_i \ (i = 0, 1, \ldots, t), \quad I_0 > 0, \\ \text{Operating cash flow: } & CF_i \ (i = 0, 1, \ldots, t), \quad CF_0 = 0, \\ \text{Cost allocation: } & D_i \ (i = 0, 1, \ldots, t), \quad D_0 = 0, \\ \text{Cost of capital: } & r \text{ (constant)}. \end{aligned}$$

7.2.2 Endogenous variables and conditions

$$\text{Assets: } A_i = \sum_{j=0}^{i} (I_j - D_j), \quad i = 0, \ldots, t, \tag{7.2}$$

$$\text{Capital charge: } CC_i = rA_{i-1}, \tag{7.3}$$

$$\text{Accounting income: } P_i = CF_i - D_i, \tag{7.4}$$

$$\text{FCF: } FCF_i = CF_i - I_i, \tag{7.5}$$

$$\text{Residual income: } P_i - CC_i = CF_i - D_i - CC_i. \tag{7.6}$$

7.2.3 The relationship between investments and cost allocations

$$A_0 + \sum_{i=1}^{t} I_i = \sum_{i=1}^{t} D_i. \tag{7.7}$$

Subject to the above definitions and conditions, it can be shown mathematically that the discounted present value of the residual incomes ($P_i - CC_i$, $i = 1, \ldots, n$) in the future is the discounted present value of the FCFs during the same period after subtracting the book value of the assets (for the proof using formulas, see the Appendix):

$$\begin{aligned} \sum_{i=1}^{t} PV(P_i - CC_i) &= \sum_{i=1}^{t} \frac{CF_i - D_i - CC_i}{(1+r)^i} \\ &= \sum_{i=1}^{t} \frac{CF_i - I_i}{(1+r)^i} - A_0 = \sum_{i=1}^{t} PV(FCF_i) - A_0. \end{aligned} \tag{7.8}$$

In order for Eq. (7.8) to be held, several conditions are necessary: the total amount of past investments after subtracting the cost already allocated must be recorded as assets [Eq. (7.2)], and the total amount of investments must be allocated entirely to the accounting profit or loss of periods before the future terminal period t [Eq. (7.7)]. However, since such definitions and conditions are consistent with the accounting principles on the equity accounts or the profit or loss account. It can be considered in general that Eq. (7.8) be held if the considering firm's lifetime is long enough.

By substituting the discounted present value of the FCFs in the formula (7.1) by the one obtained from formula (7.8) $(\Sigma PV(FCF_i) = \Sigma PV(P_i - CC_i) + A_0)$, we can conclude that the discounted present value of the future residual incomes and the current equity $(A_0 - LB_0)$ is equal to the theoretical shareholder value of a firm. The theoretical value of the stock price is the theoretical value of the shareholder value divided by the outstanding stock volume.

Based on these characteristics of the residual income, Stewart (1991) set forth his view that the EVA can be used to estimate the appropriate stock price. However, as shown from the above conditions for the proof, any residual income which meets certain conditions is capable of explaining the stock price to the same extent as the EVA. In the following section, this aspect will be examined further.

7.3 The Effects of the Accounting Procedure on the Enterprise Value

Let us now show by using a simple numerical example that the relationship proved in the preceding section between the discounted present value of FCFs and the one of the residual incomes is held under the different accounting procedures. First, let us assume that, at the beginning of the first year, the amount of 1,000 was invested; an additional 500 was invested at the end of the second year. By way of simplification, let us assume that durable assets purchased by these investments must be depreciated in four years and after the four years of service life they are disposed of with no sale value. Let us assume also that this company has no other assets than these, and that the fund for the investment was covered entirely by its own equity.

Assuming that an operating cash flow of 600 is obtainable for each term with these assets, the FCFs for each term until the end of the 8th term, when the life time of the lastly purchased asset ends, are 600, 100, 100, 600, 600 and 600 (excluding the initial investment of 1,000). For example, the discounted present value is 2,345 in total after discounting these FCFs

Year	0	1	2	3	4	5	6	PV*
(1) Investment	1,000		500					
(2) Operating CF		600	600	600	600	600	600	
(3) FCF (2)-(1)		600	100	600	600	600	600	2,345
(4) Cost allocation (depreciation)		250	250	375	375	125	125	
(5) Assets at year end	1,000	750	1,000	625	250	125	125	
(6) Capital charge		80	60	80	50	20	10	
(7) Residual income (2)−(4)−(6)		270	290	145	175	455	465	1,345

*Cost of capital=0.08.

Fig. 7.1 Comparison of PV of FCFs and PV of residual incomes (with straight-line method of depreciation)

with 8% cost of capital. Accordingly, the net present value (NPV) after subtracting the initial investment from the discounted present value of the FCFs is 1,345 (see Figure 7.1).

Furthermore, let us assume that each fixed asset is depreciated on a straight-line basis with four years' service life without estimated residual value. We consider that the difference by subtracting cost allocation by the depreciation and retirement cost of assets from the operating cash flow for each term is considered to be an accounting income. The residual income is gotten by subtracting capital charge (asset value multiplied by capital cost) from the accounting income (see the column "residual income" in Figure 7.1). The discounted present value of these residual incomes with 8% cost of capital is 1,345 shown in the lowermost cell of the column "PV" in Figure 7.1, and this figure equals to NPV of FCFs mentioned above.

This numerical example shows the equivalence relationship in formula (7.8) proved in the preceding section under the method of a straight-line depreciation. However, even if the method of cost allocation is changed from a straight-line basis depreciation to a fixed-percentage basis, the equivalence relationship between NPV of FCFs and the discounted present value of the residual incomes is maintained (see Figure 7.2). In another numerical example in Figure 7.2, depreciation of assets is calculated by multiplying fixed rate of 0.43766 by asset value at the end of previous year. The residual value of the assets (that is 10% of purchasing cost of assets) remains after the four year service life. This residual value is treated as loss on the retirement of assets.

Year	0	1	2	3	4	5	6	PV*
(1) Investment	1,000		500					
(2) Operating CF		600	600	600	600	600	600	
(3) FCF (2)-(1)		600	100	600	600	600	600	2,345
(4) Cost allocation (depreciation)		438	246	357**	301	69	89⁺	
(5) Assets at year end	1,000	562	816	459	158	89	0	
(6) Capital charge		80	44.96	65.28	36.72	12.64	7.12	
(7) Residual income (2)−(4)−(6)		82	309.04	177.72	262.28	518.36	503.88	1,345

*Cost of capital=0.08.
**Cost allocations to 3rd year and 6th year contain the retirement cost (residual value) of the assets which end their service lives.

Fig. 7.2 Comparison of PV of FCFs and PV of residual incomes (with fixed-percentage method of depreciation)

It is considered to be one of accounting accruals that the cash outflow invested in an asset at a certain period is allocated to other accounting periods as a cost. As easily guessable from these numerical examples, the discounted present value of residual incomes after accounting accruals equals to NPV based on FCFs, selecting any method of accounting accrual.

To put it the other way around, even if the discounted present value of the expected residual incomes, in any form, agrees with NPV of FCFs for a long term, it does not mean that this form of residual income can explain better the shareholder value than other form of residual income (or FCF without any accounting accrual).

This applies also to the EVA model as well as to the residual income model. That is, the EVA model and the residual income model include a calculation of economic value reflecting the time value of fund (a cost of capital), even utilizing any accounting accrual involving periodic allocation of cost. It cannot be proved however that a specific accounting income concept is superior to other income concepts or cash flow concepts.

Even if in the long term it agrees with NPV of FCFs, a residual income based on the accounting profit shows a profit or loss for a period which is greatly variable depending on selection among the methods of accounting accrual. Accordingly, the possibility is not eliminated that an arbitrary judgment of accounting managers in a firm may distorts accounting profit and residual income.

For such reasons, criticism such as "cash is king, profit is opinion" from advocators on corporate finance against the accounting profit has persisted. However, the knowledge obtained from our analysis on the EVA model or the residual income model also shows that the opinion that cash flow is free from any arbitrariness of those who draw up accounting information is independent from the other opinion that cash flow may become an effective administrative information. In the following section, an examination as to the effectiveness of cash flow information will be made from the viewpoint of management accounting.

7.4 The Limitation of Cash Flow in Terms of Management Accounting Information

The tendency toward aspiring for enterprise value (or shareholder value) during these 15 years is about to have a profound effect on the management accounting in that the measures of shareholders who evaluate corporate executives switched from the maximization of accounting profit to that of enterprise value. We assume that the definition of the management accounting is to make decisions and to evaluate performances of managers in a firm using accounting information. The change of standard for evaluating corporate executives from the maximization of profit to that of enterprise value affects the criteria of decision making and performance evaluation by middle-level executives who are the subordinate officers of the executives.

As discussed in the preceding sections, the enterprise value sought after by shareholders means a long-term economic value obtained by discounting FCFs of future periods as far as can be estimated. It has been a well-known fact that the managerial decision-making must be made based on future information. Decision-making based on prognostic information on distant future in addition to one on near future is more desirable than the judgment based on prognostic information on only near future. Therefore, the value-based management in which the managerial decision-making is based on the long-term economic value may heighten the quality of management accounting (although there still remain some technical problems, including the prediction accuracy of FCF in distant future and the issue of setting an appropriate level of cost of capital).

However, the management accounting information for performance evaluation is restricted to that on a fixed period (for example, one year or one month) and on past events. That is, an appropriate performance measures should be prepared other than the enterprise value. Those scales are required to be consistent with enterprise value while using the data obtained from a certain period in the past.

Since enterprise value is determined based on the numerical sequence of predicted future FCFs, a simplistic opinion that the maximization of one-term FCF results in maximizing enterprise value could be often asserted. Also, based on the opinion that the sum of current equity and MVA agrees with the enterprise value, the maximization of one-term EVA which is only a factor for determining MVA could be insisted to leads to maximizing enterprise value. However, the situation that the performances for the relevant future periods should be sacrificed in order to improve the performance for certain period in near future is often observed in real operations. Those insistences on maximizing single number of FCF or EVA in one period have not yet been proved in general.

Above all, in the growth period of market, it is a well-known fact that FCF tends to become negative due to active investments for the purpose of accumulating future capacity. However, the sales increase of a firm is considered to be one of value drivers by investors, and stock price of the firm increase in the stock market. In the case where the market growth is accompanied by a large amount of investments, the investors in the stock market do not consider that the enterprise value declined while FCF is negative. In many cases the enterprise value seems to be highly evaluated in the stock market in spite of negative FCF.

In this section, both the changes in the market values of an enterprise and the changes in FCFs in the growth (or decline) period of its sales were examined. First, we used the financial data from 1979 to 1999 of 378 companies (excluding those companies whose shares were listed on a stock exchange after 1995) being classified into the chemical industry, machinery industry or electrical equipment industry, whose shares were listed on the first or second section of the Tokyo Stock Exchange. Free cash flows on the growth periods and decline periods were extracted, upon defining the period in which the sales volume increased for at least three consecutive years as the growth period and the period in which the sales volume declined for at least three consecutive years as the decline period. Furthermore, for the enterprises classified into the three industries, the changes in FCFs in the growth period and in decline period and the changes of the total market values of shares were examined.

The examination of the probability of FCFs indicating negative values revealed that the negative FCFs were observed in 53.5% of fiscal years during the growth period. This figure is significantly higher than 35.3% during the decline period, that is, it can be said that the probability of FCF being negative is higher in the growth period than in the decline period (see Figure 7.3).

Also, the probability of fiscal years in which FCFs decreased (or increased) from the beginning year of the growth (or decline) periods and the probability of fiscal years in which the total market values decreased (or increased) therefrom were examined. While FCFs decreased in the fiscal years accounting for 74.0% in the growth periods, FCFs were found to increase in 74.6% of fiscal years and to decrease in 35.4% of fiscal years in the decline periods. In contrast with this, while the total market values increased in 86.9% of fiscal years in the growth periods, they decreased in 77.4% of fiscal years in the decline periods (see Figure 7.3).

The analysis hereinbefore shows that in the growth period of sales volumes, while the total market values which represent the evaluation by the capital market increased, FCFs decreased, and the probability of FCFs being negative was high.

With the aim of examining the difference in the degree of changes in FCFs and total market values between the growth period and the decline period of sales volume, we examined the differences between the value of a beginning year and one of a fiscal year in the growth period (or decline period). Then we defined the degree of change (DOC) in order to standardize differences among the different size of companies. The degree of change was carried out by dividing the difference between two values of beginning year and of a certain year in a growth (or decline) period by the difference between the maximum value and the minimum value in the same period.

	Years with negative FCF	Years with declining FCF	Years with declining market value
Growth periods	1,130ys (53.5%)	1,219ys (74.3%)	212ys (12.9%)
Decline periods	478ys (35.3%)	376ys (35.4%)	823ys (77.4%)

Fig. 7.3 FCFs and total market values in the growth and decline periods

	Growth periods		Decline periods	
	DOC in FCF	DOC in market value	DOC in FCF	DOC in market value
Chemical	−0.1521	0.4371	0.2060	−0.2911
Machinery	−0.2525	0.4304	0.1509	−0.5484
Electrical equipment	−0.1877	0.4561	0.2161	−0.5075
Total	−0.2020	0.4447	0.1994	−0.4516

Fig. 7.4 Average degree of change (DOC) in FCF and total market value

The degree of change (DOC) = (value in a fiscal year t − value in the beginning year)/(the maximum value − minimum value).

The mean DOC in FCFs were −0.202 in the growth period and +0.199 in the decline period, and the mean DOC in the total market values were +0.444 in the growth period and −0.452 in the decline period. Also, the F test showed that the mean values in the growth period were significantly different from those in the decline period with 1% reliability. About the same level of statistical results were obtained when the mean values of the DOC were calculated for each industry (see Figure 7.4).

These analysis results show the following statements:

1. The stock market considers the change in sales amount as a value driver (indicator of enterprise value).
2. The probability is high that a short-term observation of FCFs exhibits a move contrary to that of the change in sales amount.

Therefore, it is highly probable that the use of FCF as the measure of performance for a short term will give the management executives an evaluation contrary to that by the shareholders. Therefore, it can be concluded that FCF is not appropriate as a measure for performance evaluation which reflects the performance evaluation by shareholders.

7.5 Conclusions

Owing to the spread of the discounted cash flow method, the enterprise value (or the shareholder value) based on the discounted present value of predicted future FCFs has come to be widely used by investors in the capital market, and it is also affecting the management accounting in the firms. However, the theoretical enterprise value model based on multi-period FCFs in the future is quite inconsistent with the constraint condition of the performance accounting that performance should be measured only for a period in the past, and the development of a short-term measure for performance measurement, which is consistent with enterprise value, is delayed.

In the EVA model and the residual income model, the possibility of performance evaluation by residual income was suggested by showing that in the long run the sum of the discounted present value of the residual incomes and the book value of equity agrees with the discounted present value of FCF. However, in this paper we have shown that the EVA model or the residual income model lacks the capability to assert that a specific income accounting method is more consistent with the stock prices than other methods. We have also shown that FCF can not explain in the short term how the capital market evaluate a enterprise through stock prices.

As these proofs have shown, many concepts and accounting techniques associated with enterprise value, proposed in the 1990s, have not contributed much to the performance accounting. Although we could not submit any active proposal in this paper, we hope that this paper serves as a warning against the superficial development of theoretical models in the past and as a starting point for empirical studies, including the analysis of enterprise value drivers, based on the detailed analysis of the relationship between accounting data and stock price.

Appendix: Relationship Between the Present Value of FCF and that of Residual Value

$$NPV(P_i - CC_i) = \sum_{i=1}^{t} \frac{CF_i - D_i - CC_i}{(1+r)^i}$$

Substituting (7.3) and (7.2) for CC,

$$= \sum_{i=1}^{t} \frac{CF_i - D_i}{(1+r)^i} - r\sum_{i=1}^{t} \frac{1}{(1+r)^i} \sum_{j=0}^{i-1} (I_j - D_j)$$

$$= \sum_{i=1}^{t} \frac{CF_i - D_i}{(1+r)^i} - r\left\{ \frac{I_0}{(1+r)} + \frac{I_0 + I_1 - D_1}{(1+r)^2} + \frac{I_0 + I_1 + I_2 - D_1 - D_2}{(1+r)^3} \right.$$

$$\left. + \cdots + \frac{I_0 + I_1 + I_2 + \cdots + I_{t-1} - D_1 - D_2 - \cdots D_{t-1}}{(1+r)^t} \right\}$$

$$
\begin{aligned}
&= \sum_{i=1}^{t} \frac{CF_i - D_i}{(1+r)^i} - r\left\{ \frac{D_1 + D_2 + \cdots + D_t - I_1 - I_2 - \cdots - l_t}{(1+r)} \right. \\
&\quad + \frac{D_2 + \cdots + D_1 - I_2 - \cdots - I_t}{(1+r)^2} + \cdots + \frac{D_{t-1} + D_t - I_{t-1} - I_t}{(1+r)^{t-1}} \\
&\quad \left. + \frac{D_t - I_t}{(1+r)^t} \right\} \\
&= \sum_{i=1}^{t} \frac{CF_i - D_i}{(1+r)^i} - r\left\{ (D_1 - I_1)\frac{1}{(1+r)} + (D_2 - I_2)\left[\frac{1}{(1+r)} + \frac{1}{(1+r)^2}\right] \right. \\
&\quad \left. + \cdots + (D_t - I_t)\left[\frac{1}{(1+r)} + \cdots + \frac{1}{(1+r)^t}\right] \right\}.
\end{aligned}
$$

Replacing using $I_0 = A_0$ and formula (7.7),

$$
\begin{aligned}
&= \sum_{i=1}^{t} \frac{CF_i - D_i}{(1+r)^i} - r\sum_{i=1}^{t}(D_i - I_i)\sum_{j=1}^{i}\frac{1}{(1+r)^j} \\
&= \sum_{i=1}^{t} \frac{CF_i - D_i}{(1+r)^i} - r\sum_{i=1}^{t}(D_i - I_i)\frac{1}{r}\left\{1 - \frac{1}{(1+r)^i}\right\} \\
&= \sum_{i=1}^{t} \frac{CF_i - D_i}{(1+r)^i} - \sum_{i=1}^{t}(D_i - I_i) + \sum_{i=1}^{t}\frac{D_i - I_i}{(1+r)^i}
\end{aligned}
$$

Substituting (7.7) for the second term of the above formula,

$$
= \sum_{i=1}^{t} \frac{CF_i - I_i}{(1+r)^i} - A_0.
$$

References

Ogura, N. (2001). Corporate valuation and a viewpoint of management accounting, *Accounting* 159-4, pp. 531–544. (in Japanese)

Ohlson, J. A. (1995). Earnings, book values, and dividends in equity valuation, *Contemporary Accounting Research* 12-1, pp. 661–687.

Penman, S. H. (2002). Tying valuation to performance with financial analysis, *The Journal of Management Accounting, Japan* 10-2, pp. 3–12.

Saito, S. (1999). The paradigm of the study of accounting, *Accounting* 155-2, pp. 173–185. (in Japanese)

Stewart, G. B., III (1991). *The Quest for Value: The EVA^{TM} Management Guide*, HarperCollins.

Watanabe, Y. (1998). Capital charge under internal capital system, *The Journal of Cost Accounting Research* 22-2, pp. 45–54. (in Japanese)

Yaekura, T. (2000). Performance measure and stock prices: cash flow, EVA^{TM} and Ohlson model, *Journal of Management Accounting, Japan* 8-1/2, pp. 157–167. (in Japanese)

CHAPTER

8

Management of Franchise Chains and Multi-Divisional Organizations: A Comparative Study on Royalty and Corporate Costs

Noriko Hoshi

Associate Professor, Faculty of Business Management, Hakuoh University

8.1 Introduction

As a franchise chain, Seven-Eleven is the first company to successfully launch a large-scale convenience store in Japan. In a franchise chain, each store uses the same signboard and resembles a branch office. Actually, each store works independently. A franchising chain is a corporate group which is created by a franchise contract between affiliated shops (franchisees) and headquarters (franchisors).

On the other hand, in a large industry, multi-divisional organizations are known as internal organizations which are made up of many divisions. The headquarters transfer much authority to divisional managers for controlling and managing these divisions.

In fact, these two types of organizations are similar, but there are many points of difference between them. In franchise chains, the affiliated shops will pay a royalty to the central office. In decentralized organizations, the central office corporate costs are allocated to the divisions.

In this paper, the author will examine how these two organizations are different regarding the handling of royalties and the allocation of corporate costs. Further, the writer will also examine whether the construction of both organizations differs regarding the royalties and the allocation of corporate costs.

8.2 Structure of a Multi-divisional Organization and Franchising Chain

8.2.1 *Characteristics of the structure of a multi-divisional organization*

When an industry grows, it operates on a large scale and in a multidimensional way. In this situation, the diversification of market and technology is seen to create a wide range of decision problems. As a result, it would be difficult for the entrepreneur to manage the overall organization. Therefore, the organization is divided into different divisions. Then in that multi-divisional organization, the authority for making multifarious decisions would be transferred to the manager who will arrange the divisions first. The manager will be assigned to manage each organization. This representative organization structure is called functional or multi-divisional organization (see Figure 8.1).

In a multi-divisional organization, decentralization would be done on the basis of products, customers, and regions. Each division would be managed by each departmental manager. The distinguishing characteristic of a multi-divisional organization is that the authority to make most of the decisions is transferred to the divisional managers. In case of product-based departmentalization, the manager makes the product compatible with the change in environment and technology. As a result, the decisions relating to the abolition of existing products or the sale of new products would be done very promptly. Further, the transferable functions like purchases, productions, sales, materials, and accounting would be delegated to the divisional managers.

8.2.2 *Characteristics of the structure of a franchising chain*

According to the Japan Franchising Association, a franchise system unites a local entrepreneur (the franchisee) to a company (the franchisor) by a contract that gives the local entrepreneur the right to sell products or services under the franchisor's trademark, trade name, and management

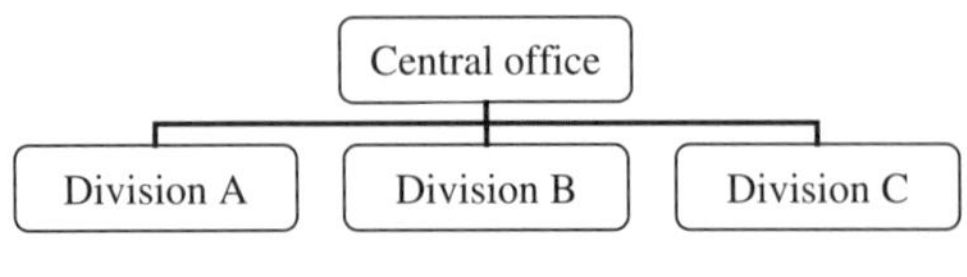

Fig. 8.1 Multi-divisional organization

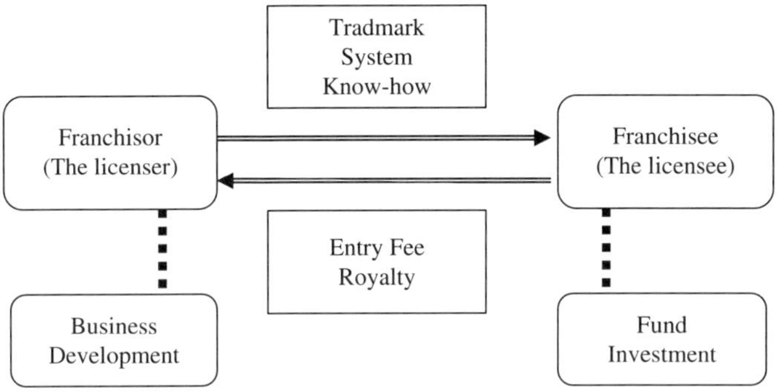

Fig. 8.2 The structure of a franchise chain. Source: JFA home page

know-how by employing a production process developed by the franchisor. The franchisee pays fixed compensation to the franchisor and invests needed capital in the business. The franchisee gets support and guidance from the franchisor and thereby runs the business as going concern of both parties. Figure 8.2 presents the structure of a franchise chain.

A franchisor's contracts are uniform across all franchisees that join the chain at the same time (Lafontaine, 1992). Generally, the contract can be terminated by the franchisor if the franchisee fails to follow company policy; the contract cannot be terminated by the franchisee unless the outlet is closed or the franchisee sells the unit. The contract typically has a finite duration and renewal is largely at the franchisor's discretion. The contractual nature of the relationship results in litigation when disputes arise. At the time the contract is signed, the franchisee pays a franchise fee. Then the franchisor provides services to the franchisee necessary to open the outlet, including employee training and operating manuals for the production and equipment, and trains employees. After opening, the franchisee manages the local unit, controlling the finances and overseeing the production process. The franchisor provides ongoing coaching and inspection of the franchise, access to trademarks, and marketing service such as advertising and new product development. In return for these services, the franchisee pays a royalty on sales to the franchisor and a royalty on sales earmarked for marketing expense, commonly called the advertising fee (Michale and Moore, 1995).

We can summarize this in the following way:

1. The franchisor (the licenser) and the franchisee (a licensee) are tied together by a contractual relationship.

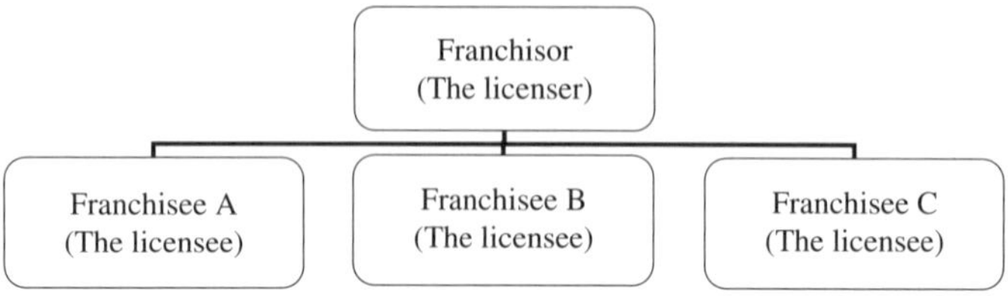

Fig. 8.3 Organization structure of franchise chain

2. By this contractual agreement, the rights and duties of both parties are established.
3. As compensation (franchise fee), the franchisee will pay a royalty to the franchisor for having the right to use the business developed by the franchisor.
4. The franchisor will continuously give support and guidance to the franchisee for successfully running the business.

The businesses that are tied together by franchise contract are operated as an independent company. The organizational relationship between the franchisor and the franchisee are built up by franchise contract. Actually, as a central authority, the franchisor will form a big organization consisting of many franchisees. Both the franchisor and franchisee will operate the business as a same identity. That is, even if they do not have any equity (capital) relationship, however, they look like an integrated company (Tamiya, 2000). Thus, it is apparent that the relationship between a franchisor and a franchisee looks very much like a multi-divisional organization. This relationship is portrayed by Figure 8.3.

8.3 Corporate Costs of a Multi-divisional Organization

8.3.1 *Function and role of the central office and the divisions*

In a product-based or region-based division the divisional head, to whom various powers or authority have been delegated, collects and understands various information that is important for the division. For each type of division this will heighten the environmental adaptability which will help in making quick decisions. Since the divisional head will take up the responsibility of divisional profit, the incentive to increase profit will be high. At the same time, the divisional manager may need to undertake training for profit improvement, since he may look for a control method for profit improvement only by himself.

On the other hand, in a central office if the authority to make various decisions is transferred to the divisional manager, the top management will be often released from decision making that happens frequently. The manager of the central office will pay attention to make decisions considering the management plan and strategy. This will help the managers of the central office in concentrating on strategic planning of the overall organization.

Further, the central office provides various service supports to the divisions regarding their type of function. These functions are, for example, handling information, research and development, fund supply, material purchase, flow of goods, labor employment, handling judicial affairs, and accounting affairs. In the central office, separate departments are established for each of the support service. All these business affairs are concentrated in the central office.

8.3.2 *Allocation of corporate costs to the divisions*

Corporate costs are incurred to support various activities in different divisions, such as general affairs, accounting, and personnel affairs. The divisions have a large benefit from the central office. That is why the corporate costs are allocated to the beneficiary divisions. In a questionnaire survey,[1] it was found that 93.1% of the respondent companies who have adopted multi-divisional organization are allocating corporate costs to the various beneficiary divisions.

In a narrower sense, the allocation of the central office control costs (e.g., corporate costs relating to the planning and control) is difficult. Therefore, some standards are determined considering the burden bearing ability of the divisions. In fixing the standards for example, the scale of sales revenue, investment amount, and total direct cost of each division are used to construct a single standard on the basis of which corporate costs are allocated. Several standards are used for this allocation.

[1]A questionnaire survey conducted in 2001 by Yasuhiro Monden (University of Tsukuba), Noriko Hoshi (Hakuoh Women's University), and Kazuki Hamada (Seinan Gakuin University) on the listed companies in the Tokyo Stock Exchange (Part I).

However, the support service cost of the central office is considered as the divisional common cost. This support service cost is in most cases allocated to each beneficiary division according to the degree of support received by each division. This system is called charge back system since the ratio of allocation for each service is the charge back rate. For example, the central office's purchase cost is allocated to each division on the basis of the number of orders placed by each division (Monden, 2001).

The purpose of corporate costs allocation is mainly an evaluation of the divisional manager's performance (Tani, 1987). Further, cost allocation might cause the following impacts (Sakurai, 2000): (1) since corporate costs allocation makes divisional managers aware that corporate costs exist, they would be very conscious about the earning of such amount of divisional profit which would recover the costs; (2) for pricing, the manager would ensure the recovery of this allocated costs; and (3) the central office renders supervision and advisory services to the divisions. As a beneficiary, each division bears part of these costs according to the degree of support received by them. When corporate costs are allocated, each division will try to prevent the increase of needless corporate costs.

Since as per charge back system, corporate costs are allocated to each division, not only each division but the whole organization would be motivated to make the most suitable decision. When corporate costs are allocated to each division, the divisional income statement will be similar to Figure 8.4.

I	Sales revenue
II	Variable cost
III	Divisional variable selling and management costs
IV	Contribution Margin (= I-II-III)
V	Divisional fixed costs controllable by division manager
VI	Controllable Profit (= IV-V)
VII	Divisional fixed costs uncontrollable by division manager
VIII	Contribution Margin for corporate costs profit (=VI-VII)
IX	Corporate costs allocated
X	Profit after allocation of corporate costs (=VIII-IX)

Fig. 8.4 Income statement of a division

8.4 Royalty of the Franchise System

8.4.1 *Sharing of the authority and function of franchisor and franchisee*

In a franchise system, the sharing of authority and function of franchisor and franchisee is clearly fixed by the contract. The franchisor presents a franchise package to the franchisee which includes: (1) the use of a franchisor trade mark; (2) the use of business know-how developed by the franchisor; and (3) the right to continually receive the advice and help rendered by the franchisor.

Generally, the franchisor will have the following rights and functions (Tamiya, 2000).

1. Franchisee development.
2. Education.
3. Supervising.
4. Marketing.
5. Flow of goods.
6. Finance.
7. Information system development.
8. Production plant development.
9. New business development.

In the restaurant franchise business, the role and function of franchisor will be the following.

1. Development of product, service, and franchisee.
2. Stable supply of materials and establishment of delivery system.
3. Advising or implementing training on store opening.
4. Inspection, scrutiny, and advice by supervisor.
5. Advertising for sales promotion.
6. Timely collection, analysis, and presentation of each type of information.

To win in the competition with the other companies of the same industry, it is important for the franchisor to differentiate its franchise package and thereby hold a dominant position in the competition. For this purpose, the franchisor should accumulate different know-how, make an effort to advise the franchisee regarding how to increase profit earning power, and try to improve the value of its trade mark.

In the Point of Sales (POS) System, which is widely used in the convenience stores, at each sales point the information relating to sales amount, and goods is transferred to the franchisor, as well as updating and accumulating this information. The accumulated information is indispensable for the franchisor for planning strategies for the overall organization. Strategic planning is also the important duty of the franchisor.

On the other hand, the franchisee operates its business by its own capital investment and by using the franchise package. The task and responsibility of the fast food franchisee are stated below (Ui, 2002).

1. Supply of funds for opening the store.
2. Royalty payment and increasing sales revenue.
3. Maintaining order in the restriction on material stocking.
4. Maintaining order in the menu structure decided by the franchisor.
5. Business operation according to the manual.
6. Recruitment and adoption of store staff.
7. Training and education of store staff.

The task and duty of the franchisee is to receive business advice as per strategic planning of the franchisor, to maintain the regulations set by the contract and to improve the amount of sales. As a result, at any time the consumers would get same service from any shop of the franchisee.

8.4.2 *Royalty*

For using the franchise package offered by the franchisor, the franchisee pays compensation to the franchisor. This is known as a royalty. In a typical franchise system, this royalty is recognized as compensation for a royalty package, which in most cases is calculated by applying a fixed rate on sales revenue or by a standard fixed amount. The method of calculating a royalty by applying a fixed rate on the sales revenue means that the franchisor holds the responsibility relating to the sales revenue. If the total profit on sales is low, in that situation also the franchisor will render support to the franchisee.

In convenience stores like Seven-Eleven, the royalty is calculated by applying a fixed ratio on the total profit on sales. From this view point, it is thought that the franchisor holds the responsibility up to the cost of sales. Since the franchisor and the franchisee have a cooperative relationship for carrying out the same business, the profit derived from this collaborative relationship would be allocated (profit distribution) according to the ratio

I	Operating revenue
	1. Franchise fee revenue
	2. Other operating revenue
II	Sales revenue
III	Total revenue (=I+II)
IV	Cost of sales
V	Gross profit (=III-IV)
VI	Selling and administrative expenses
	1. Advertisement expense
	2. Supplis expenses
	⋮
VII	Operating income (=V-VI)

Fig. 8.5 Income statement of a franchisor

of investment which includes not only cash but also labor, know-how, and trust (Kawagoe, 2001).

The royalty paid by the franchisee will become the revenue of the franchisor. Besides the royalty, other components of franchisor's revenue are advertisement costs and information costs which are calculated by using a predetermined standard, and the price paid by the franchisee for goods and materials sold by the franchisor. The franchisor's profit will be ensured by all these revenue components.

Figure 8.5 portrays the income statement of a franchisor. Here it is evident that a franchisor is a profit center. In multi-divisional organization, the central office is itself a cost center. The central office, which incorporates many divisions, takes the responsibility of profit and loss of overall organization. In a company which is profit center, the central office is also considered as cost center for carrying out main functions.

8.5 Comparison between Franchise Chains and Multi-divisional Organizations

Up to Section 4, the organizational structure, duty, and characteristics of franchise chains and multi-divisional organizations have been described. In this section, we will state similarities and differences of these two organization structures, and their duties regarding royalties and allocation of corporate costs.

Although, franchise chains and multi-divisional organizations look similar, the following differences are found.

1. Differences in organization structure
   In a multi-divisional origination, the divisions are an internal organization of the central office. On the other hand, the franchisor and franchisee are independent organizations which are tied together by a contract.
2. Differences in business strategies
   In a multi-divisional organization, since divisions are segregated based on product or region, and in most cases there is a need for different strategies and decisions for each of the divisions. In a franchise system, because franchisees are doing the same business, similar strategies can be developed for them.
3. Differences of decision making
   In a multi-divisional organization, most of the authority is transferred to the divisional managers who make quick decisions regarding different region-based or product-based divisions. However, for the overall organization, the selection and integration of the business and the related structural reorganization (including alteration of divisions) are the headquarters' strategic decision matters. In a franchise system, franchisee will make decisions needed for daily business operations. Franchisor will make all strategic decisions.
4. Differences in risk burden
   In a multi-divisional organization, since all fund investments are done by the central office, the ultimate risk would be borne by that company. In a franchise system, since the franchisee operates the business by investing its own funds, in case of failure the franchisee will take full responsibility.

There are also many similarities between a franchise chain and a multi-divisional organization. Their organization structures are not only apparently similar, their duties and responsibilities are also similar. Both the central office of the multi-divisional organization and the franchisor concentrate on developing respective business strategies. They also provide various support and guidance to franchisees or divisions, whatever the case may be, to carry out business strategies. After receiving support and advice, the franchisees and the divisions would be able to manage the business which would then enhance sales revenue and profit. As mentioned above, the decision making of the divisions, to whom most of the authorities have been delegated, is not similar with the franchisee's daily decision making. Since it also includes product-based or region-based strategic decisions,

		Franchise chain	Multi-divisional organization
Differences	Organization structure	Various enterprises are tied together by franchise contract	Internal organization
	Business strategies	Since they are doing the same business, similar strategies can be developed for all stores	Different strategies may be needed for each division
	Decision making	Franchisee makes decision on daily basis	Quick decision making for own division
	Risk	The franchisee who makes the investment takes the final responsibility	Responsibility rests with the central office
	Scale of operation	Franchisee operates on a small scale	Multi-divisional organization operates on a large scale
Similarity	Development of business strategies	Franchisor or the central office will develop business strategies for all stores or overall organization.	

Fig. 8.6 Comparison between franchise chain and multi-divisional organization

the contents of the decision for operating a business are largely different from franchisee. This can be viewed as the difference in the length of scale of business operation. The franchisees are mostly individual shops. In a multi-division organization, a product-based division is operated by integrating various production plants with many employees. If the franchisee's business operates on a large scale, the contents of decisions would be similar to that of the central office. Figure 8.6 presents the similarities and differences between the organization structures of a franchise chain and a multi-division organization.

To concentrate in developing the business strategies, it is important for both the franchisor and the central office to recover the costs incurred in the franchisor or in the central office. For this purpose, in franchise chain, the franchisee will pay a royalty (or service charge) to the franchisor. In multi-division organization, since corporate costs are allocated to the various divisions, it is important for the divisions to earn a profit which would cover these costs. For a profit center franchisor, this royalty is revenue. For a cost center multi-divisional organization, the allocated corporate costs are considered as cost recovery. Both the franchisee and the divisions allocate a part of the profit on sales to the franchisor or the central offices. For this reason, the franchisor's attainable profit should be maintained and also the recovery of costs generated in the multi-division organization also should be ensured. These two types of organizations are similar from this view

	Franchise chain (Royalty)	Multi-divisional organization (Allocation of corporate costs)
differences	Receipt and payment of royalty	Allocation of corporate costs
	Profit of franchisor	Recovery of corporate costs
similarities	Expense of franchisee and division	
	Ensuring profit for franchisor and central office	

Fig. 8.7 Comparison between royalty and head office cost allocation

point. Figure 8.7 displays similarities and differences between royalty and allocation of corporate costs.

8.6 Conclusion

A royalty is revenue for the franchisor which the franchisee pays as a price for using the know-how and knowledge of the franchisor. In a divisional organization, the sales revenue of each division is added up to constitute the total sales revenue of the overall organization. The allocated corporate costs are handled in each division as cost. In the central office it is considered as cost recovery of the cost center. Since the organization structures of the franchise chain and the multi-divisional organization differ, the account of the royalty and corporate costs also differ.

When a multi-divisional organization develops, matures, and becomes a business group that includes a related subsidiary company, the subsidiary company will pay costs to the central office for using patents, and for getting advice on technology business affairs. This type of activity is evident in the Matsushita Electric Company. This is similar to the allocation of corporate costs in a multi-divisional organization. This type of expense relating to patent use, technology advice, and business advice are similar to a royalty, which is an expense for a subsidiary company but revenue for a central office.

In order to maintain and ensure profit, it is important for a franchisee to earn sufficient sales revenue to recover the royalty cost. Similarly, in a multi-divisional organization it is important for the divisions to earn such sales revenue which would cover allocated corporate costs. This will help the franchisor and the central office to ensure profit, and help the franchisor and central office to concentrate on their business strategies.

In a franchise system, besides a royalty, the franchisee will pay advertisement costs and guarantee money to the franchisor. Further, the franchise system will build a network and the data received from it will be used to develop new business strategies and accumulation of different know-how. In the case of a multi-divisional organization, the payments of costs, besides the royalty in a franchise system, are similar to the payment to the central office for using marketing functions or an information system function (known as charge back system). However, research is needed regarding this type of cost as well as the information system.

References

Asada, T. (ed.) (1997). *The Theory and Practice of Management Information Network*, Tokyo Keizai Joho Shupan. (in Japanese)

Francine, L. (1992). Agency theory and franchising: some empirical results, *Rand Journal of Economics*, 23-summer, pp. 263–283.

Kaplan, R. S. and Atkinson, A. A. (1989). *Advanced Management Accounting*, 2nd Ed., Prentice-Hall, Inc. (translated by Asada, T. *et al.* (1996), Chuokeizaisha.)

Kawagoe, K. (2001). *The Law of Franchise System*, Shojihomu. (in Japanese)

Japanese Ministry of Economy, Trade and Industry, http://www.meti.go.jp/.

Kobayashi, T. (ed.) (2002). *The Strategy for Mega-franchisee*, Diamond Inc. (in Japanese)

Japan Franchise Association (2003). *Franchise Handbook*, Shogyokai. (in Japanese)

Japan Franchise Association, http://jfa.jfa-fc.or.jp/qa_1. html.http://frn.jfa-fc.or.jp/.

Monden, Y. (2001). *Management Accounting*, Zeimu Keiri Kyokai. (in Japanese)

Monden, Y. (ed.) (2003a). *Organization Structure and Management Accounting*, Zeimu Keiri Kyokai. (in Japanese)

Monden, Y. (ed.) (2003b). *Management Accounting Text*, 3rd Ed., Zeimu Keiri Kyokai. (in Japanese)

Okabe, T. (1987). Franchise contract and accounting information system (1), *The Business Review of Kansai University*, 32-2, pp. 79–102. (in Japanese)

Okabe, T. (1987). Franchise contract and accounting information system (2), *The Business Review of Kansai University*, 32-3, pp. 103–198. (in Japanese)

Sakurai, M. (2000a). *Management Accounting*, 2nd Ed., Dobunkan. (in Japanese)

Sakurai, M. (2000b). *Dictionary of Management Accounting*, Dobunkan. (in Japanese)

Shogyokai, (ed.) (2004). *Franchise Chain in Japan*, Shogyokai. (in Japanese)

Solomons, D. (1965). *Division Performance: Measurement and Control*, Financial Executives Research Foundation, Inc.

Steven, C. M. and Hollie, J. M. (1995). Returns to franchising, *Journal of Corporate Finance*, 2, pp. 133–155.
Tamiya, M. (2000). *Franchise Strategy to Succeed*, Diamond Inc. (in Japanese)
Tani, T. (1987). *Measurement and Control of Division Performance*, Zeimu Keiri Kyokai. (in Japanese)
Ui, Y. (2002). *Eat and Drink Franchise Business Handbook*, Ko Shobo. (in Japanese)
Yamamoto, T. (2003). *Economics of Restriction Reform*, Bunshindo. (in Japanese)

CHAPTER

9

Corporate Revitalization through Management Buyout

Naoyuki Kaneda

Associate Professor, Faculty of Economics, Gakushuin University

9.1 Introduction

Management buyout (MBO) occurs when executives and employees, on the premise of continuation of business, acquire a controlling interest in a company. In ordinary M&A, other companies of the same industry buyout the targeted company (Strategic Buyer). In the case of MBO, the executives of the company usually acquire shares, and investment funds often provide additional capital for the transaction (Financial Buyer).

Corporations subject to MBO are not venture companies but companies which are well-established businesses with steady cash flows. Financial buyers, such as private equity funds, make investment with leverage for a 3–10 year period in order to realize high returns using exit strategies such as initial public offering (IPO) or further MBO. Advantage Partners, Inc., Unison Capital, MKS Partners Limited, and other private equity funds with actual results in Japan are mainly domestic companies rather than subsidiaries of foreign companies.

I will discuss MBO in Japanese corporations from the perspective of corporate revitalization.

9.2 Background of Reorganization through MBO

9.2.1 *Historical background*

Buyouts were taking place in Japan even before the 1980s. One example is the buyout of Sega Enterprises Ltd., a subsidiary of Gulf and Western Industries. However, in the latter half of the 1990s, during the recession following the burst of the bubble economy, and amidst disclosure with emphasis on consolidated financial statements, management buyouts (MBOs) began to attract attention during a time when Japan's large corporations were focusing on "core competency" in restructuring. MBO is thought to be a viable approach for Japanese corporations, because the existing management remains in the company after the deal and employment is more stable than in ordinary mergers.

9.2.2 *Institutional reform*

The Ministry of International Trade and Industry (MITI) was aware that venture business were less prevalent in Japan than in the US. In the late 1990s, the ministry founded an MBO workshop to take advantage of the economic resources (both human and technological) of large-scale corporations in order to revitalize the economy through spin-offs (Aoi, 1999). In this research group, institutional reforms were proposed to promote MBO, and in the last few years, these proposals have been put into practice in the legal system in Japan. Listed below are the issues pointed out by this workshop in April 1999: (1) review of the required inspection of the transfer of the assets to the newly established company by the court-appointed auditor; (2) introduction of "share exchange" to facilitate corporate restructuring; (3) improvement of the takeover bid system; (4) establishment of "cash out merger" systems to eliminate minor shareholders; (5) improvement of bankruptcy proceedings; (6) introduction of a consolidated taxation system; (7) deferment of taxation for share exchange; (8) equal treatment of taxation on capital gain between public and privately owned shares; (9) facilitation of financing through preferred shares; (10) development of institutions involving "MBO funds;" (11) issuance of subordinated bonds (also, facilitation of subordinated loans); (12) development of institutions related to security interests in personal property; (13) activation of over-the-counter markets as exits for new companies; (14) examination of public support measures; (15) ensuring of portability of corporate pensions; and (16) maintaining retirement payment taxation system.

With regard to issue (1), the working group were concerned over the deterioration of the goodwill of the company, because it takes quite a while for the court-appointed auditor to inspect the assets to be transferred. Through the 2002 amendment of the Commercial Code, whereby accredited lawyers, legal professional corporations, chartered accountants, audit corporations and certified tax accountants may inspect the assets, the inspection by the court-appointed auditor is no longer necessary. (Commercial Code Article 246.)

With regard to issue (2), through the 1999 amendment of the Commercial Code, a share exchange acquisition (a corporate equity swap) was introduced. Share exchange occurs when two or more companies, (one to be the parent company and the others to be subsidiaries) mutually exchange their shares. In a share exchange acquisition, as provided for in Article 352 of the Commercial Code, a share exchange contract is drafted between the companies, if the contract is approved in the shareholders' meeting, the share exchange will be conducted mandatorily, with no regard to the individual shareholders' intentions (Ibayashi, 1999). In this way, it is easy to deal with minor shareholders who are against such an MBO.

Issue (3). When a publicly held company is strategically privatized through MBO, the shares must be purchased from shareholders at the previously announced price through a takeover bid, even if the shares are purchased from a few shareholders outside of the market. The workshop considered the burden of legal proceedings too high for the related party of MBO. Thus, this amendment was proposed.

Even through share exchange in the second proposal, minor shareholders cannot be excluded from the parent company shares. "Cash out merger" in issue (4) is a regular practice in the US, and cash is issued to minor shareholders in exchange for complete removal of those shareholders.

For the case of corporate mergers, the Legislative Council of the Ministry of Justice is currently considering a legal amendment that could be implemented in 2007, which gives the option to provide shares from other companies (including foreign ones), corporate bonds or cash money as compensation for the shareholders of the other party. In this way, a "cash out merger" may be a choice for corporate mergers in the near future (Nikkei Newspaper, June 6, 2004).

Issue (5). In the case where a part of a bankrupted company is separated through MBO, it takes time to draw up restructuring plans under the scheme of Corporate Rehabilitation Law and the working group had some concerns over the deterioration of the goodwill of the company. Under

Article 43 of the Civil Rehabilitation Law in 1999, the courts are provided with the power to permit transfer of assets of the bankrupted company and the approval of the shareholders' meeting is no longer needed. In this regime, we expect better management of the troubled companies.

Issue (6). In the Corporate Tax Law (Article 4 paragraph 2), a consolidated taxation system is introduced for hundred-percent subsidiaries (direct or indirect) of domestic corporations. The law took effect in 2002.

With regard to issue (7), in the Special Taxation Measures Law (Article 67 paragraph 9), when a fixed condition has been fulfilled, the book value of the acquired subsidiary shares is regarded as the share value at the time of exchange. Deferment of taxation on capital gain is allowed.

Issue (8). In the previous system, a taxpayer filed tax returns based on a fixed percentage of the selling price of the stocks of the public company regardless of the purchase price. This so-called "separate withholding taxation" system was abolished at the end of 2000. Now taxpayers must file their returns based on the purchase price of the stocks to calculate capital gain for both public and privately-held companies. The system is impartial toward both types of companies after the reform.

Issue (9). In the 2001 Commercial Code amendment, the classified share system was made more flexible, and restricted voting shares were introduced (Commercial Code Article 222). Also, the maximum limit on nonvoting shares was increased from one-third to one-half of the total number of issued shares (Commercial Code Article 222 paragraph 5). In this new legal system, it is easier for institutional investors to make investments to achieve higher returns without seeking voting rights.

Issue (10). Previously, "limited partnerships for investment" (*Toushi Jigyo Kumiai*), which make investment in unlisted corporations, were established as partnerships. However, partners who do not engage in the execution of partnership business have the risk of unlimited liability. "Limited Partnership Act for Investment" (*Toshi Jigyo Yugen Sekinin Kumiai Keiyaku ni Kansuru Horitsu*) guarantees the limited liability of partners who are not involved in the management of partnerships.

Issue (11). The legal issues of subordinated bonds and subordinated loans are under review. They have yet to be legislated.

Issue (12). We do not have comprehensive security interests in personal property in the current legal system in Japan. The cost of attachment of security interests is too high for the transaction related to MBO without a comprehensive system for personal property.

Issue (13). TSE (Tokyo Stock Exchange) Mothers in 1999, and Osaka NASDAQ Japan in 2000 (now Hercules), were created as share markets for new companies. Through them, more options for MBO exit strategies are now available.

Issue (14). In light of the financial situation during the deflationary period, financial support through public institutions for troubled companies was considered.

Issue (15). The defined contribution pension plan was introduced. After the pension reform of 2004, if an employee moves to a new workplace where the employer has defined a contribution pension, the employee may bring his balance in the previous pension plan to the new account. While still limited, portability was improved.

Situation (16). No amendments have been made to the system that increases the annual tax deduction for retirement allowance after 20 years of continuous service in the same company (Income Tax Law Article 30 paragraph 3). Review of tax systems for relatively new remunerations such as stock options is needed.

9.2.3 *Types of MBO*

There are five different types of MBO, listed below.

The first type is the "business reconstruction" type, which is used as a method to sell off non-core business sectors or subsidiaries, conforming to large corporations' group restructuring of business operations. It is often used when management has hesitation to sell business to rival companies in the same industry. From the viewpoint of business evaluation, the level of dependency toward the parent company becomes an important factor. A good example is the general distribution company Vantec, and the vehicle transport company Zero. These companies were involved with Nissan Motor's restructuring.

The second type is the "active independence of management" type. It is MBO without restructuring, where the management becomes the buyer and conducts an MBO. In this background, differences with the parent company's policies, and an inferior position within the group can often be seen. Many foreign-affiliated corporations have become independent through such an MBO.

The third type is the "business succession of owner-management corporation" type. In owner-management corporations, when the time for generational change arrives, the problem of securing a successor arises. There are cases where the MBO is used for the purpose of business succession to the current management personnel. While fulfilling the need to sell the owner's share, it also has the benefit of carrying out succession without the sudden changes involved with M&A. However, there is the problem of owners often having a psychological resistance to selling toward private equity.

The fourth type is the "private type through takeover bid." Private equity funds carry out non-hostile takeover bids, on the premise of privatization of public corporations. The purpose is to concentrate control and allow for quick business restructuring. This often occurs when corporations have slumping share value. High premiums are often associated with takeover bids.

The fifth type is the "corporate revival type." Corporations faced with crisis in management, corporations involved in legal bankruptcy procedure are reconstructed through a private equity fund. In the case of Japanese corporations, traditionally support has been accepted from other companies in the same industry.

The most important condition for the success of MBO is the competency of the management team. In Japan's case, management weakness in outside markets has been pointed out. Even when MBO first started in England, a similar situation existed. Management personnel were not taken from outside sources. Rather, MBO started with existing management personnel as its core (Azuma, 1999). After that, as the personnel pool increased for corporate management, MBI (management buy-in) increased. In Japan, although it may not be suitable to have a structure where all management personnel are drawn from the outside, through adding more personnel pool to management, a section of management will be accepted from outside sources, and thus we can expect to see more management that will be able to increase corporate value.

9.3 Existing Literature

Here, I summarize the existing literature dealing with MBO in academic research.

Kaplan (1989) used American corporations as a sample, and reported the increase in operating income, decrease in capital expenditures, and increase in net cash flow in the three years after the buyout. It concludes that the improvement in financial conditions is due to improved incentives rather than layoffs or managerial exploitation of shareholders through inside information.

Smith (1990) measures the change in operating returns after the management buyouts on the basis of operating cash flows. It concludes that this change was not through the reduction of advertisement expenditure, research and development expenditure, or repair costs. It suggests that the increase in the operating returns after the buyouts most likely reflects an increase in operating efficiency stemming from improved management incentives. It also suggests that the evidence provides additional confidence that operating gains documented in Kaplan (1989) are not caused by the corporate accounting procedures.

Wright *et al.* (1996) used the data of 6,500 UK and other European buyouts and analyzed the failure of MBO corporations using LOGIT model. The introduction of new products, restructuring at the time of buyouts, and solving the problem of cash flow before buyouts were the main factors behind the avoidance of failure. On the other hand, restructuring plans within three years of buyouts, the need for financing, and cash flow problems after buyouts all contributed to increasing the likelihood of failure.

Although they have statistically insignificant results in the paper, some potential factors behind the failed buyouts are listed below.

With regard to buyouts which were implemented from 1988 to 1989, many senior and subordinated loans had outstanding balances, and this may have been a reason for failure. The probability of failure is low when management takes the initiative in buyouts, and when the employees own the shares of the company and have strong commitments in the operations of the company.

Wright *et al.* (1995) carried out factor analysis on the life span of corporations after buyouts. It was shown that the scale of the corporation (larger being better) had a significant impact on the preservation of the corporation.

9.4 Qualitative Analyses Based on Cases of Japanese Corporations

9.4.1 *The merits of organizational restructuring through MBO*

With regards to merits of management through MBO, there are a number of cases that I will detail. Firstly, in the case of those in the corporate group of the large company, the salary level is high, and this may be an impediment in its management. For example, in the case of Sumisho Alis Corporation splitting off from Sumitomo Corporation, they tried their best to minimize the number of employees dispatched from the parent company, and tried every possible means to not increase the number of staff in order to improve the bottom line (Toyo Keizai, October 30, 1999). The case of Sumisho Alis shows the efforts put in managerial reform before buyouts. If such efforts had not been made, this would not have led to the buyout, and there would also have been the possibility of employment loss.

Secondly, one of the merits of MBO is that it is able to reach the previously dubbed "sacred areas." In the case of Vantec, in exchange for receiving orders from Nissan, every year it accepted loaned employees from the parent company with guaranteed salaries. After the buyouts, the company began a policy "If their work only produces 55 yen, their salary is 55 yen," and around 100 loaned employees were returned to Nissan. Thus they succeeded in reducing personnel costs (President, May 13, 2002). Also, in the case of Nissho Iwai Alconics, they withdrew from a "Pandora's box" business which used to have a connection with the powerful "old boys" of the parent company (Nikkei Business, April 7, 2003).

As pointed out in the case of Japan Pure Chemical, where business was developed from a technological base, if M&A occurs, and one segment of human resources has to leave or outflow to other companies, it becomes detrimental to the company's intangible assets, and thus it will be destructive to the company's management. Also, in the case of Advanced Life Science Institute, Inc. (a spin-off from Tonen Corp), the management chose the buyouts to protect the intangibles in the research and development, which is realized by the teamwork of all members (Keizaikai, June 13, 2000). In general, MOB would be an option for the management to preserve the value of the intangible assets attached to human resources, especially where the portion of value of those intangibles is a large part of the total value of the firm.

Also, in the case of Taka Plastic Navi (a Showa Denko intra-venture business), a new business was started as an intrapreneurship. When that business follows its desired path, MBO is thought of as a solution for independence (Toyo Keizai, November 5, 2001). For the case where a new business is started, there is much risk in starting off independently, but if it is started as an intra-venture business where most of the personnel are loaned employees, the risk is reduced, and the company increases its effectiveness in managing human resources in this scheme.

Financial institutions' stance for supplying capital to the buyouts has improved over the past few years. With respect to buyouts, nonrecourse loans borrowed in the security of future cash flows are the norm nowadays. However, when financing working capital, or providing financing through corporate bonds and warrant bonds, banks require the security interests of the individual properties (Shukan Diamond, November 6, 1999). Leverage is essential for buyouts, and hereafter, along with the interest trends, changes of systems and practices will likely have an impact on the practice of buyouts.

9.5 Conclusion

Large corporations have been restructuring themselves since the late 1990s, and buyouts have been increasing. However, there has not been much academic research done on cases of Japanese corporations. In this paper, Japan's policy trends and the category of MBO have been described. Furthermore, the qualitative characteristics are extracted from cases in Japan. From here on, the clarification of the characteristics of buyouts in Japan and their empirical analysis are challenges that, amongst others, await us.

References

Aoi, R. (1999). Necessity to allocate economic resources beyond firm boundaries, *Japan Center for Economic Research Report* 9-1, pp. 16–19. (in Japanese)

Ikeda, T. (1996). M&A for business succession in Japan (part 2), *M&A Review* 10-10, pp. 6–10. (in Japanese)

Ibayashi, T. (1999). *Nutshells in the Amendments of Commercial Code*, Zeimukeirikyokai. (in Japanese)

Shukan Economist (2003). Initial public offerings of MBOs, February 25, pp. 72–75. (in Japanese)

Keizaikai (2000). Three CEOs of MBOs, June 13, pp. 142–145. (in Japanese)

Kaplan, S. (1989). The effects of management buyouts on operating performance and value, *Journal of Financial Economics* 24, pp. 217–254.

Higashi, N. and Koyano, K. (1997). Implications of U.K. management buyouts to revitalize Japanese corporations, *Zaikai-Kansoku* May, pp. 50–89. (in Japanese)

Smith, A. (1990). Corporate ownership structure and performance: the case of management buy-outs, *Journal of Financial Economics* 27, pp. 143–164.

Iwatani, T. and Seki, Y. (2001). Current situation and future prospects of MBOs in Japan, *Capital Market Quarterly* Autumn, pp. 128–149. (in Japanese)

Seki, Y. (2003). *Investment Banking with MBO and CMBS*, Nomura Research Institute. (in Japanese)

President (2002). How to buy your company, May 13, pp. 97–99. (in Japanese)

Weekly Toyo-Keizai Special Edition (2001). Managing a company as CEO; an option of MBO, November 5, pp. 118–119. (in Japanese)

Horiguchi, W. (2003). *Securities Exchange Law*, 4th edition, Shoji-Homu. (in Japanese)

Nikkei Business (2003). MBO to revitalize human capital and business, April 7, pp. 30–39. (in Japanese)

MITI MBO Workshop (1999). Issues to proliferate MBO in Japan, April 2. (in Japanese)

Wright, M., Thompson, S., Robbie, K., and Wong, P. (1995). Management buy-outs in the short and long term, *Journal of Business Finance and Accounting* 22(4), pp. 461–482.

Wright, M., Wilson, N., Robbie, K., and Ennew, C. (1996). An analysis of management buy-out failure, *Managerial and Decision Economics* 17, pp. 57–70.

CHAPTER

10

Strategic Control and Feedforward Management Accounting

Okihiro Maruta

Associate Professor, Graduate School of Economics and Business Administration, Hokkaido University

10.1 Introduction

With regard to strategic management accounting, many articles have paid much attention to the concepts of double-loop feedback and feedforward as the key concepts in considering strategic management accounting methods which are expected to support strategic control. This chapter aims to examine the relationships between feedback and feedforward, single-loop and double-loop, and output and outcome, and then emphasize some functional limits of single-loop feedback and necessity of double-loop feedback, and also some functional limits of feedback and necessity of feedforward in case of strategic control. Moreover, it attempts to place strategic management accounting methods such as Target Costing, ABC (Activity-Based Costing)/ABM (Activity-Based Management)/ABB (Activity-Based Budgeting), and BSC (Balanced Scorecard) on a framework constituted of feedforward control and feedback control, and show theoretical shift of weight from feedback to feedforward in development of strategic management accounting.

10.2 Feedforward Control and Feedback Control

With regard to the relationship between feedforward and feedback, interesting studies have been accumulated, not only in the field of control engineering in which those concepts are originated, but also the fields of psychology (e.g., Pribram, 1971), organization theory (e.g., Jackson and Morgan, 1978), management theory (e.g., Koontz and Bradspies, 1972) and management accounting (e.g., Demski, 1969).

First of all, single-loop feedback control, which has been traditionally developed in management accounting, is a closed system which measures actual output and then compares it with target output, and recognizes actual variance between the actual output and the target output.

Double-loop feedback control, in addition to the single-loop feedback, has another closed loop that recognizes variance between target outcome expected to be realized if target output is achieved and actual outcome resulted from actual output. At this time, output is defined as quantitative result of goods and services produced from process and can be indicator for measuring efficiency of process. On the contrary, outcome is defined as qualitative consequence of goods and services produced from process and can be indicator for measuring effectiveness of process. Strategy could be interpreted as hypothetical relation between target outcome and target output.

A possible discrepancy between output and outcome needs double-loop feedback control. There is an assumption that target in single-loop feedback control must be constantly relevant and compensatory actions may not be required if there is no variance, and external and lagging target outcome must also be achieved if internal and leading target output are achieved. However, as for double-loop feedback, target could be not constantly relevant and compensatory actions might be required even if there is no variance, and target outcome may not be necessarily realized even if target output are achieved.

On the contrary, feedforward control measures input and predicts output which may be produced from process, and then compares predicted output and target output. It is an open system which doesn't have a loop to measure actual output. If target output would be possibly not achieved, it needs to modify input, process, or target output in advance.

These above three control systems comprised with single-loop feedback, double-loop feedback, and feedforward are not exclusive each other, but they should be mutually complement under a dilemma of control (e.g., Jackson and Morgan, 1978). Feedback is control based on certain post-information, thus the control can be more reliable. However, it requires analysis of causes and examination of compensatory actions after recognition of variances, thus, timeliness of control is relatively sacrificed. As for feedforward, it is control which tries to timely intervene into possible causes of problem based on prediction, and relatively gives priority to timeliness.

However, it is based on uncertain pre-information and accuracy of predictions is sacrificed, thus, reliability of control is less secured. Consequently, a relationship which mutually enhances reliability and timeliness is required between feedback and feedforward.

10.3 Strategic Control and Management Accounting

10.3.1 *Strategic control and double-loop feedback*

According to Lorange (1982), some features of strategic control could be marshaled from diverse views as follows.

For example, features in measurement are pointed out as follows: data about competitors and market characteristics from external sources are required, and they are collected in a future-oriented manner before taking action, and a controversy arises regarding adequacy of quantitative and qualitative information about external environments which become conditions for strategic decision-making, and external elements such as competitors become bases of standards for strategic evaluation, and interval of strategic evaluations are flexible and irregular (Lorange, 1982, pp. 115–116).

As for features in analysis, they are pointed as follows: data tends to be aggregate approximations and intuitive rather than evaluative, and the degree of accuracy in analysis is not always high, and in addition to changes of parameter, examinations of all assumptions and flexible changes of an analytical model itself are required in cases that unpredicted situations occurred or predicted situations did not occur (Lorange, 1982, pp. 116–117).

Moreover, as for features in compensatory action, the relationship between actions and outcomes becomes weak such as actions are not effective or it takes long time to be effective, and there is no certainty to be able to examine every action for the reasons that there is no precedent case for strategic issues and data are often inaccurate.

As for features in timing of control, it takes long period of time that strategic decision-making becomes effective, irregular responses are required every time strategies could be affected by environmental changes, and the problems tend to have structural or technological differences from the ones caused in the past, so responses could be always different (Lorange, 1982, pp. 117–119).

With regard to such external, longer, less repetitive features of strategic control, Picken and Dess (1997) pointed out the limitation of single-loop feedback and the necessity of double-loop feedback (Picken and Dess, 1997, pp. 39–42). The traditional approaches to strategic control are comprised by the process as follows: (1) strategies are formulated and goals are set by top management; (2) strategies are implemented; and (3) performance is measured against the predetermined goal. Here, only single-loop feedback is assumed after long time-lag without questioning adequacy of strategies themselves. Such traditional approaches are effective under conditions where environment is stable, complexity is not high and goals are set with certainty. However, there is a possibility that strategies themselves would become unfunctional under unpredictable conditions in which environment changes dramatically.

Therefore, as for modern approaches to strategic control, a systematic study must be incorporated to monitor, examine, and review strategies and goals constantly. In other words, strategies should be controlled from the viewpoint that organizations are "doing the right things" and "doing things right" at the same time, and an approach is required that monitors to see if strategies and goals are carried out appropriately through strategy implementation control while monitoring constantly to see if strategies and goals are fit to environment through strategy formulation control, and recognize environmental changes early and shorten time-lag to strengthen an ability to adjust to environmental changes quickly and flexibly.

10.3.2 *Strategic control and feedforward*

However, a problem arises regarding the limitation of feedback and the necessity of feedforward for strategic controls, since single-loop is not essentially different from double-loop to be a part of feedback control as Schreyögg and Steinmann (1987) and Preble (1992) pointed out. In the traditional control, leaning on feedback which monitors if plans are implemented appropriately through comparing results with standards set in advance, it will confront serious problems as follows: (1) it is post-action control; and (2) standards are taken for granted (Schreyögg and Steinmann, 1987, p. 92). Thus, as for feedback about strategic actions taken already after waiting for strategies to be accomplished, it is too late to correct strategies, and it will go on for years without having an opportunity to intervene. Even if trying to cover these problems by frequent feedback, it doesn't mean to overcome a feature as post control, and it confronts with time-lag such as between causes and occurrences, occurrences and responses, and responses and effects, and it allows strategic environment to change while compensatory actions become effective. Consequently, in order to overcome time-lags, feedforward is required to deal with critical strategic threats occurred but not yet affecting to strategies.

10.3.3 *Reconstructing framework of strategic control*

As an approach to establish a management accounting framework based on the framework of Anthony R.N. which has been traditionally and widely held, Bouquin (1997) modified Anthony's framework to "strategic control/management control/operational control" by expressly ensuring process of strategic control. In the meantime, according to Wilson and Chua (1993), a control system constituted of feedforward and feedback is introduced as a framework to replace many management accounting methods.

Thus, a framework shown in Figure 10.1 can be envisaged by integrating these approaches and making explicit two phases: control over strategy formulation process and control over strategy implementation process in strategic control. Based on this framework, four phases could be assumed deductively as phases of strategic control: feedforward strategy formulation control, feedforward strategy implementation control, feedback strategy formulation control, and feedback strategy implementation control.

10.4 Feedforward Feature of Strategic Management Accounting

10.4.1 *Feedforward feature of target costing*

In recent management accounting research, some trends to explain an attribute of target costing by applying feedforward concept has revived

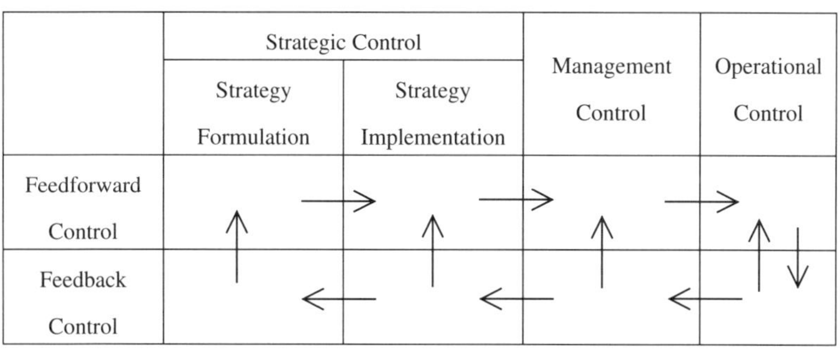

Fig. 10.1 Reconstructed framework of management accounting

awareness of its importance (e.g., Morgan and Weerakoon, 1989; Morgan, 1992; Cooper, 1995, 1996; Cooper and Slagmulder, 1997, 1999; Nishimura, 1995, 2003). Target costing could be recognized as feedforward tool for strategic control which sets target cost as criterion of strategy implementation control and positions estimated cost as an object of control, and then compare the target cost and the estimated cost in advance at the development stage and the design stage.

On the contrary, standard costing can be indicated as a single-loop feedback tool for operational control at the manufacturing stage which sets standard cost as criterion of control and positions actual cost as an object of control, and then compares the standard cost with the actual cost after the fact.

In addition, kaizen costing plays a role as a control system constituted of double-loop feedback and feedforward for management control which compares target profit and estimated profit beforehand to set cost reduction target as criterion of management control at the manufacturing stage, and then compares it to the actual cost reduction observed as positive variance through single-loop feedback which compares actual cost and standard cost.

Such perspective could bring to us an interesting understanding that the development of cost management — from standard costing to kaizen costing and then to target costing — means the process that the weight of control shifts from single-loop feedback for operational control to double-loop feedback and feedforward for management control, and then to feedforward for strategic control (Figure 10.2).

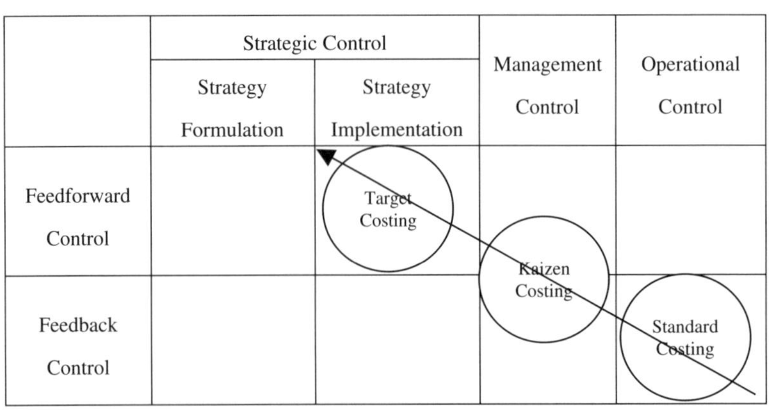

Fig. 10.2 Development of cost management

10.4.2 *Feedforward feature of ABC/ABM/ABB*

Early ABC took for granted that cost data calculated by the traditional cost accounting system after actual operations may be indefinite and deflected and that actual cost data calculated by ABC only must be correct (Kaplan and Cooper, 1998). Thus, the control logic underlying ABC can be regarded as single-loop feedback for management control for the reason that cost data produced by ABC could be implicitly placed as criterion of control for profitability analysis of products.

However, soon ABC has developed to ABM which monitors if each activity is value-added which brings expected outcome while it manages resource capacity using not actual activity driver rate based on historical data, but standard cost driver rate based on budget (Kaplan and Cooper, 1998; Kaplan, 1994). Such logic of control underlying ABM could be described that it places actual cost driver rate as an object of control under standard cost driver rate as criterion of control in single-loop feedback process while developing double-loop feedback process to evaluate activities themselves if they value-added or not. Thus, the logic of control in ABM could be understood as double-loop feedback for management control at the production stage.

In the end, ABM has also developed to ABB which tries to estimate costs of strategic value-added activities evaluated to bring desirable outcomes based on ABC data, and distinguish possible opportunities for cost improvement of each activity by proposals under strategic activity cost

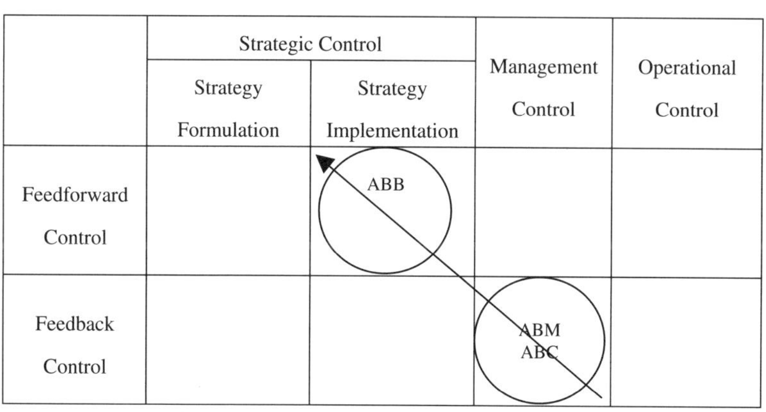

Fig. 10.3 Development of activity-based management accounting

targets derived from strategic plans to overcome the traditional budget control problem that discrepancies are not prevented and it would be too late when they are reported (Hixon, 1995). The basic logic of control in ABB has been developed to strategic feedforward control trying to recognize potential differences between actual activity costs and strategic activity cost targets.

As discussed above, activity-based management accounting could be understood that it has developed from single-loop feedback to double-loop feedback for management control, and then to feedforward for strategic control (Figure 10.3).

10.4.3 *Feedforward feature of BSC*

Traditional management control has played a role only as single-loop feedback toward strategies without suspecting relevancy of the strategy itself. However, in order to satisfy multiple outcomes, BSC has been propound so that double-loop feedback for strategies should be established to examine the effectiveness of the strategies continuously and then to improve them if needed (Kaplan and Norton, 1996).

In this regard, it should be realized that not only double-loop feedback reactively using result indicators or financial outcome indicators to evaluate output after the fact (ex post), but also feedforward proactively using process indicators or non-financial performance indicators to evaluate process before output are produced (ex ante), are built in BSC (de Haas and Kleingeld, 1999).

However, as for feedforward in BSC, reliable preliminary knowledge about process indicators to lead to achievements of outcome indicators is necessary, and it is impossible to confirm accuracy of the causal relationship assumed between leading performance indicators and lagging result indicators until monitored if outcome indicators are achieved or not. For that reason, there will be a risk which causes anti-functional and partially-optimized organizational activities if wrong process indicators based on inappropriate assumptions are selected (Nørreklit, 2000).

As discussed above, it can be described that BSC is a systematic strategic control which monitors through double-loop feedback if financial outcome indicators and lagging result indicators are achieved while monitoring through feedforward if nonfinancial performance driver and leading process indicators selected under the causal relationship. From this consideration, possible typology of BSC could be made, for example, such as double-loop

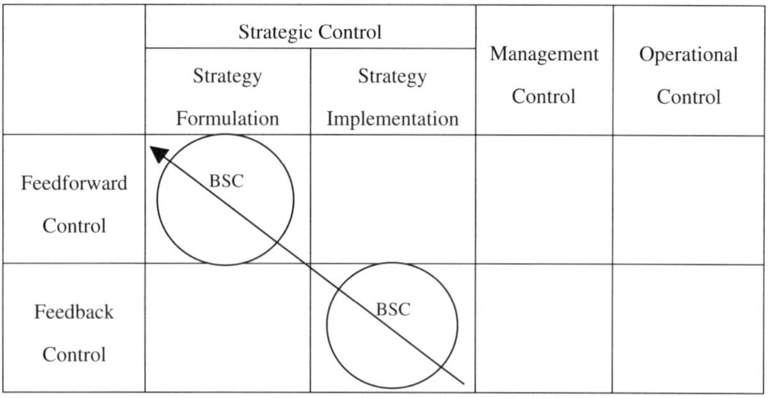

Fig. 10.4 Possible development of BSC

oriented BSC which weighs heavily on double-loop feedback monitoring lagging performance indicators at the implementation stage of strategies to improve strategy map while examining the causal relationship between performance drivers and outcome indicators, and feedforward oriented BSC which weighs heavily on elaborating leading performance indicators at the formulating stage of strategies (Figure 10.4).

10.5 Conclusion

In conclusion, some issues for the future could be indicated as follows.

First of all, the concepts of outcome and feedforward made full use in this paper could be applied to discuss and understand the framework of Simons (1995, 2000). For example, the necessity of interactive and bottom-up double-loop feedback could be understood as a result of possible constant discrepancy between output and outcome, and the system concretized in Simons theory could be recognized as a feedforward system although he himself didn't use the concept of feedforward.

In addition, even though the concept of feedforward itself has been focused in 1970s, the reason it has come to the front again now is that the control philosophy of feedforward could be understood as commonly underlying logic not only of target costing (zero variance) but also JIT (zero inventory) and TQM (zero defect), and it has been shown as a key feature supporting competitive advantage of Japanese companies (Morgan, 1992; Nishimura, 2003). It should be discussed further if Japanese management and even Japanese management accounting are theorized using feedforward as the key concept.

References

Bouquin, H. (1997). *La Comptabilité de Gestion*, ⟨⟨Que sais-je?⟩⟩, Presses Universitaires de France.

Cokins, G. (2002). Integrating target costing and ABC, *Journal of Cost Management* July/August.

Cooper, R. (1995). *When Lean Enterprises Collide: Competing through Confrontation*, Harvard Business School Press.

Cooper, R. (1996). Costing techniques to support corporate strategy: evidence from Japan, *Management Accounting Research* 17.

Cooper, R. and Slagmulder, R. (1997). *Target Costing and Value Engineering*, Productivity Press.

Cooper, R. and Slagmulder, R. (1999). *Supply Chain Development for the Lean Enterprise: Interorganizational Cost Management*, Productivity Press.

Demski, J. S. (1969). Decision–performance control, *The Accounting Review* 44-4.

de Haas, M. and Kleingeld, A. (1999). Multilevel design of performance measurement system: enhancing strategic dialogue through the organization, *Management Accounting Research* 10-3.

Hixon, M. (1995). Activity-based management: its purpose and benefits, *Management Accounting* June.

Jackson, J. H. and Morgan, C. P. (1978). *Organization Theory: A Macro Perspective for Management*, Prentice-Hall.

Kaplan, R. S. (1994). Flexible budgeting in an activity-based costing framework, *Accounting Horizon* 18-2.

Kaplan, R. S. and Cooper, R. (1998). *Cost and Effect: Using Integrated Cost Systems to Drive Profitability and Performance*, HBS Press.

Kaplan, R. S. and Norton, D. (1996). *The Balanced Scorecard: Translating Strategy into Action*, HBS Press.

Koontz, H. and Bradspies, R. W. (1972). Managing through feedforward control: a future-directed view, *Business Horizons* 15-3.

Lorange, P. (1982). *Implementation of Strategic Planning*, Prentice-Hall.

Morgan, M. J. (1992). Feedforward control for competitive advantage: the Japanese approach, *Journal of General Management* 17-4.

Morgan, M. J. and Weerakoon, P. S. H. (1989). Japanese management accounting: its contribution to the Japanese economic miracle, *Management Accounting* June.

Nishimura, A. (1995). Transplanting Japanese management accounting and cultural relevance, *The International Journal of Accounting* 30-4.

Nishimura, A. (2003). *Management Accounting: Feedforward and Asian Perspectives*, Palgrave Macmillan.

Nørreklit, H. (2000). The balance on the balanced scorecard: a critical analysis of some of its assumptions, *Management Accounting Research* 11-1.

Picken, J. C. and Dess, G. G. (1997). Out of (strategic) control, *Organizational Dynamics* Summer.

Preble, J. F. (1992). Towards a comprehensive system of strategic control, *Journal of Management Studies* 29-4.

Pribram, K. H. (1971). *Languages of the Brain: Experimental Paradoxes and Principles in Neuropsychology*, Prentice-Hall.

Schreyögg, G. and Steinmann, H. (1987). Strategic control: a new perspective, *Academy of Management Review* 12-1.

Simons, R. (1995). *Levers of Control: How Managers Use Innovative Control Systems to Drive Strategic Renewal*, HBS Press.

Simons, R. (2000). *Performance Measurement and Control Systems for Implementing Strategy: Text and Case*, Prentice-Hall.

Wilson, R. M. S. and Chua, W. F. (1993). *Managerial Accounting: Method and Meaning*, 2nd ed., ITP.

CHAPTER

11

Does Total Quality Management Generate Value?

Walid Zaramdini

Assistant Professor, Department of Business Administration
College of Business and Economics, United Arab Emirates University

11.1 Introduction

It is well known that modern quality management started in Japan, in 1950, when the Japanese Union of Scientists and Engineers (JUSE) invited different American academicians like Dr. Edward Deming and Dr. Joseph Juran in order to deliver lectures on statistical process control and company-wide quality management (another name for TQM). Generally, every book on quality management relates the enthusiasm of the JUSE members in spreading the teachings of these famous quality "gurus," and how they established the Deming Prize (DP) as an award given to the Japanese companies that showed an outstanding commitment to quality management.

More than 30 years later (in 1987) a similar award (the Malcolm Baldridge National Quality Award) was established in the USA and almost four years later (in 1991) the European Quality Award was established in Europe. Each award represents a perceived framework of TQM or Business Excellence (Porter and Tanner, 2004). The awards are based on core concepts associated with the following non-exhaustive list:

- Leaders are committed to quality.
- Customer satisfaction.
- Strategy and policy.
- Knowledge management.
- Caring about stakeholders.

- Results' focused company.
- Social responsibility.

In fact, the models on which the awards are based provide an interesting audit tool through which different organizations can assess their quality management approaches, the deployment of these approaches, and their end results (Ghobadian and Woo, 1996). Eventually winning a quality award is considered as one of the highest honors that a firm can attain.

11.2 The Financial Benefits Linked with Winning a TQM Award

A traditional question is usually asked when discussing TQM: does TQM generate value for the firm's shareholders? Our answer to the previous question is based on the study carried out by Iaquinto (1999) on the financial benefits obtained by the Deming Prize winners.

Iaquinto (1999) had studied the financial performances of large Japanese manufacturing firms that have won the DP award from 1964 to 1989. Two measures of performances were selected: Return on Sales (ROS) equal to the operating income divided by the total sales, and Market Share. Indeed Japanese companies are usually more concerned with results of market share.

Iaquinto analyzed the selected firms' performances for a period starting from three years before receiving the DP award till three years after winning the award (that he labeled as competition and post-competition periods). The performances of each selected firm were compared with the performances of two other companies operating in the same industry, which were used as controls.

Two main results emerged from Iaquinto's study:

1. In an initial analysis he found that generally speaking there is a positive relationship between winning the DP award and the firm's financial performances.
2. By applying a regression analysis, he found that the DP winners belonged to two groups:

    - Toyota group members: They were characterized by a continuous improvement in financial performances.
    - Non-Toyota group members: After winning the DP award, these firms showed a decline in their financial performances, though still better than the control firms.

In order to justify the above results, the author advanced two explanations (naming them as): "the danger of simplicity," and "the winner's curse." The first one consists in the obsession of the whole firm in obtaining the award at the expense of loosing its focus on its core competency. This will often drain the firm's human resources by making key managers entirely occupied in preparing the company for the award competition.

The second one says that the tremendous efforts undertaken by the winning company in the competition stage leads to a general fatigue at the post-award stage. Hence, the resulting decreases in financial performances that are observed.

We think that an analogy could be drawn between the Toyota group members that won the Deming Prize and marathon athletes. The marathon athletes spent gradually their energy during the competition and keep some energy for the finishing line. Also, before participating in the race they spend a lot of time exercising in order to control their pace and breathing. As Toyota considers that winning the DP is just a stopover in the quality journey, so once they have won the DP, they will deploy their knowledge to its group members and will provide a role model for them. Also before applying for the award, they already have an existing TQM system in place. As a result, the preparation for the award submission was not a difficult exercise. However, the complacent attitude presented by some of the non-Toyota group members after winning the Deming Prize could be considered as a temporarily organizational fatigue. In fact, in order to win the award, the firm had to deploy a lot of energy and resources.

We need to mention that the winners of the Deming Prize can apply for the Japan Quality Medal every five years. As quality improvement is an ongoing effort, this medal is given to the companies that keep working and ameliorating the procedures developed during the pre-winning period. Another study was carried out by Hendricks and Singhal (1997) where they had assessed the financial performances of a sample of the American TQM award winners for a period starting from six years before getting the award till three years after getting the award. They found that, firms that won quality awards presented higher sales growth than the control firms. This corroborated with Iaquinto's study although it is performed in a different economic environment.

The remaining parts of the chapter will be as follows.

First, we present the notions of shareholder's value and stakeholder's value. Next, we analyze the Deming Prize Award model from the context of value generation. Then, we present the different procedures and tools that could be a source of value generation for different stakeholders. Finally, we conclude by stressing the importance of TQM as a necessary part for the adoption of Value-Based Management (VBM) in a given company.

11.3 Stakeholder Value Versus Shareholder Value

The "stakeholder" as defined by Conti (2003) is a "collective concept used to identify the interested parties in any organization.... Stakeholders are supposed to contribute to the aims of the organization and are entitled to benefits in return." Usually the different stakeholders that are considered in various TQM awards are: suppliers, employees, shareholders, owners, partners, government, regulators and customers. So, the shareholding aspect of a firm, whether individual or institutional, is being considered as a part of a bigger framework.

Traditionally, maximizing the shareholders monetary gains was the ultimate goal of any publicly traded corporation. So if a certain company announces downsizing measures, which is usually translated by the market forces as the layoff of workers, the stock market reacts by an increase of the company's shares.

However, this behavior is contested as there are two types of shareholders: small shareholders who generally have no power in changing the firm's policy, and major or large shareholders who have a better knowledge of the inner workings of the firm. So, the top management of certain companies gives more consideration to the interest of the major shareholders at the expense of the smaller ones, as if the shareholder value is a linear function of the shareholding's size.

It is true that major shareholders have invested heavier so they are encountering a higher risk. However, if small shareholders have invested their retirement funds in a mismanaged company, then they will end up having no financial support at their retirement age which will dramatically deteriorate their living standards. Also if the top managers are not properly and ethically taking strategic decisions, then they can jeopardize the profits of the firm leading to its bankruptcy. By consequence, not only the shareholders value is lost for ever, but also the employees' jobs are lost too.

From the above viewpoints, we can deduce that maximizing the shareholders value should rhyme with maximizing the stakeholder values.

Due to the above reason, the TQM award models are now stressing the importance of the different stakeholders' interest and in order to win the award the competing organizations should identify all of them and show objective evidence on how they are well caring about them. The identification as well as addressing the needs of the stakeholders should be based on a carefully thought out process.

11.4 The Deming Prize

The Union of Japanese Scientists and Engineers (JUSE) established the Deming Prize in 1951, in honor of Dr. Deming who came to Japan in 1950 and delivered lectures on company-wide quality management. The Deming Prize is divided into three categories:

- The Deming Prize for Individuals.
- The Quality Control Award for Operating Business Units.
- The Deming Application Prize given to companies or divisions of companies.

The Deming Prize for Individuals is "given to those who have made outstanding contributions to the study of TQM or statistical methods used for TQM, or those who have made outstanding contributions in the dissemination of TQM" (JUSE website: www.juse.org.jp). Past winners include famous Japanese quality gurus like: Dr. Ishikawa who developed various quality tools like the "cause and effect" diagram known also as the "fishbone diagram" or Dr. Akao who developed the Quality Function Deployment (QFD) technique.

The Quality Control Award for Operating Business Units is "given to operations business units of an organization that have achieved distinctive performance improvement through the application of quality control/management in the pursuit of TQM in a designated year" (JUSE website: www.juse.org.jp). Past winners include famous Japanese companies like Matsushita Electric Works and Nissan Motor Company as well as foreign companies like Hi-Tech Carbon in India.

The Deming Application Prize is "given to organizations or divisions of organizations that have achieved distinctive performance improvement through the application of TQM in a designated year given to companies or divisions of companies" (JUSE website: www.juse.org.jp). In order to win the latter prize, the competing firms have to submit a document that details every step of how it is applying TQM. Also the DP assessors will visit the applying firms in order to verify the claimed improvements. The JUSE website presents the whole submission process.

The Deming Prize has been selected as a representative model for Total Quality Management because it has pioneered the quality awarding activities throughout the world. In fact it has introduced different concepts like: document submission, criteria weighting and company visits. These concepts were adopted later on by different national and regional quality awards in the world. From now on, our discussion will focus on the Deming Application Prize.

11.5 DP and Value Generation Process Model

The main question in this chapter consists in determining the relationship between Total Quality Management and Value-based Management. We have adopted the Deming Prize model as a practical representation of Total Quality Management and Figure 11.1 shows the relationship between the Deming Prize Model and the process of value generation for stakeholders.

The DP part consists of three elements:

- DP philosophy which is defined by JUSE as: "TQM is a set of systematic activities carried out by the entire organization to effectively and efficiently achieve company objectives so as to provide products and services with a level of quality that satisfies customers, at the appropriate time and price."
- DP core concepts: The DP philosophy is based on a set of fundamental concepts which translate it into a more understandable framework. These concepts are broad enough to address the concern of firms from different industries. Also, they will be used as guidelines for the formulation of the award's criteria, which include: leadership, customer focus, social responsibility, etc.
- DP examination criteria: The purpose of the criteria is not to serve as a checklist for the DP assessors but rather a set of broad practical guidelines on how to implement TQM in a certain company. Normally they are applicable for different types of companies operating in different sectors of the economy. The DP prize is composed of 10 main criteria and each criterion is also composed of several sub-criterions (see Figure 11.2).

The VGP (an acronym for Value Generation Process) is composed of three elements:

- Value Generators: To each TQM examination criterion, we have assigned different practical managerial methods, tools and indicators that we have

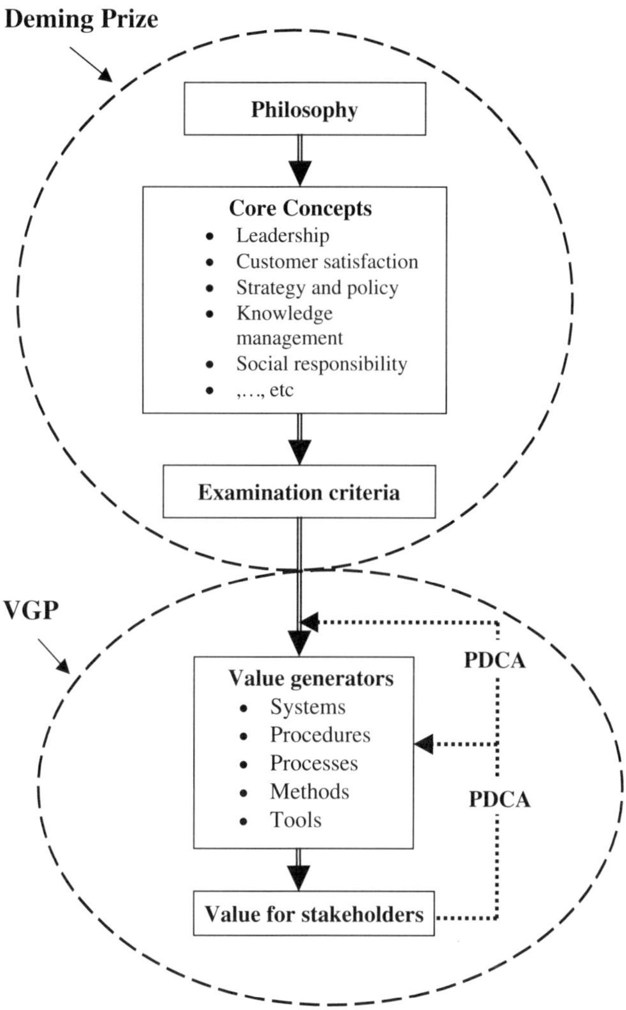

Fig. 11.1 Deming prize and value generation process model

termed as value generators. For example if we consider that customer satisfaction will lead to higher profits for a certain company, a straightforward cash value, then conducting a survey on customer satisfaction will determine the important features of the product that are well-liked by the customers. Hence, the company will obtain a high value piece of information, which if reflected on its products, will most likely generate customer satisfaction. So, the customer survey could be considered as a value generator. Also, when designing a new product or improving an existing one, the company's designers can use the Quality Function Deployment tool (which represents the "voice of the customer" during the design stage) and this will lead to a highly appreciated product by the customers. Hence a value generator for the company.

- Value for stakeholders: The concept of value varies according to the type of stakeholder chosen, and each type of stakeholder can have interest in one or more types of values. For example, when considering the shareholders of a certain firm, they are usually interested in high dividend per share of annual income and also they want a transparent accounting system applied by the firm. So, at least they are concerned with the financial value of the firm and also with the level of accountability of its top management.
- PDCA: One of the core themes in TQM is the Plan-Do-Check-Act (PDCA) cycle. It is not sufficient to generate value, but the company has to sustain the value creation process through PDCA activities. As generally nothing stays proprietary for the company for a long time, especially in this era of global competition, hence any enterprise has to systematically assess the whole process of value generation. Also, the PDCA activities should be carried out at two stages: the first one when interpreting the DP criteria into value generators and the second one when assessing whether the selected systems, methods and tools have really generated the expected values.

We note that the above model of value generation based on the DP criteria could be adapted as well for different quality awards like the Malcolm Baldridge National Quality Award or the European Foundation for Quality Management Excellence Award.

11.6 DP Criteria and Value Generators

For the different Deming Prize examination criteria (listed in the first and second column of Figure 11.2), we have associated a set of management methods, tools and indices that could concretely generate value for a given company. Eventually the proposed management tools do not represent an exhaustive list as any company can develop its own particular set of tools.

DP main examination criteria	Sub-criterion	Value generators
1. Top Management Leadership, Vision, and Strategies	1.1 Top management leadership 1.2 Organizational vision and strategies	- Hoshin Kanri (Policy Deployment): Top managers can use it for determining the quality strategy of their company and how to implement it at the different hierarchy levels. - Benchmarking - Number of top managers involved in strategic quality activities
2. TQM Frameworks	2.1 Organizational structure and its operations 2.2 Daily management 2.3 Policy management 2.4 Relationship to ISO 9000 and ISO 14000 2.5 Relationship to other improvement networks 2.6 TQM promotion and operation	- Number of project team activities (yearly growth rate) - Hoshin Kanri (Policy Deployment) - PDCA cycle on objectives achievements - Consistency between TQM and ISO 9000 and 14000 - Consistency between TQM and Just-In-Time (JIT) or Total Productive Maintenance (TPM) - Number of TQM promotion activities (yearly growth rate)
3. Quality Assurance System	3.1 Quality assurance system 3.2 New product and new technology development 3.3 Process control 3.4 Test, quality evaluation, and quality audits 3.5 Activities covering the whole life cycle 3.6 Purchasing, subcontracting, and distribution management	- QFD (Quality Function Development) - Design of Experiments (Taguchi method) - FMEA (Failure Mode and Effect Analysis) - Process Capability indexes derived from the Statistical Process Control (SPC) activities - Internal quality audits results - Indices of: % of defective products, % of scrap, % of returned items from customers and number of monthly or weekly customer complaints - Reliability tests

Fig. 11.2 Link between the value generators and the DP examination criteria

DP main examination criteria	Sub-criterion	Value generators
4. Management Systems for Business Elements	4.1 Cross-functional management and its operations 4.2 Quantity/ delivery management 4.3 Cost management 4.4 Environmental management 4.5 Safety, hygiene, and work environment management	- Production management tools (productivity, scheduling and logistics indices) - Inventory control methods and indices (work-in-process, inventory turnover, and lead time for parts delivery) - Product time to market - Cost of quality (failure costs, appraisal costs and prevention costs) - Target costing - ABC costing - ISO 14000 implementation - Life Cycle Assessment (LCA) - Occupational Health and Safety management system (OHSAS) 18001
5. Human Resources Development	5.1 Positioning of 'people' in management 5.2 Education and training 5.3 Respect for people dignity	- Employee survey (different indices could be derived from it like: satisfaction, motivation, and empowerment) - Employee turnover - Number of employees trained on the use of quality tools - Quality Circles - Number of suggestions per employee
6. Effective Utilization of Information	6.1 Positioning of 'information' in management 6.2 Information systems 6.3 Support for analysis and decision making 6.4 Standardization and configuration management	- Information dissemination technologies (intranet and internet) - Database management systems - Security level of information systems - Percentage of utilization of different software related to: statistics, project management, document processing, graphics and operations management

Fig. 11.2 (*Continued*)

DP main examination criteria	Sub-criterion	Value generators
7. TQM Concepts and Values	7.1 Quality 7.2 Maintenance and improvement 7.3 Respect for humanity	- PDCA activities - Customer satisfaction surveys - Focus groups
8. Scientific Methods	8.1 Understanding and utilization of methods 8.2 Understanding and utilization of problem-solving methods	- Statistical Process Control - Design of Experiments - Quality Control Tools (check sheet, histogram, Pareto analysis, Ishikawa chart, stratification analysis, scatter plot, control charts - Quality Management Tools (affinity diagram, relation diagram, matrix diagram, matrix data analysis, process decision program chart, procedure diagram)
9. Organizational Powers	9.1 Core technology 9.2 Speed 9.3 Vitality	- SWOT (Strength Weaknesses Opportunities and Threats) analysis - Number of registered patents - Time-scale of decision making
10. Contribution to the Realization of Corporate Objectives	10.1 Customer relations 10.2 Employees relations 10.3 Social relations 10.4 Supplier relations 10.5 Shareholder relations 10.6 Realization of corporate mission 10.7 Continuously securing profits	- Customer satisfaction survey (source of different indicators like: company image, product image, competitiveness, innovation, quality in design, reliability, price, delivery, after sales servicing, intention to repurchase,..., etc) - Employees survey - Supplier survey - Share price growth rate - Profitability measures

Fig. 11.2 (*Continued*)

11.7 Conclusion

One of the main characteristics that justifies the higher success of Japanese products all over the world is quality. Higher success is synonymous with higher market share, higher profits, and higher appeal to world wide customers. By adopting the Deming Prize criteria as a practical framework for Total Quality Management (TQM), we have presented a model that links TQM and value generation. Also, we have listed the different company's activities that, if properly implemented, can lead to wealth creation and stakeholders' satisfaction. However, the success of TQM implementation heavily depends on the sincere and continuous commitment of the top management. Other barriers consist of: The use of TQM as a quick-fix for the company's problems, expect rapid results from TQM activities, poor coordination across functions and departments, and not rallying the full commitment of the different company employees. The above listed barriers could be encountered as well by any company when launching Value-Based Management (VBM) activities. Therefore TQM is not only a source of value generation but also it represents a useful support for the implementation of VBM programs.

References

Conti, T. (2003). A strategic view of organizational stakeholders, in *Quality into the 21st Century: Perspectives on Quality and Competitiveness for Sustained Performance*, edited by Watson, G. H., Conti, T., and Kondo, Y., Milwaukee, Wisconsin: ASQ Quality Press, pp. 1–20.

(The) Deming Prize Committee (2000). *The Deming Prize Application Guide*, Union of Japanese Scientists and Engineers (JUSE), Tokyo.

(The) Deming Prize at http://www.juse.or.jp/e/deming/index.html.

Hendricks, K. B. and Singhal, V. R. (1997). Does implementing an effective TQM program actually improve operating performance? Empirical evidence from firms that have won quality awards, *Management Science* 43-9, pp. 1258–1274.

Ghobadian, A. and Woo, H. S. (1996). Characteristics, benefits and shortcomings of four major quality awards, *International Journal of Quality and Reliability Management* 13-2, pp. 10–44.

Iaquinto, A. (1999). Can winners be losers? The case of the Deming prize for quality and performance among large Japanese manufacturing firms, *Managerial Auditing Journal* 14-1/2, pp. 28–35.

Khoo, H. H. and Tan, K. C. (2003). Managing for quality in the USA and Japan: differences between the MBNQA, DP and JQA, *The TQM Magazine* 15-1, pp. 14–24.

Morisawa, T. and Kurosaki, H. (2002). The current state of value-based management in Japan and the road map for success, NRI Papers, No. 56, Nomura Research Institute, Japan.

Porter, L. J. and Tanner, S. J. (2004). *Assessing Business Excellence*, 2nd Ed., Burlington, MA: Elsevier Butterworth-Heinemann.

Williams, R., van der Wiele, T., van Iwaarden, J., and Visser, R. (2004). TQM: why it will again become a top management issue, *International Journal of Quality and Reliability Management* 21-26, pp. 603–611.

PART 3

DESIGN AND CONTROL OF DECENTRALIZED BUSINESS UNITS IN THE BUSINESS GROUP: HOLDING COMPANY, INTRA-FIRM COMPANY, DIVISION, MINI-PROFIT CENTER AND GLOBAL COMPANY

CHAPTER

12

Features of the Holding Company of Japanese Manufacturing Industries: Konica-Minolta Group Management

Takayuki Asada
Professor, Graduate School of Economics
Osaka University

Yasuhiro Monden
Professor, Faculty of Business Administration
Mejiro University

12.1 Introduction

This case objective is to find out the answer to two questions by taking a detailed examination of "the management integration in pure holding company through the mergers of the Konica and Minolta companies."

These two questions are: (1) what kind of merits does management integration have in a pure holding company structure; and (2) what kind of merits does diversification strategy have in global business?

The first theme is "what merits are realized by holding companies and manufacturing subsidiaries structure from those two independent manufacturing companies with division structure or decentralized structure when integrated." The second theme is related to that core focusing strategy, focusing on either core business or not diversification, which means stockholders value perspectives and the company, and how they should be retreated from low performance business. However, looking at Konica-Minolta, what kind of merits does this holding company have with a number of business divisions and still keep them and seek more diversification strategies?

We try to discuss the contents of the Konica-Minolta management integration and finally make our view clear with our tentative conclusions.

12.2 The Objectives of Konica-Minolta Management Integration

The objectives of Konica-Minolta management integration are expressed at their middle-range strategic planning by old-Konica company (Konica before this integration). According to this plan, the goals of this integration are fourfold: to promote enterprise value, increase stock-holders' satisfaction, increase customers' satisfaction and increase employees' satisfaction. They also stated four kinds of generic strategic means: corporate business portfolio management, Speedy market adaptation, clear corporate governance structure and strategic alliance with realizing scale-power.

12.2.1 *Turning corporate business portfolio management into practice*

This strategy is different from selecting and focusing on specific businesses that are popular in the high-tech business world. Rather, Konica had lots of experiences in implementing many kinds of businesses and this new group tries to do group management with steady revenue structures.

If a company tries to focus on a specific business, he could gain high return under a prosperous state of economy but must face the adverse wind under depression. A company that adopts such a focusing strategy would face high-risk and high-return business. The top-management of this group company who don't adopt this policy would like to keep middle-risk and middle returns in their performance and obtain steady revenue with a low coefficient between each business profitability trend.

This thought for doing business is said to be a diversification strategy including business risk for performance, and we thought this company should not measure a kind of business risk by a profit variance between business units but should measure such risk by a covariance of ROI between business units.

Also, we think a company should invest his scarce resources into growth or strategic business fields rather than averagely allocate his resources into all business units.

12.2.2 Doing rapid adaptation for market trend or strengthening division responsibilities in a division system or holding management system

This investment-center organization which was called "Division-Company Structure" was introduced in 1999 and in 2003. This company adopted "Pure Holding Company" and "Business Holding Company Structure" which was transferred from non-legal business units into subsidiaries kept by the holding company (Konica-Minolta Holdings). After this transformation, the followings objectives will be achieved.

1. To do more speedy market adaptation of each business unit. This transformation is a radical decentralization based on each business segment basis.
2. To make clear a management responsibility based on each business unit. This company at the time of "a division-company structure" used a unique Japanese division control System meaning "intra-company capital systems" and "intra-company cost of interest systems," an allocation of head quarter expenses, which was a kind of quasi-capital to be invested from a headquarter was abolished and this new decentralization was achieved.

However, owing to our opinion, there might be no essential differences between "Division Company," and "Pure Holding Company" on an accounting system's level. Thus, we try to know what kinds of merits come with this legal decentralization ("Bunsha Sei").

12.2.3 To make strength of a corporate governance

Transferring from "a division-company" to "holding-company" with American style board directors' system is to realize corporate transparency and fairness to stockholders and also to do a speed-up of management decisions.

12.2.4 To realize scale merits with the promotion of strategic alliances

Considering the future state of Konica, top management considered the growth or success in the global market being very difficult and should like to promote business alliance or capital alliances with other companies. If

Konica would become being a holding company as its first action, it is easy for them to hold other companies as subsidiaries and this holding company would reshuffle many business units and promote the efficiency for doing business and realize scale merits by reducing surplus human resources, physical assets, and monies in various business unit. Top management considered holding company systems to be effective in the state of Konica and Minolta integration for doing total business portfolio management.

However, at the time in 2001, before the integration of the two companies, Konica and Minolta did not reach the agreement for business integration but established a joint company, Konica-Minolta Supplies Co., Ltd, for producing color toner by connecting Minolta's color printing technology and Konica's new toner technology. The goal for this joint company is to realize synergy effects from the two companies' technology fusion. This fusion would indicate the two companies' integration in the near future.

After several years in such joint companies' setting up, we think the basic reasons for this business integration are to realize the scale merits and synergy effects. Also, the synergy's effects are in the following fields: as some examples, Minolta is strong in monochromatic copying low speed machines, and Konica is strong in monochromatic high-speed machines and new technology toner productions. We think this business integration is to make synergy through technology fusion. The scale effects from this integration are realized in the reductions in the number of production sites, labor costs reduction, reducing 4800 employees, reducing the number of models through the integration of the two companies' product models, and cost reductions by the synergy effects through the two companies' complementary technologies.

12.3 Some Steps of Konica and Minolta Management Integration and Business Restructurings

12.3.1 *A development of organization structures*

Generally looking at a history of business organization from American companies, pure holding companies were very popular from the 19th century into the beginning of the 20th century. Currently, American business systems developed from pure-holding structure into multi-divisions or business holding companies by the effects of anti-trust laws or anti-monopoly laws in federal government regulations. But, in Japan, except for in the age of "Zaibatu" systems before the Second World War, the anti-monopoly laws of Japan did not allow the pure-holding companies since the end of the Second World War, and multi-business companies with subsidiaries, intra-companies, and multi-business units have been developed and in 1999 the Japanese government changed Chapter 9's anti-monopoly law and pure holding companies become possible as a company system.

A kind of boom about introductions of the pure-holding company system by large-scale Japanese companies is said to achieve industry restructuring by reducing the number of companies under severe economic conditions and especially we can see such restructuring of the banking business. We can say such holding companies' booms to be a first step for restructuring. Moreover, a holding company would acquire a competitor in the same industry. For a short while a holding company could try to restructure its business units and will be able to achieve the same results from the merger of two companies. A holding company system would be able to be said to be an important one for achieving the flexible industry restructuring. Having such minds about holding systems, we try to see several steps of companies' restructuring between Konica and Minolta.

The first step (in April 2003). Konica changed all of its business units as subsidiaries and Konica became a pure holding company. After this legal change of business structure based on new commerce laws, Konica Holding Co., Ltd., has controlled four business subsidiaries and two shared service subsidiaries. After this change, Konica was still a company listed in the Tokyo stock exchange.

This kind of method for making its business units into subsidiaries was said to be the "physical splitting of business units." Pre-splitting Konica was the base for splitting, and Konica began to prepare setting up six subsidiaries and transferred all legal rights and responsibilities concerning each business unit into such subsidiaries.

The second step (in August 2003). At each stockholders general meeting of Konica and Minolta in June 2003, the integration was agreed to legally. In August 2003, Konica Co., Ltd., changed its name to Konica and Minolta Holdings Co., Ltd., and this holdings acquired Minolta as a 100% subsidiary. At this trading of stock exchange between Konica-Minolta Holdings and Minolta, Konica-Minolta Holdings exchanged its 0.621 stock with one stock of Minolta. After this trading Minolta became a subsidiary of Konica-Minolta Holdings and was taken off of the Tokyo stock exchange market.

The details of this stock exchange were the following: for several weeks before announcing this acquiring of Minolta by Konica, Minolta stock price was around 842 yen and this exchange ratio of the acquisition was 0.621, and the number of issuing stocks of Minolta was 286.87 million shares. So, 842 yen $*$ 0.621 $*$ 286.87 million = about 150 billion yen were the capital surplus of Konica and Minolta Holdings. However, the net amount of assets transferred from Minolta was about 50 billion yen. After this acquisition, 10 billion yen of after-acquisition goodwill occurred in this new holding company. This holding company announced 20 years amortizations for this asset.

The third step (in October 2003). Konica-Minolta Holdings tried to restructure pre-Konica business units and shared service units and also reshuffle pre-Minolta business units as well as pre-Minolta headquarters and pre-Minolta R&D center. Thus, this was Konica Business Technology Co., Ltd., a subsidiary of Konica-Minolta Holding, which absorbed Minolta Information business unit to become Konica-Minolta Business Technology Co., Ltd. Also, Konica-Minolta Camera Co., Ltd., was set up by the merger as a part of Konica Photo Imaging Co., Ltd., and Minolta Optical Instruments business unit. The Minolta Measurement Instruments business unit became new a subsidiary of Konica-Minolta Holding as Konica-Minolta Censing Co., Ltd. A part of the headquarters of Minolta Co. are merged into Konica Business Expert Co., Ltd. This subsidiary is a service company for business units. Also, Pre-Minolta Corporate Development Center, Knowledge Property Department, and Designing center of pre-Minolta are merged into Konica Technology Center as Konica-Minolta Technology Center Co., Ltd.

These series of organizational restructuring were mainly decided and managed by a strategic office of these holdings. This office made a project team for two companies' integration and made a master plan for these decisions with the aid from the legal office and accounting office.

The forth step (in October 2004). Additional reshuffling of organizational structure was done in the integration between Konica-Minolta Photo Imaging Co., Ltd., and Konica-Minolta Camera as Konica-Minolta Photo Imaging Co., Ltd.

12.3.2 *Restructuring related companies under the control of each subsidiary*

Konica Holding acquiring Minolta Co., Ltd, top management of these companies tried to reorganize these related companies under the control of each subsidiary. These related subsidiaries were originally controlled by Konica or Minolta Business Units and were owned 100% by stocks. One such example is an information service company of an information business unit.

The organizational restructuring after management integration through holding company systems is done as multiple steps rather than a single step. The business group portfolio reshuffling has been done by a two layer re-organization which means business group portfolio changes at the first layer and also SBU portfolio changes at the second layer. A president of each business subsidiary has an authority of investment decision-making. The president of Konica-Minolta Business Technology Co., Ltd., a core business unit of Konica-Minolta Group, has larger authority and is also an executive vice president of a holding company. This unit sales volume is 6 billion yen and also a half of 11.4 billion yen of total sale volume of this Konica-Minolta Holding.

12.4 A Method of Measuring a Subsidiary's Assets, Liability and Capital: A Transfer from a Kind of "Company Systems" to "Holding Company System"

Under the holding company systems of Konica-Minolta each subsidiary is transferred from a business unit of Konica or Minolta Co. Ltd. in principle. At the time of such transferring from intra-company business units into legal subsidiaries the following procedures or methods were used for each company's financial evaluation as post-acquisition's financial evaluation in assets, liabilities, legal capital and surpluses.

1. Assets: succession of assets from each business unit. However, account receivables are transferred from a business unit to holding company.
2. Liabilities: account payables in each business unit are transferred into a subsidiary to be under the holding company. Also cash to be transferred from an account receivable is kept in the holding and when a subsidiary is under the condition of needing cash, he can ask for a holdings to borrow money.

   And he can get some as a short-term loan of a subsidiary.

   Each subsidiary doesn't have an authority for borrowing money from a bank independently. This finance decision is held in the holding company and a subsidiary's short or long-term borrowing is only done through the way of holding company.
3. Capital: (total assets − total sum of account payable and borrowing money = subsidiary capital. The (1) amount of Legal capital supplied

from a holding into a subsidiary is 500 million yen for a large corporation being allowed under Japanese commerce law and also is less than 50 million yen for a small or medium corporation. This (2) residual amounts from capital equity less legal amount of capital is regulated as (3) capital surplus in Konica-Minolta Holding.

The methodology explained above is often used as an introduction of intra-company business unit capital systems in Japan, and this method was used under the investment center-like business unit of Konica Corporation, which was called as "intra-company systems."

The ratio of its own capital is relatively low compared to its competitor. Thus, this subsidiary needs to increase his own capital in its growing process, and only the holding company can supply cash to him and this procedure of holding company is the same to be done under intra-company business units for quasi-capital increase. As this holding has an opportunity for borrowing cash by satisfying this cash needs, but it would like to improve its group debt-equity ratio, he suggests and demands that a subsidiary's level of capital increases under the maximum amount of free cash flows.

According to the details of management accounting in this holding, we think this subsidiary corporation systems ("Bunsha Sei") under a holding is not changed.

Further explaining about the side of "unchanged," if a subsidiary wishes to use holding controlling assets (land or buildings), they must pay a rental fee to the holding company. Also, a subsidiary must pay a fee for using corporate brands when they try to use it, and the rate of this fee is constant and the volume of this cost is based on sales volume of such subsidiary. When a subsidiary uses a patent right kept at holding company, they must be allowed such usage from the holding company and pay patent's usage charge to holding company.

12.5 Performance Evaluation Methods

12.5.1 *Financial performance of division company and EVA™*

There are three kinds of performance measures in division companies

1. Operating profit at the level of consolidated statement.
2. Free cash flow at the same level above.
3. The degree of achievement about important task items at the level of total group's performance.

(There are three issues which mean integration of sales subsidiaries, the volume reduction of employees, the development of technologies).

These (1) and (2) are the consolidated financial results based on the combination of each subsidiary's performance and also total performance is the weighted sum of (1), (2) and (3) and is to score a number based with a maximum of 100. These scores are reflected into a reward for the manager and more positions' people and the level of financial performance is the degree of achievement based on budgetary goals.

This company reviewed the introduction of EVA at the day of Konica Company, and the budgetary goal of EVA was used and after these two companies merged, such trial was stopped.

This Konica Company made the specific organizational design as "KANPANY-SEI" which meant investment center systems of management accounting and they used intra-company interest charge into each business division on the basis of intra-company capital system. Now, the cost of capital is depending on the market interest rate and a subsidiary's capital is legal base. We think EVA's calculation of Konica-Minolta Company is easier than those of the old Konica's business division. However, getting a fund from a market is done by the holding company.

This company is applying division-Portfolio-Analysis into his own business group's analysis and classified their own business units into core businesses, growing businesses, and maturity businesses. However, we think an introduction of "EVA" into the classification of business units to be desirable for strategic analysis of each business unit.

12.5.2 *A kind of revenue calculation for a shared service's company*

Konica-Minolta's two shared services companies are called as Konica-Minolta Business Expert Co., Ltd. (to be showed as "BE") and Konica-Minolta Technology Center Co., Ltd. (to be showed as "TC"). These two companies are profit centers from the viewpoint of management accounting.

A criteria for a classification about a service into "TE's" or "BE's" Shared Services are the following: whether these services are professional or strategic. Environmental protection or product quality services belong to BE company while Strategic services, intellectual property management, product designing activities and corporate R&D belong to TC company.

We could say the role of TC Company has two types of activities: (1) the development and the strength of core technology to be common for several business units; (2) technology development function as corporate laboratory; and (3) incubation and growth of new business.

How to calculate this revenue from shared services are the following: (1) Shared services from BE or TC are showed as a kind of menu into each business unit and a service price of each menu is based on the fair market value. This methodology is mainly used in BE company. A service from TC is very difficult at finding out a fair market value and this service is asked from a business unit into TC and the revenue of TC is calculated based on output basis and the full production costs $*$ (1+0.04) is revenue for TC. This methodology covers fixed costs of TC. Looking at the detail of TC business activities, TC has two kinds of research activity to be entrusted from holding company or business unit company. One kind of research trust from holding is concerned with common technology development of these business units or new technology development. Another kind of research trust from Business Company is concerned with business needs of each business unit and the costs for developing such new technology from business unit need are fully charged into such customers after the end of contracts and are not related to the level of research results.

The holding company keeps significant knowledge property rights and TC supplies such property into holding. When a business unit tries to use a patent technology kept at HD, it must pay such usage charge of a patent into holding.

12.6 Conclusions

We try to say the conclusion on our research agenda. The problem is "what are the merits in this business integration of Konica and Minolta."

The main change of business design was after two companies' integration by this merger.

Why do they adopt "Holding Company System" and most of business units became subsidiaries through several steps after the merger's integration process? Looking at business organizational design in the two companies, they adopted divisional structure or intra-company systems. Thus, the main change in organizational design is to adopt the holding governance systems having 100% legal control in all business units.

Looking at the substantial function of holding systems, there are no significant changes about controlling business units at which we try to compare "Business Company with Holding Function" with "Pure Holding Company" except for pure holding company only focusing on strategic function and investment function.

However, when we compare our divisional structure with a Western one, our divisional managers generally have lower antimony or less Western-style divisional structures are adopted in our Japanese company. Also, according to some empirical studies, our Japanese company used business holding systems as complementary means for lowering autonomy's divisional structures (Odagiri, 1992). Another reason for low number of adopting Western style divisional structure is the necessity of information sharing for technology fusion and etc. between business units and if there would be some obstacles in smooth movement of human resources by a kind of wall between business units, human resource deployments or such resource support from a specified position to another one would not happen smoothly. Also, putting more weight on short-term financial performance under division structure was not appropriate for long-term growth perspectives in Japanese companies. But, according to some academics, a "Bunsha-Sei," decentralization was used for responding and defeating "scale diseconomy" when a Japanese company was enlarging its scale. This "Bunsha-Sei" is not different from Japanese division systems if their head-quarter also keeps the perfect control in human resources and money resources.

However, if headquarters begins to make smaller-scale subsidiaries and to employ new persons, labor costs are thought to be decreased. Furthermore according to the case of NEC Company, they set up their manufacturing subsidiaries in Japanese countryside and can employ a lot of younger labors because manufacturing company can not usually keep low-cost young labors in urban or large cities of Japan.

Owing to our opinion, there is no essential difference about decentralization in between pure holding company systems, business company-holding systems, or Japanese Company systems (it is a system of investment centers). The reason for saying such a viewpoint is to do severe top-down control by top management in main company (or holding company) for promoting total enterprise value maximization. As most of big Japanese company must disclose the form of consolidated financial statements for stockholders and top management should monitor and manage any intra-divisions as well as any subsidiaries under his group.

The function of corporate governance in between a division-based structure, pure holding structure and business holding structure is not significantly changed because top management demanded consolidated value maximization by stockholders.

Thus, could we say where are the merits of "holding company systems"? The merits of these systems are the following:

1. Making management responsibility to be clear: subsidiaries are different from intra-company division or business units, and they have a duty for tax declaration. Also they must instantly face the risk of bankruptcy if their performance became worse. As a subsidiary becomes a legal entity independent from his holding company, the CEO of such company becomes into a person concerned with some legal contracts or lawsuits and must have more legal responsibility of observance than the top management of a division. According to these points, the top management of such subsidiary might have higher motivation for management than intra-company division managers or a business unit leader.
2. Decreasing labor costs: each subsidiary under a holding company could pay a salary for each employee based on his own scale or his performance, total labor costs of consolidated group might be decreased in comparing with single legal company including many business units. Some reductions of labor costs are one of the very important benefits for a headquarter of holding company.
3. Easy for doing M&A: a holding company becomes easy in doing business integration between his own subsidiary and another independent company.
4. Easy for doing business decomposition: When a holding company wants to get out from unprofitable business, only it is enough for him to sell his own stocks about such business subsidiary.

References

Asada, T. (2003). Group management, in Monden, Y. (Ed.). *Management Accounting*, 3rd edition, Zeimu-Keiri Kyokai, pp. 223–238. (in Japanese)

Itoh, H. and Mochida. O. (1996). The boundary of an enterprise, in Itoh, H. (Ed.). *Japanese Enterprise Systems*, Nikkei Shinbun Publisher, pp. 153–181. (in Japanese)

Komuma, Y. (2002). *Japanese Enterprise Group Restructuring*, Diamond Publisher. (in Japanese)

Koube, M. (2003). *Konica-Minolta Business Integration Process and Future Management Policy*, Kigyo-Kenkyu Kai (Enterprise Research Council). (in Japanese)

Monden, Y. (2004). Organizational integration and divestiture: financial systems for an enterprise restructuring, *Doshisha Shogaku,* pp. 32–39. (in Japanese)

Odakiri, H. (1992). *Japanese Enterprise Strategy and Organizations,* Toyo Keizai Shinpou-Sha. (in Japanese)

Tanaka, T. (2004). Enterprise restructuring, in Tanaka, T. and Takahashi, K. (Ed.). *Management Accounting for Group Management*, Doubunkan Publisher, pp. 21–37. (in Japanese)

CHAPTER

13

Autonomy and Control in Three Types of Decentralized Organizations: Multi-Divisions, Internal-Company and Subsidiary Company

Eri Yokota
Professor, Faculty of Business and Commerce
Keio University

13.1 Introduction: Issue Awareness and Research Objectives

It is nearly ten years since Sony carried out organizational reform under the new designation of the internal-company system, and already many other companies have adopted a similar course of reform.

After 2003, though, news emerged that NEC and Fuji Xerox would scrap their internal-company systems, while Takeda Pharmaceutical, which had similarly introduced the internal-company system in 1996, announced that as a part of its business restructuring, it would hand over the running of its internal companies to other companies by fiscal 2003 and focus on its core business of pharmaceuticals.

In this chapter, we will examine the change in the Japanese company management control system of group management through the divisional system, internal-company system ("Kanpani-sei" in Japanese), and the establishment of branch companies from the perspective of organizational independence and integration. Under the internal-company system pseudo-independent companies are formed within the company, so they are seen as independent organizations, while establishing branch companies and group management can also be seen as moves toward expanding independence. We will clarify the issue of company independence and organizational integration primarily through case studies from publicly available information and interviews.

In the next section we will first examine the meaning of organizational "independence," then look into management systems for promoting and integrating independence from the examples of major US and European companies that sought to become such independent organizations. we will then review the significance that moves toward a internal-company system and the establishment of branch companies, and group management have in today's corporate environment from case studies of NEC and other Japanese companies.

13.2 Organizational "Independence"

13.2.1 *"Independence" in management control*

Tao (1991) defines independence as "the potential to participate voluntarily without coercion, conceive one's own ideas, and put those ideas into action." In this paper, the term "independence" is used uniformly, even where other terms may be used in individual company case studies. This concept is related to the concepts of self-management, self-control, and internalization. What these concepts have in common is "to determine one's own actions and carry out those actions with a certain purpose, and confirm the degree of achievement by oneself" (Yokota, 2002).

Considering this in terms of organizational independence, the organization itself commits to the goals set up by the organizational unit, and after acting, monitoring and evaluating, it proceeds to the next step. Such organizational actions are in effect "organizational independence." Leadership by the head of the organization is, of course, critical for organizational independence, but from the management of the overall organization, it is also important to establish rules to promote such actions and achieve the general goals of the organization. Rules, here, are, for example, rules for work procedures, budgets, and performance evaluation. Daft (2001) states that methods of controlling the organization include official rules within the organization, control by colleagues, market control, and independent control. Independent control arises from individual sense of values, goals, and standards, and under this control, members of the organization set their own goals and monitor their own performance. At the same time, organizations need strong leaders who can clearly define the scope of actions of members. Control by colleagues and independent control by social and intangible such as the organizational culture are effective when there are difficulties in setting rules using official and financial information such as management control.

As indicated by Itami, management control is a structure for implementing the notion of "delegating work but still retaining some supervisory control over it" (Itami, 1986). This structure is a system that uses information, especially accounting information, to maintain or change actions in the organization as required (Simons, 1991). Realizing a consistency between the overall company goals and sectional goals through this structure is a theme that the theory of management control continues to pursue.

Kagono pointed out the "non-independence" of Japan's former divisional system with the term "functionalized divisional system," and I, too, point this out in my book (Kagono, 1993; Yokota, 2003). Under the company system ("Kanpani-sei"), Japanese companies changed the organization and management structure to increase independence in which they delegate greater authority and responsibilities to line heads. Case studies on the implementation of the internal-company system in my book show that the authority of the head company actually strengthens with the introduction of the internal-company system, and this coincides with the principles of branching and integration (Lawrence and Lorsch, 1967; Yokota, 2000).

13.2.2 *"Independent organizations" and integration*

Divisional system management in companies has been highlighted by the pursuit of how an independent organizational management structure can be realized within the organization. That is, the need for independent organizations has existed for quite some time. Why, then, these days has the need for independent organizations increased, and specifically, why has the internal-company system become necessary? One factor in this is that the speed of responses and decision-making demanded by the environmental and business conditions that companies face today is becoming much faster. Amid such developments, independent organizations that can commit themselves to achieving the goals set by the organizational unit, monitor their progress, and proceed to the next step are essential. At the same time, though, the pursuit of independent organizations also require a structure of integration. So what kind of management system can realize a consistency between the overall company goals and sectional goals? We will now answer using the following examples.

13.3 Examples of Major Companies Pursuing Organizational Independence

Independent moves by a sectional organization within a single organization present a risk for those with an interest in integration. The reason for this is that the more a sectional organization pursues independence, the more difficult overall integration becomes, and this has the potential to bring down the organization. Here we will focus on an example of a company tackling this issue — ABB (Asea Brown Boveri). ABB is a major company engaged in power generation and transmission facilities, high-speed trains, automation and robots, and its head office is in Zurich. Former ABB President Hercy Barnevik built up a management system in an effort to tackle the seemingly irreconcilable issues of global and domestic, and big and small. we will therefore examine how ABB built the internal structures to deal with these irreconcilable themes.

13.3.1 *ABB organization and management approach*

In 1993, ABB comprised 1,300 companies in 150 countries, and had 210,000 employees (Kets de Vris, 1994). It was a matrix organization consisting of 5,000 profit centers each averaging 50 employees under vertical and horizontal line managers for each division, and each region or country (Yokota, 1998). Each profit center comprised two managers — one for the divisional line and a one for the regional line.

ABB's profit centers are "independent units responsible for the development, manufacture and sale of their own products, and are also responsible for their own results, and asset/liability control. They must be able to evaluate their own performance."

One structure that enables the management of the 5,000 profit centers around the world is the Asea Brown Boveri Accounting Communication System (ABACUS). ABACUS guarantees the consistency of internal data. For example, all organizations throughout the world must apply the same definition of "profit." Numerical data, management comments regarding the state of business progress, budget, and explanations of any divergence from forecasts are entered into ABACUS in English. These data are all encoded and transmitted to ABB's central data processing center. ABACUS is the only route for official internal reports. Reports are done only once, and the data are integrated in the main database. After processing through the next stage, the data are sent to ABB throughout the world, and are even used by the various profit centers.

Access to the database is restricted according to the level of authority and responsibility. For example, managers of ABB companies have access to the data of their own companies and the profit centers within their companies, but not to the data of other companies. Managers of business fields can access data relating to all units of their responsible business fields, but have no access to data in other business fields. Vice presidents have access to all data.

ABB managers receive directions on goals from the top down, undertake to strictly adhere to budgets prepared from the bottom up, and frequently follow up changes and causes. Managers who are unable to adhere to budgets must improve, and those who cannot, are replaced.

13.3.2 *Suggestions for the internal-company system from ABB*

From the ABB matrix organization and 5,000 profit centers, and ABACUS that links these together, we can gain suggestions for forming the sectional organizations within the organization into independent organizations, and integration of this management into the overall company.

First is the establishment of management accounting rules as a common language in the company. Each profit center of the ABB Group exists as independent companies in various countries. There is, however, a single meaning of "profit" in management accounting throughout the ABB Group, a collection of independent companies spread across the world. There are clear management indicators for senior management, and the concept of this is reflected in the structure. It is clearly recognized that consistent management accounting rules as a common language around the world is essential to integrate decentralized and independent organizations.

Second is the strength of the coercive power for overall company integration in which changes midway through the financial year were not authorized, and goals were set from the top down. The fact that companies around the world that are independent organizations are actually placed under strong top-down control is in line with the finding that as a number of Japanese companies changed to the internal-company system the authority of the head office actually increased (Yokota, 2003).

To managers at the various ABB profit centers, data and analyses from ABACUS are critical information to assist them in their decision-making.

One in particular that should be looked at is that top management's control over the company organizations throughout the world is extremely strong, and the common management accounting systems formed from the company's own rules has been established worldwide.

Increasing the independence of organizations under Japanese companies is dependent on the adoption of a structure for promoting independence, and how the head office establishes performance evaluation rules and a management accounting system for overall company integration.

13.4 Examples of Japanese Companies that Shifted from the Internal-company System to Other Structures

The introduction of the internal-company system by Japanese companies had meant the introduction of highly independent investment centers within a single company that, in principle, have self-support accounting and are self-contained (Yokota, 2003). Since then, though, Japanese companies began to pursue the promotion and integration of new independent organizations with the trend toward "group management" against a backdrop of the adoption of consolidated accounting and the lifting of the ban on holding companies. That is, the companies are promoting a shift to branch companies and subsidiaries that legally and explicitly require self-support accounting and self-containment to a greater degree than internal companies. On the other hand, some parent companies have discontinued their internal companies. Sony and Matsushita are among a number of companies that have started to incorporate their former subsidiaries as divisions of the parent company. What does a trend such as this signify? Here we will examine issues in the internal-company system (internal branch companies) and group management through the establishment of branch companies from examples of 2-companies that have shifted to a new stage from the internal-company system. The companies are NEC Corporation, and Fuji Xerox Co., Ltd.

13.4.1 *NEC Corporation*

NEC Corporation (NEC) shifted from an internal internal-company system to a flat organizational structure based on business lines on April 1, 2003.

Until 2000 the NEC organization was a "functionalized divisional system" in which business headquarters — cost centers — were set up separately from the business divisions. In 2000 a relationship of interdependence among the business divisions in which the attitude that "some other division will make enough profit to offset any loss" began to be noticeable, so NEC shifted to the original divisional format, and adopted the internal-company system in which companies operate independently with general responsibility from production through to development and sales for each market. Along with the introduction of the internal-company system, NEC developed a structure of internal company capital and an accounting structure as a pseudo-independent company.

The three-internal-company system introduced by NEC in April 2000 consisted of semiconductors, communications, and computers, but after the semiconductor business was formed into a branch company in 2002, it became a two-internal-company system. When the new president took over in 2003 the internal-company system was abolished. Business in the IT and network divisions were no longer in step with the business flow as the strength of the company independence acted as an "obstacle" to technological amalgamation. NEC therefore set up semiconductors, which worked under a different business model, as an independent operation, and amalgamated the two businesses that were more closely connected. NEC established nine domestic and industry business lines, including system service, software, computer broadband, social infrastructure, mobile phones, personnel solutions, and profit centers. NEC assigned eight officials responsible for IT-network amalgamation to manage these businesses horizontally. It also strengthened the staff structure by integrating the staff deployed to the companies and corporate staff. The NEC press release states that NEC intends to push ahead with the delegation of authority to the business lines with the aim of timely management closely linked to customers and the market.

With the shift to a flatter organization, the NEC president and the heads of the business lines have direct lines of communication without having to go through the internal company heads and the company vice-president, so the decision-making is expected to be quicker, and the opportunities for the president to be involved in decision-making will increase. In fact, it seems that there are now more opportunities for senior management conferences, BU head conferences and group management conferences following the abolition of companies and the flattening of the organization.

In 2004 business lines were changed to business units (BU). Eleven BU were established — the existing business lines and three new BU. Under the BU, NEC set up business headquarters and business divisions. The business headquarters linked the business divisions, and drew up balance sheets and profit and loss statements, but these were just an accumulation of the balance sheets and profit and loss statements of their subordinate business divisions, so they were artificial bodies. The actual authority to carry out business lies primarily with the business divisions.

NEC incorporated a structure to promote cooperation among the eleven business unit with the establishment of a marketing unit and R&D unit as organizations to link these business units horizontally. The marketing unit is a headquarter organization and a cost center. As the organization became flatter with the eleven business units directly linked to the company president, a similar horizontally oriented organization that could monitor new markets and put forward R&D-based business proposals became essential. Simply put, the mission of this organization is to pick up new business leads.

As indicators for evaluating the performance of the business units, NEC set comparison with the previous year's sales to assess their effort, and as absolute evaluation indicators, rate of shipment growth, and ratio of operating profit to shipments (in the case of software, ratio of profit to gross assets), and other optional items. The weight of each is one third. ROE and operating profit are used as indicators.

The NEC internal-company system serves the purpose of management for determining whether a business can become independent, and makes it possible to clarify a new direction of centralization or decentralization. Through the internal-company system process, NEC identified the need for amalgamation and independence of the company proper and the branch companies within the overall NEC Group. The issue of the internal-company system was a barrier that had been built up between companies. In an effort to tear down this barrier, NEC has placed smaller organizations of an equal standing directly beneath the company president (flattening of the organization), and established two horizontal cost center organizations as headquarter organizations. In its new strategy, NEC is pursuing a structure that seeks overall integration as a group company in which independent organizations are branch companies, and the parent company is responsible for current priority businesses.

13.4.2 *Abolition of the internal-company system by Fuji Xerox*

On March 31, 2004 Fuji Xerox announced that it was abolishing the internal-company system. In a press release, the reasons the company gave for this were "as a part of moves to improve business efficiency" and "to aim at an operating profit ratio of 10% for fiscal 2006."

Fuji Xerox introduced the functionalized internal-company system in January 2000 with the aim of improving the independence of its development, production, sales and other divisions. Functionalized means that it set up independent manufacturing and sales companies with the primary business of photocopiers. This was based on a recognition that the interdependence between the monolithic manufacturing and sales businesses was far too strong. The company therefore attempted to initiate an overall change of values by making the two businesses independent and having them compete with each other. Under this internal-company system, Fuji Xerox sought to promote competition by allowing the production division to make purchases outside the company's sales division, while the sales division was also permitted to purchase from other manufacturers. Other than hiring, Fuji Xerox is also said to have attempted to align promotions and pay rises, and recruiting with the respective qualities of the internal companies. For commercializing business seeds in new business domains that did not fall under the scope of either of the companies at that time, Fuji Xerox establish a New Business Center (NBC). Research into photocopiers was the responsibility of the internal companies, while the responsibility for other research was handed to the New Business Center.

The adoption of the internal-company system brought with it a number of negative effects, including an increase in the number of tiers within the overall company from top management to the factory or workroom floor, duplication of back-room divisions such as personnel, accounting, and general affairs, and because manufacturing and sales were transformed into independent organizations, coordination with head office departments, which were focusing on what is best for the overall company, became a burden, and the speed of decision-making fell. Moreover, setting internal company goals sparked increasing competition between the company presidents, and as a result, they were unwilling to become involved in anything that did not fall within the business scope of their respective companies.

When the new company president took over in 2003 he realized that he could not gain a good feel for the state of the company through the internal-company system, so a year after assuming the position, he restructured the company into the divisional system.

The main products of Fuji Xerox were photocopiers and printers, but in April 2003, the development, manufacture and sales of office laser printers were spun off into a branch company. By spinning off the office printer business and concentrating management resources into the subsidiary, Fuji Xerox sought to realize more fluid and timely management.

As well as abolishing the internal-company system, Fuji Xerox also "flattened" the organization by slashing the number of divisions from 390 to 230, and cutting the number of tiers from a maximum of eight to five from executives to managers. The company reviewed posts, such as making departmental directors group directors, to consolidate authority and speed up judgment and decision-making.

The new organizational structure to replace the internal-company system consolidated the company into two lines — business headquarters and functional headquarters. For the business headquarters, Fuji Xerox positioned the four business fields of "office service business headquarters," "production service business headquarters," "office product business headquarters" and "Fuji Xerox printing systems" as strategic business fields. In addition to the three business headquarters, the structure consists of the four functional headquarters of "domestic sales division," "overseas sales division," "development and production division," and "research division," and head office management divisions such as personnel and legal affairs.

The former company heads were placed in charge of the business headquarters and the development headquarters. Staff from each of the companies, whose placement had become an issue, were shifted to the headquarters, business headquarters, and the direct or indirect divisions of the business divisions.

In addition to these structural reforms, Fuji Xerox pushed ahead with its full-scale shift of production functions to China in an effort to cut costs by more than 30 billion yen during fiscal 2004 with a view to achieving an operating profit ratio of 10% in fiscal 2006.

We can see the creation of "barriers" in the Fuji Xerox internal-company system as well. The internal-company system is a structure with the characteristics of the original divisional system and investment centers of self-support accounting and being self-contained. So if the company pursues business independence, it is only natural that the internal companies will increase their independence, thereby building up "barriers" between the companies. As can be seen in the course of building the former GM divisional system, the divisional system is best suited when a company buys out an independent company to form a single company or when there is no connection between businesses. But as was the case with Japan's traditional divisional system, when there is a close connection between businesses, even though the structure may be called a divisional system, the barrier that tends to form between organizations has been thinned down through personnel transfers between the organizations, transactions between the organizations, exchange of information, and strong involvement by top management (Yokota, 1998).

In the example of Fuji Xerox as well, we can identify the management of the core business in the company itself, and the business of the overall group, and see that it is a simultaneous use of the two moves of an organizational structure that facilitates the close involvement of top management at the company and strengthening of independence through the spinning off of branch companies.

13.5 Observations from the Examples: The Internal-company System and Forming Branch Companies as Independent Organizations

The internal-company system is also an attempt to form pseudo-companies within the company. To Japanese companies, in which the investment center system has not become firmly established, this is a method of pushing ahead with decentralization, and at the same time, the authority of the head office for integrating the overall company was strengthened (Yokota, 2003).

It is interesting to note that there are examples of companies having identified the achievements of the internal-company system, and shifting to a different form of organization. From a strategic perspective, the internal-company system is to form the company into independent organizations, and has enabled top management to select the areas of business and identify the areas of focus. The internal-company system was one method of increasing the independence of the organization with the aim of expediting practical decision-making within the business, but to top management, it was also significant as a stepping stone for strategic options. That is, the internal-company system promotes the independence of the organization, and is also a trial for making judgments on the independence of subsequent business. Top management can consider business options as a group company, and as a single unit. To this end, management accounting rules under the internal-company system of Japanese companies are a device for setting internal company capital and internal company money rates similar to independent companies as much as possible. The issue that emerges here is the level of control of the head office.

One line is the spinning off of branch companies after identifying the core competence of the parent company and group management after the business becomes independent. Since the internal-company system increases the independence of decentralized organizations, a broad conscious barrier is built up between the independent organizations. Exchange of information between organizations slows down, making it increasingly difficult to achieve any form of synergy. After a number of the internal companies have been spun off into branch companies, integration of the businesses held by the parent company as internal company divisions became an issue. One method of resolving this is the formation of horizontal organizations as had been done by NEC. The drawback here was the authority of the horizontal organizations. The horizontal organizations can also lose their ability to function depending on how the authority was delegated. Another is that the head office takes the initiative to tear down the conscious barrier between organizations. By flattening the organization, the company president increases the opportunity to become directly involved in the business of the divisions, recruit personnel and acquire funds centrally, and almost compel the organizations to exchange information and cooperate with each other. ABACUS in ABB can be said to be an example that made this method possible through the management accounting structure. A third is establishing a situation in which each decentralized organization is unable to make a profit without cooperating with other organizations. For this, there are a number of possible driving forces, such as responding to market needs, or providing some form of reward for business developments accomplished through cooperation. Creating such a situation may be difficult in the short term, but if we consider the long-term function improvement of the organizations, it is a desirable method.

Similar to those mentioned above, moves to incorporate affiliated companies already listed on the stock exchange into group management as full subsidiary companies, as in the cases of Sony and Matsushita, can be considered from the viewpoint of independence and integration. The internal-company system is a process of positioning internal company business through greater independence and determining business amalgamation, and as in this case, it can be assumed that Sony and Matsushita judged that these businesses are important for the group strategy. Therefore, although they have retained the form of independent internal branch companies, at the same time they are pursuing integration at the initiative of the head office to merge technology and information by making the organizations complete subsidiaries. The key to the success of this is the introduction of a system or structure that can overcome the barrier.

13.6 Conclusion: Independent Organizations and their Integration

In this chapter we examined the moves of organizational management toward the divisional system, especially the internal-company system and the establishment of branch companies from the perspective of independent organizations and integration. It was recognized that to make organizations independent, a strong capacity to integrate was essential in the head office, including top management. Not just the strength of authority, but also the necessity for an organizational structure that supports the flow of information to the top management, and also from the top management to the lower levels.

If the internal-company system means a process of pursuing a balance between organizational independence and head office control, and a process of determination for formulating strategies, we can also understand moves for the subsequent establishment of branch companies and abolition of the internal-company system. An important viewpoint here is a clear indication of goals and examination of indicators for successful group management from a wider perspective than the internal-company system. As well as examining a structure for branching and integration, building a management accounting system for producing information that determines whether the business can become independent is also a key issue for examination.

References

Daft, R. L. (2000). *Organization Theory and Design*, 7th Edition, South-Western College Pub.

Hayashi, S. and Asada, T. (2001). *Group Management Strategies — Theory and Practice*, Tokyo Keizai Joho Shuppan. (in Japanese)

Itami, T. (1986). *Theory of Management Control*, Iwanami Shoten. (in Japanese)

Kagono, T. (1993). Functionalized divisional system and internal markets, *Kokumin Keizai Zasshi* 167-2, pp. 35–52. (in Japanese)

Kets de Vries, M. F. R. (1994). Percy Barnevik and ABB INSEAD No. 494-022-1, Keio University Business School Case. (translated by Naoto Watanabe)

Lawrence, P. R. and Lorsch, J. W. (1967). *Organization and Environment*, Harvard Business School, Division of Research.

Matsukura, H. (2004). NEC's business line system, *Kigyo Kaikei* 56-5, pp. 42–49. (in Japanese)

Simons, R. L. (1991). Strategic organization and top management attention to control systems, *Strategic Management Journal* 12, pp. 49–62.

Simons, R. L. (1992). Asea Brown Boveri. The ABACUS System, Harvard Business School Case (9-192-140), Keio University Business School Case. (translated by Haruo Takagi)

Tao, M. (1991). *Psychology of the Organization*, Yuhikaku Publishing Co., Ltd. (in Japanese)

Yokota, E. (1998). *Management and Psychology of the Flat Organization*, Keio University Press. (in Japanese)

Yokota, E. (1999). Changes in the management system through the introduction of the internal-company system — Pursuit of investment centers by Japanese companies, *Musashi University Anthology* 46-3/4, pp. 27–49. (in Japanese)

Yokota, E. (2000). Goals-based management and performance — Pursuit of speed and flexibility, *Musashi University Anthology* 47-3/4, pp. 473–501. (in Japanese)

Yokota, E. and Okazaki, H. (2002). Self-management and organizational reform — From cases of the pursuit of independent actions, *Musashi University Anthology* 49-3, pp. 345–375. (in Japanese)

Yokota, E. (2003). Internal-company system and investment centers, in *Organizational Structure and Management Accounting*, Edited by Monden, Y., Zeimukeiri Kyokai, pp. 55–78. (in Japanese)

Yokota, E. (2003). Strategy and management of the divisional system and the internal-company system, Interim report by the Special Committee for the Japan Accounting Association, Research on management accounting of company value and organizational restructuring, pp. 89–95. (in Japanese)

CHAPTER

14

Management Accounting in Japanese Multinational Corporations: Lessons from Matsushita and Sanyo

Kanji Miyamoto
Professor, Faculty of Corporate Intelligence
Osaka Gakuin University

Masanobu Kosuga
Professor, School of Business Administration
Kwansei Gakuin University

14.1 Introduction

Japanese multinational corporations are confronted with several opportunities and obstacles in their quest for creating corporate value. One way of benefiting from these opportunities and fending off those obstacles is to achieve the appropriate fit among corporate strategies, organizational structures, and management control systems.

So far several books and articles in Japan have introduced some ideas of organizational structures and management control systems for multinational enterprises to Japan and explained how these ideas have been implemented and debated in the US, UK, and other Western countries. However, not enough attention has been paid to the practical aspects of Japanese companies. The past studies in Japan have not answered the questions such as which type of organizational design and structures Japanese enterprises chose in terms of the extent of decentralization, what kind of management control systems they established, and how they use accounting information for global value-based management.

The purpose of this study is to examine the organizational design and performance evaluation practices in Japanese multinational corporations. The semi-structured interview method was used for this study. Matsushita Electric Industrial Co., Ltd. and Sanyo Electric Co., Ltd. were selected as typical multinational companies. Interviewees were senior financial directors, chief operating officers, and managers of planning department in both head offices in Osaka, Japan (for the details of both companies, see the Appendix).

14.2 Typical Development of Multinational Corporations

14.2.1 *Four stages of the development*

From our point of view, organizational structure and effective control systems are closely related. Then let us consider first the typical development of multinational corporations in this section (Hulbert and Brandt, 1980; Bartlett and Ghoshal, 1989; Miyamoto, 2003). Second, we would like to compare this theoretical side consideration and our major results of Japanese practical side research.

Although each organization has a unique structure, a structural development in many companies generally consists of four stages: export structures, international division, global structures, and multidimensional structures. Although these are described and treated here as sequential, some companies do not move beyond stage one or two; others bypass these altogether.

14.2.2 *Export structures: First stage*

Once the export strategy becomes deliberate, a company is likely to make a formal, permanent adjustment in its organizational structure. It creates an export function or department that coexists with the traditional organizational structure. This new organization is added to either a functional or a divisional structure.

In a functional organization, the export trade department is established as a revenue center. In a divisional organization, the export division is treated as a profit center. When a company's strategy recognizes foreign opportunities, but is not anxious to pursue them, then an export structure is appropriate in general.

14.2.3 *International division structures: Second stage*

Many companies move into an international division structure as foreign opportunities become more important. An international division structure implies a change in strategic focus to an increased emphasis on international opportunities. It is responsible for all product groups marketed or produced outside of the domestic area. It is generally on the same level as other corporate divisions. Head office delegates a fair degree of power and/or authority to the international division, and concentrates the international expertise in the company.

This structure is appropriate for a company that has international opportunities that require specialized attention, but believes there are more profitable opportunities yet to be exploited. To be brief, this structure is an intermediary stage between the essentially domestic firm and the international enterprise.

14.2.4 *Global structures: Third stage*

A global structure becomes appropriate when global opportunities and interests become as important as domestic ones. Three primary types of global structures are identified: a global functional structure, a global product structure, and a global regional (or area) structure.

A global functional structure has similar functions to those in a domestic company, but functional responsibilities would be worldwide. It tends to be ineffective for most firms because functional needs differ by product, by customer, and by geographic region.

A global product division structure is typical of companies with a varied product line in which each product is produced and marketed in a similar fashion around the world. It is based on global standardization within product lines. Therefore, it can lead to duplication of corporate activities, and consequent inefficiencies, within regions.

In a global regional structure, the world as a whole is divided into regions, and domestic interests are one of many. This structure is typical of companies with relatively narrow product lines that need to be differentiated regionally. However, it entails less focus on product lines and their needs, and the area focus may discourage a globally integrated approach to their operations.

14.2.5 *Global multidimensional structures: Final stage*

Global companies must coordinate a variety of functional, product, and regional needs. These needs lead to trade-offs and modifications in the organization. More than one priority may exist at the same time. This has led to multidimensional structures.

The matrix organization is a typical multidimensional structure. The most common global matrix organization combines product and region priorities. This type of organizational structure attempts to give equal weight to more than one organizational activity. From our point of view, a global matrix organization is most suitable for implementing traditional strategy.

In following sections, we would investigate which type of organizational structures Matsushita and Sanyo established, and examine some characteristics of their management control systems.

14.3 Organizational Reforms and Creating Corporate Value in Matsushita

14.3.1 *From Progress 2000 to Value Creation 21*

As a result of the *Progress 2000* plan launched in 1997, Matsushita implemented a number of business reforms, including the introduction of the internal divisional company system and the selection and strengthening of strategic key business areas to concentrate resources.

In April 2001, Matsushita started to implement the next mid-term plan, *Value Creation 21*. It was designed to take full advantage of the opportunities created by evolving digital networking society. President Kunio Nakamura said, "The goal of this plan is to enhance our contribution to society in the 21st century by transforming Matsushita into a Super Manufacturing Company, which provides truly customer-oriented services as its principal mission through the development and supply of systems, equipment and devices. Our task is to steadily expand profitability, efficiency and corporate value by forging ahead with such efforts." (*Annual Report 2001*, p. 3).

The *Value Creation 21* initiated a new corporate model based on the concept of a Super Manufacturing Company. The attributes of a Super Manufacturing Company are follows (*Annual Report 2001*, p. 4):

1. Outstanding strength in components and devices, backed by leading-edge technologies.

From: "Lean and Agile" (*Structural Reform*)	To: "Creation" (*Growth Strategies*)
IT Innovation	Business Domain-Based Structure
Headquarter Reforms	Management Focusing on Cash Flows
Closure/Integration of Manufacturing Bases	Management Quality Innovation
Employment Structure Reforms	More Efficient Organization
R&D and Design Reform	Increased Brand Value
Reform of Sales/Distribution Structure in Japan	Global Strategy
Manufacturing Innovation	Black-box Technologies
Corporate Culture Reform	V-Products

Fig. 14.1 Core concepts of *Value Creation 21* plan

2. Manufacturing products at speed with astute responsiveness to market needs.
3. A firm commitment to providing truly customer-oriented services.

Figure 14.1 shows the core concepts of *Value Creation 21.* The most important concept is the shifting all focus to "creation" for a "lean and agile" Matsushita through *deconstruction* (*Annual Report 2003*, p. 6).

14.3.2 *Business and organizational restructuring*

To maximize corporate value, *Value Creation 21* called for the reengineering of traditional business structures based on the company's successful experience in the 20th century. The core elements of the plan were i) structural reforms with an emphasis on profitability and efficiency improvements, and ii) the creation of a new growth strategy. By implementing these strategies, Matsushita have been trying to work in order to enhance capital efficiency through the utilization of Capital Cost Management (CCM). CCM is a Matsushita's own yardstick for internal divisional management control, and it is a kind of a residual income. CCM is calculated as follows:

$$\text{CCM} = (\text{Income Before Tax} - \text{Interest Earned} + \text{Interest Expense}) \\ - \text{Cost of Assets Invested.}$$

The balance of operating assets multiplied by Cost of Capital set at 8.4% is Cost of Assets Invested.

As part of *Value Creation 21*, Matsushita set a goal to increase net sales by approximately 1,400 billion yen from fiscal year 2001 to 2004. Overseas sales were projected to account for approximately 1,000 billion yen of this

	"Deconstruction"	"Creation"
Fiscal 2002	Domestic Consumer Sales and Distribution Restructuring Employment Restructuring Closure/Integration of Manufacturing Locations	Manufacturing Process Innovation More Efficient Organization
Fiscal 2003	Transformation of Five Group Companies into Wholly Owned Subsidiaries	Management Focusing on Capital Cost Management (CCM) and Cash Flows
Fiscal 2004	Organizational Restructuring by Business Domain	Business Domain-Based Organizational Structure and New Management System

Fig. 14.2 Results of implementing *Value Creation 21* plan

increase. Matsushita encouraged greater autonomy in its locally established headquarters overseas, thus enabling more prompt decisions in respective regions (*Annual Report 2001*, p. 6).

In January 2003, Matsushita reorganized their group structure to maximize corporate value of the entire Matsushita Group. As a result of this reform, 14 new business domains were established. The business domain means a strategic large business unit. President Nakamura said, "This business restructuring is aimed at providing the most effective solution services from a customer standpoint. The Company's business restructuring will eliminate counterproductive overlapping of businesses among Group companies, concentrate and make optimum use of Group-wide R&D resources, and establish an integrated operational structure that covers everything from product development and manufacturing to sales, thereby ensuring a pertinent autonomous management structure." (*Annual Report 2002*, p. 5). Indeed, this structural reformation was designed to "deconstruct" management structures of the 20th century and "create" business and products that would lead to future growth. Figure 14.2 shows the results how Matsushita restructured its business and organizations from 2002 to 2004 based on *Value Creation 21* (*Annual Report 2004*, p. 7).

14.3.3 *Roles of business domain companies and headquarters under the new organizational structure*

President Nakamura said, "The key features of our new organizational structure are empowerment, (delegation of authority) and capital governance. I believe that empowerment is a prerequisite to achieving speedy operations with a customer-oriented focus. Therefore, to ensure clear decision-making and decisive action, complete empowerment of business domain companies, which are well-versed in their respective businesses and customers, is necessary." (*Annual Report 2003*, p. 9).

Under this new structure, business domain companies were established as customer-oriented, autonomous organizations. They have complete authority over, and must take responsibility for all aspects of business activities in their respective domain, of course including not only domestic but also overseas operations, from R&D and manufacturing, to sales. By delegating such responsibilities, Matsushita tried to promote autonomous management by each business domain company, thus accelerating decision-making, and facilitating efficient allocation of management resources. The role of the Headquarters is to oversee these operations from a shareholder's perspective (*Annual Report 2003*, pp. 8–9). Figure 14.3 shows the conceptual change from internal divisional structure into business domain-based management structure (*Annual Report 2003*, p. 8).

In 2004, Matsushita implemented further reform to establish an optimum management and governance structure tailored to the Group's new business and organizational structure. Mr. Nakamura said, "Under the new structure, the Headquarters will empower each of the business domain

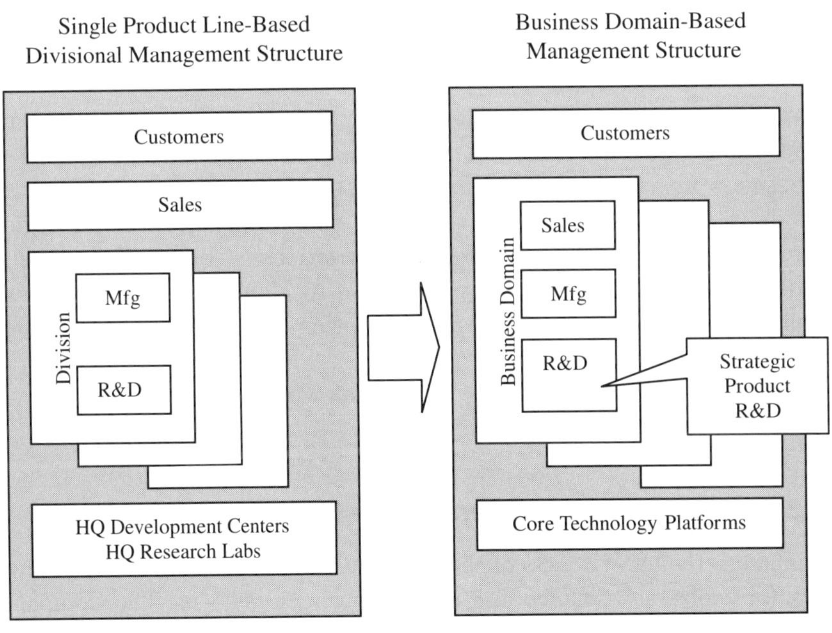

Fig. 14.3 Concept of group-wide business and organizational restructuring

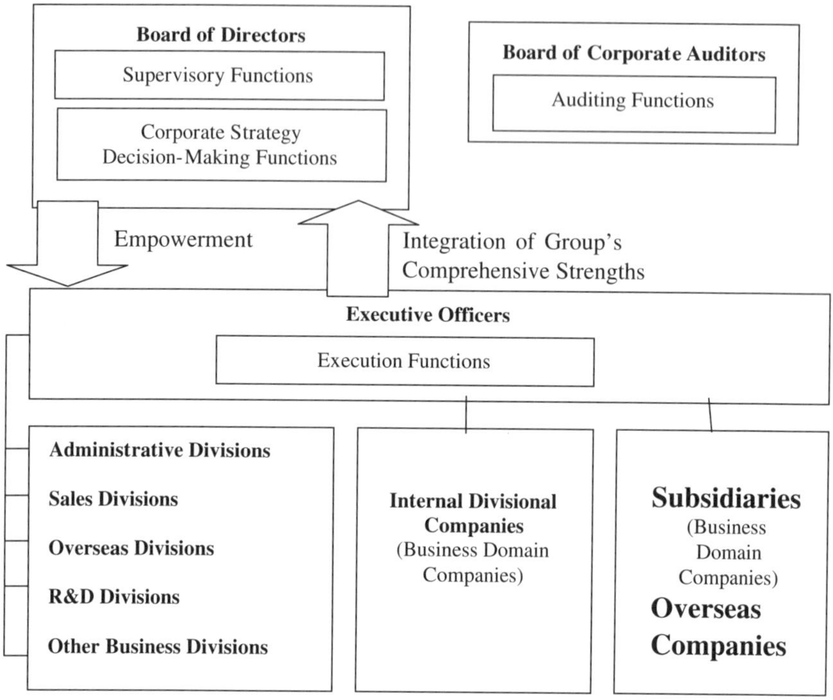

Fig. 14.4 New group management structure

companies by delegating authority in order to expedite autonomous management. At the same time, an Executive Officer System, for execution of business at various domestic and overseas Group companies, will be introduced, enabling the Headquarters to carry out corporate strategies that integrate the Group's comprehensive strengths." (*Annual Report 2003*, p. 10). Purposes of this restructuring were to eliminate several business duplications, to integrate R&D, manufacturing and sales, and to concentrate R&D resources.

Figure 14.4 shows the outline of the New Group Management System (*Annual Report 2003*, p. 10).

14.3.4 *New group management system*

To increase the effectiveness of these reforms, Matsushita created a framework for capital governance in a new management system. The Company revised the fundamental components of the previous internal divisional management system: Headquarters Fee Structure, Internal Share Investment/Dividend System, and Business Performance Evaluation Standards (*Annual Report 2003*, p. 9).

First, charges paid to the Headquarters were treated as variable under the previous system, because they were calculated based on sales amount. This treatment has been changed. They are now fixed in accordance with services provided by the Headquarters.

Second, a new standard regarding internal dividends was started, in which each business domain company pays dividends to the Headquarters at a fixed rate, based on the domain company's consolidated shareholder's equity. President Nakamura said, "Under this system, business domain companies are required to pay dividends whether or not they are profitable, thereby providing an incentive for closure/integration of unprofitable business." (*Annual Report 2003*, p. 9). Furthermore, Matsushita introduced a new overseas share investment system, where business domain companies deposit funds with the Headquarters in an amount equivalent to the share investment in the relevant overseas subsidiaries under their control, and in tern, the Headquarters, through regional headquarter companies, invests 100% in shares of such overseas subsidiaries. With this new system, business domain companies are effectively responsible for not only investment but also management of overseas subsidiaries in their domain (*Annual Report 2003*, p. 9).

Finally, Matsushita revised the performance evaluation measures for business domain companies to promote autonomous management and allow for effective delegation of authority. Their performance is evaluated based on two results-based measurements. They are CCM for evaluating capital efficiency and Cash Flow for evaluating a company's ability to generate cash. Both of these measures are applied to each business domain company's performance on a global consolidated basis (*Annual Report 2003*, p. 9). Mr. Nakamura said, "Through these management system reforms, business domain companies are shifting from the parent-alone, domestic focus of the past, to an autonomous management style that emphasizes cash flow on a global consolidated basis." (*Annual Report 2003*, p. 9). Furthermore, compensation for members of the Board of Directors and Executive Officers is linked to this new performance evaluation measures to pursue management based on shareholder interests and enhance corporate value.

14.3.5 *From Value Creation to Leap Ahead*

After *Value Creation 21* plan ended on March 31, 2004, Matsushita started the next mid-term plan called *Leap Ahead 21*. The aim of this plan is to achieve global excellence by 2010 to fulfill its mission of creating value for customers. Overseas Initiative within the *Leap Ahead 21* plan is a vital role of overseas operations as a "growth engine" in expanding business and enhancing overall earnings.

Mr. Yukio Shohtoku, former Executive Vice President (Member of the Board) in charge of Overseas Operations, said that key strategies for future growth were (1) a unified global brand; (2) matrix management; (3) superior products; (4) realizing 1,000 billion yen business in China; and (5) creation of a "lean and agile" marketing structure.

Figure 14.5 shows the structure for matrix management (*Annual Report 2004*, p. 13). Matsushita has expanded the responsibilities of regional head-quarter companies to include corporate governance functions regarding overseas operations. Mr. Shohtoku said, "As a result, overseas subsidiaries

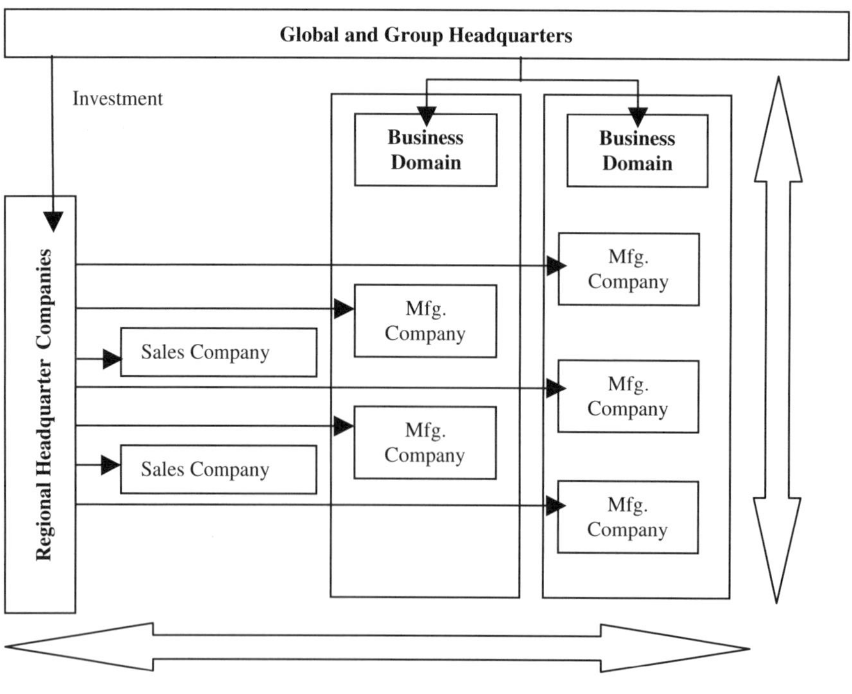

Fig. 14.5 Business domain companies and regional headquarter companies

are included not only in the consolidated operations of their respective business domain companies, but are also part of the regional consolidated management of regional headquarter companies. Overseas operations are thus managed according to a matrix with a 'business axis' for the global strategies of business domains, and a 'region axis' for the comprehensive growth strategies of regional headquarter companies." (*Annual Report 2004*, pp. 12–13). Vertical "business axis" shows the globally consolidated management by business domain companies and horizontal "region axis" shows the regionally consolidated management by regional headquarter companies.

14.4 Structural Reforms and New Management Control Systems in Sanyo

14.4.1 *From divisional organizations to business group system*

The name Sanyo means "three oceans" (that is, the Pacific, Atlantic, and Indian Oceans) and symbolizes the Company's global perspective. The Sanyo Group of companies is truly international, comprising 82 manufacturing companies, 40 sales companies, and 39 other companies around the world as of March 31, 2005.

In 1999, Sanyo introduced Business Headquarter Company System to reinforce the function of traditional divisional organizations. Eight headquarters were reorganized into five in-house company groups. And, in 2003, based on the mid-term business plan called *Challenge 21*, Sanyo reformed its business organizations into four customer-oriented Business Groups. Former Chairman & CEO, Satoshi Iue said, "With our planned conversion to a holding company structure in mind, we have reorganized our head office into a strategy Headquarters Division and Operating Division staff and further divided these divisions into business units. The strategy Headquarters Division will eventually be transferred to the holding company, and the Staff Division will be divided up among the entities of the Sanyo Group, primarily the business companies. Overseas business development strategies, too, will be transferred to business groups, with the function and role of the resulting new sections to be determined by region in accordance with the trend to greater autonomy and responsibility." (*Annual Report 2003*, p. 6). Structural reforms resulted in better profit structures. In fact, Sanyo intended to use those transformations aggressively and continually to raise its profitability, to create positive corporate value and brand value, to gain a sufficient free cash flow, and to create a strong, highly competitive structure.

14.4.2 *Business unit (BU) system*

In order to create a powerful, self-reliant group, Sanyo divided the Group into 271 Sanyo Business Units (SBUs) along product, functional lines, business process, and regions. SBUs have clearly defined goals and lines of responsibility, make it easy to judge each unit profitability (sales, profit, profit ratio) or contribution to the total profitability, and encourage a simple and quick decision-making to improve their agility.

In fiscal year 2004, Sanyo expanded Business Groups to five. International Business Group was added. As a result of this structural reform, Headquarters (comprises 54 BUs), Consumer Business Group (124 BUs), Commercial Business Group (59 BUs), International Business Group (26 BUs), Components Business Group (109 BUs), and Service Business Group (79 BUs) were established. A further clarification of roles and directions yielded 451 BUs in April 2004.

The mission of International Business Group is "to provide the products and services of each Business Group tailored to local markets." (*Annual Report 2004*, p. 5). This Group was established to focus on developing business overseas. Sanyo intended to strengthen its international presence through integrating overseas operations.

14.4.3 *Structural reformation in 2005*

On April 1, 2005, Sanyo implemented organizational reformation again to further evolve their management systems. The Company was reorganized into the eight Business Groups to clarify Sanyo's future priority business domains. These groups are Home Electronics Group, Personal Electronics Group, Component & Device Group, Power Solutions Group, Commercial Solutions Group, Sales & Marketing Group, Innovation Group, and Business & Management Group.

The focus of this reformation is on the "subdivision and reorganization of the previous business groups and business unit systems into the eight business groups" and the "realization of a small, strong headquarters." The purposes of this reformation are "to quickly cope with the rapid and severe changes in the management climate, to become a more customer- and market-oriented company, and to facilitate speedy decision-making." (*Annual Report 2005*, p. 6). As a result of this structural reform, International Business Group was deconstructed. It means that Sanyo backed away from a global matrix organization and now stays at a global product division stage.

But, in September 2005, Sanyo stated that Sanyo would establish the *Global Headquarter* to reform this new business group system. This reformation is recognized as getting back to the global matrix organization stage from a global division stage.

14.4.4 *New management system*

Sanyo started the new management system in 2003. The system was established based on the following basic concepts:

1. Business groups are responsible for operations in their respective fields.
2. They are obligated to contribute to maximizing the corporate value of the entire Sanyo group.
3. In-house companies are treated as profit centers, and are responsible both for business in their fields and for the management of BUs under them. BUs, in tern, are responsible for achieving the business goals determined for them by their in-house company's plan and for contributing to the business performance of that in-house company.

To put these concepts into effect, Sanyo introduced new control systems. Sanyo started to use some performance measures to evaluate the results of business groups and in-house companies. Sanyo uses profitability and growth as its evaluation criteria. They are based on Income Statement, Balance Sheet, Cash Flow Statement, and SVA (Sanyo's version of residual income like as economic value-added). SVA is calculated as follows:

$$\text{SVA} = \text{After Tax Income} - \text{Cost of Capital}.$$

Cost of Capital is usually 3% of the total of interest-bearing debt and capital. SVA is used as an *ex post* measure for in-house company level performance evaluation, neither as an *ex ante* nor for BUs. Performance measures for BUs are based on major items in Income Statement. BU is the smallest unit to which Sanyo apply its evaluation criteria.

14.4.5 *New personnel evaluation system*

In 2003, Sanyo reformed its personnel evaluation system for top and executive officers along with the start of the new management system. This new evaluation system is called Business Unit Leader System.

Sanyo explained this system as follows: "We have placed business unit leaders in charge of our new SBUs and included them in management as candidated for executive officers. As our future management leaders, we develop their abilities selectively. Because the performance of each SBU reflects on the capabilities of the business unit leader, the introduction of the new management system has increased motivation. We have set the term of office for business unit leader as three years. There is a clear set of rules governing incentives and penalties: business unit leaders are promoted or demoted and given salary raises or cuts depending on performance. A new contract system has been introduced for their compensation that determines their annual salaries based on a reward and penalty system dependent on whether or not they meet their performance targets." (*Annual Report 2003*, p. 9).

14.5 Conclusion

In this chapter, we summarized the results of the interview research. The major findings are as follows:

1. The core of the global strategy is to maximize corporate value.
2. The major role of headquarters is to develop and coordinate subsidiaries strongly in an integrated effort. Tax and financial issues are treated at headquarters.
3. The major role of subsidiaries and in-house companies is to carry out and support a detailed strategy developed at the business domain company or the business group.
4. Matsushita has a global matrix organization and Sanyo has a business group-based organizational structure like a global product division structure.
5. But, in September 2005, Sanyo stated that Sanyo would establish the *Global Headquarter* to reform this new business group system.
6. Matsushita uses quite simple performance measures: CCM and Cash Flow. Sanyo uses a variety of financial measures.
7. Local currency is basically used for planning and controlling overseas operations.

Appendix

a. Outline of Matsushita Electric Industrial Co., Ltd.
   Foundation: 1918
   Net Sales in fiscal 2004: 8,713.6 billion yen
   Number of Employee as of March 31, 2005: 334,752
   Global Brand: Panasonic
b. Outline of Sanyo Electric Co., Ltd.
   Foundation: 1947
   Net Sales in fiscal 2004: 2,484.6 billion yen
   Number of Employee as of March 31, 2005: 96,023

References

Bartlett, C. A. and Ghoshal, S. (1989). *Managing Across Borders*, Boston, Massachusetts: Harvard Business School Press.

Hulbert, J. M. and Brandt, W. K. (1980). *Managing the Multinational Subsidiary*, New York, N. Y.: Hold Rinehart and Winston.

Miyamoto, K. (2003). *Global Management Accounting*, Tokyo, Japan: Chuo-Keizai-Sha. (in Japanese)

Miyamoto, K. *et al.* (2005). International management accounting practices of Japanese enterprises in the electronics industry: a case study of SHARP corporation, in *Management Accounting in Asia*, Edited by Nishimura, A. and Willett, R., Singapore: Thomson Learning.

CHAPTER

15

Global Management Control: Knowledge Flows and Decentralization

Ken Lee

Associate Professor, Faculty of Business Administration
Kyoto Gakuen University

15.1 Introduction

The headquarters (HQ) of global companies make their overseas subsidiaries dependent upon them in terms of knowledge by transferring some portion of their knowledge to their overseas subsidiaries. There seems to be two kinds of knowledge concepts, one of which is knowledge stock which would be the object of technology transfer such as target costing or target cost management and just-in-time systems. The other is knowledge flow which has a broader meaning and includes routine knowledge as well as the knowledge stock. In this chapter, the latter concept of knowledge is used.

It can be argued that the relationship between HQ and overseas subsidiaries is shaped to some extent by the knowledge flows from HQ to subsidiaries. If so, it would be quite relevant to pay attention to "knowledge transfer" as one of the factors to explain global management control.

15.2 Research Framework

According to the "resource dependence perspective" which has been proposed since the late 1970s, an organization is an open system which exists as a result of dependence on other resource holding organizations.

Due to this "dependence," inter-organizational relationships are formed and maintained over acquisition and/or disposal of resources. Organizations try to enlarge their control areas by avoiding being dependent on other organizations and reversely making other organizations depend on them. They seem to have a behavioral principle of dealing actively with their dependence on others when they have to tolerate it (Iwabuchi, 1995, pp. 139–140).

If we apply the "resource dependence perspective" to the context of a global company, the extent of resource dependence would be closely related to the extent of HQ's control over its subsidiaries. The more overseas subsidiaries depend on HQ in terms of resources, the bigger HQ's power becomes.

To add to this, there are many kinds of tangible and intangible resources with "knowledge" being one of the most representative intangible resources. In this chapter, we focus on "knowledge flows" and examine global management control from the viewpoint of knowledge transfer. In this sense, it could be called a "knowledge dependence perspective" as a special type of "resource dependence perspective." Iwabuchi (1995) set up a hypothesis based on the "resource dependence perspective" saying;

> The higher the extent of overseas subsidiaries' resource dependence on HQ, the stronger the influence of HQ on the decision making processes of the subsidiaries.

He went on to conduct a questionnaire survey which verified the above hypothesis. Similarly, from the viewpoint of a "knowledge dependence perspective," Lee (2003) derived the following hypothesis which will be tested in this chapter.

H1: *The more HQ's knowledge is transferred to overseas subsidiaries, the more decision making authority is centralized.*

15.3 Findings from Preceding Researches

The relationship between knowledge transfer and delegation of decision making authority has been analyzed by a series of papers by Lee (1996, 1998, 2001, 2003). In these papers, the volume of knowledge transfer from HQ to overseas subsidiaries was measured. Lee (1996) first measured the volume of knowledge transfer in five areas (purchasing, manufacturing, distribution, marketing and product development) by using 7 point Likert scale (1 = none, 7 = all). The paper introduced a composite variable called "volume of knowledge transfer" by averaging out the scores from the five areas. Using principal component analysis the composite variable was divided into

	Component	1	2
	Interpretation of Component	Market related Knowledge	Product related Knowledge
Purchasing related knowledge		0.85439	0.14454
Manufacturing related knowledge		0.13780	0.88093
Distribution related knowledge		0.87696	0.11603
Marketing related knowledge		0.68278	0.35611
Product development knowledge		0.23586	0.85298
Eigenvalue		2.66521	1.03942
Contribution rate		53.3%	20.8%
Accumulated contribution rate		53.3%	74.1%

Source: Lee (1996), p. 72.

Fig. 15.1 Market related vs. product related knowledge

two factors. These were "market related knowledge" and "product related knowledge."

As seen in Figure 15.1, the "market related knowledge" measure was derived by averaging the scores of purchasing related knowledge, distribution related knowledge, and marketing related knowledge. On the other hand, the "product related knowledge" measure came from averaging the scores of both manufacturing related knowledge and product development knowledge.

Similarly, as seen in Figure 15.2, decision making was also divided into two categories using principal component analysis of seven decision making areas. The first category "strategic decision making" was derived by averaging the scores of four decision making areas and included new product introduction, withdrawal from established product lines, supplier selection, and facility enlargement investment. The second category "administrative decision making" was derived by averaging the scores of three decision making areas including budget draft preparation, bonus determination for subsidiary vice president, and promotion of directors within each subsidiary. Meanwhile, credibility of all composite variables has been positively assessed by the coefficient of Cronbach's alpha.

Based on the correlation analysis shown in Figure 15.3, a negative correlation was verified between "volume of knowledge transfer from HQ to subsidiaries" and "delegation of decision making authority." It is noteworthy that a strong negative correlation was identified specifically in relation to "delegation of strategic decision making authority."

	Component	1	2
	Interpretation of Component	Strategic Decision Making	Administrative Decision Making
New product introduction		0.87423	0.07177
Withdrawal from product lines		0.83611	0.02556
Supplier selection		0.49283	0.46798
Facility enlargement investment		0.66652	0.13670
Budget draft preparation		0.38869	0.50710
Bonuses for vice president		-0.00468	0.82720
Promotion from within		0.05403	0.85688
Eigenvalue		2.78536	1.43829
Contribution rate		39.8%	20.5%
Accumulated contribution rate		39.8%	60.3%

Source: Lee (1996), p. 76.

Fig. 15.2 Strategic vs. administrative decision making

	Volume of knowledge transfer from HQ to subsidiaries
Delegation of strategic decision making authority	-0.307***
Delegation of administrative decision making authority	-0.163*
Mean	-0.290***

N=164, *p<0.05, ***p<0.001.

Fig. 15.3 Correlation between volume of knowledge transfer and delegation of decision making authority (from HQ survey)

The negative correlation between the two variables signifies a positive correlation between knowledge transfer and centralization of decision making authority. The above results show that the more knowledge HQ transfers to subsidiaries, the more decision making authority is centralized. Transferring knowledge to subsidiaries by HQ is just like investing in subsidiaries by HQ. Just as the investment enhances corporate governance, so knowledge transfer strengthens the power of HQ. These findings from preceding research lead to Figure 15.4.

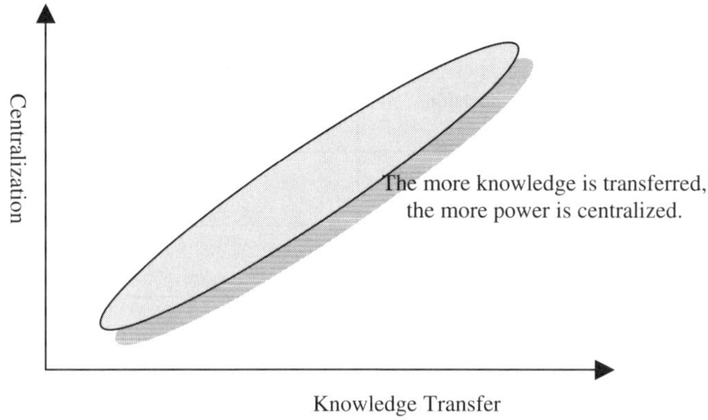

Fig. 15.4 Knowledge transfer and centralization

15.4 Homogeneity Hypothesis Regarding Knowledge Transfer

In relation to knowledge transfer and decision making authority, Lee (2003) has derived two different hypotheses. The first one is called the "homogeneity hypothesis." When we consider management control of global companies from the viewpoint of knowledge transfer, it is not so important which country the HQ is located in. Instead, what seems to be more relevant is the pattern of knowledge transfer and the level of decentralization. As a result, the following hypothesis could be derived from the perspective of knowledge dependence.

H2: *There exists homogeneity in management control systems among knowledge dependent companies despite the differences of national cultures.*

For example, knowledge dependent Japanese companies and knowledge dependent western companies should belong to the same type according to the view of knowledge dependence. The question here is whether these firms show a similar level of homogeneity in management control systems. A survey of foreign companies in Japan gives us some clues to this question. Lee (2001) found that the delegation of both strategic and administrative decision making authority is negatively correlated with the volume of knowledge transfer (Figure 15.5). In other words, the more knowledge is transferred from western HQ to Japanese subsidiaries, the more decision making authority is centralized around HQ.

	Volume of knowledge transfer from HQ to subsidiaries
Delegation of strategic decision making authority	-0.359†
Delegation of administrative decision making authority	-0.323†
Mean	-0.380*

N=21, †p<0.1, *p<0.05.

Fig. 15.5 Correlation between volume of knowledge transfer and delegation of decision making authority (from foreign company survey)

15.5 Heterogeneity Hypothesis Regarding Knowledge Transfer

The second hypothesis by Lee (2003) about knowledge transfer and decision making authority is called the "heterogeneity hypothesis" which deals with regional differences among Asia, North America and Europe. It is very much the case that there is some difference in the volume of knowledge transfer between regions of relatively lower economic status and those of relatively higher economic status. By using the knowledge dependence perspective, this kind of regional difference also can be analyzed. Lee (2003) derived the following hypotheses regarding knowledge transfer and decision making authority.

H3: *There are regional differences in knowledge transfer from HQ to overseas subsidiaries among three regions.*

H4: *There are regional differences in the extent of delegation of decision making authority among three regions.*

These hypotheses were analyzed based on the data from the preceding HQ survey (Lee, 1996), where the number of effective cases is 61 which have more than one subsidiary in each region respectively. Figure 15.6 shows the results of an analysis of variance regarding the transfers of product related knowledge. As the original mean value did not come within a normal distribution, algebraic conversion was used. Both F-statistic and p-value in Figure 15.6 are based on the scores after algebraic conversion.

As shown in Figure 15.6, the regional difference in the volume of knowledge transfer is identified in product related knowledge ($p < 0.05$). In other words, the volume of knowledge transfer from HQ to Asian subsidiaries is

	# of Cases	Mean	Value after Conversion	SD	*F*-statistic	*p*-value
Asian subsidiaries	61	6.0574	1.7803	0.2209	3.688	0.027
N.American subsidiaries	60	5.4083	1.6426	0.3277		
European subsidiaries	60	5.5250	1.6653	0.3365		
Total	181	5.6657	1.6965	0.3037		

Fig. 15.6 Regional differences in knowledge transfer (in case of product related knowledge)

greater than that from HQ to North American or European subsidiaries. The same is true of market related knowledge as shown in Figure 15.7 ($p < 0.05$).

Based on the results of the variance analysis above, H3 was verified. Meanwhile, H4 examines the differences in the delegation of decision making authority among three regions which would result from the regional differences in the level of knowledge transfer from HQ to subsidiaries. Figure 15.8 illustrates the regional differences regarding the delegation of strategic decision making authority.

As the original mean value did not come within a normal distribution, algebraic conversion was used. Both F-statistic and p-value in Figure 15.8 are based on the scores after algebraic conversion. The results, however, do

	# of Cases	Mean	Value after Conversion	SD	*F* statistic	*p* value
Asian subsidiaries	61	4.1257	1.3493	0.3932	3.350	0.037
N.American subsidiaries	60	3.5219	1.1713	0.4442		
European subsidiaries	60	3.5601	1.1715	0.4734		
Total	181	3.7359	1.2307	0.4438		

Fig. 15.7 Regional differences in knowledge transfer (in case of market related knowledge)

	# of Cases	Mean	Value after Conversion	SD	*F*-statistic	*p*-value
Asian subsidiaries	61	3.8238	1.2955	0.3173	1.534	0.219
N.American subsidiaries	61	4.1366	1.3842	0.2794		
European subsidiaries	61	4.0751	1.3665	0.2900		
Total	183	4.0118	1.3487	0.2969		

Fig. 15.8 Delegation of strategic decision making authority

not indicate any significant differences among three regions in delegation of "strategic decision making authority." And the same is true of "administrative decision making authority" as shown in Figure 15.9.

To sum up, regional differences in knowledge transfer (H3) were statistically supported although regional differences in delegation of decision making authority (H4) were not. From the knowledge dependence perspective, it would be natural that the delegation of decision making authority from HQ to overseas subsidiaries is low in the regions with higher level of knowledge transfer from HQ to subsidiaries. This kind of causal relationship, however, could not be verified.

	# of Cases	Mean	Value after Conversion	SD	*F*-statistic	*p*-value
Asian subsidiaries	61	5.1475	1.5932	0.3262	1.486	0.229
N.American subsidiaries	61	5.5191	1.6768	0.2769		
European subsidiaries	61	5.4918	1.6696	0.2851		
Total	183	5.3862	1.6465	0.2977		

Fig. 15.9 Delegation of administrative decision making authority

15.6 Correlation between Knowledge Transfer and Delegation of Decision Making Authority

In the preceding section, we divided knowledge into "product related knowledge" and "market related knowledge" and also divided decision making into "strategic decision making" and "administrative decision making." In this section, we further investigate the relationships among these four variables. Figure 15.10 illustrates the results of a correlation analysis which includes 183 subsidiaries of 61 Japanese global companies.

As shown in Figure 15.10, there are some significant correlations. First of all, a strong positive correlation was found between "transfer of PK" and "transfer of MK." This correlation indicates that the more product related knowledge (PK) is transferred, the more market related knowledge (MK) is also transferred. Secondly, there is a strong positive correlation between "delegation of SDMA" and "delegation of ADMA." This means that the higher the delegation level of strategic decision making authority (SDMA) is, the higher that of administrative decision making authority (ADMA) becomes.

Next, we can see a strong negative correlation between "transfer of PK" and "delegation of SDMA." Product related knowledge (PK) consists of the knowledge of product development and manufacturing. This kind of knowledge is likely to be a part of a company's core knowledge and HQ tends to take the responsibility for it. On the other hand, strategic decision

	Transfer of PK	Transfer of MK	Delegation of SDMA	Delegation of ADMA
Transfer of PK	1.000	0.473***	-0.338***	-0.080
Transfer of MK	0.473***	1.000	-0.202**	-0.160*
Delegation of SDMA	-0.338***	-0.202**	1.000	0.356***
Delegation of ADMA	-0.080	-0.160*	0.356***	1.000

PK=Product related knowledge, MK=Market related knowledge, SDMA=Strategic decision making authority, ADMA=Administrative decision making authority, N=183, *p<0.05, **p<0.01, ***p<0.001.

Fig. 15.10 Correlation between knowledge transfer and delegation of decision making authority

making authority (SDMA) tends to be centralized and relatively hard to delegate. Therefore a strong negative correlation between the two could be interpreted as follows; the more HQ transfers product related knowledge (PK) to its overseas subsidiaries, the more dependent the subsidiaries are on HQ in terms of product related knowledge. As a result, strategic decision making authority (SDMA) would be centralized to HQ.

Finally, there is a negative correlation between market related knowledge and strategic/administrative decision making. Market related knowledge seems to be peripheral knowledge rather than a part of a company's core knowledge. A high level of transfer even in this knowledge means that the level of knowledge transfer is significantly high. As a result, administrative decision making as well as strategic decision making authority are likely to be centralized.

The illustration in Figure 15.11 summarizes the results of the preceding correlation analyses. The horizontal axis represents the level of knowledge transfer which increases in order of "low transfer," "transfer of PK," and "transfer of both PK and MK." Similarly, the vertical axis represents the level of centralization (i.e., the reverse of authority delegation) which increases in order of "low centralization," "centralization of SDMA," and "centralization of both SDMA and ADMA." As shown in Figure 15.11, the two plus (+) cells represent significant correlations between the level of

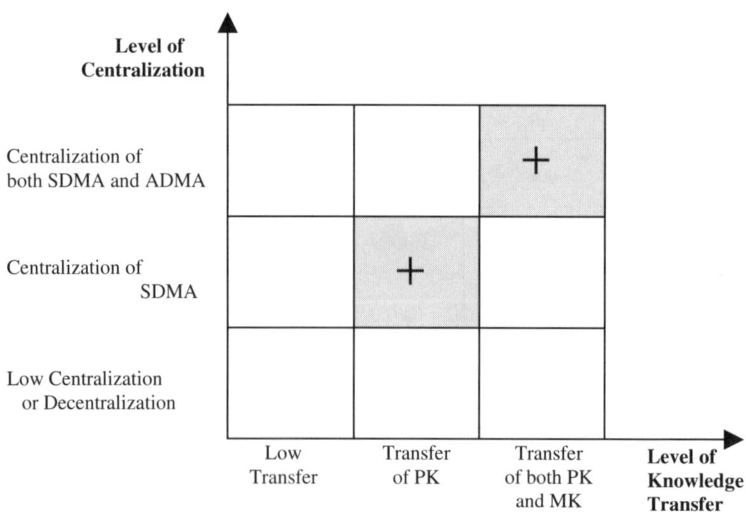

Fig. 15.11 Illustration of correlation analyses

knowledge transfer and the level of centralization. As the level of knowledge transfer increases, the level of centralization also increases. This result supports our hypotheses derived from the knowledge dependence perspective.

15.7 Knowledge Transfer and Network Organization

In the preceding sections, we tried to verify the hypotheses regarding knowledge transfer and authority delegation which were derived from the knowledge dependence perspective. Knowledge flows, however, are not limited to those from HQ to subsidiaries. Reverse flows (i.e., knowledge flows from subsidiaries to HQ) and/or horizontal flows among subsidiaries also exist. Gupta and Govindarajan (1991) set up a subsidiary role model as in Figure 15.12 by focusing on the complicated patterns of knowledge flows.

In this model, for example, the "global innovator" is a subsidiary with low knowledge inflows from the rest of the company and high knowledge outflows to the rest of the company. Similarly, "integrated player" represents a subsidiary with high knowledge inflows as well as high knowledge outflows. The IBM subsidiary in Japan would be a typical example of "integrated player." In this model, global companies are viewed as network organizations where subsidiary roles are varied. A similar idea is also found in

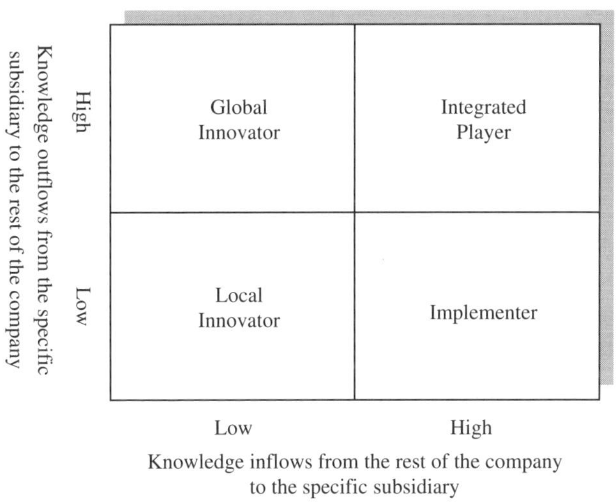

Source: Gupta and Govindarajan (1991), p. 774.

Fig. 15.12 Subsidiary role model based on the knowledge flows

Bartlett and Ghoshal (1986, 1989) where four distinct subsidiary roles are defined depending on the level of two variables, "strategic significance of local environment" and "capability level of local organization."

The implication from these models is that there exist different types of subsidiaries with strategically different roles which consist of a network and interact with each other to increase the value as a group. These kinds of models are called "integrated network organization models" and also quite close to "transnational model" of Bartlett and Ghoshal (1989). In terms of knowledge transfer, it is assumed that subsidiaries around the world develop knowledge by themselves or cooperatively and then share it within the group. This is the opposite of a one-way relation where HQ develops knowledge and then transfers it to overseas subsidiaries. Bartlett and Ghoshal (1989) have positioned the "integrated network organization" as an ideal organizational type. By using network synergy resulting from integrated network organizations, global companies could enjoy high knowledge levels which could not be obtained from traditional organizations with centralized power.

However, in integrated network organizations which are based on the role differentiation and specialization of subsidiaries, horizontal dependency among subsidiaries also comes to the front along with vertical relation between HQ and subsidiaries. Although we found that vertical knowledge transfer increases dependency of subsidiaries upon HQ and as a result leads to centralization of power, horizontal dependency among subsidiaries shown in integrated network organizations is unlikely to entail delegation of authority. This is why a new mechanism is essential for promoting horizontal knowledge flows. Since the success of an integrated network organization depends on the density of both vertical and horizontal interactions, it is an important issue to investigate appropriate control systems to activate horizontal interaction including knowledge transfer.

15.8 Summary and Conclusion

According to the "resource dependence perspective," whether HQ controls its overseas subsidiaries centrally or not is closely related to the global strategy of the company. By deciding the patterns of knowledge dependence, HQ could manage its subsidiaries either in a centralized mode or in a decentralized mode. For example, it is said that Japanese global companies tend to rely heavily on centralized global management without delegating sufficient authority to overseas subsidiaries. This may result from considerable knowledge transfer from HQ to subsidiaries because decision making authority would be centralized by making subsidiaries heavily dependent on HQ in terms of knowledge. Similarly, if western companies are said to rely on local based global management, it might mean that HQ transfers its knowledge to local subsidiaries only partially or to a lower extent, for it is the implication of knowledge dependence perspective that low knowledge transfer leads to low level of centralization.

To sum up, it is possible to explain the differences in global management control by introducing the concept of knowledge dependence. As a result, there is no need to resort to the differences in national cultures as has often been the case in the past to explain the differences in global management control. Meanwhile, as global companies evolve into integrated network organizations, horizontal knowledge transfer has a significant meaning along with usual vertical knowledge transfer. It is one of the challenges for global management accounting to design control systems which promote both vertical and horizontal interactions within the network.

Finally, if it is possible for the pattern of knowledge transfer to shape HQ-subsidiary relations and even management control systems of a global company, it is important to pay more attention to the significance of global strategy itself as it might direct the pattern of knowledge transfer. It is also necessary to focus on the potential of the balanced scorecard (BSC) as one effective tool to implement global strategy. More research is needed to examine the link between global strategy, knowledge transfer and the BSC.

References

Bartlett, C. A. and Ghoshal, S. (1986). Tap your subsidiaries for global reach, *Harvard Business Review* 64-6, pp. 87–94.

Bartlett, C. A. and Ghoshal, S. (1989). *Managing Across Borders: The Transnational Solution*, Harvard Business School Press.

Bartlett, C. A. and Ghoshal, S. (1995). *Transnational Management: Text, Cases, and Readings in Cross-border Management*, 2nd edition, IRWIN.

Dent, J. F. (1996). Global competition: challenges for management accounting and control, *Management Accounting Research* 7-2, pp. 247–269.

Ghoshal, S. and Nohria, N. (1993). Horses for courses: organizational forms for multinational corporations, *Sloan Management Review* Winter, pp. 23–35.

Gupta, A. K. and Govindarajan, V. (1991). Knowledge flows and the structure of control within multinational corporations, *Academy of Management Review* 16-4, pp. 768–792.

Gupta, A. K. and Govindarajan, V. (2000). Knowledge flows within multinational corporations, *Strategic Management Journal* 21-4, pp. 473–496.

Itoh, Y. (ed.) (1995). *Globalization of the Company and Management Accounting*, Chuo-Keizaisha. (in Japanese)

Iwabuchi, Y. (1995). Resource dependence relationship and management control in the global companies, in *Globalization of the Company and Management Accounting*, Edited by Itoh, Y., Chuo-Keizaisha. (in Japanese)

Kato, Y. (1994). National cultures and management control, *Kaikei* 145-3, pp. 60–75. (in Japanese)

Lee, K. (1996). *Empirical research on global control systems*, Doctoral Dissertation, Kobe University. (in Japanese)

Lee, K. (1998). Strategy, organization, and control systems of global companies, *Genkakeisan-Kenkyu* 22-1, pp. 36–50. (in Japanese)

Lee, K. (2001). Global management control: from the viewpoint of foreign companies, *Genkakeisan-Kenkyu* 25-2, pp. 47–57. (in Japanese)

Lee, K. (2003). Knowledge transfer and HQ-subsidiary relationship, in *Organization Structure and Management Accounting*, Edited by Monden, Y., Zeimukeiri-Kyokai. (in Japanese)

Miyamoto, K. (2003). *Management Accounting for Global Companies*, Chuo-Keizaisha. (in Japanese)

Nakagawa, M. (2004). *Globalization of Management Accounting*, Moriyama Shoten. (in Japanese)

Yoshihara, H. (ed.) (1992). *International Management of Japanese Companies*, Dobunkan. (in Japanese)

CHAPTER

16

Designing Micro-Profit Centers to Promote Organizational Learning

Katsuhiro Ito
Associate Professor, Faculty of Economics
Seikei University

16.1 Introduction: What is a Micro-profit Center?

Some companies have introduced a cost management method called a "micro-profit center" to promote or revitalize cost improvement (GENKA-KAIZEN) at the point of production; it has been a great success. There are many variations of the micro-profit center,[1] and it bears many names, depending on the company implementing it. In general, the micro-profit center is a management method of dividing an organization into units comprising a few people at minimum (in some cases, only one) to about 50 people at maximum, setting up profit centers (profit responsibility centers) and then putting the management of the unit into the hands of a manager or the employees at the production line. Micro-profit centers are mainly introduced to promote the development and evolution of Japanese business improvement methods (cost improvement activities conducted by small groups and routine cost reduction activities such as TQC/TQM or TPM). Well-known companies and facilities which have introduced micro-profit centers include the Higashimaru Shoyu Co., Ltd., the Kyoto factory of the Kirin Brewery

[1]The micro-profit center is also called a pseudo-profit center, because it does not make comprehensive decisions on procurement and sales. If it is a department in the factory, procurement decisions regarding suppliers of materials, timing, and prices, and sales decisions regarding buyers, sales channels and sales prices cannot be changed and are regarded as given. The Japanese department system (departmentalized organization) can be regarded as a type of pseudo-profit center.

Co., Ltd. ("profit management system at the workplace"), the Tatsuno and Ina plants of the Olympus Corp. ("group management"), the 3B plant of the Texas Eastman Co., the KOA Corp. (KPS, or KOA Profit System), the Ayabe and Mishima factories of the Omron Corp. (WSM, or Work Shop Management), and the Sumitomo Electric Industries Group, NEC Saitama, the Kikusui plant of the Kyushu Matsushita Electric Co., Ltd., the Hino Site of the Konica Corp., and the Sakai Plant of the Kubota Corp. (these facilities employ the "line company system").[2]

This paper tries to address two points. The first is to figure out the mechanism, purpose and effects of the micro-profit center. In short, the micro-profit center is a mechanism for introducing strategy in view of improving the activities carried out at a factory. The second is to examine the causes of the diversity in the methods of measuring micro-profit center performance. After an interview survey of companies which have adopted micro-profit centers in Japan and abroad and an examination of published documents, it quickly becomes clear that the methods of measuring micro-profit center performance vary among companies or even within the same company. The details are explained later, but the following three causes of this diversity can be presented briefly. These causes are important in designing a micro-profit center matching the management strategy.

1. Handling unrealized profit: Orientation of cost improvement activities.
2. Method of organizing micro-profit centers.
3. Priority items in implementing business strategy (strategic priorities).

16.2 Preceding Studies on Micro-profit Centers

Pioneering studies on micro-profit centers used for promoting cost improvement include the works by Cooper (1995), Tani (1996), Kaplan and Cooper (1997), and Tani and Miya (1998). The micro-profit center is a management method whose aim is to encourage organizational learning activities via a comprehensive indicator "profit," based on traditional small-group activities (like TQC). It is called a pseudo-profit center or a mini-profit center, because the business results are measured on a small-group (team) basis.

Cooper has discussed at Harvard Business School a series of Japanese companies and their cost management methods, emphasizing MPC

[2]Profit management based on small groups in the distribution industry has been discussed by Sakurai (2004, pp. 501–504).

(micro-profit centers) as an important component. He has classified micro-profit centers into real and pseudo (Cooper, 1995).

The research on the micro-profit center initiated by Cooper has been expanded by researchers in Japan. For example, Miya, Tani and Kagono (1999) have studied the "amoeba management" of the Kyocera Corp. and the management accounting system originated by that company. Ito (1998) has chosen to study the profit management system at the workplace at the Kyoto factory of the Kirin Brewery Co., Ltd., to clarify how the situation has evolved since Cooper's description. Excellent work focusing on motivational aspects at the micro-profit center has been done by Watanabe (2002, 2003, 2004).

Since the micro-profit center has only attracted attention in recent years and the research has just started, no dominant theory has been established yet on which to base a calculation system (a profit-and-loss system), and it is highly expected that research on this topic will evolve dramatically in the near future. It is essential to continue to gather detailed results through field surveys, as Sugamoto has done (2003). In this sense, the micro-profit center is a tool which can only be designed by someone with ingenuity as well as the willingness to undergo the strenuous process of trial and error.

16.3 Reasons for Implementing a Micro-profit Center

In general, a micro-profit center is introduced in anticipation of the following two advantages:

1. Acquisition of an appropriate navigation system
   Traditional cost improvement methods, including TPS (Toyota Production System), TQC and TPM, focus on such quantitative (sub-goal) indicators as productivity, yield and utilization rate. Given only these quantitative indicators, the frontline (the person in charge of the production line) cannot decide which improvement activities to prioritize and which improvement investment plan to adopt. Once the improvement activity reaches a certain level, the amount of cost improvement tends to diverge from the amount actually influencing the profit. This means that an improvement of the quantitative indicator which bears no relationship to the bottleneck cannot lead to progress in business financial performance. The accumulation of cost improvement experiences further worsens this phenomenon.

The adoption of a micro-profit center can give the production line its improvement goal based on the profit-and-loss indicator, as well as guidance on which improvement project to prioritize. As a result, decision making in view not of sub-optimization but of total optimization is encouraged. "Once the early rewards from picking low-hanging fruit have been achieved, however, further improvements are not always free. That is, to get to pick the next level up, someone may have to buy a ladder."[3] As in this maxim, the more experience a company has in cost management, the harder it is to find an improvement project which is easily accomplished. Often, further improvement requires investment, and comprehensive management based on a profit-and-loss indicator is important in deciding on the investment.

2. Improving the frontline's motivation
The longer the company has been implementing improvement activities, the more weary and tired of improvement activities its frontline tends to be. When business results are measured by a quantitative indicator, it is hard for the frontline of the production process to realize the true scope and significance of the results of the improvement activities.

   However, the motivation of the frontline can be reinvigorated by introducing a micro-profit center, because the more positive goal of increasing profit is given and the business performance is measured by a profit-and-loss indicator instead of such goals as cost saving or progress (a qualitative indicator).

Now, let us look at the three design variables (the handling of unrealized profit, the method of organizing micro-profit centers, and the prioritization of items in implementing business strategy), which are apt to become particularly problematic when implementing micro-profit centers.

16.4 Design Parameter 1: Handling Unrealized Effects

16.4.1 *Classification of cost improvement effects*

The effects of cost improvement are classified in Figure 16.1. It is important in the design of a micro-profit center to handle the unrealized effects properly, namely to decide whether or not the unrealized effects should be included in the profit amount of the micro-profit center.

[3] Kaplan and Cooper (1997), pp. 144–145.

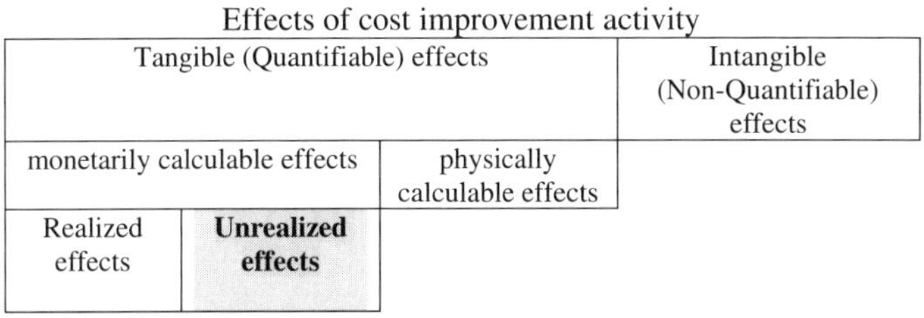

Fig. 16.1 Classification of the effects of cost improvement activities

The effects of cost improvement activities can be divided into "intangible effects" and "tangible effects." The former are impossible to calculate (or hard to calculate), and the latter are calculable. Although the two types of effects cannot be strictly separated, the improvement of willingness and the reform of consciousness at the production line as well as the accumulation of experience are often categorized into the former type, while the improvement of the material yield, the reduction of the production lead time and the squeezing of inventories are generally classified into the latter.

Tangible effects are further divided into "physically calculable effects (at the basic unit)" and "monetarily calculable effects (in money)." The division into these two categories is dependent not on the characteristics of the activity result but on the kind of measurement system adopted. To take the reduction of the production lead time as an example, if the former measurement method shows a reduction from 20 minutes to 15 minutes, the latter will show a reduction by 40,000 yen (assuming the conversion rate of 8,000 yen/minute). The adoption of a micro-profit center is the expression of a policy whose intention is to expand the area where monetary measurement is applied.

Attention should be paid to the two types of monetarily calculable improvement effects. One comprises the "realized effects" and the other the "unrealized effects." A realized effect is an improvement effect actually linked to the company's cash flow and differential revenue (or the differential cost) within the framework of traditional management accounting theory. For example, let us say that, as a result of cost improvement activities, the production lead time of a process has been reduced to 90% of the past result. If this reduction by 10% is not utilized elsewhere in the production process and just increases the outage of the machine and equipment, the effect does not bring in any cash flow. This is an *unrealized effect* even if converted to money. Meanwhile, if the saved capacity (the operating time) of the equipment is diverted to other production uses and the production and sales volumes of the company increase, or if the consolidation of equipment advances and extra equipment can be retired, the cash flow of the company increases. This is a *realized effect*.

The fact that unrealized effects exhibit the potential profitability of the company in the future is pointed out as a reason to measure and report not only the realized effects directly linked to the cash flow of the company but also the unrealized effects. In short, the larger "the accumulation of unrealized effects," the more the management can understand the progress of the "constitutional reform" of the company, one of the major purposes of cost improvement activities. In other words, the realized effect is "a short-term effect directly linked to the cash flow" and the unrealized effect is "a potential (long-term) effect linked to the strengthening of the company."

Now let us look at reasons for introducing micro-profit centers and the methods of measuring their effects.

1. Logic of the theory of constraints (TOC): Orientation toward cost improvement activities — not sub-optimization but total optimization. The necessity of focusing the cost improvement activity on the most efficient phase in the whole company is pointed out as a reason for introducing a micro-profit center. In short, when quantitative indicators are given in different dimensions, it is impossible to judge the priority of the solutions at the production line, whose employees are to be practically engaged in cost improvement activities, due to the inability to prioritize such improvement activities. For example, the dilemma whether to first shorten the lead time or to improve the yield cannot be solved based exclusively on quantitative data (minutes or percentage). When the cost is improved according to a quantitative measure, ineffective improvement activities increase as time goes by.

   This symptom must be paid attention to in the Japanese production system or in companies tackling cost improvement activities. Efforts should focus not on the improvement of non-bottleneck parts of the business process but on that of the bottleneck part, after combining conventional cost improvement activities with the philosophy of the TOC.

   The micro-profit center can be understood as a concrete deployment of this approach. It is intended to provide the frontline with an appropriate navigation scheme in view of effective cost improvement, by setting up the production line as a micro-profit center and converting the cost improvement effects into money. Measurement of the cost improvement effects should be strictly limited to the realized effects, in order to emphasize total optimization and maximize the short-term effects. This can be seen as an application to the cost improvement activity of the TOC notion of focusing on the balance of the production line and measuring the business result of the production activity based on the cash-flow effect.

2. Requirement of empowerment: Revitalizing small-group activities
Another factor is mentioned as a reason for introducing a micro-profit center. This is a response to the problem of the gradual loss of a sense of participation and the willingness to accomplish good work at the production line, where full exhibition of individual initiative is normally expected. Countermeasures against this loss of interest focus on setting up not a "negative" goal, such as the cost improvement amount (the saved cost), but a "positive" goal, such as the profit amount, thereby revitalizing cost improvement activities in times of generalized gloom.

While the logic of the TOC is related to "the direction of the vector" of cost improvement activity, the revitalization of cost improvement at the production line is related to "the length of the vector" of activity (improving willingness). This is conceived as the "promotion of empowerment" by the micro-profit center.

Attention should be paid to the fact that the logic of the TOC and the promotion of empowerment are totally different in their approaches to solving problems. Companies and managers make a variety of judgments on how to balance these two requirements. Due to these differences in judgment and policy, each company has introduced its own business result measurement system in order to assess its micro-profit center. The differences in management philosophy appear very clearly in how the unrealized effects are handled. Emphasis on the TOC tends to completely exclude the unrealized effects from the measurement of the business result, while emphasis on the promotion of empowerment is not sensitive in excluding the unrealized effects.

16.5 Method of Organizing Micro-profit Centers

The problem of how to organize a micro-profit center is related to the above item and is very important. Methods of organizing a micro-profit center include the method of organizing "by process (by production process attribute, i.e., horizontally) and the method of organizing "by product variety (by goods manufactured, i.e., vertically) (see Figure 16.2).

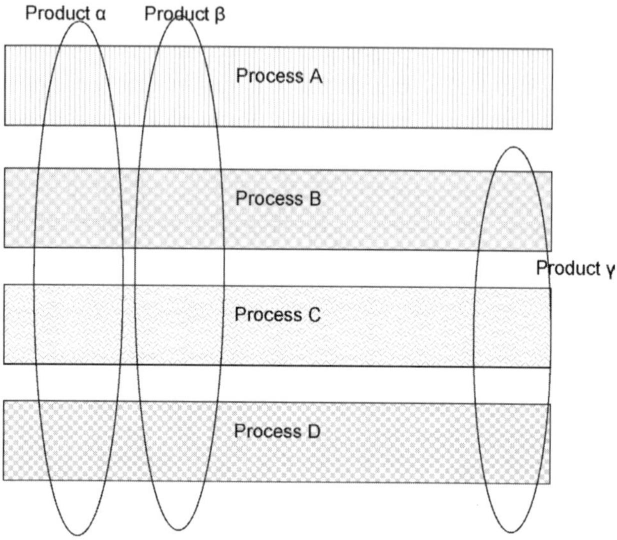

Fig. 16.2 Method of organizing micro-profit centers

While organization by process reflects the result of cost improvement efforts at the production line easily and straightforwardly, it is relatively incompatible with the TOC principle because it counts the unrealized effects. If a micro-profit center is introduced with the intent of optimizing the total production process, it is desirable to adopt a micro-profit center organized by product variety. This is because it is difficult for a micro-profit center organized by process to induce balance across the production line. On the other hand, organization by process is easy to introduce, because it requires a relatively small change in the conventional system in terms of technology and personnel distribution, which means that much of the existing infrastructure and experience of the conventional small group can be used.

16.6 Problems in Implementing Business Strategy

The difference in business strategy among companies and the subsequent difference in the missions given to each micro-profit center (sub-unit) is the source of differing business result measurement systems used to assess the performance of micro-profit centers. There might even be different business result measurement systems within the same company.

For example, let us imagine ABC Company, which has introduced and is managing a micro-profit center which focuses on the efficiency of the company-wide cost improvement activities and emphasizes the realized effects. Because of a change in the corporate environment, however, it is now imperative to substantially change the mix of products and acquire new clients. What is most important in acquiring new clients is the delivery of the ordered prototype exactly on schedule by the sales department (or even earlier than the scheduled delivery time in some cases). Under these circumstances, the business result measurement system of the test production department (the auxiliary department) must be thoroughly reviewed, after which it must to motivate the early delivery of the prototype (by updating the organizational routine so as to make this possible). Concretely speaking, a bonus (a positive item in the micro-profit center's profit) shall be given in case of earlier delivery, and a penalty (a negative item in the micro-profit center's profit) shall be imposed in case of late delivery. In the case of big orders received as a result of the quick delivery of a prototype according to the specifications requested by the client, a royalty (a certain percentage of the sales) is added to the profit of the test production department over a certain period.

Attention should be paid to the fact that the newly adopted bonuses, penalties and royalties have the unrealized effect of cost improvement, in that they do not accompany a cash effect. ABC Company has succeeded in inducing cost improvement activities which match its problems by implementing sound business (competition) strategy with this mechanism.

16.7 Conclusion: Impact on Japanese Companies

Several Japanese companies are well known in the world for their thorough and continuous improvement of sub-goal indicators in their cost improvement activities. It is, however, often pointed out that this kind of improvement at the basic unit has reached its natural limit. It is called the "strong factory and weak head office" syndrome,[4] and the current situation is that

[4]According to Fujimoto (2003, 2004), the cause of this "strong factory and weak head office" syndrome is believed to be the traditional lack of strategic conceptual power. A similar remark on the phenomenon that positioning strategy has been neglected in Japanese companies is also found in Porter and Takeuchi (2000). In that study, the authors use the expressions "competition based on operation efficiency" and "competition without strategy."

even a serious accumulation of creative organizational capability and potential competitiveness does not necessarily lead to increased profit. To overcome this deadlock, the review of traditional cost management methods is essential. A possible way out is the micro-profit center.

To implement a cost improvement activity effectively, it is important to find a way to smoothly direct the trial-and-error activates of the employees at the production line and systematically absorb the resultant knowledge. From the perspective of cost management, consistent compatibility between the outer-directed *positioning approach strategy* (how to differentiate oneself from other companies) and the inner-directed *learning approach strategy* (how to enhance one's own organizational capability) is required. Japanese companies have been weak in the positioning approach. The micro-profit center has the potential to smoothly combine the two approaches, positioning and learning, in the following two problem areas:

1. Acquiring information
   The profit-and-loss indicator of the micro-profit center can affect the decision making of the employees at the production line regarding the situation, field of expertise and intensity of the study activity. Which direction the organizational study activity focuses on depends on the analysis and recognition of the external environment where all companies are active. It is expected that the business result measurement system of the micro-profit center will clarify in advance what the employees should prioritize.
2. Evaluating and selecting information
   Besides the micro-profit center, the contribution of management accounting to information sharing has been greatly emphasized in discussions on cost management methods in recent years. In addition, a variety of the business result measurement systems are practically devised to ensure the provision of information (private information sharing). In cost improvement methods based on small-group activities, such as TQC/TQM and TPM, the number and the grade of improvement proposals have been conventionally thought of as important business result measures. Monitoring the number of improvement proposals and their qualities can motivate employees toward further acquisition and provision of knowledge.

   In the process of organizational learning, however, each frontline conducts various trial-and-error activates, according to its own judgment. Without the evaluation and the selection of information, total and effective organizational learning is impossible and organizational routines (work habits) cannot be improved. It is important to judge which information (improvement proposal) is valuable enough to incorporate into the routine and which should be rejected, depending on the positioning approach. The micro-profit center is useful as a system of measuring the results of the learning activity, and provides an infrastructure therefor.

References

Cooper, R. (1994a). Kirin Brewery Company, Ltd., Harvard Business School Case #9-195-058.

Cooper, R. (1994b). Olympus Optical Company, Ltd. (B): Functional Group Management, Harvard Business School Case #9-195-073.

Cooper, R. (1995). *When Lean Enterprise Collide, Competing through Confrontation*, Harvard Business School Press.

Cooper, R. (1997). Olympus Optical Company, Ltd. (A): Cost Management for Short Life-Cycle Products, Harvard Business School Case #9-195-072.

Fujimoto, T. (2003). *Competition for the Resource Accumulation: Why Japanese Automobile Industry is so Competitive?*, Tyuukousinsyo. (in Japanese)

Fujimoto, T. (2004). *Philosophy of Japanese Manufacturing*, Nihon Keizai Shimbunsha. (in Japanese)

Ito, K. (1998). A study of psuedo-profit centers, *Sangyou Keiri* 58-3, pp. 85–92. (in Japanese)

Ito, K. and Sugamoto, E. (2002). Management control systems to promote cost improvement activities: a case study, *Research Bulletin of Accounting*. (in Japanese)

Kaplan, R. S. and Cooper, R. (1997). *Cost and Effect, Using Integrated Cost System to Drive Profitability and Performance*, Harvard Business School Press.

Miya, H. (2003). *Amoeba Management System of Kyocera*, Touyou Keizaisinhousya. (in Japanese)

Okamoto, K. (1991). How to measure the effect of TPM: part 1, *Journal of Japanese Plant Maintenance Association* 3-2, pp. 55–60. (in Japanese)

Okamoto, K. (1992). How to measure the effect of TPM: part 2, *Journal of Japanese Plant Maintenance Association* 3-3, pp. 55–60. (in Japanese)

Porter, M. E. and Takeuchi, H. (2000). *Competitive Strategy of Japanese Companies*, Diamond-sha.

Sakurai, M. (2004). *Management Accounting*, 3rd edition, Doubunkan. (in Japanese)

Sugamoto, E. (2003). Management accounting of Japanese manufacturing company: case study on Sumitomo Electric Industry, *Journal of Accountancy* 29, pp. 1–33. (in Japanese)

Tani, T. and Miya, H. (1998). Line-company system in NEC Saitama: how to design mini-profit center, *Kokumin Keizai Zassi* 177-3, pp. 17–34. (in Japanese)

Watanabe, T. (2002). Management accounting and organizational culture: implication for recognition and motivation, *Business Research* 1. (in Japanese)

Watanabe, T. (2003). Management accounting and motivation: consideration on influential effect, *Shougaku Ronsou* 45-1, pp. 49–90. (in Japanese)

Watanabe, T. (2004). Empirical research on line company system of Sumitomo Electric Industry, *Journal of Cost Accounting* 28-2, pp. 12–26. (in Japanese)

Yoshida, E. and Matsuki, S. (2001). Pseudo-profit center systems to promote empowerment: case study of Sumitomo Electric Industry, *Syukei Gakusou* 47-3, pp. 171–190. (in Japanese)

CHAPTER

17

A Case Study on Design and Implementation of Micro-Profit Center System

Eizo Sugamoto
Associate Professor, Faculty of Commerce
Chuo University

17.1 Foreword

There have recently been noteworthy cases of businesses which have transformed the awareness and behavioral patterns of their organization members by introducing a management method aimed at reducing the size of the responsibility center and setting profit as a comprehensive evaluation indicator; this revolutionary management method is the micro-profit center (MPC) system. In this article, we will examine the characteristics of the management accounting information provided by the MPC system and the implementation of the MPC system at Harima Chemicals, Inc. This particular MPC system was introduced after the Kyocera Corporation's amoeba management system was customized to suit the needs of Harima.

This article is structured as follows. First, we will present the reason why Harima introduced the MPC system. Next, the problems related to the structure of Harima's MPC system will be discussed from the viewpoint of the *direction of motivation*. Then, I will present my views on the characteristics of the management accounting information provided by Harima's MPC system from the viewpoint of the impact on the *strength of motivation* of the organization members. Finally, the problems related to the implementation of Harima's MPC system will be examined.

17.2 Definition of the MPC System and the Organization at Harima

As shown in Figure 17.1, Harima Chemicals completely revamped its management accounting system in June 1996. It abolished its standard cost and flexible budgeting systems, and constructed a new management accounting system in consultation with the Kyocera Communication Systems Co., Ltd. This management accounting system, called the "unit saisan system" in Japanese is a system where a module comprised of a few people is designated as a profit center and the person in charge of the module manages profit and loss.

At Harima, organizational modules such as subsections, sections, factories and departments are called "units," and the heads of these modules, i.e., the subsection chief, the section chief, the factory manager and the department manager, are responsible for the profitability of their own units. The full-time employees numbered 480 in 1996 and the company was an aggregate of some 140 profit centers.

17.3 Design of the MPC System

In this section, the problems related to the structure of Harima's MPC system will be discussed from the viewpoint of the direction of motivation.

17.3.1 *Designing the income sheets for the manufacturing and sales departments*

Under the MPC system of Harima Chemicals, the manufacturing, sales and technological development departments are operated as profit centers.

Before the introduction	After the introduction (since June 1996)
Standard/direct costing.	Income sheet in the form of a household account book.
The administrative department prepared the results/plans.	Each unit prepares its results/plans.
The profit and loss of the whole company was divided among the units.	The profits and losses of the units are summed up.
The profitability of the whole company was emphasized.	The units are financially independent.

Fig. 17.1 Changes in the management accounting system at Harima Chemicals

First, let us look at the design of the income sheet of the manufacturing and sales departments. The content of the income sheet of the technological development department will be described later.

The basic concept of the income sheet of the manufacturing departments is shown in Figure 17.2. Please note that the real income sheet is more detailed than this conceptual table. Remarkable are the inclusion of the raw material cost in the expenses and the exclusion of the personnel cost.

Similarly to amoeba management in general, it is set up so that the sales to the customers are directly understood as the turnover of the manufacturing department: it conveys the market price directly to the manufacturing department, and the sales department receives a certain percentage of the sales of the company's products in the form of a sales commission from the manufacturing department.

Next, in Harima's MPC system, the turnover of the manufacturing department is recognized when the sales are posted (shipment). Regarding shipment, the conflation of the posting of sales with the posting of production reflects the reality that the accumulation of inventory in the warehouse does not imply payment from the customer on the income sheet, and promotes the production and purchase of raw materials in view of salability.

Total sales	A = B + C
Extra-company sales	B
Intra-company sales	C
Intra-company purchases	D
Gross contribution margin	E = A − D
Total expenses	F
Direct material costs	
Tools & supplies costs	
Maintenance costs	
Power costs	
...	
Allocated divisional overheads	
Allocated plant-overheads	
Sales commissions	
Intra-company tech. royalty	
Value added	G = E − F
Total labor hours	H
Value added per hour	G ÷ H

Fig. 17.2 Income sheets for manufacturing departments

On the other hand, recognizing the raw material cost at the time of purchase (acceptance) of raw materials is a rule. This rule is based on the fact that the purchase of raw materials requires payment on the income sheet. Therefore, with this mechanism, actions aimed at reducing the inventory of raw materials are to be expected. Management targets of top management, including the improvement of cash flow and capital efficiency, are built into the MPC income sheet.

Harima adopts the market price as the transfer pricing among manufacturing MPCs. When no market price is available, negotiations between the parties decide the price, and the manufacturing cost is not applicable. Most important is an acute awareness of the market all times, and this can be readily achieved because there are few complicated manufacturing processes and the design of the MPC is easy.

Let us now look at the allocated expenses. There are three types of allocated expenses: head office expenses, basic research laboratory expenses and the indirect expenses of factory department. The head office expenses are allocated per head (the number of personnel). The reason for this is as follows. A decrease in personnel means a reduction in the injected work hours, a substantial drop in the allocated expenses and eventually a boost of profitability per hour. On the contrary, an increase in personnel is designed to enhance the per-hour denominator and thus inflate the allocated expenses. A willingness to improve productivity while not increasing (or while decreasing) the personnel can be expected in this setup. We will discuss the basic research laboratories is later.

17.3.2 *General concept of the income sheet*

Like ordinary amoeba management, Harima's MPC system calculates the monthly result of each MPC not in volume but in the amount of money. The profit of each unit is called the "value added." In ordinary accounting terms, the manufacturing department does not subtract the personnel cost in the formula "manufacturing sales minus purchased raw material cost minus expenses plus non-operating profit and loss." In other words, operating profit plus the personnel cost is the value added. The personnel cost is excluded because personnel mobility is hindered due to the differences in employee payroll and because each MPC income sheet is specifically prepared for a particular unit.

Next, this income sheet, which calculates the value added per hour by dividing the profit of each MPC by the working hours, also calculates the profit per working hour and compares the profitability and the improvement ratios fairly, regardless of the size of the MPC. The reason for not evaluating the absolute amount of value added per hour is its heavy dependence on the business structure, the rules and the type of operation. For example, some operations are now profitable while others are unprofitable. A profitable operation improves the absolute value, and an unprofitable one worsens it. The absolute amount is not used in the evaluation because any evaluation relying solely on the profitability of the assigned operation is unfair.

Another emphasis of the design is to put substantial authority (external transactions for raw materials, capital investment, personnel exchange, work plans, and work assignments, etc.) in the hands of the manufacturing department, enable the MPC leaders related to manufacturing to get a proper feel for the real market by disclosing actual information on the sales prices and the raw material prices required for self-management, and thereby strengthen the manufacturing department.

17.3.3 *Designing the income sheet for the technological development section*

There are three types of research and technological development sections at Harima Chemicals. First, the Tsukuba Research Laboratory is in charge of developing new businesses and technologies and is not a profit center. The expenses arising from this laboratory are not allocated anywhere and are treated as a part of the head office budget. Next, the Central Research Laboratory is in charge of basic technologies, the development of new products, the improvement of existing products and the development of new technologies for all departments, and is not a profit center, either. The expenses arising from the Central Research Laboratory are shouldered by the beneficiary departments in proportion to the derived benefit. Finally, the technological development sections in charge of applied research are profit centers. Harima is currently divided into three product business departments. This technological development section is incorporated into each business department to develop new products, improve existing products and develop new technologies for the departments, and is required to be independently profitable.

The internal royalty system of the technological development section of the business department comprises three areas: new products, improved products, and new technologies and processes. It applies different royalty rates, shouldering departments and periods, depending on the situation.

The system is set up in order to improve profitability, as new products and improved products are developed and the sales and income increase. Its point is to embed the top management strategy of promoting the development of salable new products, improved products and new technologies in the income sheet of the technological development section.

17.4 Characteristics of the Management Accounting Information of the MPC System at Harima

In this section, I would like to present my views on the characteristics of the management accounting information of the MPC system at Harima, especially from the perspective of the strength of motivation.

17.4.1 *Meaningful goals*

As far as the management of Harima led the introduction of the MPC system, the value added per hour as a target indicator was established for the both leader and the members of each MPC. The transition from the cost center system to the profit center system resulted in the clarification of the causal correlation between the contribution of one's own section to the profit and loss of the whole company.

17.4.2 *Understanding goals simply and easily*

The factors improving the profitability per hour are limited to the following three: (1) increasing the sales; (2) cutting the expenses; and (3) reducing the working time. Since the idea is simple, anybody can understand and master it. It is also crucial to be able to understand it in a daily sense.

17.4.3 *High goals*

In deciding the annual and monthly plans, the company must establish the highest possible profitability per hour as a target, because this makes employees eager to take on the challenge. Unless a high target is established, the company cannot expect a satisfactory outcome. The plan is just a tool for achieving the desired result, not a goal.

17.4.4 *The results of efforts (actions) are easily reflected upon and understood*

In the MPC system, both the leader and the members of the MPC can understand their own individual contributions easily. All participants can cultivate a vivid sense of participation in the game, and the results of individual efforts are easily grasped by all because each unit has a small number of people. As the number of members increases, it becomes more difficult to clearly define who contributed to the result and in what way.

Because each individual can prepare the income sheet by himself or herself and clearly understand his or her own activities and profitability, the purchase and the resultant expense can be precisely specified and the difference between the plan and the result can be clearly explained. Because the absolute amount is displayed rather than the cost variances, the leader can grasp the situation easily.

When defective products come out of the production line, the impact on the awareness of the employees at the workplace is enormous, because everyone involved knows the absolute cost and the wastefulness of substandard performance. In contrast, mistakes expressed in percentages or the cost variances are not so convincing.

17.4.5 *The outcome is timely and available*

Leaders can decide how much effort should be put into achieving the target value established beforehand, by pinpointing the outcome not necessarily daily but in a timely manner. They can also complete the income sheet of their section by themselves daily if necessary.

17.4.6 *Market orientation*

Although some companies which have introduced amoeba management still use the standard cost, Harima does not use it anymore. This is because Harima's aim is to enable all employees to get an accurate feel for the real market, as well as to secure the top spot in global competition by eliminating the theoretical figure of the standard cost.

Providing the employees at workplace with real information has traditionally been deemed unnecessary, and the move toward transparency faced particularly strong resistance from the sales department at Harima. Sharing real information with the employees has been found to foster the kind of trust which is indispensable to success, and encouraging cooperation and a sense of unity with the company is now thought to be advantageous.

17.5 Implementation of the MPC System at Harima

17.5.1 *A small number of people*

This is related to the control span of the MPC leader. Harima considers that an MPC leader can control a maximum of 10 to 15 people. If the number reaches 20 to 30, the leader does not understand what he is doing. Therefore, the company intends to solve the control span problem by placing its MPC leaders in a nested structure.

17.5.2 *Information revealed to all people*

Although it is natural to clarify one's own performance to oneself, the MPC system discloses one's performance to all other people, including superiors and colleagues. One also has access to the performances of other people. The main purpose of this policy is to enhance personal satisfaction at the workplace, by letting the leaders enjoy their big moment, and give all employees a chance to assert themselves. One side effect of this openness is the creation of a competition arena. As will be discussed later, however, the company is trying to make the participants enjoy the competition like a game, because the result does not affect the personnel evaluation directly.

17.5.3 *Self-evaluation*

The superiors eventually evaluate their subordinates. The company wants the MPC leaders to recognize that they must evaluate their own performances also by obliging them to set up goals related to the income sheet, appraise the results, and compare the plan with the results. The major premise is that one must be able to prepare the income sheet by oneself, and for this appropriate training is needed.

17.5.4 *Education*

The disclosure of information is meaningless if the employees do not understand the disclosed management figures. A basic understanding of the value added per hour, its calculation and the ways of improving it are needed.

With such an understanding, wastefulness is reduced and high-quality decision making at the workplace is made possible.

17.5.5 *The internal terms are unified in management accounting*

The profit and loss figure of the MPC system do not naturally correspond to those of financial accounting and tax accounting. The accounting of the company is unified under the MPC system in order to avoid unnecessary confusion.

17.5.6 *The PDCA cycle is implemented at the monthly management meeting at the unit level*

The core meeting in the MPC system is a monthly management meeting at the unit level. This meeting focuses on the announcement of the results of the previous month and the action plan for the current month. In the beginning, separate meetings in the east and west blocs were usually held once a month, in which those above the section/group level took part, and expanded management meetings were held once every three months, in which those above the subsection/team level participated. Executives and directors also attended meetings in which the results of the value added per hour of the MPC income sheet were scrutinized. Because of these regular and frequent meeting, the MPC leaders were encouraged to understand and manage the actions conducted in their respective sections and their own influence on profitability.

17.5.7 *Initiative is respected*

Fairly substantive authority is now put in the hands of the MPC leader, in contrast to past practice. He is given authority over capital investment, sales volume, external transactions for raw materials, exchange of personnel with other sections, work plans and allocations. Each leader is allowed to think and act independently, and the company benefits from individual initiative and the independent completion of challenging management tasks.

17.5.8 *High goals (values) are required: Experimentation*

As mentioned before, Harima forces the MPC leaders to establish challenging goals in formulating the annual plan and the monthly action plan. However, the risks undertaken by the leaders in setting up a challenging plan with high goals must also be reduced as much as possible. Otherwise, the leaders tend to set low goals. Therefore, the performance of the section is evaluated at the fiscal year level with particular emphasis on improvement against the result rather than achievement (the plan achievement ratio).

On a monthly basis, however, the plan achievement ratio is emphasized, in order to clarify how many of the planned tasks have been successfully completed. In establishing high goals, a corporate culture unafraid of failure is crucial, as well as the absence of a direct link to personnel evaluation, as will be discussed below. It is essential for top management to always focus on nurturing this type of corporate culture.

17.5.9 *Absence of a direct link to personnel evaluation*

Business decisions and performance evaluations are not made solely based on the absolute value/result of profitability per hour, because the employees may be assigned to a booming department or a struggling department independently of their will, and the condition of the department to which they are assigned would reflect on their work unfairly. Also, profitability per hour changes substantially, depending on the business structure and rules. In Harima's case, for example, the paper and chemical department often has hit products, but the electronic material department sells few items and has difficulty in improving the value added per hour. These departments cannot be compared consistently and fairly. Therefore, the MPC system does not evaluate personnel.

17.5.10 *Energy is injected*

The MPC system is not a management method where the executives take the easy road and leave the management of the company to the employees at the workplace. For example, it is important for a director to always attend the management meeting of the unit, to support and encourage the employees and provide helpful comments in order to solve problems. This seriousness and passion at top management level is extremely important.

Acknowledgments

I would like to express my gratitude to Mr. Nobuo Makino, senior executive director of Harima Chemicals, Inc., for his warm cooperation in preparing this article. Please refer to the following website for information on the company: http://www.harima.co.jp/. This article is a part of a research endeavor sponsored by Grant-in-Aid for Young Scientists (B) 17730286 and Chuo University Grant for Special Research for fiscal 2005 and 2006.

References

Case, J. (1995). *Open-book Management*, HarperCollins Publishers.

Cooper, R. (1995). *When Lean Enterprises Collide: Competing Through Confrontation*, Harvard Business School Press.

Hamada, K. and Monden, Y. (1989). Profit management at Kyocera Corporation: the Amoeba system, in *Japanese Management Accounting*, Edited by Monden, Y. and Sakurai, M., Cambridge, MA: Productivity Press, pp. 197–210.

Inamori, K. (1998). *Practical Expertise of Inamori Kazuo: Management and Accounting*, Tokyo: Nihon-keizai Sinbun. (in Japanese)

Kaplan, R. S. and Cooper, R. (1998). *Cost & Effect: Using Integrated Cost Systems to Drive Profitability and Performance*, Harvard Business School Press.

Miya, H., Tani, T. and Kagono, T. (1999). *Amoeba System Can Change the Management*, Tokyo: Daiyamondo. (in Japanese)

Monden, Y. (2002). The relationship between mini profit-center and JIT system, *International Journal of Production Economics* 80, pp. 145–154.

CHAPTER

18

Japanese Micro-Profit Center: A Case Study of the Amoeba System at the Kyocera Corporation

Hiroshi Miya

Associate Professor, Graduate school of Business Administration Kobe University

18.1 Introduction

Empowerment can be the key to successful management (Johnson, 1992). Some Japanese companies use micro-profit center systems to this end (Cooper, 1995).[1]

Kyocera Corporation, one of the most profitable and fastest growing companies in Japan, was founded in 1959 as a small-scale producer specializing in fine ceramic parts (see Figures 18.1 and 18.2). Since then, the company has diversified to become a vertically integrated manufacturer with fine ceramic technologies as the foundation of its business (see Figure 18.3).

Kyocera has been armed with a micro-profit center system which creates a large number of self-support units called "amoebas." Amoeba is a small autonomous organization composed of 10 people in average. Like a unicellular animal, it is continually disunited and united. A single step of the manufacturing process or a small regional area of sales offices can be divided into this unit. Once becoming an independent amoeba, it becomes self-sufficient. It is supposed to earn its own living not only by reducing

[1]In addition to Kyocera, Cooper provides the examples: Higashimaru Shoyu, Kirin Kyoto Brewery, Olympus, Taiyo Group. Tani and I have conducted field researches at NEC Saitama, Sony Minokamo, and so on.

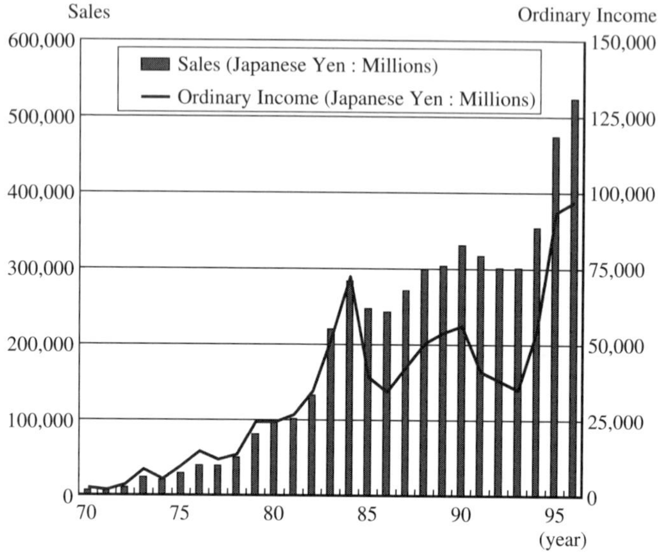

Fig. 18.1 Sales and ordinary income

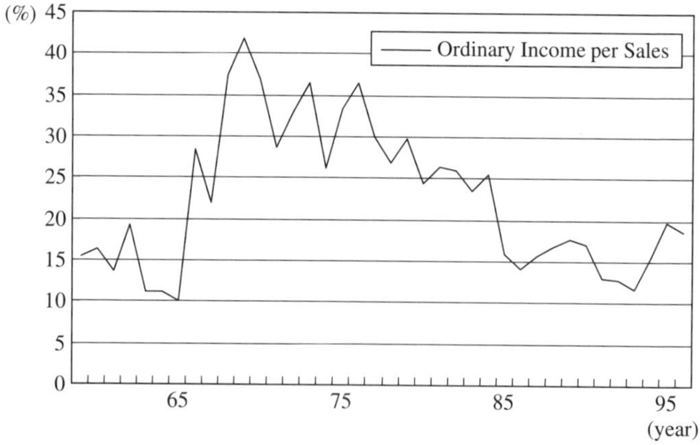

Fig. 18.2 Ordinary income per sales

the cost of its products or services, but also by selling them to internal and external customers.

The ultimate purpose of this system is to raise the entrepreneurial spirit in the leaders. Under the pressure to run assigned businesses, the amoeba leaders are expected to learn what management is about and to realize

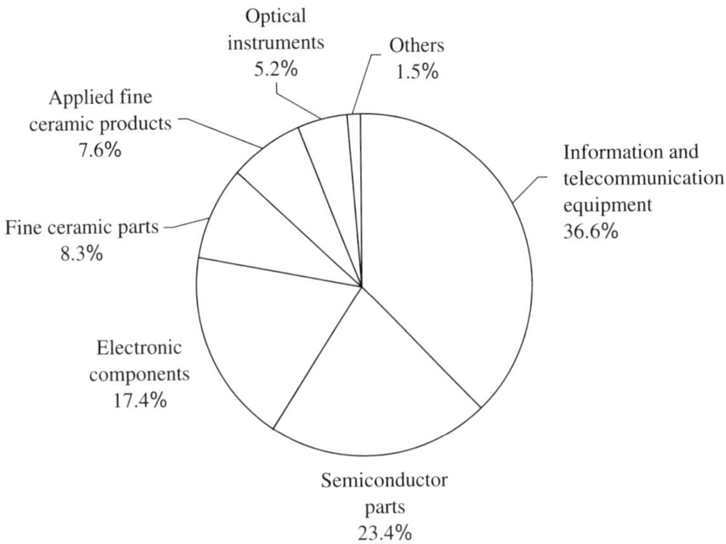

Fig. 18.3 Sales information by product (1996)

how enjoyable it is. Though all the leaders do not have enough experience to manage the profit centers, they have to be responsible for the entire business just like the presidents of real companies. The leaders are required to make decisions on such matters as the volume of production, selling prices, investment, and the appropriate size of the amoeba.

The first question of this study is how those inexperienced leaders can make such difficult decisions. And the second question is how such highly autonomous micro-profit centers can join their forces. Little attention has been given to the precise mechanism of the amoeba system.[2] Based on our intensive case study, we provide evidence that a well-designed management accounting system, together with the corporate philosophy and the flexible organization, plays an important role to support empowered amoeba leaders.

18.2 Research Method

Our concern is not to verify "grand theory," but to discover the "grounded" theory of the amoeba system (Glaser and Strauss, 1967). As qualitative

[2]Exceptions are Cooper op. cit., pp. 303–316, and Hamada and Monden (1989).

information is suited for this purpose, Tani[3] and I have conducted intensive case studies at Kyocera Corporation and its subsidiaries since 1995. We investigated various aspects of the amoeba system such as accounting, administration, organization, leadership, marketing, manufacturing, R&D, new business, corporate culture, and corporate philosophy.

Research materials were collected mainly from semi-structured interviews and direct observations. We had interviews with executives of administration, manufacturing, R&D, and new business, and with amoeba leaders of manufacturing, management, and accounting. We observed shipment, manufacturing, monthly meetings, morning meetings, and so on at Kokubu plant and Shiga plant of Kyocera. Additional research materials were gathered from analysis of planning and control materials, documents of "the amoeba management workshops"[4] and so on.

18.3 The Micro-profit Center

Except for some administrative and R&D sections, amoebas are usually operated as profit centers regardless of their size. In the case of manufacturing amoebas, sales to internal and external customers are recognized as their revenues. To make profits, amoebas try to minimize their controllable costs. Moreover, it is peculiar to Kyocera that they are allowed to negotiate the buying prices of parts and services with the selling amoebas, not simply following the pre-determined transfer prices on market-basis or cost-basis.

Buying and selling between amoebas does not always take priority over the dealings with the external companies. If the terms of the external offer are more favorable than those of internal one, "the buying amoeba" can make a deal with the external suppliers. In order to continue the dealing, "the selling amoeba" needs to offer quicker delivery or higher quality as well as lower costs than external suppliers. On the other hand, the selling amoeba is also permitted to sell the external customers its products at higher prices, as far as these dealings do not damage the Kyocera's competitive advantages.

By removing the boundaries of a company, market mechanism prevails among every amoeba including upstream ones that do not face the end

---

[3]Professor Takeyuki Tani, Kobe University.

[4]The amoeba management workshops are held at regular intervals to promote the amoeba system to other outside companies by Kyocera's consulting subsidiary, Kyocera Communication Systems.

consumers. Amoebas are expected to be competitive in the market and always improve themselves, even though they possess fewer resources than external competitors.

18.4 Entrepreneurial Leadership

What amoeba leaders need is entrepreneurship. They are responsible not only to make their own amoebas profitable by carrying out the given tasks efficiently, but also to grow them up in the long run by planning monthly, yearly, and mid-term (5 years) targets and innovating on the existing conditions.

On selling products, leaders ought to consider the long-term relationship with customers and set appropriate prices to satisfy both sides. When making production plans, leaders estimate the yield rates and place the right amount of orders. If it is possible to gain the economy of scale from the tie-in order, leaders will try to make a contract with the supplying amoebas for harmonizing each operation and sharing the merit. Since deciding appropriate investment is also the leaders' duty, they will make efforts to keep in touch with other sections as marketing and R&D to gather the up-to-date information.

Moreover, how to organize amoebas is particularly important in the amoeba system. As there is no fixed rule to divide them, the judgment depends on leaders' management ability. Taking advantage of the amoebas' flexibility, the leaders can freely modify the organizational structures. For example, the size of an amoeba may be reduced and the criterion for dividing amoebas may be changed from the manufacturing process-basis to the product-basis. Kyocera employees believe that it is time to revise the organization when leaders feel difficulties in grasping the situation of their amoebas or when the members' motivation decline as well as when their performances become worse. The new organization is expected to raise their motivation and support leaders' decision making.

Though the size of amoeba is even smaller than the smallest unit of the divisional organization system, the responsibility of the leader to amoeba is as great as that of the divisional manager. An amoeba is so small that it may look inefficient to delegate authorities, but this micro-profit center has many benefits such as good face-to-face communication among members, acute sensitiveness to the environmental changes, and quick responses to problems. Furthermore, more than one thousand ordinary people — about one employee in a dozen at Kyocera — are given chances to become leaders, who can learn by experience how difficult and how enjoyable management is. As a result, this system develops entrepreneurship of the leaders to play the principal roles in the empowerment management, and consequently leads to high profitability and fast growth of Kyocera.

18.5 The Amoeba Accounting System

While leaders are responsible for the entire business, just like the presidents of real companies, all of them do not have enough experience to manage profit centers. Thus, the first question of this study is how those inexperienced leaders can make such difficult decisions. The key point is the use of management accounting information. The first feature of the amoeba accounting system is its simplicity. There is only one performance measure, added value per labor hour, which is calculated as follows[5]:

Step 1. Total Amount of Shipments − Purchasing Costs from the Company's Other Amoebas = Total Outputs.
Step 2. Purchasing Costs from Outside the Company + Operating Costs + General Administrative Costs = Total Expenses.
Step 3. Total Outputs − Total Expenses = Deduction of Sales.
Step 4. Deduction of Sales/Total Labor Hours = Added Value per Hour.

These numbers are reported to every single amoeba by income statements. The income statements are as simple as household account books and are useful for pinpointing problems. Leaders can know the amoebas' performance at a glance. By comparing added value per hour with in-house standard wage rate, each amoeba will know if it is earning its living, because labor costs are excluded from total expenses. (Figure 18.4 is a sample of a manufacturing amoeba's statement.) Accounting often gives the impression that it is something like a black box only accounting experts can read and handle. When starting the amoeba system, Kazuo Inamori, founder of Kyocera, was not satisfied with conventional management accounting systems because they were too complicated for amoeba leaders having limited accounting knowledge. To derive potential ability from ordinary people, Inamori, who used to be an engineer, strongly believed that the management accounting system should be designed for leaders running amoebas

[5]These steps are prepared by referring to Hamada and Monden, op. cit., p. 203.

instead of accountants. That is why the added value per hour and the income statement were invented.

Without the help of accounting sections, it is easy for leaders to understand the statement and to calculate their income and expenditure. Because each category of the accounting report indicates the impact on the bottom line, and because amoebas are small organizations, leaders can fully grasp the situation of their amoebas and point out the confronting problems. To be brief, there are only three ways to raise the added value per hour: increasing sales, cutting costs down, and reducing labor hours, therefore even inexperienced leaders can analyze internal and external circumstances and can plan proper strategies to run their amoebas.

18.6 Feedback of Performance

The second feature of the amoeba accounting system is its quick and frequent feedback cycle. In many companies the results are returned once a month after some weeks, but in Kyocera everyday and the following day. Kyocera employees think monthly feedback data is so late and so aggregated that leaders cannot utilize those data to promote continuous improvement. Quick feedback can bring out early discoveries of problems and quick actions to cover failures. Additionally, frequent feedbacks deepen members' awareness of profit. Thus, such reporting system is indispensable to supplement the leaders' inexperience and eventually to achieve empowerment.

The third feature is the openness of information. Necessary and sufficient accounting results on the amoebas' performance are passed not only to executives and leaders but also to all amoeba members including part time workers. At the morning meeting, the results of the previous day and the targets of this day are announced to every employee, who can understand those numbers in the same way as leaders.

Under the given condition, added value per hour can be simply compared among amoebas because the measure is not influenced by the number of amoeba members, function, or products, but by the efficiency and effectiveness. Thanks to feedback information, all members enjoy such competitions as games and are self-motivated to win. Besides, anyone can know whether his or her amoeba is able to continue to earn its own living. If it seems hard to survive, all amoeba members will try to unite efforts. As empowerment relies on bottom-up suggestions, sharing accounting information enhances their commitments and furthers workers' participation and continuous improvement. In this way, no matter how inexperienced leaders may be, they can count on other members' small but many ideas, and can run their amoebas well.

Although the management accounting system to materialize those three features over numerous amoebas is likely to initiate a large amount of administrative expenses, Kyocera considers that these expenses are indispensable for the amoeba system and can be paid off. On the other hand, the company has accumulated know-how about the operation of the accounting system and has been reducing its running costs.

18.7 Education of Corporate Philosophy

Empowerment inevitably has some risks that might encourage leaders and members to take their selfish actions and to get the whole company to fall into confusion. When extremely tight profit targets are set for such small centers as amoebas, leaders should regard not only their centers' interests but also the whole company's. Thus, the second question of this study is how such highly autonomous micro-profit centers can join their forces.

Inamori thinks it is the key to successful empowerment to train leaders to be persons of good judgment who can take suitable actions by themselves in any situations. For this purpose, the company tries to educate them about its credo, Kyocera Philosophy. The philosophy of striving to "do what is right as a human being" shows leaders the aim of the amoeba management, required mental attitude, and code of conduct. In Kyocera Philosophy, cooperation is emphasized. According to Inamori's idea, necessary condition to work the amoeba system effectively is to have absolute mutual trust among all corporate members, such as between executives and employees, and among fellow workers. If there is no corporate culture to regard the right way of life, this system would excessively arise rivalry among amoebas or would cause their improper acts, and would bring about the ruin of companies in the end (Inamori, 1997).

Actually, no amoeba has sufficient resources to succeed without support from others, though they are regarded as self-support units. Paradoxically speaking, amoebas cannot help living together in mutual prosperity. The way to manage such collaboration is one of the most important matters for micro-profit centers, just as same as the importance of forming strategic alliances for real companies. Therefore, well-educated leaders do not neglect cooperation and always communicate with other amoebas to maintain good relationship.

18.8 Communication Supported by Accounting

It should be added that empowerment does not mean leaving leaders alone. To complement the education of the corporate philosophy, executives and superiors also have to make firm commitment to the amoeba management. Since forcing their opinion on leaders is against the spirit of the amoeba system, they are to give leaders impartial advice from broader points of view. When two amoebas do not reach agreement on dealing, superior above them will arrange meetings, mediate between the conflicting claims, and adjust their activities.

It is the management accounting information that let executives and superiors know the actual situation of amoebas and communicate fully with leaders. Kyocera's accounting system is proud of its accuracy as well as the simplicity as discussed above. As shown in Figure 18.4, the accounting system calculate income and expenditure per amoeba, which includes common expenses and administrative expenses. What executives have to do to get the whole company's profit is just to subtract total labor costs from the sum of all the amoebas' deduction of sales. By dividing or combining the

Total Amount of Shipments	A=B+C	--,---
External Shipments	B	-,---
Internal Shipments	C	--,---
Internal Purchases	D	-,---
Total Outputs	E=A-D	--,---
Total Expenses	F=a+b+...+p	--,---
Raw Material Costs	a	---
Conversion Costs	b	--,---
Repair Costs	c	---
Electricity	d	---
......	...	......
......	...	......
Interest and Depreciation	m	---
Common Expenses	n	---
Factory Expenses	o	---
Selling and Administrative Expenses	p	---
Deduction of Sales	G=E-F	--,---
Total Labor Hours	H	-,---
Added Value per Hour	I=G/H	---

Fig. 18.4 Income statement of manufacturing amoeba

amoebas' results at their own discretion, they can freely reach income and expenditure per division, function, factory, manufacturing process, product, sales area, and customer.

Because the size of amoeba is small, and because the accounting system is accurate, amoebas do not have any room to hinder their bad results caused by their selfish acts or neglect of cooperation. Executives and superiors can monitor all the amoebas regardless of their size and, if necessary, can give the leaders proper guidance. So long as every Kyocera employees share the accounting information and knowledge, communication supported by accounting data has advantages of making discussion concrete and practical. Since the visibility of organization is enhanced in this way, the accounting system works as a useful communication tool among executives, superiors, leaders, and amoeba members. In the end, coordination among highly autonomous micro-profit centers is realized.

18.9 Summary and Conclusion

Kyocera uses the amoeba system to promote empowerment. Developing entrepreneurial leadership is the ultimate purpose of this system, which brings the perfect harmony between organization, management accounting, and corporate philosophy (see Figure 18.5).

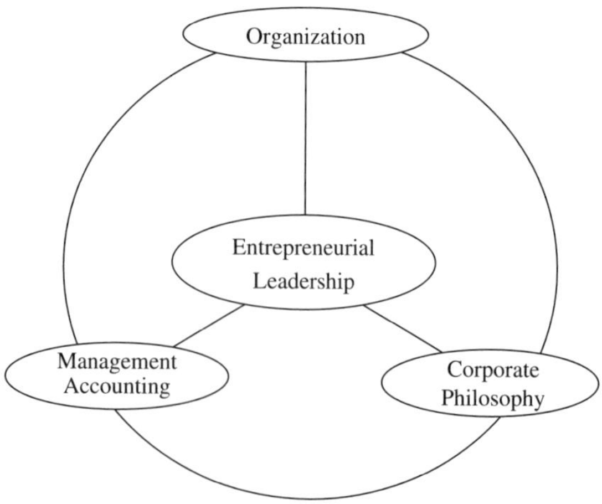

Fig. 18.5 Empowerment by the amoeba system

Though leaders do not have enough experience in business, they are required to run their micro-profit centers like the presidents of real companies. Our first question is how those inexperienced leaders can make proper decisions. The key point is the use of management accounting information. Kyocera's accounting system is proud of the simplicity of calculation, the quickness and the frequency of feedback, and the openness of information. Such reporting system is indispensable to supplement the leaders' inexperience.

However, empowerment has some risks that might encourage leaders to take their selfish actions and to neglect cooperation among amoebas. The second question is how highly autonomous micro-profit centers can join their forces. Kyocera tries to train leaders to be persons of good judgment who can take suitable actions by themselves in any situations. For this purpose, the company educates them in the corporate philosophy. And executives and superiors are also supposed to give advice, mediate between the conflicting claims, and adjust their activities. The accounting system is so accurate that it can work as a useful communication tool among all the members of the company.

To conclude, let us consider the implications of this study. The first point to notice is the relationship between empowerment and accounting. Though Johnson (1992) emphasizes the importance of empowerment, he argues that accounting information must be removed from the operational control system. Tani (1996) argues against Johnson that as long as management accounting system is well designed, it can promote empowerment at least in the case of the micro-profit center management. In Kyocera, this accounting system has practical utility to amoeba management, and plays the important roles. This fact supports Tani's opinion.

The second point is the ways to implement and control strategies. Simmons (1995) describes that there are four basic levers to control them: beliefs systems, boundary systems, diagnostic control systems, and interactive control systems. And it requires a balance among them to implement strategy effectively.[6] Simmons's idea can be applied to the case of Kyocera.

[6]Simmons writes, "Beliefs systems are used to inspire and direct the search for new opportunities. Boundary systems are used to set limits on opportunity-seeking behavior. Diagnostic control systems are used to motivate, monitor, and reward achievement of specified goals. Interactive control systems are used stimulate organizational learning and the emergence of new ideas and strategies." (Simons, p. 7.)

Its accounting system works as a diagnostic control system and an interactive control system, and its corporate philosophy works as a beliefs system and a boundary system. Besides, the accounting system and the philosophy complement each other. Kyocera has been armed with such unique and excellent management control system, which is its core competence (Hamel and Prahalad, 1994). However, to discuss these issues is beyond the scope of this brief paper. Further investigation is expected for further understanding of the amoeba system, micro-profit center system, and empowerment.

References

Cooper, R. (1995). *When Lean Enterprises Collide: Competing through Confrontation,* Harvard Business School Press.

Glaser, B. G. and Strauss, A. L. (1967). *The Discovery of Ground Theory: Strategies for Qualitative Research*, Aldine Publishing Company.

Hamada, K. and Monden, Y. (1989). Profit management at Kyocera Corporation: the amoeba system, in *Japanese Management Accounting: A World Class Approach to Profit Management*, Edited by Monden, Y. and Sakurai, M., Productivity Press.

Hamel, G. and Prahalad, C. K. (1994). *Competing for the Future*, Harvard Business School Press.

Inamori, K. (1997). *Respect the Divine and Love People*, PHP. (in Japanese)

Johnson, H. T. (1992). *Relevance Regained: From Top-Down Control to Bottom-Up Empowerment*, The Free Press.

Simons, R. (1995). *Levers of Control: How Managers Use Innovative Control Systems to Drive Strategies,* Harvard Business School Press.

Tani, T. (1996). Management accounting for micro-profit center: the pursuit of empowerment, *Zeikei Tsusin* 12. (in Japanese)

CHAPTER

19

Micro Finance: Towards a Business Model in Bangladesh

Mahfuzul Hoque

Associate Professor, Faculty of Business Studies
University of Dhaka

19.1 Introduction

The term "microfinance" is not new in the domain of business and economics anymore. In short, it can be defined as an endeavor for ensuring the access of poor people to loans and saving services. Micro finance programs extend small loans to very poor people for self-employment projects that breed income and permit them to care for their families. Today, microfinance is very popular all over the world and it can be said that poor people will continue to need and use this.

Nowadays, microfinance is recognized worldwide as a successful tool used for poverty alleviation. The movement of microfinance started in 1976 in Bangladesh in the name of Grameen Bank by the worldwide renowned Bangladeshi economist Professor Muhammad Yunus. In Bengali (the mother tongue of Bangladeshi people) the word "Grameen" means "something related to village." The bank works only for the poor in the society. There is no doubt that from her independence since 1971, Bangladesh was suffering from low level of income and pervasive poverty. So, an efficient growth policy through providing basic services to the poor became a substantial issue in this village based agricultural economy. Grameen Bank with microfinance came as a blessing to the poor. Initially, it was formed to verify the unproved theory that if financial resources were accessible to the poor at reasonable rates of interest, they would be able to procreate fruitful self-employment without outside assistance. Professor

Yunus identified that the rural poor people are unable to acquire credit at a reasonable interest rate. With this thought of providing loans to the poor at a reasonable charge, he started his Grameen Bank. Grameen Bank fought with poverty by creating entrepreneurs at the grassroots level. Most of the members of the bank were women, intensely insolvent and rural.

Initially, Professor Yunus started Grameen Bank as his personal initiative in Chittagong, Bangladesh in 1976. Later Bangladesh Bank (the central bank of Bangladesh) took it as their own project and in 1983, this project was transformed into a bank by passing legislation. At the beginning Yunus started the bank by investing some money from himself. After that he personally took loans from several banks and invested in this venture. Later he collected funds from several banks under a project of Bangladesh Bank. Grameen Bank started taking loans from several donor agencies of the world from 1982. The first fund was given by IFAD to Bangladesh Government in 1982 at 1% service charge over a term of 50 years. The Government of Bangladesh provided this fund to Grameen Bank as loan at 3% interest for 15 years. After that it collected funds from NORAD (Norway), SIDA (Sweden), CIDA (Canada), Ford Foundation and the Government of Netherlands. From 1995, Grameen bank stopped taking aids and started collecting loans from commercial sources. Now it operates with the help of its deposits and assets. By the year of 1997, Grameen Bank could develop a portfolio of $260 million and the number of total members became 2.3 million. They could collect almost 98% of their payments. It is said that the total loan disbursed in a year by this bank alone is more than the sum-total of all the loans disbursed by all other banks in the country to the rural people (Yunus, 2004). At present, the activities of Grameen Bank are running successfully in more than 40,000 villages in Bangladesh. They have more than 70,000 branches in these areas. Almost 90% of their members are rural women.

The success of Grameen Bank was remarkable and now the Grameen micro credit model is very popular worldwide. Till this date the Grameen model is established and followed by many countries of Africa (like Chad, Egypt, Somalia, South Africa, Sudan, Uganda, Tanzania, etc.), Asia (Afghanistan, Bhutan, Cambodia, China, Fiji, India, Indonesia, Nepal, Pakistan, Philippines, Lebanon, Vietnam, etc.), Europe (Albania, France, Netherlands, Norway, Cosovo, Bosnia, England, Poland), Australia and America (Argentina, Bolivia, Uruguay, Brazil, Canada, USA, Mexico, Peru, etc.).

19.2 Grameen Bank — Micro Credit Model

The target groups of Grameen Bank are the poorest of the poor, and are mostly women. The program was initiated with the objective of providing poor people with credit without collateral. Professor Yunus called the process of substituting the provision of collateral with group harmony and other aspects of micro credit as "freeing of credit from the bondage of collateral" (Yunus, 1997). The potential borrowers need to complete several steps in order to ensure loan repayment as described in Figure 19.1.

At the outset, the members have to select five persons of their own to form a group. Experience has taught the bank that loans are more likely to be repaid if groups include only individuals of the same gender, from the same village and from similar economic backgrounds (Khandker, Khalily and Khan, 1995).

Then, groups participate in a weeklong training program where they are taught the rules and regulations of the bank. If the bank is satisfied with the group's response to this training then loan is issued. Each member

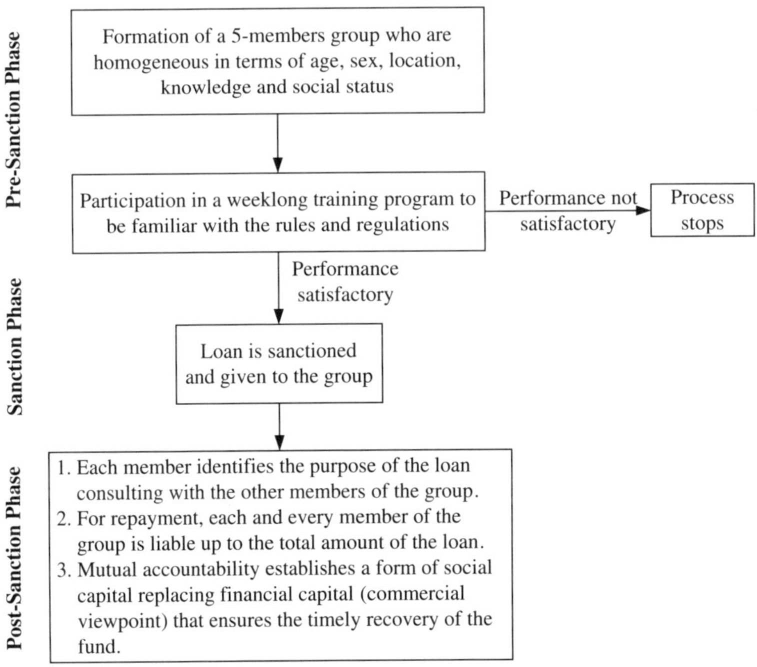

Fig. 19.1 Grameen model of microfinance at a glance

identifies the purpose of his or her loan with guidance from other members of the group (McDonnel, 1999).

To overcome problems of loan defaults, the Grameen Bank has developed a system of *joint liability* based on a group lending structure. Under this structure the group as a whole becomes ineligible to receive any additional loans if any member of the group defaults. This joint liability reduces risk in three ways (Conning, 1998). First, joint liability gives members an incentive to exclude known bad risks. For outsiders, knowledge of individual character is costly, but, for villagers, it is often a sunk cost. Thus, joint liability can cut the cost to screen potential borrower. Second, joint liability gives members an incentive to make sure that their fellows do not waste their loans. This can cut the cost to monitor borrowers. Third, joint liability gives members an incentive to convince group members out of arrears or even to repay their debts for them. Members may also guide each other. This can cut the cost to enforce repayment. The fright of social criticism and solid rural community reliance make poor client superior in loan repayment.

The interest rate paid by the borrowers is not subsidized. Charging a comparatively high interest rate (that covers the full cost of the program), and which the poor are apparently willing to pay, appears to be a win-win proposition (Morduch, 1997). This strategy is consistent with the lessons learnt from the experience of earlier cooperative and other government aided credit programs for the poor, whose failure has been blamed on the subsidized interest rate policy (Adams *et al.*, 1984).

At this moment Grameen is providing several types of loans like general loans, housing loans, collective loans, seasonal loans, and lease/loan arrangements. Micro credit, nowadays, is very popular in Bangladesh and there are more than 1,000 Micro Finance Institutions (MFIs hereafter) in Bangladesh at present. Among these, Grameen Bank is ranked within the top two.

19.2.1 *Sustainability of the micro finance program*

In 1998, *Micro Banking Bulletin* (Murdoch, 1999) performed a survey and the survey results revealed that even poverty-focused programs with an obligation to attain financial sustainability cover only about 70 percent of their full costs. According to Murdoch (1999), sustainability is generally measured at two levels. The first one is called the *operational sustainability.* It refers to the capacity of institutions to produce enough revenue to cover operating costs (it may not represent the full cost of capital). The second level is called *financial sustainability*. This indicates whether or not the institution requires subsidized contribution in order to run. If the institution is not financially sustainable, it cannot survive if it has to attain all inputs (especially capital) at market. In the same survey, it is found that, most of the programs have crossed the operational sustainability but many fewer could cover full capital costs. As a program relating to poverty alleviation, most of the MFIs are substantially subsidized and for this reason, it can be said that the financial sustainability of these institutions does not reflect the real profit. In order to reflect real profit, the opportunity cost of cheap funds should be accounted for and this is referred to as *economic sustainability* (Khalily, 2004).

It is also identified that the use of cheap fund creates several management problems. Cheap funds or subsidized funds negatively affect the behavior of the top management and as a result it distorts the efficient allocation of funding, increases default costs and operating costs and affects the viability of lenders (Adams *et al.*, 1984; Von Pischke *et al.*, 1983).

Another important issue is that, Grameen Bank is facing immense problem towards its sustainability because of its highly formal nature of operation. In terms of its structure, it is the only MFI in Bangladesh that is registered under special ordinance. It gives all financial benefits to its employees as per the rules and regulations of Government. The salaries of the employees are also paid according to national pay scale. In Bangladesh, another MFI naming The Association for Social Advancement (ASA) followed a highly successful approach of cost control. Their practice is much different from that of Grameen. Khalily, Imam, and Khan (2000) said that the program of ASA is *quasi-formal* whereas Grameen focuses on formal operations. They identified that after a long fifteen years of experience, Grameen Bank is close to sustainability, but ASA has achieved a higher degree of sustainability within seven years of its operation. The reason is that these two micro credit institutions differ largely in their design of programs, coverage, financial efficiency, and financial structure. To remain sustainable, ASA made its operations simplified. For instance:

1. They have made their activities simpler by providing only one type of loan. This is not the case of Grameen. As discussed in the previous section, Grameen is providing several types of loans.
2. Grameen looks for employees with genuine formal qualifications but ASA does not care about this strict rule of hiring employees of exactly this qualification. Rather ASA is flexible in this issue and hires staffs with

less formal aptitude and staff retention is a matter of high significance to them. In this way ASA control its costs by providing a low average salary.

3. In order to control costs, ASA eliminated their mid level branch offices.
4. Unlike the Grameen Bank practice, ASA concentrates on large groups of 40 members. Grameen focuses on a much smaller group of 5 members.

Thus, ASA is considered to be a sustainable organization and praised for its quasi-formal operational structure. Other than Grameen Bank, most of the MFIs in Bangladesh are following this quasi-formal structure and their average salary to the employees is much lower than Grameen Bank. This quasi-formal structure demands less cost than the formal one (Khalily, Imam and Khan, 2000).

Most of the MFIs are having an ownership structure that does not provide enough incentives for the management. Other than Grameen Bank, not a single MFI in Bangladesh is equity based. Even in Grameen Bank, management does not enjoy any equity interest (Khalily, 2004). The management in these institutions is not motivated enough for the sustainability rather they show an "expense-preference behavior." Literature provides substantiation that this kind of behavior is more apparent when such form of organization is financed by cheap or subsidized funds (Khalily and Imam, 2001).

These are the several causes that hinder the sustainability of MFIs everywhere. But in order to survive in the long run, sustainability is imperative. The urge for sustainability gave birth to another concept called "commercialization," that is going towards a business model.

19.3 Commercialization

Commercialization refers to the idea that rather than high dependence on donor funds, the activities of Micro Finance Institutions should be managed on a business basis within the framework of regulated financial system. Most of the MFIs rely on grant funds or funds provided at a highly concessional interest rate by various agencies. ADB (2000) in its Rural Asia Study identified that commercial approach is essential for micro finance development. It is now considered that the regulated commercialized MFIs are highly sustainable. It is believed that this recent trend in the Micro Finance Industry will ensure long term sustainability. The main objective of commercialization is to reduce the level of poverty of the poor households by allowing them access to flexible financial services but this should be done with a view to keep a balance between customers and the institutional growth. Commercialization encourages rendering profitable operations, maximizing equity, and achieving financial sustainability. Surviving in the competition is also an important consideration in commercialization.

In 1992, *BancoSol*, an NGO in Bolivia transformed into a commercial bank and became the first regulated microfinance institution. Soon, it outperformed the other Bolivian commercial banks and entered into the international capital market. *BancoSol's* main focus is on banking and not the service to the society. Interest rate is also relatively high and because of this, it makes reasonable return on their lending and does not have to depend on subsidies. The bank's repayment schedule is also accommodating, means, it allows some borrowers to make weekly payment and others monthly. The duration of loan is also not rigid.

Like *BancoSol*, *Bank Rakyat Indonesia* (BRI) also focuses on business and not social services. It uses a system called *unit desa* which is self-sufficient and focuses on providing loans to both poor and non-poor households. It emphasizes on collateral and as a result, very poor section of the society cannot afford it. But the matter of collateral is not so rigid. The officials are allowed to practice some discretion in case of reliable borrowers who may not be able to back the full amount of loan with the assets. The bank reduced its costs by creating a network of branches and posts (Murdoch, 1999). It does not provide its clients with training and guidance.

There is no doubt that this drift towards commercialization is to guarantee sustainability in the long-run. But it is seen that this particular movement towards commercialization distracts the main objective of micro finance. Means, the focus on only the poor section (and mostly the very poor section) becomes blurred. In the thought of commercialization, most of the organizations have focused on increased loan sizes. This may be a trouble in the process for the poor to reach the support.

19.3.1 *Towards a business model targeting the poor*

There is no doubt that if the main objective of micro finance is to be fulfilled, the very poor section of the society cannot be ignored at all. The concept of commercialization can ensure sustainability but the very poor section of the society is ignored. As both commercialization and sustainability are important issues, a business model on micro finance should concentrate on "helping the poor with a business motive." The mission of the MFIs should be to provide diverse, appropriate and market responsive financial services at reasonable prices to extremely poor, poor, and weak non-poor customers at the same time, the institutions should be run in a cost-effective way. Their objective should be to:

1. Make best use of equity for sustainability by rendering profitable operations;
2. Increasing net cash flow;
3. Concentrating on business expansion.

A balance between customer and business welfare should be the target. For this, they should concentrate on the following initiatives (Figure 19.2):

1. Lack of rigidity in providing loans: The financial services should be such that it can be availed by the poor section. There should be different kinds of loan products which will be attractive to the poor people. There should be flexibility in case of loan terms (monthly, quarterly etc.). The issue of collateral should be avoided as much as possible. *Social capital* will be the base on which the total matter should stand. Theses flexibilities of the loan packages will attract the poorer section even if the interest charges are kept little high. Larger loans can be given to a group having more number of members (like ASA).

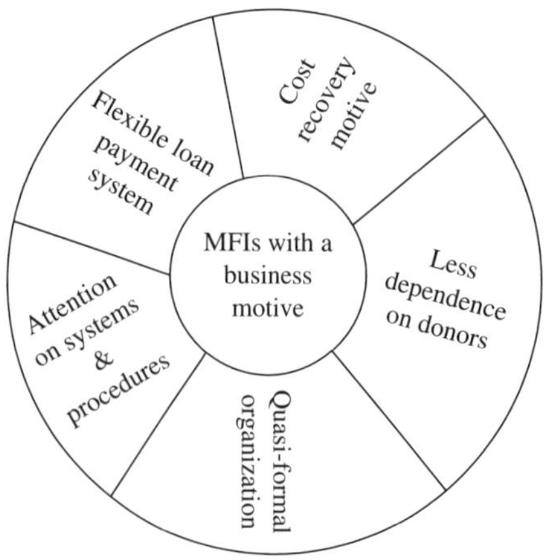

Fig. 19.2 MFIs with a business motive

2. Quasi-formal operating approach: The average salary of the employees should be reasonable. Rather than hiring high qualified employees, people having lower qualifications can be hired. Salary structure should be flexible. To motivate employees a performance related pay system can be introduced. Using marketing intelligence, obsolete products, and services should be cut off from the product line.
3. Cost recovery: The financial viability should be the target and the revenues should cover all costs. A full cost pricing approach should be followed. The revenue plan should cover all provisions related to administrative costs, financial costs, and loan loss provisions. Thus, the institution will become operationally and financially self-sustainable. The pricing of lending interest rate should be done by appropriate costing system.
4. Less dependence on donors: As cheap and subsidized financing creates motivational problems among the top management, the dependence on donor fund should be reduced. Rather top management should be encouraged to maximize shareholder's wealth by giving them some interest in equity. Commercial sources of funds should be used.
5. Attention on systems and procedures: An overall awareness on loan provisioning, liquidity management, capital adequacy, asset management, human resource management, and risk management should be shaped under appropriate governance, like the practice of several business organizations.

19.4 Conclusion

MFIs originated with a mission to help the poorer section of the society. As sustainability became a significant issue, commercialization, or business approach came in the MFI scenario. As a result, the problem of sustainability disappeared but the mission appeared to be tough to achieve. Now a new solution, that will help in serving the poor of the society and at the same time ensure profitability, is needed. The literature reveals that "reaching the poor" is a constraint to the business profitability as it increases the cost with the number of non-feasible sized loans. This excessive cost can be significantly reduced by giving feasible sized loans to groups with large number of members. If it is done, it will also be feasible for the poor people. The very presence of social capital will reduce the risk of loan default, minimize cost, and improve fund utilization with efficiency. Moreover, the poor are good business as it is a big market to explore. The business approach towards sustainability with a concentration on the poor section of the society will lead to a considerable growth of MFI industry at the same time it will lead to a growth of entrepreneurship at the lower class of the society.

References

Adams, A. W., Graham, D. H., and Von Pischke, J. D. (eds.) (1984). *Undermining Rural Development with Cheap Credit,* Westview Press: Colorado.

ADB (2000). *Rural Asia Study: Beyond the Green Revolution*, Manila.

Conning, J. (1998). Outreach, sustainability and leverage in monitored and peer-monitored lending, *Journal of Development Economics* 60, pp. 51–77.

McDonnel, S. (1999). The Grameen Bank micro-credit model: lessons for Australian indigenous economic policy, CAEPR, Australian National University, Australia.

Murdoch, J. (1997). Micro finance sustainability: a consistent framework and new evidence on the Grameen Bank, Discussion Paper, Cambridge: Harvard Institute for International Development.

Murdoch, J. (1999). The role of subsidies in microfinance: evidence from the Grameen Bank, *Journal of Development Economics* 60, pp. 229–248.

Khalily, M. A. B. (2004). Quantitative approach to impact analysis of microfinance programs in Bangladesh — what have we learned?, *Journal of International Business* 16, pp. 331–353.

Khalily, M. A. B., Imam, M. O., and Khan, S. A. (2000). Efficiency and sustainability of formal and quasi-formal microfinance programmes — an analysis of Grameen Bank and ASA, *The Bangladesh Development Studies,* XXVI-2&3.

Khalily, M. A. B. and Imam, M. O. (2001). Expense preference behavior of micro finance institutions and the case for regulation and supervision, in *Poverty and Finance: The Emerging Institutional Issues,* edited by Sharif, I. and Woods, G., Dhaka: Oxford University Press.

Khandker, S. R., Khalily, B., and Khan, Z. (1995). Grameen Bank: Performance and Sustainability, World Bank Discussion Papers No. 306, World Bank, Washington D.C.

Von Pischke, J. D., Adams, D. W., and Donald, G. (eds.) (1983). *Rural Financial Markets in Developing Countries: Their Use and Abuse,* Baltimore: John Hopkins University Press.

Yunus, M. (2004). *Grameen Bank o Amar Jibon (in Bengali),* Dhaka: Maola Brothers.

PART 4

DESIGN AND CONTROL OF BUSINESS PROCESSES: PROCESS REENGINEERING, SUPPLY CHAIN, SHARED SERVICES AND OUTSOURCING

CHAPTER

20

Japanese TQM as the Origin of Balanced Scorecard

Gunyung Lee

Professor, Faculty of Economics, Niigata University

20.1 Introduction

Kaplan and Norton's 1990 research on "a new performance-measurement system" led to the development of the Balanced Scorecard, which took the industrial and academic fields by surprise. The "Corporate Scorecard (CS)" of the Analog Devices Inc. (ADI) was also known as a corporate case based on this research (Kaplan *et al.*, 1996, preface). The CS is a sheet that shows the five categories of performance measurement: quality improvement process (QIP), manufacturing metrics of products, manufacturing metrics of assembled products, new products and a traditional financial performance, though ADI's CS will be described later.

ADI introduced Japanese Total Quality Management (TQM) earlier than other companies in America. The evaluation of QIP activity based on TQM in the ADI's CS derived from the Half-Life concept of Yokogawa-Hewlett Packard (the company name changed in 1995 to Japan Hewlett Packard Inc.) (Kaplan, 1993, p. 3). Furthermore, the former professor of Tsukuba University in Japan, Shoji Shiba was included in the diagnoses of ADI's Hoshin management related to TQM activity (Shiba *et al.*, 1995). One may thus infer that the relationship of Japanese TQM and ADI's CS is deeply entrenched. I think that ADI's CS is a key element in understanding the connection of Japanese TQM and Balanced Scorecard.

Therefore, I will examine the features of ADI's Corporate Scorecard that influenced the Balanced Scorecard, and the management tools of ADI. Then, I will clarify its connection with Japanese management techniques.

Finally, it will evaluate the differences between Balanced Scorecard and Japanese management techniques in terms of TQM.

20.2 ADI Overview

ADI, founded in 1965 in Massachusetts, is a manufacturer that develops, manufactures, and sells the integrated circuits that convert between analog and digital data. The company is one of the world's top ten IT companies that has experienced significant growth. Sales increased from $1.45 billion in fiscal year 1999 to $2.58 billion in fiscal year 2000 (Business Week's investigation). According to a March 1999 study by Fortune magazine, ADI ranked 4th in the United States' most respected semiconductor companies. The company is renowned for its "development of employee" culture and its low attrition rate (ADI's URL). One of their major management systems is TQM, which is introduced in their website as:

> Analog Devices continues to be committed to the long-term adoption of TQM into our overall organizational culture. We believe that TQM is a major means to achieving our business objectives. The involvement of all Analog employees has been critical to meeting our goals and will continue to be essential in the 21st century.

ADI's chairman, Ray Stata is the president and chairman of "The Center for Quality of Management (CQM)." The CQM was founded in 1989 by CEOs and senior executives from seven major New England companies who wanted to work together to study and implement cutting-edge management practices (CQM's URL). CQM's main activities are to build upon a foundation of TQM and address the three areas critical to long-term business success: planning, operations, and managing change.

20.3 ADI's Half-Life System

In 1983, ADI introduced TQM due to customers' complaints about the delivery and quality of goods. However, rather than a full TQM implementation, it only entailed literature review and participation in seminars. As a result, the expected outcome of implementing TQM was not fully realized. The Half-Life concept of quality improvement was then introduced to break such a situation in 1986 (Anthony *et al.*, 2001, pp. 464–465). General features for the Half-Life system and CS of ADI taken up by Kaplan (1993) is summarized in this section.

20.3.1 *Changing the market strategy*

Historically, ADI focused its attention on developing new products that would earn high profit margins in the niche marketplace. However, the increased demand for some products required that ADI adopt a new market strategy. The demand-change in the market led ADI to switch to a high-volume products market. It usually needed the strategy matched to the market trend that required the on-time delivery at the low price there. Gradually, ADI set the strategic focus to the production-volume and new products to maintain and expand market-share in such a market at the product quality, on-time delivery, and the lead-time.

20.3.2 *Application of Half-Life concept in improving quality*

ADI worked on various improvements that centered on TQM according to its strategic focus. However, the company did not have any notion of what rate of improvement was satisfactory or what would be needed to accelerate the improvement process, which expectedly led to the below target results. This led to the subsequent hiring of Art Schneiderman as the vice president, who was a follower of the Juran TQM philosophy. The Half-Life concept in improving quality was introduced under his leadership. The Half-Life concept is an approach that identifies the root causes of defects, and ranks them in order of importance, and then solves the problems using the Plan–Do–Check–Action (PDCA) cycle of TQM (Anthony *et al.*, 2001, p. 465).

The chance of the introduction of the Half-Life concept in improving quality resulted from the Half-Life graph of defective rates of quality for the improvement activity of Yokogawa Hewlett Packard (YHP) that the vice president had found by chance. The Half-Life graph of YHP shows a decreasing trend on a straight line when the defective rate is plotted on semi-log graph against time. It is showing of the cycle when a defective rate reduced by half. Schneiderman got a hint from the Half-Life graph, and collected data concerning all the quality improvement programs, and made up the activity model of Quality Improvement Process (QIP). This problem solving model was employed throughout Schneiderman's leadership (Kaplan, 1993, pp. 3–4).

The QIP activity model continually solves the problems using the Half-Life concept as the yardstick for measuring how fast the organization accomplishes the PDCA cycle as shown in Figure 20.1.

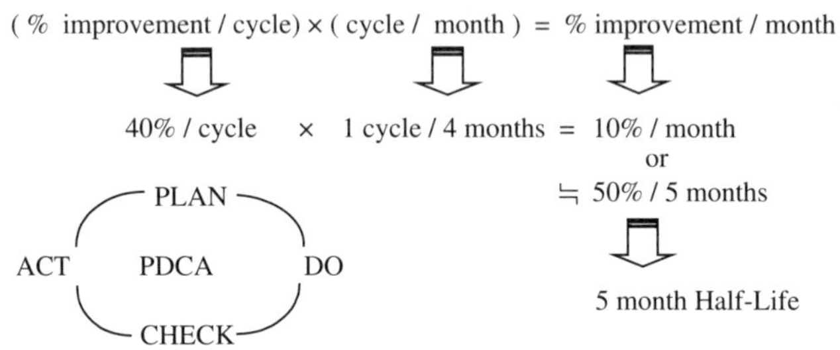

Source: Kaplan R.S., "Analog Devices: The Half-Life Metric," *Harvard Business School Case,* #9–190–061, 1993.

Fig. 20.1 Metric of continuous improvement

20.3.3 *Corporate Scorecard and application of Half-Life concept in ADI*

ADI established the five-year plan started in 1987 as shown in Figure 20.2.

Especially, the target of the sales growth rate is a challenge target. However, because this target could be achieved when ADI recognized by its customers, ADI established the targets for the customer as the following top-down performance measurement targets (see Figure 20.3).

These target values were established based on what were expected from major competitors in 1992. However, the target values were established based on the 1992 target specified by extrapolating from current half-lives if ADI could not meet the competitor.

To achieve such targets, four performance measures were established internally for every division over the course of five years (see Figure 20.4).

Performance measurement	Target value
Sales growth	20% to 25% per year
Operating profits	17% of Sales
Profit after tax	9.4% of Sales
Return on capital	15%

Source: Kaplan R.S., "Analog Devices: The Half-Life Metric," *Harvard Business School Case,* # 9–190–061, 1993.

Fig. 20.2 ADI five-year plan for fiscal year 1987 to 1992

Performance measurement	1987	1992	Half-Life (months)
On-time delievery	85%	> 99.8%	9
Outgoing defect level	500PPM	< 10PPM	9
Lead time	10 wks	< 3 wks	9

Source: Kaplan R.S., "Analog Devices: The Half-Life Metric," *Harvard Business School Case*, # 9–190–061, 1993.

Fig. 20.3 ADI's specific target for customers

Performance measurement	1987	1992	Half-Life (months)
Manufacturing cycle-time	15 wks.	4–5 wks.	9
Proces defect level	500PPM	< 10PPM	6
Yield	20%	> 50%	9
Time to market	36 months	6 months	24

Source: Kaplan R.S., "Analog Devices: The Half-Life Metric," *Harvard Business School Case*, # 9–190–061, 1993.

Fig. 20.4 Four measures of internal performance

On the other hand, to see the predicted performance of each division as mentioned above, the quarterly Corporate Scorecard was designed as shown in Figure 20.5. The scorecard is a one 8.5 inch by 11 inch sheet of paper with 12 points or bigger fond (Anthony *et al.*, 2001, p. 472). First of all, Schneiderman filled in the scorecard for upcoming next years with benchmarks based on Half-Life improvement rates from prior years. Then, the division managers established their bottom-up targets. Finally, the targets were decided through negotiations.

On the other hand, single page trend-table with all key indicators was reported monthly and quarterly. It is said that a high level of internal competition by the scorecard introduced in all divisions in 1988, could generate the faster learning curve (Anthony *et al.*, 2001, p. 468).

20.3.4 *The feature of ADI's Corporate Scorecard*

The relation between Corporate Scorecard and the Half-Life system can be summarized as shown in Figure 20.6.

20.4 ADI's Hoshin Management

In 1990, ADI experienced its first loss despite the company's dramatic improvements on quality measures. The company introduced Hoshin

Indicators	Description
FINANCIAL	
Revenue Revenue growth Profit ROA	presents information of interest to stockholders
QIP	
On time delivery % CRDs not matched Excess lead-time Labor turnover	presents data on how ADI looks to its customers and employees
MANUFACTURING METRICS: PRODUCTS	
Outgoing PPM Process PPM Cycle time Yield	presents measures of internal manufacturing performance for products
MANUFACTURING METRICS: ASSEMBLED PRODUCTS	
Outgoing PPM Process PPM Cycle time Yield	presents measures of internal manufacturing performance for assembled products
NEW PRODUCTS	
Bookings pre-86 products Bookings post-85 products Total bookings	presents how well ADI is doing in introducing new products
1992 ratio (Fiscal year 90 plan / fiscal year 87 plan)	the achieving level of the strategic goals

Source: Kaplan R.S., "Analog Devices: The Half-Life Metric," *Harvard Business School Case,* # 9–190–061, 1993.

Fig. 20.5 Indicators of ADI's Corporate Scorecard for fiscal year 1990

management due to the financial crisis. While the Half-Life system improved quality and reduced cost, the company decided to shift its strategy due to the lack of wealth creation (Anthony *et al.*, 2001, pp. 469–472). Hoshin management is an extension of the QIP effort at ADI, and is regarded as a tool to center the company's energies on wealth creation (Anthony *et al.*, 2001, p. 472).

Overall, the type of continuous improvement is possible to divide into the incremental improvement and the breakthrough improvement like Hoshin management. On the other hand, the incremental improvement often appears as "burnout syndrome" if the goal is not given clearly because

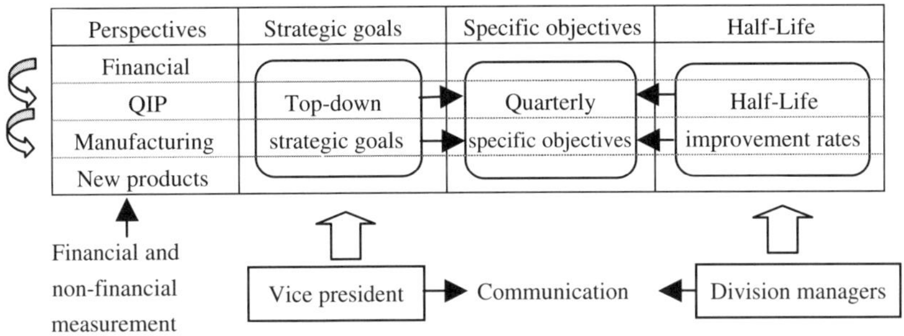

Fig. 20.6 Relation between Corporate Scorecard and the Half-Life system

it is repeated in every period. To break the syndrome, the Half-Life system had been introduced at ADI. The incremental improvement system also has a limit for wealth creation, though it works well at stopping wealth-reducing (Anthony *et al.*, 2001, p. 470). Therefore, Hoshin management was introduced at ADI to promote wealth creation. However, the company does not clearly distinguish between incremental improvement and breakthrough improvement. The company uses the terms Hoshin, breakthrough goals, and incremental improvement goals interchangeably (Shiba *et al.*, 1995). That is, it is guessed that the incremental improvement tools like the Half-Life system are applied to "plan solution" shown in Figure 20.7 in Hoshin deployment.[1]

ADI uses Hoshin management to solve critical problems that cannot be solved in each division as used in Japanese companies. That is, Hoshin management is used as a methodology for aiming at breakthrough improvement by cross-functional cooperative activities. ADI is executing Hoshin management by repeating four processes of (1) Setting the Hoshin; (2) Deploying the Hoshin; (3) Monitoring the Hoshin; and (4) Diagnosing the Hoshin, though its detailed feature is described in this section (Shiba *et al.*, 1995).

20.4.1 *Setting the Hoshin*

Setting the Hoshin is a decision-making process of what "should" be accomplished based on long-term vision, past experiences and environmental

[1] ADI uses the Half-Life Concept as a tool to solve long-term problems. (Kaplan *ibid.*, p. 8)

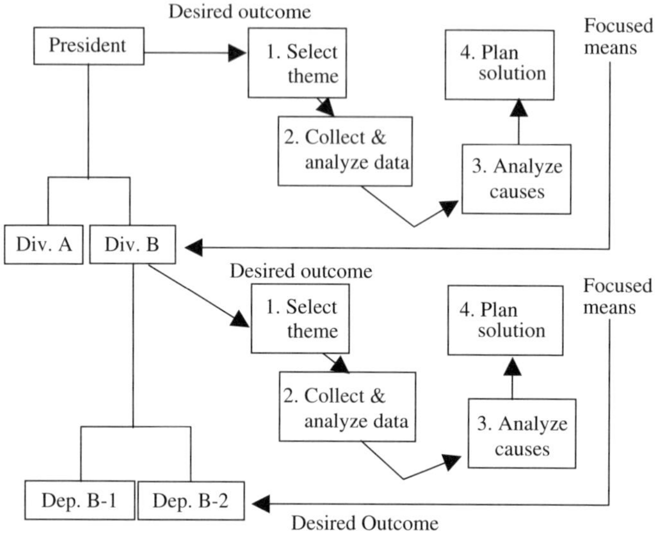

Source: Shiba S., Pursch T. and Stasey R. (1995), Introduction to Hoshin management: Achieving Alignment at Analog Devices and Teradyne, *Center for Quality of Management Journal,* Fall, pp. 22–33

Fig. 20.7 Hoshin deployment

change, and is the P (Plan) step in the PDCA cycle. ADI learned that customers wanted improvements in delivery through the customer satisfaction surveys. Although delivery performance showed continuous improvement, the improvement was not meeting customers' expectation. Therefore, a breakthrough of delivery was established as the main objective of Hoshin management.

First, ADI used the Pareto chart to identify the major contributors to late delivery. In analysis process of each contributor, Ishigawa diagram was used to determine the root causes of the late delivery problem. In the last step, solution-planning was performed to develop the focused-means for improving late delivery. Focused-means planning included quantifying problems, identifying required resources, determining time to completion, and determining the main means to achieve the Hoshin. In the decision of the main means, it is focused on means with high contribution level at which a breakthrough improvement is enabled. It is important to concentrate few resource and organizational ability on the specified breakthrough goals. Incremental improvement is focused on other fundamental business issues (Shiba *et al.*, 1995).

20.4.2 *Deploying the Hoshin*

Deploying the Hoshin is a process of "vertical" and "horizontal" alignment down the organization, and is the D (Do) step in the PDCA cycle. At this time, Hoshin is given by the top down, and deployed with the chain of focused means and desired outcome. The main means to accomplish the desired outcome are found by using the Pareto chart and Ishigawa diagram mentioned above. At ADI, Hoshin is deployed down three levels (i.e., Top management level, Division level, and Department level). On the other hand, desired outcome, performance measures, target values, focused means, and the deadlines are written in a Hoshin sheet at each level. ADI's focused means are obtained by repeating the analysis process to narrow the focus down the organization as shown in Figure 20.7. The deployment process is called *cascading* and the joint analysis between levels is called *catchball.*

In ADI's Hoshin management, the focused means to accomplish Hoshin goals are squeezed to 2–3 means unlike Japanese companies who use many means to accomplish the goals. Furthermore, "solution planning" step is accomplished by Management by Objectives (MBO) rather than Hoshin management at ADI (Shiba *et al.*, 1995).

20.4.3 *Monitoring the Hoshin*

Monitoring the Hoshin is a process of monitoring the execution of focused means to meet the desired outcome, and is the C (Check) step in the PDCA cycle. In ADI, monitoring the Hoshin is done based on the business plan review sheet. The desired outcomes with target values, the actual performances, the symbols, the weakness analyses, and the corrective actions are in the business plan review sheet. The symbol is distinguished by an easy sign based on the concerning degree, the improved performance, and so on.

20.4.4 *Diagnosing the Hoshin*

Diagnosing the Hoshin is a process of evaluating the overall process or system of Hoshin management to identify areas of improvement, and is the A (Action) step in the PDCA cycle. In ADI, diagnosing the Hoshin was done by top management included Prof. Shoji Shiba as an outside subject matter expert.

20.4.5 *The feature of Hoshin management of ADI as strategy execution system*

Hoshin management of ADI described above can be summarized as shown in Figure 20.8.

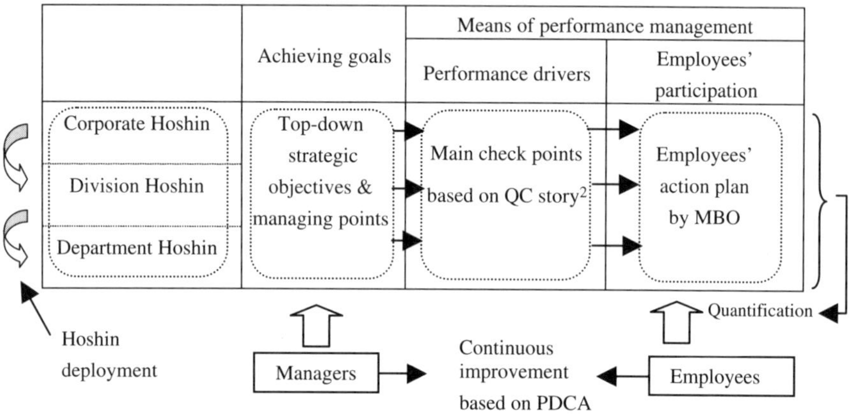

Fig. 20.8 Essence of Hoshin management

20.5 Comparison between Japanese TQM and ADI's TQM

The continuous improvement of Japanese companies is divided into the breakthrough improvement like Hoshin management and incremental improvement. In general, the outcome increases rapidly with breakthrough improvement. However, any mechanism that improves it further cannot be developed. It is because only the employee accepted the breakthrough improvement, but not sympathized with it. Therefore, the incremental improvement activity as a routine work is needed to synchronize with a breakthrough improvement, and improve continuously, then the culture and the know-how of the improvement get fixed in the company (Takahashi, 1997). Of course, unless the employee appreciates their objectives of daily improvement, employees' burnout syndrome will appear. ADI

[2] QC story is the following processes: (1) process to navigate the problem-solving; (2) process to summarize the activities; and (3) process to interpret the activity-result to employee (Kano N. ed. (1996). *Kadai-tasseikata QC story ni Yakudatsu Syuho*, Nikkagiren, p. 10) (in Japanese).

uses a method different from Japanese companies to overcome the limitation in such an improvement.

ADI uses Hoshin management, QIP, the Corporate Scorecard, and critical success factors to create, deploy, and implement strategy (Anthony *et al.*, 2001, p. 473). ADI's TQM can be summarized as: Hoshin management is first used to accomplish the strategic goal, and Management by Objectives is linked with the solution planning in the deploying the Hoshin, and the objectives are given to the employee individually in ADI's TQM. The Half-Life concept is also used to sustain a sense of accomplishment for the continuous improvement. The performance measurements linked with the corporate strategy goal are shown in the Corporate Scorecard of single paper.

On the other hand, in a Japanese company, corporate culture influences Hoshin management, and is various, and then more original methods are developed and executed. As a result, it is not easy for a company to introduce Hoshin management for the first time, because Hoshin management is not standardized. That is, it is not clear how to have to perform Hoshin management. Moreover, it is not clear at which level the implemented Hoshin management is positioned, and how to have to value it (TQM committee, 1998, pp. 189–201).

While the Hoshin management style is not standardized, Japanese companies can learn from ADI's experience. ADI's TQM can be called the model of American TQM. It can be said that ADI's TQM modified Japanese TQM as:

1. In deploying the Hoshin, the quantified important means that become the desired outcome at the next level is squeezed to 2–3, and it applies to accomplish the objectives. Other means with few contributions are accomplished by an incremental improvement.
2. The means specified by deploying the Hoshin are linked to each employee's goal using Management by Objectives (MBO).
3. The breakthrough improvement objectives are deployed by applying Hoshin management. However, the Half-Life system is applied to fix the continuous improvement.
4. Both a breakthrough improvement objective and the incremental improvement objective can become the objectives of Hoshin management.
5. Corporate Scorecard is used to understand and evaluate the relationship of the long-term management goals.

6. Corporate Scorecard is used to urge an inter competition as a performance trend table.

20.6 Comparison between Balanced Scorecard and ADI's TQM

Balanced Scorecard is a management tool that adds the focused measures for customers, the focused measures of internal business process and the learning and growth measures for employees to financial performance measures, and the focused measures in the same perspectives are linked to them with distinct perspectives by cause-effect relationship. It is a management tool that establishes the outcome measures and the performance drivers, and fulfils the PDCA cycle. On the other hand, ADI's Corporate Scorecard is a simple performance measurement sheet checked from four perspectives that added the focused new product measures, the focused manufacturing measures, and the focused QIP measures to the focused financial measures as previously stated. Especially, because CS is used as one of the management tools of ADI, the ADI's TQM including CS almost includes the essence of Balanced Scorecard.

Nomura Research Institute summarizes the essence of Balanced Scorecard based on their experiences consulting Japanese companies as shown in Figure 20.9. On the other hand, when Balanced Scorecard and above-mentioned ADI's TQM (Figures 20.5, 20.6 and 20.8) are compared,

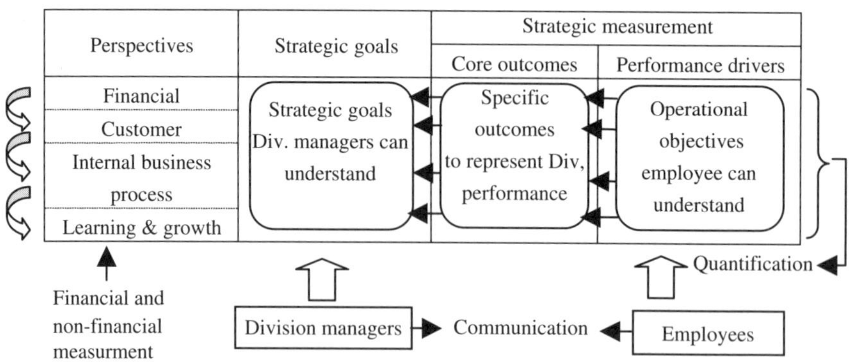

Source: Ito Y. and Kobayashi Y. (2001). *Neo Balanced Scorecard*, Chuokeizaisya, p. 47 (in Japanese).

Fig. 20.9 Essence of Balanced Scorecard framework

the only difference seems to be the four "how to fix" and "how to summarize" perspectives.

20.7 Conclusion

In general, a lot of Japanese companies combine financial (especially total sales) and non-financial performance measures together. The view that emphasizes the total sales is due to the logic of relating the total sales to the profit according to economics of scale and experience curve. On the other hand, the extending sales are possible in the case that offers cheaply the wanted service or goods to the customers when it is necessary. Therefore, methodologies such as TQM, TP (Total Productivity) managements, and TPM (Total Productive Maintenance) are developed and improved as a management tool to attain these purposes in Japan. However, these methodologies mean a trade-off between quality and profits sometimes. Kaplan and Norton (1996, pp. 32–34) gave the example that breakthrough improvement in quality, productivity, and customer service failed to deliver financial benefits. The example is to highlight the importance of having financial performance measurement as a final outcome measure. As a result, Kaplan and Norton developed Balanced Scorecard as a new management tool to overcome the problems that TQM and the MB prize have.

Japanese TQM advocators insist that a lot of methods of Europe and America are similar with the manual of the target-oriented type that pursues "what to do." On the other hand, they insist that Japanese TQM is a process-oriented exploring the "How to do" that emphasizes the methodology and results of quality improvement (TQM committee, 1998, p. 333). Such a comment seems an important point that should be noted when Balanced Scorecard is discussed.

On the other hand, Japanese TQM was introduced to U.S. companies, and was amended as a method matched to the situation of the United States, and was developed as today's Balanced Scorecard. Nowadays, Japanese companies begin to introduce Balanced Scorecard that performs such a transition process. In general, the mannerism by "systemic fatigue" also becomes a problem in executing any management tool, and it is the reason to expect a new management tool. However, a revised Japanese TQM matched to the situation of United States' companies is introduced into Japanese companies again. We need to search carefully how it will be developed in the future in Japan.

References

ADI's URL (http://www.analog.com).

Anthony, R. N. and Govindarajan, V. (2001). *Management Control Systems*, 10th ed., McGraw-Hill Irwin.

CQM's URL (http://www.cqm.org/about/index.html).

Kaplan, R. S. (1993). Analog Devices: the half-life system, Harvard Business School Case # 9–190–061.

Kaplan, R. S. and Norton, D. P. (1996). *The Balanced Scorecard — Translating Strategy into Action*, HBS Press.

Shiba, S., Pursch, T. and Stasey, R. (1995). Introduction to Hoshin management: achieving alignment at Analog Devices and Teradyne, *Center for Quality of Management Journal*, Fall, pp. 22–33.

Takahashi, H. (1997). The meaning of TQM in Toyota Motors, monthly text of quality 268. (in Japanese)

TQM Committee (1998). Total "quality" management in the 21st century, Nikkagiren, pp.189–201. (in Japanese)

CHAPTER

21

Process Management System by KPI Towards Challenging and Evolving Organizations

Noriyuki Imai
Vice President, Toyota Financial Services Corporation

21.1 Introduction

The term "management" was coined in America in the mid-19th century and saw its ascendancy in the 20th century. Its meaning underwent gradual change during that time. In the 21st century, its meaning and implications are set to undergo further transformation.

Chandler claims that the first modern corporate organization with a structure wherein managers manage other managers and each manager reports to his line manager in the hierarchy developed in America after the 1830s (Chandler, 1997). The competitive advantage of a modern corporation depended on the "capacity for administrative coordination."

According to Drucker, the definition of a business manager that was current immediately after the Second World War was someone who was accountable for the work of his subordinate(s). In other words, a manager was the boss and management signified "status and authority." However, by the early 1950s the business manager had come to be regarded as someone responsible for how well his subordinates worked. Eventually, the business manager came to "be responsible for the application of knowledge and its efficiency" (Drucker, 1993). The focus of management in the post-1990 era is shifting toward the realm of "knowledge creation" in the knowledge-worker.

Within this context, the Process KPI (Key Performance Indicator), which is the subject of this paper, is deemed a tool for adapting product-making management to the mega-competition of the 21st century.

In short, 20th century management fought its battles using "head office capability" and "staff capability," and achieved a degree of success thereby. In the 21st century, however, "head office capability" and "staff capability" are prerequisites with which "all-out war," or more precisely, a battle of "theater-war capability," is fought. So long as the nature of this competition is clearly discerned, the chances of Japan's manufacturing sector maintaining its vantage position are not too small.

"The will toward self-initiating evolution," and "people and processes that think thoroughly in simple honesty and undergo perfect combustion" were on a plane well beyond the framework of 20th-century shareholder-value based management, agency theory, or managerial accounting mechanisms such as budget control or performance evaluation systems. However, the key task for the 21st century is to attain the aforementioned new level of management consciousness. Based on such understanding, this paper sets out to explore the potential of Process KPI, a conceptual device built on a new philosophy.

21.2 Concept of Process KPI

21.2.1 *Definition of terminology*

Although already a popular term, what we mean by "process" is the flow of goods from receipt of product order right up to completion of manufacture. In the narrow sense of the word, we may understand "process" to mean "manufacturing process," but in the wider sense "process" includes the total cyclical process of materials, from the point at which they are extracted from the earth as resources up until they are ultimately returned to the earth. In this paper, "process" shall signify a concept with a horizontal vector, as opposed to a concept governed by vertical alignment, such as "business unit," "section" or "responsibility center." In practice, for an organization to maintain its vitality, the long and narrow pitfall of an "octopus trap" must be avoided; thus, it is highly important to ensure the operation of a horizontal vector, a cross-functional mobility unconstrainable by the straightjacket of a vertical divide.

Meanwhile, KPI (Key Performance Indicator) is already a widely used term, just as "process" is, and refers to a "leading measure of output." It can be considered almost synonymous with the word "driver" in the terms "activity driver" or "cost driver."

In a traditional view of management, whether it be KPI or driver, a control mindset operates at its core, in the belief that exercising control over key indicators that govern a certain domain would enable the manager to optimally run that domain and the organization as a whole.

By contrast, the Process KPI described in this paper only regards the measurement of process to be its mission, and does not aim to control the process. Rather, the thinking is that indicators are not independent vehicles that can implement reform; or, to put it another way, no reform is brought about by data. It is people who are the movers that exercise control, and the object of such control is the process itself. This is what Toyota refers to as "genchi genbutsu" (literally, actual site, actual object, meaning "going to the source to make correct decisions"). Just as we find an automobile difficult to drive if it has no rear-view mirror, indicators are essential for checking our current position. However, we cannot drive a car just with a rear-view mirror. In this regard, the implication of Process KPI seems much more logical than the assumptions of American-style managerial accounting.

From the viewpoint of accounting structure, traditional accounting knowledge hinges on the periodic control of term profit; existing optionally are project-type controls, such as life-cycle costing and product-specific calculation, under the heading "special cost accounting."

In the case of Toyota, product control via cost planning is implemented meticulously at the model planning and design stage, the cost thereby being virtually determined before manufacture. This means that there is less room for control intervention at the operational stage.

The operational stage is controlled by the Toyota Production System (TPS), which is a control system of people and "genchi genbutsu;" the result is the realization of profit as targeted. Therefore, those involved in operations do not need to know what the target profit is. This does not mean that there is only loose control over profit. Instead of profit, which is an indirect indicator, the system works on the premise that so long as control over people and "genchi genbutsu" is implemented, the resultant accounting profit will inevitably be realized. In this sense, the drive toward profit realization is after all a stringent one.

Let us delve further into the characteristics of the knowledge model of "traditional accounting knowledge," down to the level of epistemology. The traditional accounting framework is based on reductionism, or the separate and independent existence of observer and observed. In contrast, Process KPI is based on the stance of interactionism, which believes that observer and observed are in a mutually bonding or interdependent relation (Johnson and Bröms, 2000).

Interactionist knowledge has its origins in the 1920s, within quantum mechanics in theoretical physics. From the second half of the 1980s, it became accepted as standard knowledge in complexity adaptation theory and molecular biology (Waldrop, 1992). Likewise in the theory of production, Just-In-Time and restriction theory, which regard the individual manufacturing process not as a non-continuous entity but as an interdependent continuous entity, are becoming the *de facto* standard (Goldratt and Cox, 1992).

In the mature mega-competitive environment, what is needed is a breakthrough mentality that transcends the dualistic framework of "manager and managed" and pushes with the attitude of all-out war to tear down the barrier of limitation. The need has now arisen to incorporate into management process "a mechanism that ignites the world of tacit knowledge itself."

An additional notable feature of Process KPI that was unknown to traditional managerial accounting is the "front-loading of risk management." In other words, the early detection of management risk. The traditional financial indicator KPI was a result indicator that pointed to the results of business activity and was a lagging indicator of risk, whereas Process KPI is a leading indicator of risk, a current indicator that expresses the here and now of a business process in an inclusive and multi-faceted manner. The quintessence of Process KPI as discussed in this paper is the early detection of signs of risk by looking at the curves of the measured values of Process KPI, dealing with risk quickly as it becomes apparent. Process KPI could therefore be called a "feed-forward indicator."

To summarize, Process KPI belongs to a management philosophy that is totally different in nature, alien to budget-control type indicator control management using ROI and such tools of traditional managerial accounting. There are four striking characteristics of Process KPI: (1) it is underpinned by product control: it is not period-based; (2) it takes no recourse to operation control through accounting indicators; (3) rather, it emphasizes control of the tacit knowledge domain that extends beyond the reach of indicators; and (4) it is geared toward front-loading of risk management.

Let us now discuss the architecture of management information as conceived by Process KPI.

21.2.2 Hierarchical model of management information in Process KPI

Figure 21.1 is a conceptual device of Process KPI, incorporating knowledge of complexity that refers to "a hierarchy of science on a different plane, wherein the most fundamental information is found at the very base and non-fundamental information is on top" (Gell-Mann, 1994).

The model in Figure 21.1 conveys the fact that old-style management could attempt control of Levels 2 and 3, but was unable to directly control Level 1, whereas new management strictly limits itself to measurement on Levels 2 and 3 and seeks to design a management mechanism such that control occurs in a self-initiating and autonomous manner on Level 1.

Level 1, at the bottom of the hierarchy, is the deepest level and constitutes the frontline of marketing, technology and production. We can view this level as a group comprising non-data scene information, for example mechanical breakdown, work running short, and complaint calls from customers, in the state before they are transformed into data.

If we describe as "on-site capability" the capacity of instantaneous response to scene information to meet standards and to attain optimization," then, the clear imperative of 21st century product-making management is to create a process design in which the inter-relationships between non-data scene information constituents on Level 1 move dynamically in a self-initiating and autonomous manner, constantly making adjustments toward attaining the overall optimum.

The perfect design of Level 1 is aimed ultimately at eliminating the necessity for Levels 2 and 3. The key to the product-making management in the 21st century is to break free of the conventional mindset that it is important to exercise control by manipulating the indicators of Levels 2 and 3.

Level	Image Type	Information Category	Information Property	Information Subject	Expression Format	Old-style Management	New Management
3	Architectural	Data	Monetary	Accounting info	Numerical	Control	Measurement
2	Descriptive	Data	Quantitative	Production info	Numerical	Control	Measurement
1	Actual	Non-data	Scene/"Genchi genbutsu"	Scene info	Phrase	None	Control

Fig. 21.1 Hierarchy model of management information

Let us refer back to the epistemology of KPI. The upper echelons (Levels 2 and 3) are historical consequences that appear after the lower levels. The moment the condition of Level 1 is turned into a typical data indicator, many of the constituents of relational information from Level 1 fall below the level of vision of the people working on Level 2 and are forgotten.

Although it may be possible to siphon scene information upward to higher levels, it would be impossible to control scene information from the upper levels. This is an irreversible process. In principle, it is not possible to control Level 1 from Level 2 in a reductionistic way.

Above all, we are no longer in the era of planned/mass production, when the production process was relatively stable. Under the conditions of order/product type/quantity variation, existing calculation technology is incapable of measuring, for instance, when and to what extent the process kaizen (improvement) conducted in a certain process on Level 1 would show itself quantitatively in cost and profit in accounting terms on Level 3. The complexity of the situation has multiplied astronomically.

In reproach to the over-reaction toward the scientific quality control proposition of the 20th century, which said "let the data speak the facts," 21st century management should perhaps disseminate the proposition, "you must not let data control the domain of tacit knowledge."

To continue the explanation of the hierarchical model of management information, let us suppose that the core tacit knowledge of TPS on Level 1 is a proposition encapsulated in the phrasal expression, "adjust to the speed of the following process."

On Level 1, in accordance with this proposition, innumerable "relational networks" are spread throughout the process, and scene information is at work. Next, on Level 2, Level 1's phrase "adjust to the speed of the following process" is turned into a data indicator on a quantitative level, in the form of "Tact-Time," a term used in Toyota to refer to the time which should be taken to produce a component or vehicle.

Furthermore, in the higher level, Level 3, the quantitative information of Tact-Time is changed into monetary information, such as work-in-progress turnover. Thus a chain of meaning that links all three levels is formed. Level 1 projects the "actual image" of the process, Level 2 the "descriptive image" and Level 3 the "architectural image."

Gaps constantly open up between these three images. It is important to constantly adjust and renew the lens of Process KPI so that the actual image is correctly projected. In other words, Process KPI must in itself reflect the changes in the management environment and the terms and conditions of orders, and must be of a nature such that the content and importance of these elements are revised moment by moment. There is nothing more dangerous to the survival of an organization than a decayed or rigidified KPI.

21.2.3 *The aims of Process KPI*

TPS's proposition of adjusting to the speed of the following process is, to put it another way, to realize "a seamless flow of goods," even in order-made production. This seamless flow of goods means, in other words, that goods do not come to a halt. In reality, randomness of load, error in reading or other trouble tends to cause the flow to falter. Inventory is an expedient used to prevent this flow stoppage from becoming a problem. The core aspiration of TPS is to prevent the occurrence of gaps without using of inventory. (Even at Toyota, this core task is not necessarily 100% achieved, and stock is deployed at crucial points on the line.)

The flow is especially apt to be interrupted in the border regions between different functions. Therefore, Process KPI sets out to designate KPI in these interface regions, with a view to ensuring non-interruption of flow.

If the production organization is divided by functional sections and responsibility centers, each section or center becomes an "octopus trap" and what results is a "spatial constriction" of the scope of human vision. When such an octopus trap works only in accordance with a person's own convenience or guesswork, the flow stops immediately and information quality deteriorates.

When the head office emphasizes period performance and the line overreacts to this, short-termism holds sway, leading to "temporal constriction" of the scope of human vision.

Thus, the aim of Process KPI is to release human vision from spatial and temporal constrictions. It digs deeply, delving into KPI associated with the interface between different functions, until it reaches the network of relationships in the frontmost line and the deepest level of the actual scene aspect of Level 1. Delving does not mean mere analysis. It means persistent pursuit until a path is formed that autonomously evolves the relationships among operational functions that surround the workplace.

It then becomes possible for all those involved in a job with a certain operational function to perceive the overall state of the process through Process KPI and to realize wherein lie the challenges of "muri," "muda," "mura" (meaning: overburden, non-value added, unevenness); this leads to everyone involved in the process sharing awareness of the problem, breaking organizational barriers and creating a condition in which autonomous kaizen occurs. This is surely what a "healthy organization" is. Next, let's take a look at "autonomy," essential to a healthy organization.

21.2.4 *What is autonomy?*

In the design and operation of Process KPI, autonomy is a key word: an analogy can be made with the way nerve cells of the autonomous nervous system work on their own to maintain the overall optimum without receiving any command from the cerebrum.

The autonomous evolution of TPS can be illustrated by Toyota's purchasing. Toyota does not simply choose a supplier that is cheap in price, but finds a supplier that it perceives as having the potential for further development if given training. The chosen supplier will at first be trained using the "design drawing on-loan method." In the next step, a designer may be dispatched from Toyota so as to enable the supplier to acquire the necessary technology. Eventually, the supplier is allowed to draw its own design under the "design approval method." This evolution takes place over the long-term development process of a ten-year cycle.

Shibata and Kaneda (2002) claim that "the procedure of the Toyota-style system of change means colleague group activity." Taking up the case of Taiichiro Ono's "Incorporation of the Autonomous Nervous System into the Production System," they explain how the Toyota system of corporate innovation is conducted. The place where the seeds of such autonomy are sown and nurtured within the organization is most certainly the "non-data world of the tacit knowledge level," described earlier as Level 1. The seven items listed in Figure 21.2 can be cited as conditions that encourage autonomic evolution in Level 1.

Conditions (1)–(7) would be satisfactory requisites of autonomic evolution. As Level 1 management, most should be commitments of the shop-floor line, as frontline players.

Next, it is important to build the IT portal mentioned in (2). Process KPI now presents a highly promising vista if it can be combined with IT, which has rapidly evolved in recent years thanks largely to the development of the web. That is, by speedily gathering KPI information from various information sources scattered throughout the process and turning them into a format that enables comparison, the reality within the process

(1) Standardization of procedure that makes visible the scene information contained in the deepest level of the process, the relational network; the path to attain tacit knowledge, and its current status
(2) Existence of an IT portal (system) of Process KPI in the visualized state
(3) Creation of activity framework that expressly forms the operation program of kaizen within the company
(4) Presence of a Knowledge Manager who leads KPI information content and system revision, maintenance and management, and creation of the operation program for kaizen
(5) *Post facto* incorporation of kaizen operation program in to organization, policies of individuals and mission statement
(6) Multifaceted evaluation, in human resources management terms, of results of kaizen operation program
(7) Existence of medium to long-term vision that gives common directionality to thinking behind kaizen operation program

Fig. 21.2 Conditions promoting autonomic evolution in Level 1

and the kaizen task can be visualized (called "mieruka" by Toyota) or, in other words, be brought within sight with an accuracy, frequency and scale expansion hitherto unknown.

Above all, the presence of a system designer familiar with all levels of management information, but particularly well versed in the circumstances that prevail in Level 1, is crucial. It is the designer that makes it possible to proceed while checking that the kaizen activity conducted is not a partial optimization in octopus-trap fashion, but is contributing toward overall process optimization.

Lastly, it goes without saying that support from top management and head office, listed under (7), is absolutely essential.

21.3 Introducing Process KPI

21.3.1 *Standard implementation procedure of Process KPI project*

As shown in Figure 21.3, (1)–(5) is a standard implementation procedure for actually introducing process KPI into process management, generalizing the method adopted at Toyota Motor Corporation.

(1) Identify the important business processes that operate cross-sectionally within the corporate organization; then, with respect to each process, create a Total Link System Chart (TLSC) so that the complete picture of work flow and data flow of each key process can be visualized.

(2) From the TLSC, list the KPI that is already operational or any item that can be used in future as promising KPI, then weigh the impact each would have on the performance ofthe entire company so as to assess importance; finally,designate the priority KPI.

(3) Analyze the interrelationship and cause-and-effect relationship of the selected KPI using work flow and real data analysis; based on the result, organize and draw up a Process KPI System Chart; this relational analysis will more or less enable localizationof the problem and revealits nature.

(4) Pinpoint the problem that requires kaizen within the operational process concerned, by observing changes in the performance levels of each KPI, their inter relations and cause-and-effect relations; define the problem and conduct a deep search for the root cause of the problem.

(5) Based on the results of (1)–(4) above, create a Process KPI system as an IT portal; make this accessible as an information sharing tool to all staff involved in work related to the relevant operational process; using the perspective of (4) as a starting point, induce awareness and autonomic kaizen of the problem within each operational process.

Fig. 21.3 Standard implementation procedure of Process KPI project

The normal implementation procedure of Process KPI is as follows. At first glance this may seem to be pretty much common sense, but what should be noted is that there may be a big difference in result, depending on the meticulousness and thoroughness of implementation; in other words, the weighting of impact on performance of the company as a whole in (2), analysis of the relationship between KPI in (3) and definition of the issues that require kaizen and deep search for the real cause of problems in (4). We wish to emphasize that the success of Process KPI depends especially on interactive benefit, with relation to the mechanism of "autonomy."

21.3.2 *General operability of Process KPI*

How far can Process KPI be generally extended in application? We now discuss the process characteristics that would be suitable for Process KPI utilization.

Let us think of corporate process properties by dividing them into two groups. First, there is the multiple type product business, such as the electronic device industry; then there is the single-product business, such as the automobile industry. The former generally uses a self-completing organizational management format for each product. The profit center is clearly identified and responsibility is allocated by separating centers using financial target KPI. When using this type of vertically organized format, traditional managerial accounting employing divisional performance assessment can function relatively effectively.

By contrast, a single-product business such as car manufacturing requires the establishment of a gapless flow in the process functions of technological development, purchasing, manufacturing and sales, so that there is no break in flow of goods and information. The different arms and functions of the company must move smoothly in coordination. The processes of close contact and detailed discussion become vital, as the majority of the line production processes are linked together in a network of interrelationships across the entirety of the sub-line chains, thus being mutually dependent and mutually interacting.

There is a limit as to how far one can arbitrarily cut up such an organization into independent management units, such as a profit center, or to make different constituents compete against each other. Not only that, there is the danger that such an attempt would be counterproductive, diminishing the mobility of an organic body or impeding the sharing of know-how. Rather, the most effective and crucial step in management would be to introduce Process KPI management in a cross-organizational way, along the lines of the priority operational processes; in other words, by implementing process management that aims to achieve the overall optimum through kaizen that focuses on the interface between different functions.

21.4 Conclusion

This paper has argued that Process KPI is aimed at creating a new manufacturing management paradigm that transcends the 20th century views on management and initiates innovative kaizen autonomously. In conclusion, we touch upon the future challenges facing this Process KPI approach.

The first challenge is to achieve greater efficiency in transforming into formalized knowledge such things as scene information found at the deepest level that stimulates information sharing and awareness, the real images and world of tacit knowledge within the process, and the network of interrelationships. The present method of discovering the optimal KPI of the interfaces between functional divisions is only close liaison and finalization through thorough dialog and inter-functional communication.

What is more, a market risk identification method and its procedure must be established. Then, there is the standardization method, as well as the visualization method of how best to truly and accurately convey the current situation in a readily understandable manner. A method is required to systematize these tasks. All of these need to undergo repeated processes of hypothesis, experiment and verification, achieving evolution by relying on partial success while adopting a preemptive approach.

The second of the big challenges facing Process KPI is how to create a framework for constantly and actively initiating autonomic kaizen. There is much scope for consideration and improvement, namely the creation of an operation program that induces autonomic kaizen activities and a method of firmly establishing such a program, the policies of the management body, compatibility with mission management and determining the ideal way of designing a Process KPI system that maintains stability while undergoing unstable change.

The shareholder value-based management and managerial accounting that prevailed in the 20th century tended to excessively promote interest in short-term financial results. In the competitive environment of the 21st century, a precondition for survival would be to hone the skills of management in dealing with "real-time," which is even more immediate than short-term, and in taking account of the medium to long-term, which is farther ahead of short-term. As well, there remains a challenge for Toyota Motor Corporation itself, that of linking real-time with the medium to long-term, using Process KPI as the medium, which is equivalent to taking TPS, which TMC and everybody else interpreted as manufacturing know-how, and sublimating it into a management system.

References

Chandler, A. (1997). *Visible Hand — The Managerial Revolution in American Business*, Belknap Harvard.

Drucker, P. (1993). *Post Capitalist Society*, Butterworth Heinemann.

Fujimoto, T. (1997). *Evolutionary Theory of Production Systems*, Yuhikaku. (In Japanese)

Gell-Mann, M. (1994). *The Quark and the Jaguar — Adventures in the Simple and the Complex*, W. H. Freeman & Co.

Goldratt, E. M. and Cox, J. (1992). *The Goal — A Process of Ongoing Improvement*, The North River Press.

Goldratt, E. M. (1997). *Critical Chain*, The North River Press.

Johnson, T. and Bröms, A. (2000). *Profit Beyond Measure — Extraordinary Results through Attention to Work and People*, The Free Press.

Kaneda, H. and Shibata, M. (2002). *Strongest Management Toyota Style — Why Toyota Keeps Changing*, Nihon Keizai Shimbunsha. (In Japanese)

Kaneda, H. (1997). *Instabilization Theory Innovates Companies — Toyota-style Paradigm*, Pal Publishing. (In Japanese)

Kauffman, S. (1995). *At Home in the Universe — The Search for Laws of Self-organization and Complexity*, Oxford University Press.

Kauffman, S. (2000). *Investigations*, Oxford University Press.

Kawada, S. (1996). *Product Management Accounting — New Framework for Production System and Accounting*, Chuo Keizaisha. (In Japanese)

Kawada, S. (2001). Product value assessment approach and knowledge management, *Meijo Discourse* 1-4, pp. 5–25. (In Japanese)

Konno, N. and Nonaka, I. (1995). *Knowledge Power Management*, Nihon Keizai Shimbunsha. (In Japanese)

Okano, H. (2002). *Development of Japanese-style Managerial Accounting — Historical Perspective on "Cost Planning"*, 2nd edition, Chuo Keizaisha. (In Japanese)

Tasaka, H. (1997). *Management of Complex Systems*, Toyo Keizai Shimposha. (In Japanese)

Toyota Motor Corporation (June 26, 2002). News from Toyota, Toyota Motor Corporation PR Division. (In Japanese)

Yoro, T. (2002). *Human Science*, Chikuma Shobo. (In Japanese)

Waldrop, M. (1992). *Complexity — The Emerging Science at the Edge of Order and Chaos*, Touchstone.

CHAPTER

22

A Combinational Model for Organizational Change

Mohammad Aghdasi
Associate Professor, School of Engineering
Tarbiat Modares University

Farzad Movahedi Sobhani
Researcher, School of Engineering
Tarbiat Modares University

22.1 Introduction

Can an organization change for the better without accepting "learning" as a principle and incorporating it into its agenda? According to Garvin (1993): "Solving a problem, introducing a product, and reengineering a process, all require seeing the world in a new light and acting accordingly. In the absence of learning, companies and individuals repeat old practice. Change remains cosmetic, and improvements are either fortuitous or short-lived."

The term learning as an organizational phenomenon has existed in management literature in the last 50 years, but it was only when Senge introduced learning organization concept in his book *The Fifth Discipline* that the essential tools for incorporating learning in a change process, were systematically brought together. Senge (1990, p. 1) described learning organization, as places, "Where people continually expand their capacity to create the results they truly desire, where new and expansive patterns of thinking are nurtured, where collective aspiration is set free, and where people are continually learning how to learn together."

To achieve these ends, Senge (1990) suggests the use of the following five "disciplines:" systems thinking, personal mastery, mental models, shared vision, team learning.

In the last two decades many business executives have mastered these learning disciplines and have begun to reorganize the process of change around them. In such companies, organization change is done through the development of skills and proficiencies — learning capability — among individuals, teams, and larger communities, which improve the capacity of people for producing the results that are really important to them.

Making changes through enhancement of learning capabilities among individuals, teams, and work groups is another camp for organizational change that Sugarman (2001) has called *learning based approach to change* and Senge has mentioned its dynamism in his book *The Dance of Change.* In this camp, change is self-sustaining and does not depend on a heroic CEO.

The principles and theories of change in a learning based approach are different from those of a traditional approach. Sugarman (2001a), through a comparison of these two approaches, has shown them to be as two contrary models that are based on two different theories. He has concluded: "The two contrasting models that I identify are: (1) the "Push" model (short term, top-down, financial emphasis) versus (2) the "Grow" model (longer term, building up of capacity, with a human resource perspective)."

In the same way, Beer (2001) has determined two theories or strategies — E and O — for change. Theory E is a hard approach to change and involves heavy use of economical incentives, drastic layoffs, downsizing, and restructuring. Executives, who subscribe to E strategy, manage change the traditional way: from the top down. They set goals with little involvement and input from lower levels. On the contrary O change strategy is based on organizational capability. It is a soft approach to change and is focused around culture and the behavior of the employees.

Both Sugarman (2001a) and Beer (2000) have led to the conclusion that the most successful change initiatives would come about as the result of a positive combination of these two approaches. Beer (2000) ascertains: "Clearly, if the objective is to build a company that can adapt, survive, and prosper over the years, theory E strategies must somehow be combined with theory O strategies. But unless they're carefully handled, melding E and O is likely to bring the worst of both theories and the benefits of neither."

In this chapter we introduce a practical example of combinational model and show how appropriate combination of these two models can offer a practical model for organizational change. This model was developed based on a research done by Tarbiat Modarres University and Iran Khodro Company[1] (IKCO), one of the leading Iranian companies in automobile industry. The objective of this research is to provide a better understanding of organizational change process in Iran's industries.

It is important that a word of caution be added in regard to this study. We believe that all organizational change models are context depended, and thus the details of every successful change model will not necessarily be applicable to other organizations or companies per se. Nevertheless, the readers will benefit from this study and will find a host of constructive ideas and concepts which can be used for designing and implementing an appropriate organizational change model applicable to their own companies.

22.2 Case Study

Iran Khodro Co. was established in 1965 by the private sector in Iran. The government took over its ownership and management after the Islamic revolution of Iran in 1979. The State management style, the war between Iran and Iraq and the economic stagnation in the aftermath of the war, made the company a mere single-product assembly line with time-worn technology with little responsiveness towards the customers' needs. Moreover, because of domestic market demand pressures, there were very little attention paid to quality control, customer satisfaction and reliable services. After the war and the economical reconstruction and as a result of new socioeconomic conditions, IKCO faced new challenges and some crises. Accordingly weaknesses were felt in the area of meeting the customer needs. The CEO of the company in 1994 decided and planned three change strategies: (1) changing from a mere assembling line company to an independent car manufacturer; (2) product diversification; and (3) quality improvement and productivity enhancement.

However, due to particular organizational and contextual relations that existed, IKCO faced serious difficulties in implementing of the above-mentioned change strategies. The dominant workplace mentality that existed in IKCO was a traditionally governmental way of thinking and

[1]Iran Khodro (IKCO), with the production of more than six hundred thousand cars in different models per year, is one of the largest automotive companies in the Middle East. IKCO strives to become a global automotive company with a production capacity of more than one million cars per year.

the employees did not see any relations between their individual performances and organizational results. Employees in the technical and production departments had many years of experience and consider themselves as the sole experts in their own particular fields. Therefore talking about any changes to the existing working methods were not simply acceptable or possible. The organizational structure was a very complex one with many different layers of hierarchical management and a complicated power structure. Any possible changes to the existing status of employees in organization would have confronted serious resistance. Furthermore, the governmental rules and regulations didn't permit downsizing and drastic layoffs, and all the employees had secure job positions. Making fundamental changes that challenged the existing formal and informal power structure would have caused serious organizational tensions. Strategically, due to the particular political and socioeconomic conditions that existed, the automotive industry was the center of attention which prevented the CEO to make any serious decisions.

Owing to all the above-mentioned contextual factors, deploying any changes by Push and top-down approaches, would have been very venturesome. On the other hand, using any Grow model was confronted by time restriction and the prior leaning limitations. In such situation, the CEO at the time decided to implement changes through a combination of Grow or O strategy and Push or E strategy. To achieve this goal, since the development of many other organizational capabilities depended on the enhancement of new product development capability, the enhancement of this capability was selected as a lever of change. Since IKCO was basically facing with a lack of practical experience in new product development and also the essential organization infrastructures for teamwork were not available, the following two strategies were decided on:

1. The establishment of an Isolation Center in the heart of the company as a liable place for enhancing of the new product development capability (Push).
2. Creating a learning environment for acquiring external knowledge and transferring it to the company (Grow).

Acquiring new product development capability at this center, made a suction force for developing supplementary capabilities, at the rest of the company. The employees of the center, that until that time, were isolated, gradually, got involved with the entire company, in order to disseminate

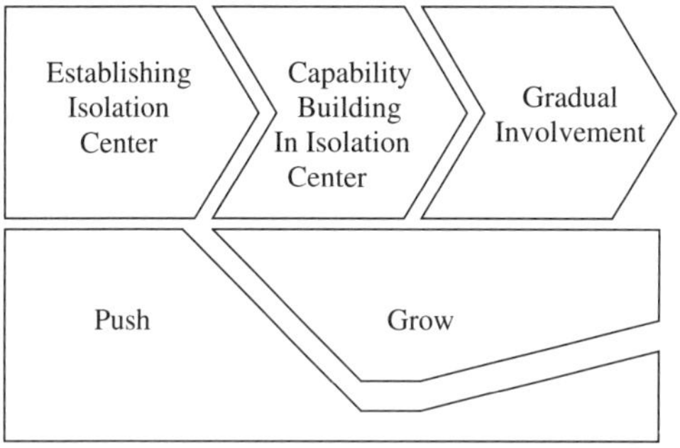

Fig. 22.1 Organizational change process in IKCO

the acquired capabilities. The consequences of this suction and dissemination dynamism caused other organizational elements such as internal processes, social relationships, customer relations, and supplier relations, to change accordingly. In fact, during this process, the formation of new product development capabilities performed a key role in bringing about the developments in the company (Figure 22.1).

In order to build organizational capability in Isolation Center and activate suction process, a set of technological components and dynamisms were designed and implemented. Some of these components are based on Grow strategy, some are based on Push strategy, and some are based on a combination of both strategies.

22.2.1 *Highlighting organizational achievements for the employees*

Creating interest and incentives in employees and motivating them to reach for higher organizational achievements, was one of the goals in creation and development of Isolation Center. What gave impetus to the efforts of employees for organizational success was personal needs for success and aspirations that caused shared vision. It was necessary that the employees be informed of their aspirations and create a common goal and a shared sense of understandings for the organizational achievements. This occurred in Isolation Center through creating an informal and friendly atmosphere among employees. At this casual environment, employees talked about their real aspirations and commitments, and allowed their colleagues to evaluate the governing variables and dominant frameworks. The creation of this cordial and informal relationship among employees and managers led to an indirect, but effective system, through which common understandings of organizational and personal results could be evaluated consequently.

In fact, this dynamism functions as a tool that defines and clarifies individual aspiration and aligns it with organizational goals and results. Without such measures, people are not motivated to enter the process of changing their previous ways of thinking and doing work. This dynamism is based on Grow model or O strategy of change, whose objective is to reinforce the process of building learning capability among employees.

22.2.2 *Sustaining the importance of organizational achievements for employees*

Although creating a shared vision is important, it is equally important and even essential to make sure it is sustained and dealt with as an ongoing process. This job was carried out in the Isolation Center by the top level management. Because of the sensitivity of the management toward the success of the Isolation Center and its well-being, the employees' psychological condition was always the center of attention. This attention was mostly paid implicitly and through an indirect evaluation system by interpretation and expounding of the occurred events. These interpretations were exchanged and discussed in various meetings of top level management and necessary decisions were taken.

The most important result of this indirect evaluation system was that it gave impetus to the top level management to show more support for organizational results. The CEO's support and encouragement was conveyed to the employees through an internal system of communication. The internal communication system had at least three functions.

The first function was that the employees were informed of the importance of organizational results and top management's commitments. This was carried out through periodical visits by top management, general meetings and use of internal and external publications. At this function, the internal communication system also played a supplementary role to the indirect evaluation system, and whenever this implicit evaluation system showed a decline in the morale, measures were taken to boost the collective commitments of the employees.

The second function of the internal communication was highlighting the importance of organizational results from a national point of view and the reinforcement of employees' commitment. This function was usually carried out through the public media which was helpful in boosting the commitment of employees and in turn in enhancing their abilities.

The third function of the internal communication system was informing the employees body and focusing attention on the organizational achievements. Informing employees of their organizational achievements led to their motivation and a higher level of commitment on their part and strengthened their continued support. This function generally was done through public and periodical meetings.

Taking care of creating shared vision is a supplementary process for the highlighting dynamism. According to this dynamism, the CEO Pushes the organizational goals into lower levels. However, they do this duty, not through hard approaches but by soft approaches that assure employees of management's commitments and their support.

22.2.3 *Surfacing and challenging individual deep rooted assumptions*

During the process of capability building, it is sometimes necessary that the employees surface and challenge deep rooted assumptions that have become embedded in individual and organizational frameworks and routines. Criticism of frameworks and routines, when employees have not acquired enough learning capabilities, would seldom happen by itself. So the leadership of the organization should find some appropriate techniques for such situations. The following methods and techniques were applied in the Isolation Center.

22.2.4 *Providing an atmosphere of observing the results*

The dynamism of challenging the deep rooted assumptions will be activated when the employees can see the result of their performance. The use of virtual experimental environment, such as simulation and or real environment tests, can help employees see the results of their performance. Without seeing the results almost there will be no feedback to reflect the individuals' dominant frameworks and routines.

But seeing the results are not the only needed condition and it is also necessary to establish relation between results and rooted assumptions. In companies that employees have not acquired enough learning capabilities, this duty will be carried out by the leaders. The technique that was employed in Isolation Center was creating an open atmosphere of discussion which was promoted through friendly formal meetings and informal gatherings. These meetings and gatherings were the most important techniques for surfacing and challenging the rooted assumptions in Isolation Center. In every meeting the results were discussed and the causes of the mistakes were studied and examined.

Generally organizing such meetings was faced with some difficulties, because the employees didn't permit criticism of their dominant frameworks and routines, but consequently, presenting the result of their performances in real and virtual environments aided them to reflect on their mental models. Moreover instilling a sense of confidence in employees for accepting risks was very essential in order to create a fear free environment of making mistake and accepting their responsibilities in this regard.

In the environments that employees are penalized for making mistakes, process of challenging dominant frameworks are rarely formed. In such environments, employees want to justify rather than find out the causes of their faults. In order to prevent such cases, the Isolation Center assured employees that making a mistake is not a crime, but making a mistake, hiding it and moreover repeating it, can be considered a misdeed.

The tools and techniques that are used under this dynamism create some kinds of learning capability to aid individuals for reflecting on their mental models. Aiding people to reflect on their mental models is the key component of the Grow approach. However, it is obvious that in Isolation Center, this does not happen unless the top management get involved and promote their ideas for creating a constructive atmosphere for observing results, an open discussion and a fear free environment.

22.2.5 *Energizing the employees*

The process of building capabilities is difficult, time consuming, and challenging. Moreover, the fact that results do not immediately follow actions and it takes some time for them to show effect, makes it even more complex. In such situations, employees' level of motivation in getting involved in exploration process is constantly threatened. When the employees' level of motivation diminish, they are less inclined to get involved in problems solving process. Learning process will also slow down and finally process of capabilities building might eventually collapsed.

In Isolation Center the task of energizing the employees and making sure that they stay motivated was delegated to those leaders that had been able to earn the employees' respect and trust and therefore could act as a role model to them.

22.2.6 *The role of Leaders' real commitment in setting example*

Most of employees look up to the leaders, adopt their methods and performance style as their own work patterns and are prepared to follow their direction as their workplace role models. Leaders' sincere commitment and their adherence to the standards they promote and an overall positive performance will provide a role model for employees and encourage them to strive more and get involved in the process of exploration and change. This was achieved through many techniques such as the system of internal communication. However, the formal techniques only played a small role. More important factor was the setting an example by the leaders through their overall performance at work. Developing relationships among families, group tours and business trips, are some other methods that can be employed to energize the employees and maintain and maximize their level of motivation.

In fact, the leaders at IKCO played according to the roles and responsibilities set in both approaches (Grow and Push). The CEO moves the organization forward and convey the organizational vision to the lower levels and simultaneously acts as a role model.

22.2.7 *Information distribution and communication capacity*

The information exchange method in Isolation Center was both formal and informal. Although the managers emphasized on the efficiency of the formal methods, but in practice, there were some efficient but informal ways of information distribution. Formal methods such as archives, weekly seminars, documentation etc., and also some informal methods such as friendly atmosphere, that enhanced the capacity of organization for information exchange.

According to Grow model, increasing the capacity of information distribution enhances employees' awareness in all fields of their work. The improvement of this aspect also provided the organizational achievements that consequently enhanced the individual results and the level of motivation for more exchanges of information.

22.2.8 *Suction process and shadow teams*

The process of acquiring new product development capability, will be done in at least two layers, the first layer was related to research and development. In IKCO, the first layer mostly was developed in the Isolation Center. The second layer was related to acquisition of the skills of manufacturing in production workshops. Unlike the employees of the Isolation Center, all employees of production workshops had worked and developed in the old culture of the company. Thus, according to new requirement, changes in some of existing methods of manufacturing workshops were inevitable. Most of the employees in the past years had used the existing methods and had become skillful in them. Any criticism of such methods would have led to their annoyance and met their defensive reactions. Making changes to these methods required a lot of time and energy. To overcome this challenge and bring about new methods, shadow teams were utilized. They were groups of employees trained at the Isolation Center whose mission was to convince the production employees of the importance of learning and applying new methods. Moreover, shadow teams took it upon themselves to enhance the individual learning capacity and familiarize the individuals with new technologies by introducing individuals to new tools and methods. To achieve this goal, shadow teams developed friendly relationships with employees without interfering with their routine work. They not only had a major constructive impact on the work teams but also were successful in creating a positive atmosphere for exchanging information and sharing knowledge.

Cooperating with the work teams accompanied by presenting new methods, enhanced the capacity of the employees for accepting criticism of the existing methods. By the same token, becoming aware of new demands and difficulties related to the old methods helped them greatly in realizing the need to change old working methods.

Shadow teams and suction process provided a powerful mechanism that is based on combination of Grow and Push approaches for dissemination of acquired organizational capability in the company.

22.3 Organizational Capability Based Approach to Change

The studied model presented for organizational change is a compound approach that is created from a combination of the two theories of Push and Grow approaches to change. Some properties of this approach have been compared with the other two approaches, suggested by Sugarman (2001a),

	Organizational capability based	Learning based	Push model
Leadership	Local change leader who are supported strongly by top manager	Local change leader	Top manager
Change leverage	Organizational capability and suction process	Creating new business model through learning teams	Executive authority to change structure
Learning Type	Double loop learning especially at local change leader	Double loop learning	Single loop learning
Driver	Individual aspiration and demands	Personal mastery intrinsic motivation	Empowerment

Fig. 22.2 Comparison of capability based approach with Push and Grow model

and have been reviewed in Figure 22.2. Since building of organizational capability acts as a lever of change, the mentioned approach is called Organizational Capability Based Approach to change.

According to Figure 22.2 organizational capability based approach can benefit local leaders and support top managers. The change lever is organizational capability in order to achieve better performance. The change process initiates with some interventions in organization structure. Learning in low layers of organization is single loop[2] and in top layers, particularly in top management, is double loop.[3] The change driver in capability based approach is personal aspiration and demands.

As pilot group and personal aspiration, have vital roles in capability based approach, so it is similar to the Grow model. It is also similar to the traditional model in being top-down and because of selecting the type of organizational capability and preparing a proper place by top management.

[2]Single loop learning occurs when errors are detected and corrected and individuals/organizations carry on with their present policies.
[3]Double loop learning occurs when, in addition to detection and correction of errors, the individual/organization is involved in the questioning and modification of existing norms, procedures, policies, and objectives.

Furthermore, the Isolation Center will not be run autonomously in the same way as pilot group in learning based approach, and the top management sometimes interferes in its management.

Accordingly, the model of capability based approach is as follows:

1. Choosing an effective organizational capability with total chain of supplementary capabilities by top management.
2. Establishing a proper place for the development of organizational capabilities (if a proper culture and organizational infrastructure for capability building didn't exit, the place should be as an isolated department).
3. Development of leadership capacity.
4. Designing and implementing of proper organizational learning tools and techniques.
5. Creation of suction dynamism.

22.4 Summary and Conclusion

The aim of this chapter is to provide a combination model of organizational change that draws from the two approaches of change (Grow and Push). Furthermore, this chapter demonstrates how a successful change needs learning capability.

Background and a brief descriptive overview of technological components of the model were covered. Comparing technological components with organizational learning literature shows some similarities. In fact, the component of highlighting organizational achievements for the individuals is equal to the concept of shared vision, introduced by Senge (1990), Templeton (2002), and Goh (2003, 1997). The component of sustaining and taking care of the importance of organizational achievements for individuals is equal to creative tension of Senge (1990). The component of challenging and surfacing rooted assumption, is equal to mental models of Kim (1993), Senge (1990), and the double loop learning of Argyris (1999). Representing the sincere commitment and energy of the leadership, implies the leadership commitment and empowerment of Goh (1997, 2003). The open discussion atmosphere and information distribution implies the dissemination of Yeung (1999) and the social learning of Templeton (2002). The component of enhancement of accepting criticism from current methods implies the personal mastery of Senge (1990).

These findings reveal a kind of proficiency and skill or learning capability accompanying the organizational change process.

References

Ackoff, R. L. (1999). On learning and the systems that facilitate it, *Reflection* 1-1, pp. 14–24.

Argyris, C. (1997). Initiating change that preserver, *American Behavioral Scientist* 40-3, pp. 299–311.

Argyris, C. (1999). *On Organizational Learning*, 2nd ed., Blackwell Publishers Inc.

Beer, M. and Nohria, N. (2000). Cracking the code of change, *Harvard Business Review* 78-3, pp. 133–142.

Berdish, D. (1999). Learning for operational excellence: a manager's story, *Reflection* 1-1, pp. 37–58.

Burke, W. (2002). *Organization Change Theory and Practice*, London: Sage Publication.

Coghlan, D. (2000). The interval dynamics of systemic learning and change, *Reflection* 2, p. 2.

Garvin, D. A. (1993). Building a learning organization, *Harvard Business Review* July–August, pp. 76–81.

Garvin, D. A. (2000). *Learning in Action: A Guide to Putting the Learning Organization to Work*, Boston: Harvard Business Press.

Goh, S. C. (1997). Benchmarking the learning capability of organizations, *European Management Journal* 15-5, pp. 575–583.

Goh, S. C. (2003). Improving organizational learning capability: lessons from two case studies, *The Learning Organization* 10-4, pp. 216–277.

Huy, Q. N. (1999). Emotional capability, emotional intelligence and radical change, *Academy of Management Review* 99, p. 24.

Kim, D. H. (1993). The link between individual learning and organizational learning, *Sloan Management Review* 35-1, pp. 37–51.

Kim, L. (1998). Crisis construction and organizational learning capability building catching-up at Hyundai, *A Journal of the Institute of Management Science* 9-4, pp. 506–522.

Kotter, J. P. (1995). *Leading Change*, Boston: Harvard Business Press.

Nonaka, I. and Takeuchi, H. (1995). *The Knowledge-Creating Company: How Japanese Companies Create the Dynamics of Innovation*, Oxford University Press.

Schein, E. H. (1999). Kurt Lewin's change theory in the field and in the classroom: notes toward a model of managed learning, *Reflections* 1-1, pp. 59–74.

Schreyogg, G. and Noss, C. (2000). Change in organizations: the equilibrium logic and beyond, *Academy of Management Proceedings* 1-7.

Senge, P. (1999). *The Dance of Change — The Challenges of Sustaining Momentum in Learning Organizations*, New York: Doubleday Dell.

Senge, P. (1994). *The Fifth Discipline Fieldbook Strategies and Tools for Building a Learning Organization*, New York: Doubleday Dell.

Senge, P. (1990). *The Fifth Discipline: The Art and Practice of Learning Organization*, New York: Doubleday Dell.

Sugarman, B. (2001). A learning based approach to organizational change: some result and guidelines, *Organizational Dynamic* 30-1, pp. 62–76.

Sugarman, B. (2001a). Push and grow theories in change management: gateways to understanding organizational learning, based on a paper presented at the Fourth International Conference on Organizational Learning and Knowledge Management at the Ivey School of Management, University of Western Ontario.

Templeton, C. F. and Lewis, B. R. (2002). Development of a organizational learning construct, *Journal of Management Information Systems* 19-2, pp. 175–218.

Yeung, A. K. and Ulrich, D. (1999). *Organizational Learning Capability*, Oxford University Press.

CHAPTER

23

Managerial Roles of Financial and Non-Financial Measures in Supply Chain and Engineering Chain Management

Kazuki Hamada

Professor, Department of Commerce
Seinan Gakuin University

23.1 Introduction

SCM regards the business flow (the purchase of materials, production, sales, distribution and the delivery to end users) as a big chain and attains global optimization by managing this business flow. Sometimes one company manages the total supply chain, sometimes several companies do. But actually SCM usually focuses on only a part of the chain, for example only the direct vendors and customers, only the purchase of parts and production, only production, sales and distribution. Also, some SCM aim at global optimization from the view of total supply chain (the global type of SCM); others aim at the optimization of their own companies from the view of own company (the individual type of SCM). I will consider the latter type of SCM especially, and I will lay stress on the view of own company even when considering the optimization in the total supply chain.

Since it has been recently indicated that the connection between the information from customers in supply chains and product development is important, the linkage between SCM and engineering chain management (ECM) is needed. ECM is the information management about the function and the composition of products, and it is the series of chain management from research development and design to purchase, production, and retention regarding technology information. This linkage type is also interpreted as SCM when it includes planning and development in a broad sense.

In this paper, the first, I will consider SCM and ECM by financial measures, then I will indicate the necessity of management by financial and non-financial measures to improve the corporate value from a long term point of view.

23.2 SCM and ECM

23.2.1 *Efficiency improvement type of SCM and market response type of SCM*

SCM is classified into several types, but two of the most important groupings are an efficiency improvement type of SCM and a market response type of SCM. The main subjects of the former SCM are the efficient utilization of facilities, efficient inventory movement, and the reduction of wages and expenses. This type of SCM is led by manufacturers in many cases and adapts to functional products. As the demand of functional products is stable, forecasting is easy. The life cycle of those products is also long and the rate of return per product is low.

On the other side, the main subjects of the latter SCM are the reduction of market adaptation cost (the opportunity cost by supply deficit, the price-cut and sales with loss on cost by oversupply, etc.) and the build-up of a flexible operation process which makes for rapid adaptation. This type of SCM is led by retailers in many cases and is suited to the product whose demand is unstable. The demand of an innovative product is particularly unstable and can hardly be foreseen. Its life cycle is short, and its rate of return per product is high.

However, it is difficult to attain an increase of sales by only the efficiency improvement type of SCM. It is necessary to adapt to the customer's needs for the increase. But the efficient supply can be hardly attained by only the market response type of SCM. In either case, SCM needs to integrate demand chains and supply chains. That is to say, the integrated demand-supply chain management (DSCM) is needed.

23.2.2 *The relationship between SCM and ECM*

When we try to reflect the customer's needs by demand chains, there are two considerations. First, we need to take into account the simple functions and services of product, and second we need to be able to develop new product. In the latter case, it is necessary to integrate SCM and ECM. ECM makes good use of the information from all members of supply chains (suppliers, customers, distribution companies, retailers and so on.) to develop a better product, and ECM also connects the design information with the total supply chain. It is particularly important to integrate SCM with ECM in the case of the market response type.

Traditionally, SCM focuses on the information needed for the current production, sales, and distribution of products, while ECM focuses on essentially the information needed for product development and its technique in future periods. So as the two are different essentially, they are dealt with independently in general. However, recently the shortening of product lead time and the flexible supply of product are demanded because of the rapid change of market needs and the shortening of product life cycle. Accordingly, it is necessary to integrate SCM with ECM as Fig. 23.1 indicates, and it is also necessary for the planning & development department, design department and all members of supply chains to share the information. Information sharing is an important problem as the frequent change of design is essential for supplying products to the market in a short time.

The Internet Platform division in Hitachi, Ltd. adopts PDM (product data management) systems and gives employees all information about the completion of products if necessary. The information is exchanged once per five minutes between PDM systems and SCM systems (Nikkei Sangyou Shinbun, 2002.4.5). Moreover, the information about the proposal of planning and the revision of operation is in a common data base. The persons concerned can comment freely on it and approve. When they approve, the

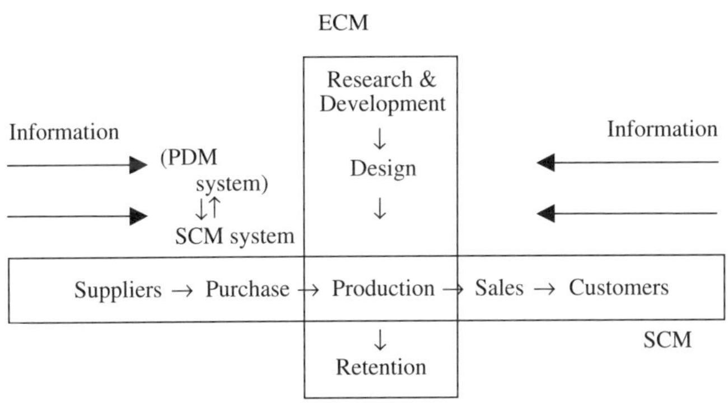

Fig. 23.1 Relationship between SCM and ECM

proposal can also be executed. The more rapid SCM is, the more the burden of planning, development and design operation increases. So it is important to integrate SCM and ECM efficiently.

23.3 SCM and Management by Financial Indicators

23.3.1 *Cost and profit management in supply chains*

I will explain the part of management or total management by financial information in supply chains which have been executed until now. The following can be used for both the individual type of SCM and the global type of SCM. But what I will mention in Sections 23.3.1.1 and 23.3.1.2 has been mainly used when we execute the former type of SCM. The information of total supply chain cost which I will mention in Section 23.3.1.3 is significant in the former type as well as the latter type.

23.3.1.1 *Purchase management by activity-based costing and the total cost of ownership*

If activity-based costing (ABC) is used for purchase management, costs of each supplier and costs of each activity are clarified. The feasibility of cost reduction and how to share cost reduction activities between suppliers and own company are clarified. ABC is useful because there are few costs concerned with unit level outside of purchase price. The costs of orders, receiving, inspection, transportation and payment are concerned with batch level. The costs concerned with designing specifications of materials and parts are costs of product support level. We can also evaluate suppliers if ABC is used. The best supplier is not the company which supplies at the lowest price, but the one which delivers at the lowest purchase related costs (purchase price + costs concerned with purchase).

But the range of the purchase related costs focused by ABC is narrow because they include only the costs of direct purchase activities. On the other hand, the total cost of ownership (TCO) includes not only purchase price and the direct purchase related costs but also the indirect costs which include the usage and maintenance costs of purchase goods, failure costs and so on. Therefore, the range of TCO is broader than the range of costs focused by ABC. Generally speaking, we should consider the cost range broadly like the TCO when we manage and evaluate suppliers. To execute the management by the TCO efficiently, we had better relate with ABC as we need to consider each activity separately. But the TCO does not include the costs of total supply chain because it is subject to purchase activities mainly. Recently analysis shows that it is important that we consider both the improvement of product value and the supplier support costs on top of basic product costs.

23.3.1.2 *Management of each sales channel and customer by ABC*

The costs of each activity in sales channels are computed if ABC is used. So the feasible activities and the amount of cost reduction in each sales channel are clarified. Moreover, discrimination between advantageous channels and disadvantageous ones is feasible and discrimination between advantageous customers and disadvantageous ones is feasible too.

Recently it is important to clarify the costs of the many activities to increase customer value (ex. the technique support for products, the improvement of service level and so on) and how these activities connect with the increase of revenue. We say that it is service to decide the product value. So when a product and services are sold as one, it is more important to analyze costs by ABC and to decide reasonable prices.

23.3.1.3 *Profit management of total supply chains*

We receive the following advantages by computing the costs of total supply chains.

1. Each activity and a process performance can be evaluated from the total view of supply chains.
2. The structures in supply chains can be evaluated and improvement points can be clarified.
3. We can recognize how the improvement of operations and technologies influence the total supply chain cost.
4. It helps to organize total supply chains.
5. It gives the means to allow supply chain members to consider from the total point of view.
6. It helps to decide the allocations of costs and benefits among supply chain members. It is also necessary to clarify how costs create customer value in the cost computation.

Solectron (Handfield and Nichols, 2002, p. 229) computes the total supply chain cost by the following equation.

$$\begin{aligned}\text{Total supply chain cost} &= \text{buying price} + \text{supplier performance cost}\\ &\quad + \text{cost of acquisition} + \text{out-of-sync planning}\\ &\quad - \text{speculation returns(ability to meet upside demands)}\\ &\quad + \text{speculation cost} + \text{manufacturing cost}\\ &\quad + \text{selling cost} + \text{distribution cost.}\end{aligned}$$

"Speculation returns" and "speculation cost" are influenced by the strategic decision of inventories and production capacities and by the degree of correspondent ability. The above equation indicates that cost decreases (profit increases) by several means.

Matsushita Electric Industrial Co. Ltd. computes the total SCM cost intended for stores, sales companies, factories. In this case distribution cost is main. It is as follows.

$$\begin{aligned}\text{Total SCM cost} &= \text{transportation cost} + \text{data processing cost}\\ &\quad + \text{material abolition cost} + \text{operation cost to balance supply}\\ &\qquad \text{with demand/interest of inventories.}\end{aligned}$$

Shiseido Logistics Co. Ltd. (Japan Management Association, 1999) considers not only the means to contribute to all Shiseido group but also the means to increase the profit of own company. To reduce the cost of total group decreasing the sales of Shiseido Logistics Co. Ltd. is needed because the sales of the company is the distribution cost in the view of all Shiseido group, as Figures 23.2 and 23.3 indicate. The company considers the means to decrease the sales and increase the profit simultaneously from this point of view.

In the above example, those companies consider not only the cost of own company but also the supply chain cost in inter-company in decision making. Therefore those companies enlarge the sight of competitive advantage.

If the cost computation by ABC is applied, costs can be traced to activities in detail and can be computed accurately. The step of analysis by ABC is as follows.

1. Analysis of the supply chain process.
2. Dividing the process into activities.
3. Identification of resources (ex. labor, facilities, materials, services and so on) needed to act.

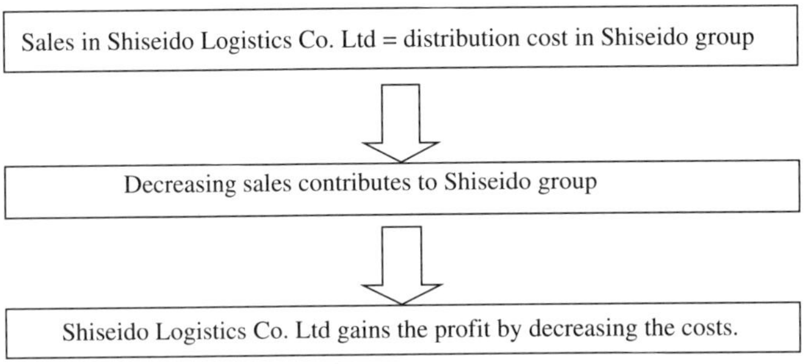

Fig. 23.2 Relationship between Shiseido Logistics Co. Ltd and Shiseido group

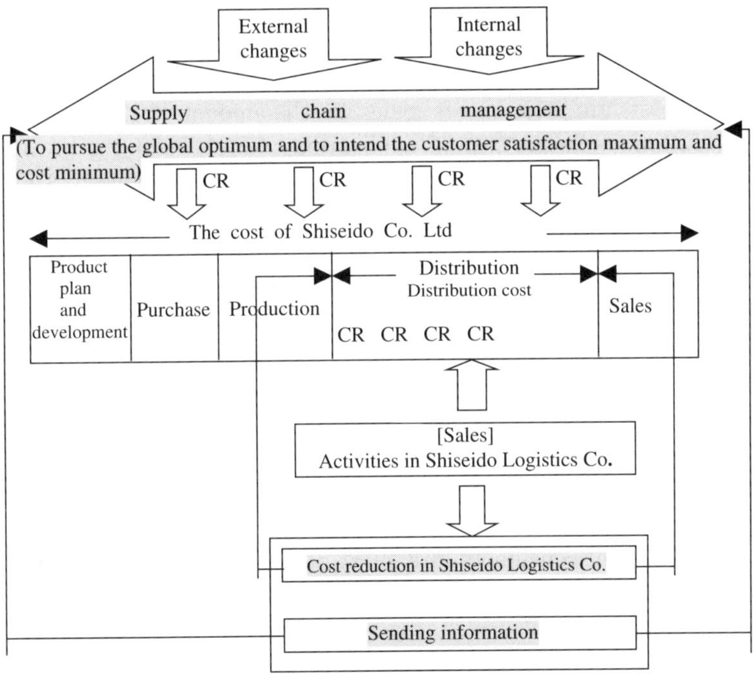

Fig. 23.3 Relationships between the cost in Shiseido group and distribution cost

4. Assigning costs to activities.

   It is difficult to trace resource costs when activities are spread over inter-company. In some cases activities also consume resources from several companies. Professional knowledge, standard values, and estimation values are utilized.

5. Tracing the total supply chain cost to each sales channel and each customer.
6. Analysis and simulation.

23.3.2 *Cash flow management in supply chains: Theory of constraint*

The speed flowing through supply chains is important to make a profit. The theory of constraints (TOC) is suitable for speed-based management and the theory is based on throughput accounting. A profit is generally computed as follows in throughput accounting.

$$\begin{aligned}\text{Profit} &= (\text{sales} - \text{direct materials}) - \text{operating costs}\\ &= \text{throughput} - \text{operating costs}.\end{aligned}$$

Operating costs are period costs. Sales are the amount of which a company sells to customers in the case of application to SCM. But the meaning of customers is different by how broad the range of SCM is focused. To intend global optimum in a total supply chain, the sales are the amount of which a company sells to final consumers. Salaries and expenses in the supply chain are operating costs and period costs not allocated products. In the theory if a company produces products which customers do not buy, salaries and factory expenses which accrue from it decrease the equivalent profit. However the inventories of direct materials are carried with the accounts of direct materials.

As follows, to make a profit in throughput accounting we need to perceive salable products rapidly and reflect it in production activities, to save operation costs by reduction of inventories and shortening the lead time and to sell to final consumers in a short period. This is the direction that the TOC intends and the way of thinking suited for SCM. Moreover, as the profit in throughput accounting is computed on the basis of the non-processed data in high grade, this is suitable for SCM.

23.4 Management by ECM and Financial Indicators: Target Costing by Information Owned Jointly

It is necessary to rapidly gain the demand information about customers' needs by using demand chains in product development. Demand information is about the demand situation of products and services being sold at that time, trend of customers' needs in the future, derivative demands and maintenance demands etc. It is necessary to make good use of them in the product development. The information about product functions and techniques is essential in ECM, but it is necessary to relate the information with cost information. The management by which cost reduction is achieved on the basis of the relation between functions and costs in the developing and designing phase of a new product is popular as target costing.

There is the case in which only a maker (a buyer) executes target costing and the case in which both a buyer and suppliers execute it. The latter is the combined target costing system. The target cost of each part in a buyer's target costing system is the target sales price in a supplier's target costing system. If both are maintained in an independent relationship, the designs of parts cannot be revised and invented freely and both must bear the higher cost. Conversely if the product design team of a buyer and suppliers collaborate with each other, it is possible to design in the high cost-efficiency. The collaboration needs to own cost information jointly, but this makes the positions of suppliers weaker.

Recently it has become important to consider products and services as a whole, so we need a great variety of information. Moreover, we should not consider that customers, suppliers, partner companies, coalition companies are only passive parties concerned, but should consider them active contributors in the creation of value.

23.5 Importance of Management by Financial and Non-financial Indicators

SCM is executed by each product group in a company generally. One case is that a product in the same group is set in a different supply chain and another case is that a product is not set in a supply chain. So a great variety of SCM are executed in a company. Moreover as the purposes are diverse, it is impossible to execute SCM by only financial information. Therefore non-financial indicators are very important. In a questionnaire to a professional meeting, "inter-company system" meeting, in the Japanese association of management accounting, it shows that both indicators are used. Especially from the long term point of view, the management by non-financial indicators (ex. customer' loyalty, improvement of the supply chain efficiency in long term and so on) is more important.

Zimmermann (2000) gives an example of the supply chain relationship between a chemical production company and its distributors. Only one of the nine performance measures is a financial measure (turnover) at the company. Other measures (market share, customer satisfaction index, complaint number, complaint quota, delivery reliability, inventory, sales days' coverage, sales volume) are non-financial measures.

Management measures of SCM intended for stores, sales companies and factories in Matsushita Electric Industrial Co. Ltd. are as follows.

1. Total lead time: Production lead time + distribution lead time.
2. Days of all inventories: Inventories in divisions + inventories in sales companies + inventories on the way + inventories in stores.
3. ROA in SCM: Cash flow/inventories

$$\text{Cash flow} = \text{sales} - \text{purchase costs of materials} - \text{SCM cost}$$

$$\text{Inventories} = \text{materials} + \text{work in process} + \text{products.}$$

4. Fill rate.
5. On time arrival ratio.
6. SCM cost: As described above in Section 23.3.1.3.
7. CCM (capital cost management): Original modification of EVA.

Recently to establish a corporate strategy, we need to consider both SC and EC as described above in Section 23.2.2. When we manage not only supply chains but also engineering chains, we need measures of product development efficiency, information collection and co-ownership in the product development, etc. Therefore, management by only financial measures is less complete.

23.6 SCM, ECM and the Management by Balanced Scorecard

23.6.1 *Management by balanced scorecard and increase of corporate value*

We should understand that SCM and ECM are not parts of operation strategies, but they promote and realize corporate strategies. Namely, the kinds of delivered products and services, customers and regions which should be oriented, etc. are decided by supply chain and engineering chain strategies. Therefore, supply chain and engineering chain strategies must be connected with the increase of corporate value which is the corporate goal for the long run. To increase the corporate long-term value, a company needs to satisfy all stakeholders, maintain the collaboration with them continuously, keep the balance of several goals and adapt to environmental changes appropriately. SCM and ECM which I explained in Sections 23.3 and 23.4 were not considered from the standpoints of all stakeholders. I also considered the management which focuses on one aspect of increase of corporate value by only financial measures.

However, management by balanced scorecard (BSC) is a type of management that considers the interests of all stakeholders and increases the corporate long-term value. The merits of using the BSC in SCM and ECM, besides the adjustment of interests among stakeholders, are as follows:

1. We can monitor the attainment levels continuously.
2. We can focus on the critical measures to attain.
3. We can recognize the potential of improvement in supply chains and engineering chains.
4. We can give an effective framework to discuss improvement points.
5. We can evaluate the results of activities executed collaborately.
6. Reliability among partners increases by the information exchange.

The BSC designated by Kaplan and Norton is composed of four perspectives and measures relevant to suppliers are included in the "internal process perspective" and the "learning and growth perspective." If the "supplier perspective" among stakeholders is especially important in SCM and ECM, it is good to add that perspective as a fifth one in certain circumstances, because they need not only the customer perspective but also the supplier one. By it, we can consider upstream stakeholders and downstream ones separately. We can also add clearly the requirements of not only first layer's suppliers but also second and third layer's suppliers by adding the supplier perspective. Moreover, by it supply chain members can own jointly measures to solve the problems of suppliers. The relationships among the five perspectives in which the supplier perspective is added are shown in Figure 23.4.

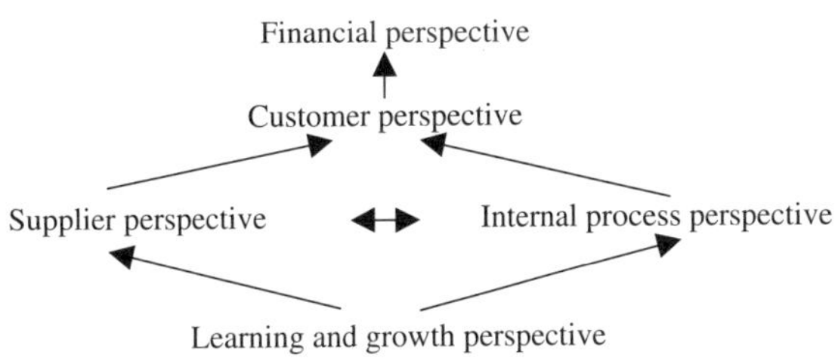

Fig. 23.4 Relationships among five perspectives

23.6.2 *An application of the BSC in SCM and ECM*

An example of the BSC for the individual type of SCM is shown in Figures 23.5 and 23.6. I use the "business process perspectives" instead of the "internal process perspective" in the both tables, because it is desirable to consider the meaning of process broadly in the case of SCM. The examples are classified into the efficiency improvement type of SCM and the market response type of SCM, and the measures based on the five perspectives including the supplier perspective are shown. They include the measures which reflect the interests of own company directly and the collaboration with other companies. Especially in the latter type of SCM, it is important to consider SCM and ECM simultaneously. It is impossible for the BSC to be described in detail and broken down to individual member companies of the supply chain the strategic goals and attainable measures of total supply chains and engineering chains even if own company is a core company, except when the total supply chains and engineering chains are

Financial perspective	Increase of profit, rate of return and EVA Increase of cash flow (throughput) Shortening of cash-to-cash cycle Increase of ROA
Customers perspective	Increase of market share Increase of the rate of customer retention Improvement of customer satisfaction Reduction of the number of complaint
Business process perspective	Improvement of supply chain cycle efficiency Reduction of total supply chain cost Improvement of the rate of punctuality of the appointment date of delivery Reduction of the rate of returned goods Inventory reduction Increase of inventory turnover Effective usage of resources
Supplier perspective	Increase of the number of data owned jointly Increase of effective relational contracts Increase of effective relationship-specific investments Improvement of supplier satisfaction
Learning & growth perspective	Improvement of employee satisfaction Increase of the preparation of IT for stable supplies Increase of investment related with employee education

Fig. 23.5 Critical measures in the efficiency improvement type of SCM

Financial perspective	Increase of profit, rate of return and EVA Increase of cash flow (throughput) Shortening of cash-to-cash cycle Increase of ROA Increase of the growth rate on sales
Customers perspective	Improvement of the rate of new customer acquisition Increase of the rate of customer retention Improvement of customer satisfaction Increase of the number of contacts with customers
Business process perspective	Prompt and flexible adaptation for demands Improvement of supply chain cycle efficiency Reduction of market adaptation costs Reduction of the costs by oversupplies Reduction of total supply chain cost Reduction of lead time Improvement of the attainment level in the cost of product development Improvement of the level in the market-oriented product development Improvement of the attainment level in the goal of new product development
Supplier perspective	Increase of the number of data owned jointly Increase of effective relational contracts Increase of effective relationship-specific investments Improvement of the collaboration in product development Improvement of supplier satisfaction
Learning & growth perspective	Improvement of employee satisfaction Increase of the preparation of IT for flexible adaptation Increase of investments related with employee education Improvement of the accuracy level in demand forecast

Fig. 23.6 Critical measures in the market response type of SCM

executed by a company. Therefore I consider the applications as follows.

1. The case that companies of supply chain members collaborate and that own company is a core company.

   The BSC is arranged by a core company. There is a case that only critical measures are owned jointly by linkage scorecards. In this case, the performances are evaluated by the core company, but details are entrusted to each company. As an example, the case of Mobil North America Marketing and Refining (Kaplan and Norton, 2001, pp. 194–196) gives much information though it is not an example of SCM. If the BSC can be arranged in detail considerably, a goals/means deployment method, for example TP (total productivity) management

(Japan Management Association, 1999) which is popular in Japan, can be used.

2. The case that companies of supply chain members collaborate but that a core company does not exist.
   It is useful for all supply chain members to make out the BSC based on strategic themes from the view of total supply chains and engineering chains if it is possible, because each member company can know how it can contribute to total supply chains and engineering chains.
3. The case that companies of supply chain members do not collaborate and that the relation is temporary.
   It is favorable to use the BSC in a contract. Because if it is a contract composed of one condition, there are many cases that other matters are neglected. Therefore a complex contract is desirable.

23.7 Concluding Remarks

As I mentioned in this paper, a company needs SCM as well as ECM which makes the most use of information gained from SCM to develop a new product. Therefore, it is necessary to consider SCM and ECM simultaneously in strategic decision making. I arranged and examined the existing management of SCM and ECM by financial information in this paper. I also pointed out that management by both financial and non-financial information is necessary in the management of SCM and ECM, and the management by BSC is very useful for this. I think that inter-company management will be a critical theme in management accounting in the future.

References

Abo, E. and Yazawa, H. (2000). *Supply Chain: Cost Down*, Chuo-Keizaisha. (in Japanese)

Ackermann, I. (2003). Using the balanced scorecard for supply chain management — prerequisites, integration issues, and performance measures, in *Strategy and Organization in Supply Chains*, edited by Seuring, S., Müller, M., Goldbach, M., and Schneidewind, U., Physica-Verlag.

Brewer, P. C. and Speh, T. W. (2000). Using the balanced scorecard to measure supply chain performance, *Journal of Business Logistics* 21-1.

Carr, L. P. and Ittner, C. D. (1992). Measuring the cost of ownership, *Journal of Cost Management*, Fall.

Cooper, R. and Slagmulder, R. (1999). *Supply Chain Development for the Lean Enterprise: Interorganizational Cost Management*, Productivity.

Ellram, L. M. (1995). Activity-based costing and total cost of ownership: a critical linkage, *Journal of Cost Management*, Winter.

Hamada, K. (2001). *Application the TOC into SCM/BSC,* Kigyo-kaikei. (in Japanese)

Handfield, R. B. and Nichols, Jr E. L. (2002). *Supply Chain Redesign: Transforming Supply Chains into Integrated Value Systems*, Prentice Hall.

Japan Management Association (1999). *Essays in Celebration of 15th Anniversary of TP Management Award: Convention in 1999.* (in Japanese)

Kaplan, R. S. and Norton, D. P. (2001). *The Strategy — Focused Organization*, Harvard Business School Press.

Lalonde, B. J. and Pohlen, T. L. (1996). Issues in supply chain costing, *The International of Logistics Management* 7-1.

Monden, Y. (2003). *Organization Structure and Management Accounting*, Zeimukeiri-Kyokai. (in Japanese)

Sakurai, M. (2003). *Balanced Scorecard*, Dobunkan. (in Japanese)

Zimmermann, K. (2002). Using the balanced scorecard for interorganizational performance management of supply chains—a case study, in *Cost Management in Supply Chains*, edited by Seuring, S. and Goldbach, M., Physia-Verlag.

CHAPTER

24

Impacts of Revenue Sharing on Incentive Alignments in Supply Chains

Yoshiteru Minagawa
Professor, Faculty of Commerce
Nagoya Gakuin University

24.1 Introduction

Supply chains perform two different types of functions, as in Fisher (1997, p. 107) and Ross (1998, p. 12). First, a partner of supply chains has access to customer demand; information of which will be shared within the entire supply chain. Second, supply chains yield timely and cost-effective movement of goods throughout the whole supply chain.

In studying supply chain management, it is important to differentiate between internal and external networks. Internal supply chains hold organizational units inside a firm responsible for all operations. In contrast, an external supply chain is made up of legally independent entities. The study addresses external supply chains. The member organizations of an external supply chain enter into an inter-firm link yet simultaneously seek their own specific interests. This leads to a strong likelihood that some partners will behave in a self-benefiting fashion. Alternatively speaking, partners would never dare to take unjustified economical risk only for the interest of others (Das and Teng, 1998, p. 504). How to cope with this tendency is essential to supply chain management.

One of the biggest challenges being currently faced with by many firms, regardless of which stages of a supply chain they are in, is to satisfy end-consumers of its own products and services in the best possible way. A key to resolving this issue properly is enhanced collaboration with other partners. As a result, choosing which supply chains to participate in will become increasingly critical for managers. If all participating member organizations in a supply chain can improve their operational performance drivers including quality, cost and delivery, the supply chain has a good chance to outperform others. Accordingly, successful supply chain management requires that all parties be willing to make investments aimed at reducing the supply chain's costs and raising the value of the supply chain's output (Baiman and Rajan, 2002, p. 213). However, this is not always achievable automatically without resorting to some management techniques. This stems from partly that different firms in the same supply chain may have different interests. Therefore, the promotion of investments by all partners, as a competitive edge of supply chains, rests with creating the right alignment of incentives to invest in order to improve their supply chain performance. How is it possible to motivate partners to invest in order to maximize the supply chain's profits? This can be achieved through the incentive schemes of sharing revenue among the partners. The paper will further focus on revenue sharing.

Che and Hausch (1999) divide organizational investments into the following three types. An investment is "selfish" if it benefits the investor. An investment is "cooperative" if it generates direct benefit for the trading partners. An investment is "hybrid" if it has both cooperative and selfish elements (Che and Hausch, 1999, p. 126). Based on Che and Hausch (1999), the study distinguishes between the following two types of supply chain investments. First, each partner invests to reduce the partner's own cost. Second, individual partners invest to satisfy end-consumers whom the supply chain serves. These investments commonly lead to expanding profit or the size of the "pie" of the supply chain as a whole and thereby increasing each partner's share of the entire "pie."

Once a firm comes to be part of a supply chain, there is potential to benefit from all the partners' investments directed to improving the value of the supply chain's output. Participating firms gain a competitive edge over firms who do not belong to any supply chain. In addition, the growth of investments within a supply chain will greatly affect its competition with other supply chains. However, securing cooperative investments under information asymmetries in a relationship among partners requires using managerial practices relevant to controlling partners' opportunistic behaviors and hence inducing supply chain investments. There are several reasons why investment-incentive issues arise in supply chains. For instance, when partners cannot observe other partners' actions, they cannot confirm whether those partners have invested (e.g., Arrow, 1985; Narayanan and Raman, 2004). Moreover, the existence of information asymmetries in supply chains engenders a disincentive to continue to make cooperative investments. Suppose that a partner made a cooperative investment but has no information on whether other partners have invested. Under the situation, the partner would most likely determine to discontinue cooperative investments.

One of the purposes of the paper lies in considering theoretically and normatively revenue sharing's impacts on supply chain investments under information asymmetries based on prior related studies. This chapter is organized as follows. First, I propose reasons as to why incentive issues related to the promotion of cooperative investment arise. Next, focusing on Cachon and Lariviere (2000), the cooperative investment-inducing mechanisms of revenue-sharing are examined. Moreover, I review Atkinson *et al.*'s consideration on incentive mechanism of revenue sharing in the case of The National Football League (1988). Lastly, I present requirements necessary for inducing revenue sharing that motivates all participants in supply chains to make cooperative investments.

24.2 Literature Review

24.2.1 *Supply chain members' cooperative investment under information asymmetries*

A researching framework in the paper is based on Porter's competitive strategy (1985). Porter shows that the profitability of an industry as a whole is a determinant of the performances of the separated firms. This is true of supply chain member firms; each partner's profitability is influenced by the performance of the supply chain as a whole. This means that the growth of partners requires, above all, enhanced profitability of the whole supply chain. Thus, partners ought to address the issue of how the supply chain's overall profit can be boosted in their management decision-making. The paper continues to focus on investment valuation.

The study, as mentioned above, divides supply chain investments into the following two types. First, partners invest to reduce their own cost. Moreover, all partners cooperatively invest to reduce the supply chain's costs and improve the perceived value of the supply chain's output to the final consumers. Both types of supply chain investment benefit investors in the sense that those result in the growth of the earnings of the supply chain. Nevertheless, as for an investment leading to increased profits of the supply chain as a whole or the other partners, each partner hardly voluntarily and automatically implements it. Rather, the promotion of such investments in supply chains requires incentive-boosting schemes.

Why do investment incentive-related issues as mentioned above arise?[1] There are the following two reasons. First, if a partner in a supply chain cannot observe the other partners' actions, the partner has no information of whether the others have made investments or not. Consequently, the partner finds it hard to detect the other partners' opportunistic behaviors (Wathne and Heide, 2000, p. 42). The problem is referred to as hidden action (Arrow, 1985). In the worst case, hidden action most likely leads to the result that partners who have invested to improve the value of the supply chain's output will never conduct such investments again.

The development and implementation of managerial plans to maximize the integrated profit of a supply chain require sharing accounting information among the partners. The relevant financial data to control partners include their own costs. Seidmann and Sundararajan (1998) study the cost and benefit of inter-organizational information sharing. According to Seidmann and Sundararajan (1998, pp. 110–112), a firm's transmission of one's information to the trading partners decreases one's bargaining power. Hence, it is likely that partners of supply chains never transmit their own information to others lest they should lose their bargaining power. This issue is referred to as hidden information (Arrow, 1985). Here it should be pointed out that there exists a difference in the levels of both verifiability and disclosure among financial data. In contrast to firms' internal cost, sales as well as prices are highly published.

A way for principles to control agents is contracting. However, when the principle can neither monitor the agent's action nor have information on the agent due to the existence of information asymmetries between them, the principle cannot even confirm whether the agent had fulfilled the contract. Even though partners in supply chains agreed on the level of investments, the existence of asymmetric information causes each of all the partners to be unable to verify whether other partners have implemented the investments. Therefore, it can be concluded that investment incentive mechanisms are of great value to the growth of supply chains.

24.2.2 *Dysfunction of profit sharing*

The conception of a practice relevant to aligning the incentives of the firms in supply chains is to share their effort-driven financial earnings among them. This includes profit sharing as well as revenue sharing.

[1] The discussion on incentive issues engendered under the existence of information asymmetries here is based Narayanan and Raman (2004).

According to Chwolka and Simons (2003, p. 53), "if supply chains wish to employ profit sharing, there are various ways to calculate the basis of profit sharing." The various schemes of profit sharing differ in terms of the range of cost components incorporated into the sharing basis. For example, profit derived from retail revenue less partners' variable costs is shared among them. Alternatively, profit derived from revenues less partners' variable costs as well as investments is shared (Chwolka and Simons, 2003, p. 53). Regardless of how to establish the sharing basis, profit sharing requires each partner of a supply chain to be able to monitor other partners' costs. In addition, partners' truthful revelation of their own costs is required. Hence, it is hardly possible for profit sharing to eliminate asymmetric information. To solve this, it is imperative to change the sharing basis from profit to revenue. The reason as to why revenue sharing can resolve information asymmetries is that "its sharing basis consists of verifiable and externally published data only." (Chwolka and Simons, 2003, p. 66)

Consider a supply chain that employs profit sharing. Assume also that a partner of the supply chain succeeded in cost reduction and thus increased profit. However, profit sharing leads the partner to receive only a fraction of the partner's profit, thereby engendering disincentives for the partner to invest to reduce the partner's cost. In contrast, revenue sharing does not adversely affect motivation for partners to cut down their costs.

24.2.3 *Revenue sharing schemes*

24.2.3.1 *Revenue sharing*

Cachon and Lariviere (2000, 2005) built a revenue sharing model and studied the impact on supply chain coordination. The section initially examines how revenue sharing influences supply chain performance based on Cachon and Lariviere (2000, 2005).

Consider a supply chain comprised of two risk neutral firms: a supplier and a retailer. The supplier provides q units of a product to the retailer, who achieves revenue $R(p, q)$ through sales of these products at a retail price, p.

Assume that the supply chain employs a revenue sharing contract developed by Cachon and Lariviere (2000, 2005). Under the contract, before transactions commence, the supplier and the retailer must agree on the following parameters. First, the agreed parameters are Φ and $(1 - \Phi)$ which represent the retailer's and the supplier's respective shares of the retail revenue $R(p, q)$. In addition, the unit wholesale price ω the retailer pays must be agreed upon. Such revenue sharing achieves coordination as follows. The supplier offers to the retailer a unit wholesale price ω lower than the supplier's own marginal cost per unit. This in turn allows the retailer to increase its purchase quantity from the supplier. Hence the retailer can boost its retail revenue $R(p, q)$. Here we should note that the heightened revenue of the supply chain is achieved partly from supplier's sales of its goods to the retailer at the price below its own cost. In order to induce the supplier to charge a lower price to the retailer, the revenue sharing scheme compels retail revenue $R(p, q)$ to be shared between the supplier and the retailer. That is, while the retailer keeps only a portion Φ of its revenue $R(p, q)$, the rest $(1 - \Phi)R(p, q)$ is transferred to the supplier.[2]

24.2.3.2 *Impacts of sharing downstream firms' revenue on investments in supply chains*

Under the above-mentioned sharing revenue scheme, the downstream firms' revenue is shared among the supply chain members. The previous studies show that employing the method of sharing downstream firms' revenue in a supply chain results in partners' underinvestment relative to investment level that maximizes the overall profits of the supply chain (e.g., Cachon and Lariviere, 2000, 2005; Baiman and Rajan, 2002). The section examines how sharing the revenue of downstream firms influences cooperative investments within the supply chain based on mainly the studies by Cachon and Lariviere (2000, 2005).

Consider a supply chain consisting of two partners: a supplier and a retailer. The supplier sells a product to the retailer, who in turn serves the market demand. The supply chain employs a revenue sharing contract described by $\{\Phi, \omega\}$: the retailer keeps the share Φ of retail revenue and the supplier receives the fraction $(1 - \Phi)$ of retail revenue. ω is the unit price that the supplier charges to the retailer. The remainder of the section concentrates on investment valuation of the supplier.[3]

Assume that the supplier invests to increase the value of the supply chain's final products and thus boosts retail revenue of the supply chain.

[2] As for revenue sharing, Giannoccaro and Pontrandolfo (2004) expand Cachon and Lariviere (2000) into a revenue-sharing model in a three-stage supply chain.
[3] Cachon and Lariviere (2000, 2005) consider the impacts of revenue sharing on a retailer's investment-incentive.

Let $I(e)$ be the amount of capital invested by the supplier. Suppose that the supplier conducts the capital expenditure at the beginning of a certain year and benefits from the investment for one year.[4] e means the level of investment effort chosen by the supplier (Cachon and Lariviere, 2005, p. 41). The retailer purchases q units of products from the supplier. The retailer's expected profit function is $R(q, e)$. The supplier's cost function is $C(q)$. Let us assume these functions to be continuous and differentiable.

The integrated profit function of the supply chain is given by[5]:

$$\Pi(q, e) = R(q, e) - C(q) - I(e). \tag{24.1}$$

From Eq. (24.1), the quantity and level of investment effort that lead to the maximum consolidated profit of the supply chain must meet the following conditions, respectively:

$$\frac{\partial \Pi(q, e)}{\partial q} = \frac{\partial R(q, e)}{\partial q} - C'(q) = 0. \tag{24.2}$$

$$\frac{\partial \Pi(q, e)}{\partial e} = \frac{\partial R(q, e)}{\partial e} - I'(e) = 0. \tag{24.3}$$

With revenue sharing contract, the supplier earns the following profit $\Pi_s(q, e)$:

$$\Pi_s(q, e) = (1 - \Phi)R(q, e) + \omega q - C(q) - I(e). \tag{24.4}$$

The requirement to achieve goal congruence of the whole supply chain is that if the supplier chooses the supply chain's optimal level of investment effort as the amount of its own invested capital, the supply chain's optimal quantity must be the supplier's optimal. For this to be met, the following condition must be satisfied.

$$\frac{\partial \Pi_S(q, e)}{\partial q} = (1 - \Phi)\frac{\partial R(q, e)}{\partial q} + \omega - C'(q) = 0. \tag{24.5}$$

From both Eqs. (24.2) and (24.5), the following equation is derived:

$$\omega = \Phi C'(q). \tag{24.6}$$

By rewriting Eq. (24.4) using Eq. (24.6), the following is given:

$$\Pi_s(q, e) = (1 - \Phi)R(q, e) + \Phi C'(q)q - C(q) - I(e). \tag{24.7}$$

---

[4]This condition is not set in Cachon and Lariviere (2000, 2005).

[5]Equations (24.1)–(24.8) are based on Cachon and Lariviere (2000).

The supplier's optimal investment capital is given by the equation below. This is proven to be negative using Eq. (24.3) and $0 < \Phi < 1$ (Cachon and Lariviere, 2005, p. 41).

$$\frac{\partial \Pi_S(q,e)}{\partial e} = (1-\Phi)\frac{\partial R(q,e)}{\partial e} - I'(e) < 0. \tag{24.8}$$

In case of $\Phi = 0$, Eq. (24.3) holds true. This means that when Φ equals 0, namely if the supplier can gain the whole amount of retail revenue, the supplier chooses the supply chain optimal level of investment effort in its own decision-making. However, in case of $0 < \Phi < 1$, that is, when the supplier captures only a portion of retail revenue, the supplier's optimal amount of capital investment is less than the supply chain optimal. Revenue sharing schemes normally set retailers' retention rates that fall between 0 and 1. Such a revenue sharing scheme results in the supplier's underinvestment as the supplier chooses to invest an amount that is less than the supply chain optimal. The reason is that under the revenue sharing scheme, even though the supplier has invested, it will receive only a fraction of *ex post* surplus. This provides the supplier with disincentives to invest aiming at improving the performance of the supply chain as a whole (e.g., Baiman and Rajan, 2002, p. 220).

In the above-mentioned researching case, it was assumed that while the supplier invests to increase retail revenue of the supply chain, the retailer neither conducts capital expenditure nor shares in contributing to the supplier's investment. This might weaken the supplier's incentive to enhance the level of its investment effort. Here, assume that the retailer had invested its funds in the relationship. In addition, let us suppose that the supplier is able to confirm whether the retailer had invested. In that case, the supplier would heighten its investment level. However, the existence of both issues of hidden action and hidden information forces the supplier to choose the amount of invested capital lower than the supply chain optimal.

24.2.3.3 *Revenue sharing in the National Football League*

Atkinson *et al.* (1988) examine how revenue sharing in the NFL (National Football League) can motivate the teams to behave in the league's best interest. Under the revenue sharing of the NFL, respective teams retain the identical fraction α of their own revenues. Each team's remaining revenue, (1-α) of its own revenues, is remitted so that all teams can share the revenue pool equitably; the revenue sharing of the NFL allows each team to receive the equitable fraction of the revenue pool made up of all teams' revenues. Consequently, subtracting each team's operational expenses incurred from total revenue received, namely, each team's kept portion (α) of its own revenues added to equal share of the pool revenue, arrives to its own profit. Among team's expenses is wage paid to players.

The revenue sharing in the NFL makes it possible for all teams to possess capital sufficient to hire players who attract the substantial number of fans and thus are worth the high wage being compensated. This benefits the performance of the league. A key to each team's success is to increase the number of fans. To do this successfully, each team must increase its number of wins. This means that hiring excellent players is of most importance for teams to achieve their sustainable growth. Moreover, the total number of audiences increases with the number of close games. The increased number of close games is achievable not only by enhancing the technical level of the i's team's players, but also by the intensified techniques of all other teams' players (Atkinson *et al.*, 1988, p. 29). However, hiring skillful players results in augmented costs of teams. Consequently, the NFL requires each team to remit a fraction of its revenue and then share the pooled revenue equitably among all teams, thereby providing all teams with capital enough to hire the desired talent.

However, the revenue sharing scheme in the NFL raises the following two incentive-related issues. First, it is likely that teams do not invest their equal shares of the revenue pool in the employment of talents. Second, the revenue sharing in the NFL is not formalized based on equalization. Under the revenue sharing in the NFL, each team's share of revenue does not increase with the amount of their own actual invested capital. Namely, both the amount of funds for each team to pool and the share of revenue each team receives out of the pool are not related to such sacrifice made by each team as capital investments. That explains why the revenue sharing in the NFL is lacking equalization.

24.3 Revenue Sharing as an Investment Incentive under Information Asymmetries

This section examines revenue sharing rules that can lead supply chain members to raise the level of their own investments based on Cachon and Lariviere's (2000) model and Atkinson *et al.*' study on the NFL's revenue sharing (1988).

Prior studies show that when revenue sharing contracts are being employed in supply chains, the member firms choose an investing capital level that is lower than the supply chain's entire optimal (e.g., Cachon and Lariviere, 2000, 2005; Baiman and Rajan, 2002). The reason is that the revenue sharing contract disallows a partner to capture the whole amount of revenue generated through the partner's investments.

Conventional studies about incentive mechanisms of revenue sharing in supply chains shed light on individual member firm's investment decisions. However, a feature of supply chain management is cooperative investments made by all members. Hence one of the most important issues in supply chain coordination is how to motivate member firms to invest aimed at improving the supply chain overall performance.

A key for supply chains to outperform the competition is "networking effects of each partner's investment;" each partner can invest to raise other partners' revenue as well as efficiency and ultimately increase the integrated profit of supply chain. To gain such a competitive edge, it is imperative to employ incentive schemes that can induce each partner to invest directed at raising all other partners' value and increasing consolidated profit of supply chain.

Among incentive schemes conducive to boost investments, made by partners to raise integrated profit of the supply chain, is revenue sharing with a rule that mandates each partner's revenue to be affected by other partners' performances. Such schemes include the NFL's revenue sharing that is formalized based on the concept of each team's revenue being affected by overall league performances. Hence, revenue sharing in the NFL requires each team to retain a portion of its revenue and remit the remaining revenue. The revenue pool made up of all teams' revenue is shared among them. Of the NFL's revenue sharing rules, one is that each team keeps a certain fraction of revenue generated, thereby yielding a self-benefiting incentive to invest.

Here, let me focus on another rule of revenue pool sharing. Respective teams' share of the revenue pool rests with the capabilities of all teams to raise their operational efficiency and boost the value of their output. Therefore, it would seem at a glance that sharing of the revenue pool allows them to potentially make an investment directed at improving other teams' profits. The point here is how the revenue pool should be shared among partners. As to this issue, the NFL's revenue sharing scheme provides the amount of the revenue pool divided by the number of teams to the respective teams. Hence, each team's share of the revenue pool is related not to the amount of capital actually invested. Instead, each team receives an equitable share. This shows that the NFL's revenue sharing scheme lacks equitability. How is this drawback of revenue sharing in the NFL being overcome? For example, the issues might be resolved by basing both individual partner's retaining rate of revenue and sharing fraction of the revenue pool on each partners' asset turn over, defined as follows: sales revenue ÷ total assets. The whole process of the revenue sharing must include for a cross-partner team to decide on the retainable percentages and receivable portions ranked in terms of asset turnover within the supply chains. The revenue sharing rule allows partners to boost the two sharing fractions only if they can raise their ranking in asset turnover.

Is there any rationale for applying asset turnover in the evaluation of supply chain performance? In order to boost asset turnover dramatically, capital investments aimed at fostering agile responsiveness to changes in demand are mandatory. Meeting customers' needs timely results in the growth of sales revenue. In order for firms to respond to variations in demand agilely, collaborative relationships with their partners are necessary. These are the reasons as to why asset turnover is an important financial indication to successful supply chain management. Furthermore, publicly disclosed financial items, sales and total assets, are used to calculate asset turnover.

24.4 Concluding Remarks

Once firms are part of supply networks, they have a potential to benefit from cooperative investments by all other partners. In order for firms to gain the benefit, it is important to make other partners refrain from behaving opportunistically concerning cooperative investments. A factor to trigger opportunistic behavior is "hidden actions" and "hidden information." The paper examined revenue sharing relevant to make partners raise their supply chain investments under the existence of information asymmetries. The paper focused on Atkinson *et al.* (1988) study on revenue sharing in the NFL. The NFL's revenue sharing scheme engenders incentive issues in that each team's share is neither related to the amount invested nor its contribution to the performance of supply chain as a whole. Consequently, the NFL's revenue sharing lacks equitability. As for solutions to this issue, the paper proposes the concept of incorporating a rule that mandates individual partners' revenue be shared among themselves according to their ranking in asset turnover.

References

Arrow, K. J. (1985). The economics of agency, in *Principals and Agents: The Structure of Business*, edited by Pratt, J. W. and Zeckhauser, R. J., Harvard Business School Press, pp. 37–51.

Atkinson, S. E., Stanley, L. R., and Tschirhart, J. (1988). Revenue sharing as an incentive in an agency problem: an example from the National Football League, *RAND J. Econom.* 19-1, pp. 27–43.

Baiman, S. and Rajan, M. V. (2002). Incentive issues in inter-firm relationships, *Acc. Organ. Soc.* 27, pp. 213–238.

Cachon, G. P. and Lariviere, M. A. (2000). Supply chain coordination with revenue-sharing contracts: strengths and limitations, Working Paper, The Wharton School of Business, University of Pennsylvania, Philadelphia.

Cachon, G. P. and Lariviere, M. A. (2005). Supply chain coordination with revenue-sharing contracts: strengths and limitations, *Manage. Sci.* 51-1, pp. 30–44.

Che, Y.-K. and Hausch, D. B. (1999). Cooperative investments and the value of contracting, *The American Eco. Rev.* 89-1, pp. 125–147.

Chwolka, A. and Simons, D. (2003). Impacts of revenue sharing, profit sharing and transfer pricing on quality-improving investments, *European Acc. Rev.* 12-1, pp. 47–76.

Das, T. K. and Teng, B.-S. (1998). Between trust and control: developing confidence in partner cooperation in alliances, *Acad. Manage. Rev.* 23-3, pp. 491–512.

Dekker, H. C. (2004). Control of inter-organizational relationships: evidence on appropriation concerns and coordination requirements, *Acc. Organ. Soc.* 29, pp. 27–49.

Fisher, M. L. (1997). What is the right supply chain for your product?, *Harvard Business Review*, March–April, pp. 105–116.

Giannoccaro, I. and Pontrandolfo, P. (2004). Supply chain coordination by revenue sharing contracts, *Int. J. Production Econom.* 89, pp. 131–139.

Narayanan, V. G. and Raman, A. (2004). Aligning incentives in supply chains, *Harvard Business Review*, November, pp. 94–102.

Porter, M. E. (1985). *Competitive Advantage*, The Free Press.

Ross, D. F. (1998). *Competing through Supply Chain Management: Creating Market-Winning Strategies through Supply Chain Partnerships*, Chapman & Hall.

Seidmann, A. and Sundararajan, A. (1998). Sharing logistics information across organizations: technology, competition and contracting, in *Information Technology and Industrial Competitiveness: How IT Shapes Competition*, edited by Kemerer, C. F., Kluwer Academic Publishers, pp. 107–136.

Tomkins, C. (2001). Interdependencies, trust and information in relationships, alliances and networks, *Acc. Organ. Soc.* 26, pp. 161–191.

Wathne, K. H. and Heide, J. B. (2000). Opportunism in interfirm relationships: forms, outcomes, and solutions, *J. Marketing* 64, pp. 36–51.

CHAPTER

25

Multi-Goals Coordination in Supply Chain Management: A Mathematical Model

Tomonori Inooka

Associate Professor, Faculty of Political Science and Economics, Kokushikan University

25.1 Introduction

The management of business-to-business (B2B) transactions used to focus on the local optimization of each company (supplier, manufacturer, dealer, etc.). In contrast, Supply Chain Management (SCM) seeks global optimization for the purpose of B2B management. The normal practice in B2B transactions as well as intra-company transactions is to manage the workflow (which involves the procurement of raw materials, components, etc, production, sales and distribution) by coordinating the tasks in pursuit of the local optimization of each task as well as the global optimization of the series of tasks. It is therefore important how local optimum is coordinated under SCM, regardless of whether the transaction is B2B or intra-company, for the purpose of achieving a global optimum. Various studies have been conducted in this area, including the development and application of management techniques and the analysis of the coordination process for a global optimum and a local optimum in SCM.

Management techniques for SCM have been implemented in various ways. Studies have been conducted from various angles, as exemplified by studies on the use of information technology (IT), and studies on the application of the Theory of Constraints (TOC), the application of production management techniques such as Total Production Maintenance (TPM) (Hamada, 2001, pp. 31–37), and the implementation of a business model which takes demand risks into account (Mita, 1999, pp. 91–113). However, not enough studies have been conducted on the mathematical approach to analyzing the process of coordinating a local optimum and a global optimum in the supply chain. Further, in order achieve multiple goals in SCM, it is important to look into how to coordinate them and how to obtain a optimal solution. For this reason, the following section examines the mathematical model for coordinating a local optimum and a global optimum in SCM.

25.2 Supply Chain Management System

25.2.1 *Extension of supply chain management*

In SCM, it is important to coordinate a local optimum and a global optimum in both intra-company transactions and B2B transactions. However, not enough analysis has been conducted on the process of how the local optimum is coordinated to achieve a global optimum in the SCM system. To address this, the coordination problem in a decentralized organization based on a division system should be examined with respect to SCM. To begin with, the Dantzig-Wolfe Decomposition Principle, which examines the process in relation to the allocation of resources in decentralized organizations, is explained below.

25.2.2 *Decomposition principle model*

In cases where there is more than one division, as in a division-based organizations, suppose there are constraints on common resources that cut across all divisions, in addition to the constraints in each division. The formula for profit maximization in such cases will be as follows.

$$\begin{aligned} \text{Max} \ & \sum_{i=1}^{n} c_i x_i \\ \text{s.t.} \ & \sum_{i=1}^{n} A_i x_i \leqq b \\ & B_i x_i \leqq b_i, \quad x_i \geqq 0, \quad i = 1 \sim n. \end{aligned} \tag{25.1}$$

Where c_i is a $(1 \times n_i)$ vector of marginal profit of output of the ith division.
x_i is an $(n_i \times 1)$ vector of quantity of output.
A_i is an $(m_0 \times n_i)$ matrix of technological coefficients of common resources.

b is an $(n_{jk} \times 1)$ vector of stipulations for common resources.

B_i is an $(m_i \times n_i)$ matrix of technological coefficients of common resources.

b_i is an $(m_i \times 1)$ vector of stipulations for the resources of the ith division.

The Dantzig-Wolfe Decomposition Principle examines the allocation of resources in a decentralized organization (Dantzig and Wolfe 1961, pp. 767–778). Its approach is to express overall profit as an objective function and maximize it under a single criterion, while satisfying the constraints on common resources and in each division. When applied to the problem in SCM, it may be expressed by the following formulations based on a simple example according to expression (25.1). Let subscript i denote the distinction between divisions, and j represent the distinction between the commodities (products). Also assume that $v_{Si,j}$ is the inventory cost (opportunity cost) per unit.

$$\begin{aligned} \text{Max} \quad & \sum_{i=1}^{n} \sum_{j=1}^{n_j} c_{ij}\, x_{ij} - \sum_{i=2}^{n} \sum_{j=1}^{n_j} v_{Si,j}(x_{i-1,j} - x_{i,j}) \\ \text{s.t.} \quad & \sum_{i=1}^{n} a_{ij}\, x_{ij} \leqq b_j \\ & \sum_{j=1}^{n_j} b_{ij}\, x_{ij} \leqq b_i \\ & x_{ij} - x_{i+1,j} \geqq 0, \quad x_{ij} \geqq 0. \end{aligned} \tag{25.2}$$

The objective function takes into account the opportunity cost in the form of inventory cost as in the second term of the objective function in expression (25.2), and represents the profit after deducting this cost. The third term represents a constraint which requires the output of division i to satisfy the output of division $i+1$. While production volume is expressed as variables in expression (25.2), hourly production volume or hourly processing volume (production speed) may be expressed as a variable, which will make it possible to manage the production time or the processing time. However, the assistance of fractional programming will be required here, as output is expressed by the cap on the available time or the processable time at each division, etc. divided by the production speed. The objective function here expressed a situation in which the same goal applied throughout the supply chain, assuming the singularity of profit, etc. The following section looks into a model that applies the Goal Programming (GP) approach to a case in which there are conflicts between multiple goals in the supply chain.

25.3 Goal Programming (GP) Approach

25.3.1 *Generalized Goal Decomposition Model (GGDM)*

The basic idea of GP is that if the "aspiration level" of multiple goals cannot all be achieved simultaneously, the most desirable compromise solution should be sought instead, by minimizing the sum total of the regrets attributable to the extent of the non-fulfillment of each goal (Fushimi *et al.*, 1987, pp. 18–19).

This involves seeking a compromise solution by weighting and prioritizing the conflicting goals when striving to achieve multiple goals, and is applicable to various management planning problems.

The use of GP is exemplified by Ruefli's Generalized Goal Decomposition Model (GGDM) (Ruefli, 1971, pp. B505–B518), which applies GP to a planning problem in a decentralized organization and logically validates how a global optimum can be achieved via decentralized optimization and decision-making and the exchange of coordination information by the central unit. This model addresses the process of determining the goal allocation based on a three-tier organization structure: m management units are allocated to the central unit, and n_k operating units are allocated to management unit k, as shown in Figure 25.1. The problem concerning management unit k on the second level is formulated as shown in expression (25.3). With the application of GP, the formulation aims to achieve a satisfactory solution by determining the optimal mix for n_k projects, in

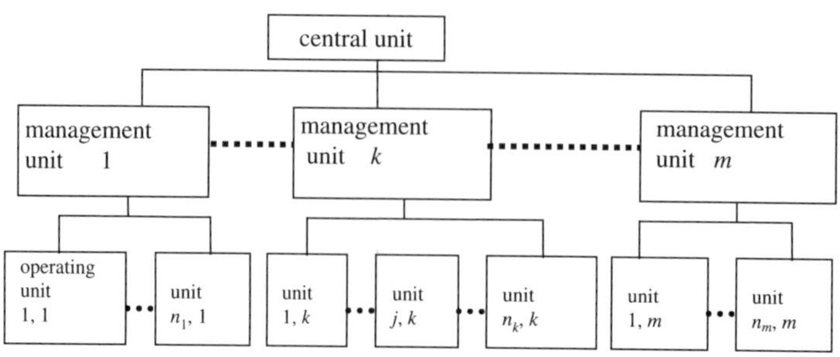

Source: Ruefli (1971).

Fig. 25.1 General organization structure

consideration of the weighted and prioritized m_k goals.

$$\begin{aligned} \text{Min} \quad & w_k^+ y_k^+ + w_k^- y_k^- \\ \text{s.t.} \quad & \sum_{j=1}^{n_k} a_{jk} x_{jk} - y_k^+ + y_k^- = g_k \\ & 0 \leqq x_{jk} \leqq 1, \quad j = 1 \cdots n_k, \quad y_k^+, y_k^- \geqq 0. \end{aligned} \tag{25.3}$$

Where w_k^+ is a $(1 \times m_k)$ vector of weights assigned to the positive goal deviations.

w_k^- is a $(1 \times m_k)$ vector of weights assigned to the negative goal deviations.

y_k^+ is an $(m_k \times 1)$ vector of positive deviations from goals.

y_k^- is an $(m_k \times 1)$ vector of negative deviations from goals.

a_{jk} is an $(m_k \times 1)$ vector of attribute levels of the jth $(j = 1 \cdots n_k)$ project of management unit k.

x_{jk} $(0 \leqq x_{jk} \leqq 1)$ is the activity level of the jth $(j = 1 \cdots n_k)$ project of management unit k.

g_k is a vector $(m_k \times 1)$ of variable coefficients giving the goal of levels for the kth management unit k.

The central unit problem is about determining the goal allocation based on the shadow price of the goal constraints obtained from the problem concerning management unit k, for the purpose of achieving the overall goal as shown in expression (25.4).

$$\begin{aligned} \text{Max} \quad & \sum_{k=1}^{K} \pi_k g_k \\ \text{s.t.} \quad & \sum_{k=1}^{K} A_k g_k \leqq g_0, \quad g_k \geqq 0, \quad k = 1 \sim K. \end{aligned} \tag{25.4}$$

Where π_k is the $(1 \times m_k)$ vector of weights shadow prices of management unit k.

g_0 is an $(m_0 \times 1)$ vector of stipulations.

A_k are $(m_0 \times M_k)$ matrices.

The problem concerning operating units j, k is about performing optimization between projects through cost minimization assigned by management unit k as shown in expression (25.5).

$$\begin{aligned} \text{Min} \quad & \pi_k a_{jk} \\ \text{s.t.} \quad & B_{jk} a_{jk} \geqq b_{jk}, \quad a_{jk} \geqq 0. \end{aligned} \tag{25.5}$$

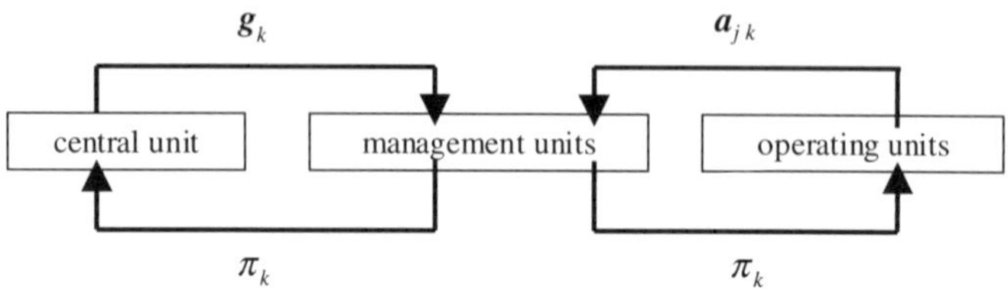

Fig. 25.2 Solution process

Where B_{jk} is an $(n_{jk} \times m_k)$ matrix of technological coefficients.
b_{jk} is an $(n_{jk} \times 1)$ vector of stipulations.

The calculation process for these problems is as shown in Figure 25.2: the central unit assigns goal value g_k to each management unit, and each management division calculates vector π_k of the shadow price of the goal constraint using expression (25.3) based on g_k, and passes it on to the central unit and each operating unit. Based on this, the central unit calculates goal value g_k by using expression (25.3), and assigns it to each management unit. Each operating unit calculates a_{jk} by using expression (25.5), and reports it to each management unit. Each management unit calculates π_k by using expression (25.3) based on g_k and a_{jk}, and passes it on to the central unit and each operating unit. The same process is repeated until an optimal solution is achieved.

The calculation process regarding the central unit, each management unit and each operating unit shown in Figure 25.2 finishes after a finite number of times.

25.3.2 Generalized Goal Decomposition Model approach to supply chain

The aforementioned GGDM is applied to intra-company transactions in cases where company-wide optimization is sought instead of local optimization of each task (procurement of raw materials or components, production, sales, etc.). In the organization structure of GGDM shown in Figure 25.1, assume that the respective operating divisions in charge of the procurement of raw materials or components, production, sales, etc. consist of management units, and operating units which comprise the management units. Weighting the objective function involves the use of an interactive solving method: weighting is decided through trial and error by the manager in relation to the calculation results. It may, however, be useful to build a scale by implementing the method of paired comparisons with respect to the manager in weighting.

Suppose the goal in expression (25.3) is time (e.g., delivery date) or inventory volume, etc., and create a formula for the respective operating divisions in charge of the procurement of raw materials or components, production, sales, etc. as a management unit problem based on GP. The formula is created on the basis of expression (25.5) with respect to projects in the respective operating units in charge of procurement, production, sales, etc., and on the basis of expression (25.4) with respect to the central unit problem.

Goal value g_k is assigned by the central unit to each management unit. Based on g_k, vector of the shadow price of the goal constraint, π_k, is calculated by using expression (25.3) for each management division. In the central unit problem, each management unit is assigned goal value g_k calculated by using expression (25.4) based on this. With respect to each operating unit, a_{jk} is calculated on the basis of expression (25.5) and reported to the central unit. The central unit calculates π_k by using expression (25.3) based on g_k and a_{jk}, and assigns it to the central unit and each operating unit. The same process is repeated until an optimal solution is achieved. As for the goal, it is possible to develop a model by determining the deviation from the cumulative processing time in each operating unit, and by minimizing the deviation which is regarded as the inventory volume, assuming that the output (processing volume) of each operating unit is the volume supplied to downstream operating units, in consideration of delivery date management. In contrast with cases in which GGDM is applied to an intra-company supply chain as described above, no central unit exists in cases where GGDM is applied to the local optimization and global optimization of B2B transactions such as those of suppliers, manufacturers, dealers, etc. To achieve a global optimum in such cases, assume that coordination would function, create a formula for the central unit problem as if a central unit exists, while assuming that suppliers, manufacturers, dealers, etc. are management units which consist of subordinate management units, and create a formula with respect to each of them in the form of a management unit problem and an operating unit problem.

25.4 Mathematical Programming Model for SCM

25.4.1 *Mathematical programming model*

The previous section described an explanatory model to look into the coordination process in SCM from the viewpoint of behavioral science, by applying GGDM. The next section examines a mathematical programming model of a supply chain aimed at global optimization rather than the local optimization of each company (supplier, manufacturer, dealer, etc.) in SCM.

There are various types of mathematical programming models, such as the cost minimization model, profit maximization model, multi-goals optimization model, and model based on game theory. The following section explores the multi-goals optimization model for the entire supply chain.

25.4.2 *Multi-goals optimization model for SCM*

A mathematical programming model for the supply chain of suppliers, manufacturers, dealers, etc. is described below. Assume that suppliers, manufacturers and dealers are denoted by business unit j ($j \leqq 1$), and consider a situation in which product k is handled at a business unit engaged in delivery such a distribution ($j = 0$). Assume that the processing or preparation/order-filling volume of product k per unit period (e.g., 1 day) at business unit j is x_{Ijk}, the target period is h_{Ijk} unit period, and the capacity volume (e.g., number of lines) is θ_{Ijk}. Then, the preparation/order-filling volume of product k during the target period at business unit j, q_{Ijk}, is expressed by the following equation.

$$q_{Ijk} = \theta_{Ijk}\, h_{Ijk}\, x_{Ijk}. \tag{25.6}$$

As the sum of the volume at the beginning of the period q_{Bjk} and the preparation/order-filling volume during the period q_{Ijk} is equal to the sum of the volume at the end of the period q_{Ejk} and the volume corresponding to completed preparation and fulfilled orders q_{Ojk}, the preparation/order-filling volume is expressed by the following equation.

$$q_{Bjk} + q_{Ijk} = q_{Ejk} + q_{Ojk}. \tag{25.7}$$

For example, suppose that the preparation/order-filling volume is to be processed at business unit j; the relationship among the volume at the beginning of the period Q_{Bjk}, the volume corresponding to completed preparation and fulfilled orders q_{Ojk}, the processing volume during the period Q_{Ojk}, and the volume at the end of the period Q_{Ejk} is expressed by Eq. (25.8). Further, the processing volume during the period Q_{Ojk} is expressed by Eq. (25.9), as a product of the processing or preparation/order-filling volume per unit period (e.g., 1 day) at business unit j, x_{Ijk}, the number of unit periods which constitute the target period, h_{Ijk}, and the capacity volume (e.g., number of lines), θ_{Ijk}.

$$Q_{Bjk} + q_{Ojk} = Q_{Ejk} + Q_{Ojk}. \tag{25.8}$$

$$Q_{Ojk} = \theta_{Ojk}\, h_{Ojk}\, x_{Ojk}. \tag{25.9}$$

Suppose that the processing volume of business unit j during the period, Q_{Ojk}, equals the preparation/order-filling volume of business unit $j+1$ during the period, q_{Ijk}.

$$Q_{Ojk} = q_{I,j+1,k}. \tag{25.10}$$

Assume that the distinction of business unit j is n based on $j = 1$, let $j = n$ denote a dealer, and consider a situation in which the product is to be sold to user u.

Here, let the volume of product k ordered by user u be denoted by Q_{uk} and the ratio of the volume of supply that can fulfill the ordered volume in the period be denoted by fulfillment rate r_{unk}.

Accordingly, the volume of product k traded by dealer n with user u, Q_{Onk}, is expressed by the following equation.

$$Q_{Onk} = \sum_u r_{unk} Q_{unk}. \tag{25.11}$$

Quantitative constraints on various resources d required for producing or processing each product at business unit j is expressed by the following expression, assuming that a_{jkd} is a technical coefficient and resources are capped at l_{jd}.

$$\sum_k a_{jkd}\, q'_{Ojk} \leqq l_{jd}. \tag{25.12}$$

$$q'_{Ojk} = h_{Ojk}\, x_{Ojk}. \tag{25.13}$$

Profit π_j of business unit j is expressed by the following equation, which involves taking into account the variable costs associated with preparation, ordering and processing and the fixed costs associated with changes in inventory costs and capacity (e.g., number of lines), and deducting them from sales.

Assume that the sales generated by dealer at $j = n$ correspond to the sales volume based on the product-by-product fulfillment rate with respect to each user according to Eq. (25.11).

$$\begin{aligned}\Pi_j = \sum_{k=1} \{ & p_{Ojk} Q_{Ojk} - (v_{Ijk}\theta_{Ijk}h_{Ijk}x_{Ijk} + v_{Ojk}\theta_{Ojk}h_{Ojk}x_{Ojk} \\ & + \frac{q_{Bjk} + q_{Ejk}}{2} v_{Mjk} + \frac{Q_{Bjk} + Q_{Ejk}}{2} v_{Cjk} \\ & + \theta_{Ijk}F_{Ijk} + \theta_{Ojk}F_{Ojk})\}. \end{aligned} \tag{25.14}$$

$$p_{Ojk} = v_{I,j+1,k}. \tag{25.15}$$

Further, profit π_0 in distribution ($j = 0$) is expressed by the following equation based on the delivery volume of each product between the business divisions.

$$\Pi_0 = \sum_j \sum_k (p_{Djk} - v_{Djk})\theta_{Djk} h_{Djk} x_{Djk} - \theta_D F_D. \tag{25.16}$$

$$q_{Ijk} = \theta_{Djk} h_{Djk} x_{Djk}. \tag{25.17}$$

Marginal profit is calculated by deducting the opportunity cost associated with not being able to fulfill orders from users in the period from the sum of the profits in distribution ($j = 0$) and the profits of each business unit, and is expressed by Eq. (25.18). C_{Ouk} represents the opportunity loss per unit due to not being able to fulfill the user's order in the period.

$$\Pi = \Pi_0 + \sum_j \Pi_j - \sum_u \sum_k (1 - r_{uk}) C_{Ouk} Q_{nuk}. \tag{25.18}$$

The lead times, namely, the lead time for preparation/order T_{Ok}, the lead time for processing T_{Ik}, the lead time for delivery T_{Dk}, and the lead time of the entire supply chain T are expressed by the following equations.

$$\sum_j \frac{1}{x_{Ojk}} = T_{Ok}, \quad \sum_j \frac{1}{x_{Ijk}} = T_{Ik}, \quad \sum_j \frac{1}{x_{Djk}} = T_{Dk},$$
$$\sum_j \left(\frac{1}{x_{Ojk}} + \frac{1}{x_{Ijk}} + \frac{1}{x_{Djk}} \right) = T. \tag{25.19}$$

For example, suppose that the lead times are weighted as follows: 4 to the lead time of the entire supply chain, 2 to the lead time for delivery, and 1 each to the lead time for preparation/order and the lead time for processing. Suppose that the highest priority is given to each of these lead times, the second-highest priority to weighting each profit goal (omitted with respect to each weight w_j), and the third-highest priority to weighting the product-by-product fulfillment rate with respect to each user (omitted with respect to each weight w_j). The objective function in this case is expressed by expression (25.20). The constraint estuation is expressed by expression (25.21), which assumes the relationships described by Eqs. (25.14) through (25.19) but simplifies and trims the overlapping sections in those formulations.

Here, a model for multiple goals was constructed, assuming constraints on resources in each business division, while giving the highest priority to the respective lead times for preparation/order, processing, delivery and the entire supply chain, the second-highest priority to the profit goal of each business unit and the profit goal in distribution, and the third-highest priority to the product-by-product fulfillment rate with respect to each user. It is possible to set various goals other than those mentioned here, and to study models assuming other various situations. The same applies to the intra-company supply chain.

$$\begin{aligned}
\text{Min}\ & P_1(4d_T^+ + 2d_{TD}^+ + d_{TO}^+ + d_{TI}^+) + P_2\Big(\sum w_j d_{\pi j}^- + w_0 d_{\pi 0}^-\Big) \\
& + P_3\Big(\sum\sum w_{uk} d_{uk}^-\Big). \qquad (25.20)\\
\text{s.t.}\ & \pi_j + d_{\pi j}^- - d_{\pi j}^+ = \pi_j^*, \quad \pi_0 + d_{\pi 0}^- - d_{\pi 0}^+ = \pi_0^*, \\
& T_{Ok} + d_{TO}^- - d_{TO}^+ = T_O^*, \quad T_{Dk} + d_{TD}^- - d_{TD}^+ = T_D^*, \\
& T + d_T^- - d_T^+ = T_T^*, \quad r_{uk} + d_{uk}^- - d_{uk}^+ = r_{uk}^*, \\
& Q_{Onk} = \sum_u r_{uk} Q_{uk}, \quad \sum_k a_{jkd} q_{Ojk} \le l_{jd}, \\
& q_{Ijk} = \theta_{Ijk} h_{Ijk} x_{Ijk}, \quad q_{Bjk} + q_{Ijk} = q_{Ejk} + q_{Ojk}, \\
& Q_{Bjk} + q_{Ojk} = Q_{Ejk} + Q_{Ojk}, \quad q_{Ojk} = \theta_{Ojk} h_{Ojk} x_{Ojk}, \\
& Q_{Ojk} = q_{I,j+1,k},\ q_{Ijk} = \theta_{Djk}\, h_{Djk}\, x_{Djk}, \quad \theta_{Ojk}\,, \theta_{Ijk}\,, \theta_{Djk} \in I \\
& d_{\pi j}{}^+\,, d_{\pi 0}^+\,, d_{TO}^+\,, d_{TD}^+\,, d_T^+\,, d_{\pi j}^-\,, d_{\pi 0}^-\,, d_{TO}^-\,, d_{TD}^-\,, d_T^-\,, \\
& x_{Ojk}, x_{Ijk}, x_{Djk} \ge 0. \qquad (25.21)
\end{aligned}$$

25.5 Conclusion

In intra-company transactions, if company-wide optimization is to be sought through the optimization of a series of tasks instead of the local optimization of each task in the workflow (such as the procurement of raw materials or components, etc, production, sales and distribution) or if local optimization of each company in the B2B supply chain (supplier, manufacturer, dealer, etc.) is to be expanded towards global optimization, these have to be coordinated and thus managed in SCM. In studying SCM, it may be instructive to examine the coordination process in situations where conflicting goals exist from the viewpoint of behavioral science by applying GGDM. This involves assuming GP, weighting and prioritizing multiple conflicting goals, and working out a compromise solution. If the problem is about creating a formula based on the combination of an ordering method and a weighting method, imagination must be demonstrated in regards to the shadow price. While there is a wide range of programming models aimed at the global optimization of the supply chain other than the one examined in this paper, varying by objective and by situation, useful approaches to tackling uncertainties may include approaches based on sensitivity analysis, which involves gradually changing the parameters according to changes in the management environment and other circumstances, as well as stochastic approaches.

References

Dantzig, G. B. and Wolfe, P. (1961). The decomposition algorithm for linear programs, *Econometrica* 29.

Dantzig, G. B. (1963). *Linear Programming and Extensions*, Princeton University Press.

Fushimi, T. Fukukawa, T., and Yamaguchi, T. (1987). *Multicriteria Programming for Management*, Morikita Publishing Company. (in Japanese)

Hamada, K. (2001). An application of TOC to the BSC in SCM, *Kigyo-Kaikei* 53-11, pp. 31–37. (in Japanese)

Handfield, R. B. (1999). *Introduction to Supply Chain Management*, Prentice-Hall.

Kuroda, M. (2004). *Supply Chain Management*, Asakurasyoten. (in Japanese)

Mita, H. (1999). The optimum order requirements of trade partners and the supply chain optimization management, *Management Accounting* 7-12, pp. 91–113. (in Japanese)

Monden, Y. (1978). *Multi-Goal-Level Management Accounting*, Dobunkan Publishing Company Ltd. (in Japanese)

Ruefli, T. W. (1971). A generalized goal decomposition model, *Management Science* 17-8.

Ruefli, T. W. (1971). Behavioral externalities in decentralized organizations, *Management Science* 9-5.

CHAPTER

26

Electronic Markets in Support of Procurement Processes Along the Automotive Supply Chain*

Henry Aigbedo
Assistant Professor, School of Business Administration
Oakland University

Mohan Tanniru
Professor, Eller College of Management
University of Arizona

26.1 Introduction

Faced with strong competition, manufacturing firms in many industries are striving now more than ever to look for different ways to reduce costs, improve their operations, and increase the profitability of their business. Until recently, the procurement function in most firms had been largely considered an operational activity and, hence, played minimal role in formulating corporate strategy. This pattern is changing, as many companies such as DaimlerChrysler, Ford Motor Company, and Honda Motor Manufacturing Company are beginning to accord due recognition to the procurement function, thereby using it as a source of competitive advantage. (e.g., Fitzgerald, 1995; Krause, 1997; Vonderembse and Tracey, 1999). Furthermore, Debra Bell, chief procurement officer at AT&T, states that

*Originally published by Taylor and Francis in the Journal, *Production Planning and Control*, 15 (7), 2004 (http://www.tandf.co.uk/journals/titles/09537287.asp).

procurement is viewed as strategic from operational and cost management perspectives (Fredette 2001).

This increased focus on procurement is largely due to the realization that procurement costs constitute a substantial portion of manufacturing as well as total costs. For example, Degraeve and Roodhooft (2001) observed that the percentage of the cost of purchased goods and services can differ significantly by industry, ranging from about 35% in the service industry to 90% in the petrochemical industry. For many manufacturing firms, a significant portion of this cost relates to the purchase of raw materials and parts used for production. (e.g., Bresnen and Fowler, 1994; Watts *et al.*, 1995), as well as the cost of Maintenance, Repair, and Operating (MRO) supplies — items that do not go into the product, but are essential for the effective operation of the firm. Furthermore, the growing trend in outsourcing and the importance of managing supply chains to meet changing customer demands has brought procurement to the forefront of management discussions (e.g., Rota *et al.*, 2002).

Recent attention on the use of Internet and the electronic markets it supports has made many firms look to improve their procurement efficiency, especially when these costs constitute a substantial portion of manufacturing as well as total costs (Degraeve and Roodhooft, 2001). In the case of a complex supply chain that connects various suppliers with customers in succession, the electronic markets have to support many of the companion activities relating to the procurement activity; such as supplier validation, some supplier relationship management (especially, when some of the products are jointly developed and serviced), training, etc.; if procurement efficiencies are to be realized. For these reasons, we broadly define procurement to include all activities in the supply chain that have a direct impact on the selection of suppliers and acquisition of materials needed in support of a firm's production of goods or delivery of services. The objective of this paper, hence, is to explore the role of electronic markets in support of the procurement function, under this broader definition, of one manufacturing industry — the automobile industry.

The remaining part of the paper is organized as follows. Section 26.2 discusses some prior research on procurement in general and the role of electronic markets in support of such procurement along the supply chain in particular. In Section 26.3, we describe our research study that uses both informal discussions and in-depth analysis of a segment of an automotive supply chain to better understand the issues of support needed along such supply chains. Section 26.4 discusses the implication of this study and provides some directions for future research, and Section 26.5 ends the paper with some concluding comments.

26.2 Prior Research

In recent years, firms have become more cognizant of the importance of building synergies with partners in the downstream and upstream sides of their value chain, often under product life cycle management. Such synergies increase the efficiency and effectiveness of the operations, leading to reduced costs and increased profits. For example, Towill *et al.* (2002) discuss the importance of integration within the context of the seamless supply chain, with an idealized material flow system. By carrying out an in-depth analysis of 20 European automotive supply chains, they position each supply chain along four stages of supply chain integration: baseline, functional, internal, and external. Among other things, they report that although none of the supply chains studied has attained the seamless status, about 20% have come close to this ideal, and therefore can serve as good sites for benchmarking visitations.

In an earlier study, Lee and Sasser (1995) describe the importance of supply chain integration within the framework of design for supply chain management (DFSCM), and they focus on how Hewlett Packard used this approach to design one of their products, Rainbow. Both of these articles incorporate procurement activities from logistics and early supplier involvement in design perspectives (also see Dowlatshahi, 1997). By viewing the procurement process strategically, three critical issues come into play in managing the supply chain: *sourcing, selection, and development* of suppliers. While sourcing strategy relates to a company's policy regarding the number of suppliers needed to meet its material or sub-assembly requirements, supplier selection relates to the choice of suppliers that will meet these requirements. Supplier development is a special type of relationship a firm nurtures with a few select suppliers in order to meet certain strategic requirements. The following discussion elaborates on these three issues, as they impact the support of a firm's procurement function.

Two major types of sourcing strategies are recognized in the literature: *sole and multiple sourcing.* Sole sourcing, which is purchase of a given part from one supplier, can help a firm realize savings in transaction costs as well as opportunities to develop close collaboration and mutual trust. On the other hand, multiple sourcing increases a firm's bargaining power by allowing it seek reduced purchase prices on a product and reduce the risk of delivery failure if an unanticipated event occurs. The fire that interrupted the operations at one of Toyota's supplier plants (Nishiguchi and Beaudett, 1998), and the excitement that preceded the entry of electronic exchanges (e.g., Covisint) to support competitive bidding and potential price reductions are some of the reasons for multiple sourcing. However, there is evidence that many companies have been moving in the direction of reducing their supplier base (e.g., Liker and Yu, 2000).

Dowlatshahi (1999) characterizes buyer-supplier relationships into six types, including, one buyer/one supplier (cooperative system), few buyers/few suppliers (balanced power system), multiple buyers/multiple suppliers (adversarial system). He notes that a "balanced power system" provides protection for the buyer and the seller, as it enables the buyer to alter levels of business to its suppliers based on their performance, and protects the seller against possible sales reduction or loss of business from a given buyer. Hence, any procurement support has to consider the sourcing strategy of the firm and the associated buyer-supplier collaboration in product development and requirement definition.

Supplier selection is a crucial issue especially for firms that deal with complex products. This is important not only to reduce the procurement costs, but also to respond to a firm's competitiveness both in the short and long run. Lee *et al.* (2003) echo this point by observing that supplier selection is a strategic issue to consider in supply chain management. Some of the issues here include price flexibility, ability to react quickly to changing customer requirements in terms of volume and mix, and ability to effectively address quality issues. Thus, procurement has to consider coordination of information between the suppliers and the firm in support of this flexibility, along with other basic price-related factors.

Supplier development typically occurs between a firm and the suppliers with which it has strategic partnerships. Supplier development varies in scope and depth, depending on the company policy and the degree of strategic importance of the procured components. It can range from simple communications regarding product needs and quality issues, to training and technical support in product development. These practices vary from country to country as well. In a comparative study of supplier relationships within the automotive industry in the US, Japan, and Korea, Dyer *et al.* (1998) found significant differences in the level of communication and technical support a firm provides its suppliers. A number of world-class firms have used such strategic partnerships effectively for competitive advantage.

For example, Dell Computers has formed strategic partnership with computer monitor suppliers (Magretta, 1998) and the automotive manufacturers have used strategic partnerships with some of their key suppliers (Liker and Yu, 2000). In other words, procurement support may vary depending on how firms view their relationship with a supplier, and the nature of support may include joint product development, sharing of key design data, and exchange of quality and schedule interruption information.

In summary, a procurement activity has to be tied to a firm's strategy on sourcing, selection and development of suppliers, and any support provided for this activity has to consider collaboration of the firm with its suppliers on product development and requirement definition. This also includes sharing of data on product quality, schedules, customer preferences, etc., in addition to conventional procurement activities such as bidding and transaction handling. The issue then is, how can an electronic market support such a complex set of supply chain requirements? Next, we will look at some prior research in this arena.

The growth of Internet in support of B2B e-commerce, which includes procurement function along with other types of information exchange, was anticipated to grow to $7.29 trillion in 2004 from about $145 billion in 1999 (Noyce, 2002). While the growth in the use of Internet in B2C markets is somewhat mixed (Chopra and Van Mieghem, 2000), its use in support of Business-to-Business (B2B) transactions, especially through technologies such as exchanges (i.e., virtual locations on the Internet that bring corporate buyers and sellers together to trade with one another) was expected to grow significantly. A major motivation for the use of exchanges by firms is the anticipated cost reduction and improvement in efficiencies that can be derived. For example, in 2000, more than twenty North American energy and utility companies, including America Electric Power, Detroit Edison, and Edison International, formed a consortium exchange, called the Pantellos Group, to reduce their procurement costs (Senia, 2000). Owens and Minor, a health care firm in the United States, operates a private exchange to reduce procurement costs through use of competitive bidding for its parts and supplies (Nelson-Rowe, 2001).

The relative successes of some of these consortium and private exchanges have created the impetus for the formation of an automotive exchange, called Covisint, by companies such as General Motors, Ford, DaimlerChrysler and Nissan, and its initial intent was to reduce procurement costs and improve efficiencies along their supply chain. While on-line, dedicated, interface between automotive firms and their suppliers is not new (technologies such as EDI have been in place for quite some time), exchanges are supposed to provide a broader set of opportunities for customer/supplier interaction. However, even here the receptivity to such exchanges has been mixed. Covisint's intent to attract a large number of suppliers has run into some difficulties (Tie, 2001; Moozaki, 2001), and part of it can be attributed to the perception that the exchange owners (i.e., the automotive manufacturers: OEMs) are the primary beneficiaries of any value received. Barua *et al.* (2001) observe that the success of any e-business initiative depends on the readiness of a firm's customers and suppliers to engage in electronic interactions in support of their operations, as well as the value they perceive in such participation. In order to better understand the critical issues that appear to impact the adoption of exchange technology such as Covisint on the automotive supply chain, the authors initiated a two-phase research study in 2002 and the results of this study are discussed next.

26.3 Research Study

In the *first phase*, the authors interviewed several industry executives from the automotive sector (see Figure 26.1 for a profile of the participant group) and some of their observations are summarized below:

- Significant *mistrust* exists with respect to "order" information provided by the OEMs to lower tiers, as such information may be changed by the OEMs with short notice so as to enable them meet changing customer preferences on certain items.
- Beyond tier 2, the *degree of technology sophistication* is low, as many suppliers in these lower levels include many small shops. This creates a significant challenge for an electronic exchange that is intent on supplier integration.

Firm	Description (supplier sales over $1B, OEMs are in the top 6 in market share)	Person Interviewed
Alpha	Tier 1 supplier	VP of Information Technology
Beta	Tier 1/Tier 2 supplier	IS Manager in Supply Chain
Gamma	Tier 1/Tier 2 supplier	IS Manager in Operations
Delta	OEM	IS Manager in Supply Chain
Epsilon	OEM	Procurement Manager (Parts/Supplies)

Fig. 26.1 A few participants in the study

- Lower tiers (beyond tier 2) are not willing to take significant risk in managing large inventories using the OEM's long-term forecasts. So, they rely on orders officially placed by their immediate customers, thus *limiting the value of any long-term forecast* information provided by the OEMs.
- Some lower tiers that supply bulk materials such as plastic, fabric, and metal are *not easily influenced* by the OEMs, because their total sales to OEMs is relatively small in comparison with their overall sales to all other customers such as major chemical and clothing manufacturers.
- OEMs have special interest in parts that relate to safety of the automobile and those that distinguish the product in the eyes of the customer. Therefore, they typically dictate to their tier-one suppliers the firms (e.g., tier-two or tier-three suppliers) OEMs consider appropriate. This alters the control structure from a direct tier-to-tier hierarchical structure to one where a higher-level tier could by-pass the next tier in making critical decisions regarding the supplier base of lower level tiers.
- A supplier of a highly customized part such as fabric needs to be able to respond promptly to requirements of the OEMs since changes in product mix usually occur. The suppliers usually carry more inventories than immediately needed or for which payment by the customer is guaranteed, so as to meet this responsiveness requirement. Excess inventories arising from the above often lead to "deadstocks" at the end of a program. Negotiations between the supplier and the customer to absorb the costs of these deadstocks tend to be very arduous and the issue typically takes a long time to be resolved.

Given the wide ranging technical as well as organizational issues the automotive supply chain has to address, a *second phase* (phase 2) of the study focused on one segment of the supply chain in-depth. This phase focused on one particular component of an automobile — *the interior*. See Figure 26.2 for a segment of the supply chain of the interior.

On the extreme right of the figure, we have three plants of an OEM X. In order to understand the factors influencing the decision process, we analyze each customer/supplier dyad (an agent pair) moving from right to left. The three interior plants shown are co-located with the three OEM plants to facilitate just-in-time delivery of parts to the plants. Each tier 1 plant supports different programs for the manufacture of different models of an automobile. Although not shown in details in the figure, we note that the same interior manufacturer supplies to other OEMs as well. In like manner, other tier 1 suppliers also supply to the same OEM assembly plants to

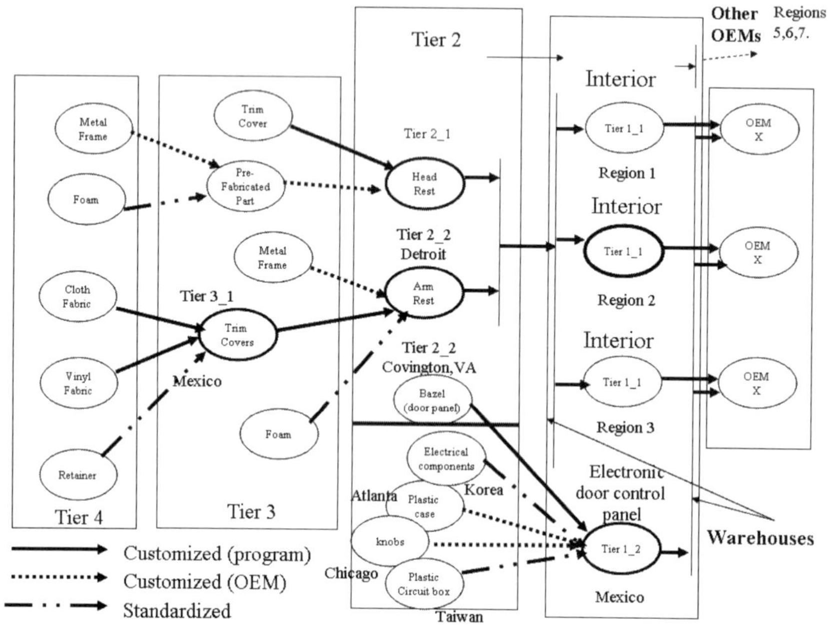

Fig. 26.2 A supply chain segment for an automotive OEM

which the interior plants deliver their products. An example of this latter scenario is the tier 1 supplier of electric door control panel: the plant that manufactures these door control panels is in Mexico, and it ships the needed material in bulk to a warehouse near the plants for distribution as needed. Critical attributes of this Supplier/Customer dyad are the *distance between supplier/customer and time constraints relating to just-in-time delivery of items to the OEM's plant.*

Moving to the next level (tier 2), we focused on the plant that manufactures *headrest and armrest* and those that manufacture items that go into the electronic door control panel. Headrests and armrests are manufactured and shipped to the interior assembly plants for this OEM as well as others. Since the firms are different and programs are different, these items are unique to the OEMs to which they are supplied. Similarly, the plant that manufactures the electronic door control panel gets its components from various other plants around the world, including Taiwan and Korea. This global sourcing of certain items such as the plastic circuit box (from Taiwan) and the electronic components (from Korea) introduces some logistics challenges to the supply chain.

The component called "bazel" used for the door control panel brings to light some special characteristics that we find in some automotive supply chains: a firm playing a dual role depending on the products it supplies. The firm that assembles the "interior" owns the plant that makes the "armrest" and "headrest." Second, the bazel is actually manufactured by the firm that assembles the interior, even though these activities occur at different plant locations, partly due to the color matching requirements and varying core competencies. In other words, a firm that is viewed as "tier 1" supplier for one product (i.e., interior) may be playing the role of "tier 2" supplier for some other products (i.e., bazel), and a single firm may own plants that operate at both tier 1 (i.e., interior assembly) and tier 2 (i.e., armrest and headrest) levels of the same supply chain. So, a hierarchical classification of the product is probably more appropriate for understanding the supply chain than a firm's classification as tier 1 or tier 2. Therefore, the relevant attributes such as *who the customer is and who owns the plant that manufactures a product* are critical in understanding the technical sophistication of the firm making the product and the organizational dynamics within the supply chain.

Next, the *headrest* requires two suppliers for its major components at the tier-3 level (*pre-fabricated part and trim cover*) and the *armrest* requires three suppliers for its major components (*metal frame, foam, and trim cover*) also at the tier-3 level. One of the reasons for using different supply frameworks for the headrest and the armrest is the available capacity to make both and the need to maintain flexibility and cost advantages. The *metal frame* that goes into a headrest is common across many programs, but is unique to a particular OEM. On the other hand, the *foam* is a commodity product and is common across programs and OEMs. The *trim cover*, however, is unique to each program as it captures the color and texture characteristics of the interior for that program. This product variation impacts the *level of flexibility* needed in the supply chain. Following on to the plant that makes the electronic door control panel, we note that the component, "bazel," is customized to match with the fabric of the interior in a given program; the door knobs and plastic casing are customized for an OEM; and other items are relatively standard.

Moving further along to the lower left portion of the fourth supply panel of Figure 26.2 (tier 4 level), we see that the firm that manufactures "trim covers" uses two major components: fabric (vinyl or cloth) and the retainers, which hold the cloth in place. The fabric that is used in a given program is customized to fit the customer preferences on the color and style, while the retainers are "standard" products. So, the relevant attributes for link between a customer/supplier dyad include *product characteristics (e.g., differences in the product customization such as standard, standard over a particular range of products, customized for a particular program).*

Given the importance of having the right fabric for a particular program, often the fabric supplier is pre-selected by the OEM and the trim cover manufacturer does not have a say in that part of the supply chain, other than coordinating the procurement and shipment of the supplier's product. In other words, some of the sourcing and selection decisions are outside the control of a customer, thus adding another attribute to the supplier/customer link: *The firm that makes the sourcing and/or selection decisions of each component.*

In summary, the analysis of this short supply chain segment points out that each link in the customer/supplier dyad along the supply network exhibits different properties, and hence may need different types of support. However, if we are to improve the overall efficiency and effectiveness of the supply chain, the support provided for each of these links has to be integrated. This is similar to any information systems application integration that is needed to provide an executive view of an organization's financial health, while at the same time supporting the disparate needs of individual business units. The major difference however is that the business drivers of various individual entities along the supply chain are different. Also, the executive view an OEM would like to take to establish the overall price and quality for the automobile are influenced by units that are not part of the same organization, thus making the integration of support much harder. Some of the observations made during phase 1 of the study reinforce these difficulties. Hence, the issue of exchange support along the supply chain has to include not only the technology integration of application support at each level, but also the business value synchronization and this is examined further in the next section, using several frameworks from prior research.

26.4 Discussion and Research Directions

Mass customization as a strategic business framework has been widely discussed in the literature (e.g., Kotha, 1996; Da Silveria *et al.*, 2001) as it applies to provision of tangible goods to meet the needs of individual customers in a cost effective manner. Similar framework may be used to develop the type of services an exchange may provide to meet the varying needs of customers along the supply chain in a cost-effective way. These services have to support the sourcing, selection, and supplier development of each customer/supplier dyad along the supply chain.

While similar services can be provided to many different customer/supplier dyads, one has to recognize that each of them exhibits different attributes as seen from the discussion in the earlier section. In addition, the suppliers have varying technological maturity and deal in transactions that differ in volume, timing and travel distance, thus calling for differences in the pricing and scope of services offered. The frameworks discussed in the building of decision support architectures in the Management Information Systems (MIS) literature can help an exchange develop a myriad set of tools, databases, and interfaces, which can be selected and used in an ad-hoc manner by the individual customer/supplier dyad, and some of the exchanges such as Covisint have proposed such an approach.

The biggest challenge, however, is convincing various users to adopt this technology, especially considering the fact that these services are to support entities in different organizations, not always with significant goal congruence on the objectives of such supply chain integration. In fact, the innovative/functional framework proposed by Fisher (1997) recognizes that supply links and chains associated with highly customized products (i.e., innovative products) exhibit significant risk of obsolescence (i.e., changing consumer behavior may make certain inventories quickly obsolete) and have to be managed differently than the supply links and chains associated with commodity type products, where the focus is on efficiencies in inventory and logistics management.

Hence, it is not just the scope and price of a service offering of an exchange that will impact its adoption, but other factors such as technological support, having confidence in the way the information is used, and agreement on how to share risk. While the "portfolio of services" offered by an exchange, in a manner similar to what is offered in the development of any intra-organizational Decision Support System (DSS), can provide a technical architecture, perceived lack of inter-organizational goal congruence, and asymmetry in the technical and process maturity play a significant role in its adoption by various players in the supply chain.

Given the myriad features that are needed to support a supply chain and the complexities related to their adoption by various supply chain members, there appears to be a need to introduce the concept of core competencies. Two broad frameworks could possibly be adopted for articulating these core competencies: the horizontal framework and the vertical framework. Under the horizontal framework, the exchange focuses on certain services that are generally used by all players in the supply chain (such as portal or auction tools). Under the vertical framework, an exchange offers a focused set of services to certain segment of the supply chain, thus reducing the variability in the organizational goal congruence or technical maturity. An example of the vertical framework could entail offering in-depth product development support to OEM/Tier 1 or Tier1/Tier 2. Developing a horizontal or vertical focus may allow, over time, for the development of a federation of exchanges, each providing targeted set of services independently, yet collaborating to ensure that these application services are integrated.

The role of targeted services in support of vertical or horizontal supply chain focus has become even more critical, as discussions in product lifecycle management (e.g., PLM 2003) are calling for both a horizontal integration of supply chain with demand chain (from OEM to customer and eventually to the disposer of the product), and a vertical integration of these supply and demand chains with product design and development. The support services needed to manage horizontal integration include alternative supplier sourcing, when interruptions occur on the supply side and volatility exists on the demand side. The services needed to support vertical integration include collaborative diagnosis and design of parts, when design flaws are detected or core supplier interruptions occur. In other words, not only do electronic markets that support procurement have to look at the context within which the tiered supply chains operate, but they also have to work with technologies that support the entire product life cycle such as the integration of inter-organizational databases and Radio Frequency Identification (RFID) technologies to track products, etc.

26.5 Conclusion

In summary, procurement activity in this paper is viewed in a broader context by making it encompass a firm's strategy on sourcing, selection, and development of suppliers. This makes it necessary for any electronic market, intent on providing supply chain support, to consider possible collaboration of the firm and its suppliers on product development and requirement definition, as well as sharing of data on product quality, schedules, customer preferences, besides conventional procurement activities such as bidding and transaction handling. Based on some in-depth analysis of a supply chain segment and some brainstorming discussions with some key executives in the automotive industry, the broader role of an exchange is shown to be critical. The exchange has to support different players in the supply chain with varying requirements based on where they are in the supply chain and what particular program/product they are supporting. Several frameworks were discussed to provide guidance for future research in the way electronic markets can effectively support complex supply chains, such as the automotive supply chain discussed in this paper.

References

Barua, A., Prabhudev, K., Winston, A., and Yin, F. (2001). Driving e-business excellence, *Sloan Management Review* 43-1, pp. 36–44.

Bresnen, M. and Fowler, C. (1994). The organizational correlates and consequences of subcontracting: evidence from a survey of South Wales businesses, *Journal of Management Studies* 31-6, pp. 847–864.

Chopra, S. and Van Mieghem, J. (2000). Which e-business is right for your supply chain? *Supply Chain Management Review* July/August, pp. 32–41.

Da Silveria, G., Borenstein, D., and Fogliatto, F. (2001). Mass customization: literature review and research directions, *International Journal of Production Economics* 72-1, pp. 1–13.

Degraeve, Z. and Roodhooft, F. (2001). A smarter way to buy, *Harvard Business Review* 79-6, pp. 22–23.

Dowlatshahi, S. (1997). The role of product design in designer-buyer-supplier interface, *Production Planning and Control* 8-6, pp. 522–532.

Dowlatshahi, S. (1999). Bargaining power in buyer-supplier relationships, *Production and Inventory Management Journal* 40-1, pp. 27–35.

Dyer, J., Cho, D., and Chu, W. (1998) Strategic supplier segmentation: the next "best practice" in supply chain management, *California Management Review* 40-2, pp. 57–77.

Fisher, M. (1997). What is the right supply chain for your product? *Harvard Business Review* 75-2, pp. 105–116.

Fitzgerald, K. (1995). For superb supplier development — Honda wins, *Purchasing* 119-4, pp. 32–40.

Fredette, M. (2001). An interview with Debra Bell: one on one, *Journal of Supply Chain Management* 37-2, pp. 2–3.

Kotha, S. (1996). From mass production to mass customization: The case of the National Industrial Bicycle Company of Japan, *European Journal of Management* 14-5, pp. 442–450.

Krause, D. (1997). Supplier development: current practices and out-comes, *International Journal of Purchasing and Materials Management* 33-2, pp. 12–19.

Lee, H. and Sasser, M. (1995) Product universality and design for supply chain management, *Production Planning and Control* 6-3, pp. 270–277.

Lee, M., Lee, Y., and Jeong, C. (2003). A high-quality-supplier selection model for supply chain management and ISO 9001 system, *Production Planning and Control* 14-3, pp. 225–232.

Liker, J. and Yu, Y. (2000) Japanese automakers, U.S. suppliers and supply chain superiority, *Sloan Management Review* 42-1, pp. 81–93.

Magretta, J. (1998). The power of virtual integration: an interview with Dell Computer's Michael Dell, *Harvard Business Review* 76-2, pp. 72–84.

Moozakis, C. (2001). Auto exchange adds apps — Covisint hopes to attract members with expanded supply chain offerings, *InternetWeek* 30 July, 14.

Nelson-Rowe, L., Case study — Medical exchange wins fans — Owen & Minors private e-marketplace drives medical suppliers, customers to the Web, *InternetWeek* 27 August, 28.

Nishiguchi, T. and Beaudett, A. (1998). The Toyota Group and the Aisin fire, *Sloan Management Review* 41-1, pp. 49–59.

Noyce, D. (2002). eB2B: analysis of business-to-business e-commerce and how research can adapt to meet future challenges, *International Journal of Market Research* 44-1, pp. 71–95.

PLM (2003). September 16-17, Scottsdale, Arizona, Organized by Worldwide Business Research (http://www.wbresearch.com/).

Rota, K., Thierry, C., and Bel, G. (2002). Supply chain management: a supplier perspective, *Production Planning and Control* 13-4, pp. 370–380.

Senia, A. (2000). Exchanges cut costs and improve efficiencies, *Utility Business* October 14.

Tie, R. (2001). Get ready for the world of B2B, *Journal of Accountancy* 191-6, pp. 49–55.

Towill, D., Childerhouse, P., and Disney, S. (2002). Integrating the automotive supply chain: where are we now?, *International Journal of Distribution and Logistics Management* 32-1/2, pp. 79–95.

Vonderembse, M. and Tracey, M. (1999). The impact of supplier selection criteria and supplier involvement on manufacturing performance, *Journal of Supply Chain Management* 35-3, pp. 33–39.

Watts, C, Kim, K., and Hahn, C. (1995). Linking purchasing to corporate competitive strategy, *International Journal of Purchasing and Materials Management* 31-2, pp. 3–?.

CHAPTER

27

Management of the Shared Services Subsidiaries as Cost Centers

Tomoaki Sonoda
Professor, Faculty of Business and Commerce
Keio University

27.1 Introduction

27.1.1 *The definition and organization of shared services*

Many large Japanese companies have adopted shared services since 1999, which is a new method to manage administrative functions. Shared services centers require (1) centralization; (2) reexamination; and (3) standardization of administrative function of the parent company and group companies.

There are three basic types of shared services centers (SSC).

Type A: Internal Organization in the Parent Company
Type B: Shared Services Subsidiary
Type C: Centralization of Several Corporate Groups' Activities

Sonoda (2001a, 2001b, 2003d) examined the basic characteristics of each type of SSC. Since then, we have witnessed some variations of the basic types of the shared services centers. This chapter focuses on the shared services subsidiary (Type B).

27.1.2 *General effectiveness of shared services and growing corporate value*

SSC has five general advantages.

1. Restructuring of the administrative function from the viewpoint of the group management.
2. Centralization of the administrative function makes fixed costs decrease.
3. Economics of scales by the centralization cuts fixed costs per one activity.
4. Redundant and non value added activities are dropped through reexamination.
5. Customized activities at each organization are standardized.

These five merits of shared services enhance corporate value. Companies can reduce costs by restructuring the administrative department, and invest management resources in the core business. Labor hours are reduced by the discontinuation of the non value added activities and the standardization of activities. Companies use these surplus hours to enhance the quality of activities and to implement strategic activities.

27.1.3 *Shared services subsidiaries as cost centers*

Because a shared services subsidiary is an independent corporation, it is required to make profits. But there are some shared services subsidiaries which are cost centers without profits. This is one of the unique management styles of the shared services subsidiaries in Japan. Chapter 27 examines the cases of Teijin Creative Staff and Sumitomo Shoji Financial Management as shared services subsidiaries of this type.

27.2 Problems of the Shared Services Subsidiaries

27.2.1 *Shared services subsidiaries as administrative function companies*

There are many shared services subsidiaries in Japan: Teijin Creative Staff, Sumitomo Shoji Financial Management, Asahi Management Service, NTT Business Associe, JP Business Service, Pioneer Shared Services Japan, etc.

When shared services subsidiaries sell their services to the companies outside their groups, it adds revenues and profits to the consolidated financial statements.[1] However, many of Japanese shared services subsidiaries sell their services only to the group companies. In this case, their mission is not to earn revenues from out of the groups, but to provide services to the group companies as administrative departments in the head office would do. This chapter defines this type as Administrative Function Company.

When companies make consolidated financial statements, transactions between group companies are eliminated, because sales of shared services subsidiaries and commissions of group companies are intra-group transactions. Administrative function companies have accounting missions: reduce costs and realize price down. They have other missions: improve the quality of activities and concentrate the administrative activities of group companies at shared services subsidiaries.

27.2.2 Responsibility centers of shared services subsidiaries

Shared services subsidiaries as administrative function companies can be defined as cost centers from the viewpoint of consolidated financial statements because they do not contribute to revenues and profits. On the other hand, they are profit centers from the viewpoint of independent companies. This ambivalence of responsibility centers makes it difficult to manage administrative function companies. Figure 27.1 shows the present condition of administrative function companies and three solutions to this ambivalence (C means cost centers, P means profit centers).[2]

Solution 1: Shared services subsidiaries are absorbed into their parent companies and positioned as cost centers. It means they change to internal organizations in the parent companies (internal functional administrative department or SSC of Type A). It makes them cost centers both of independent and consolidated organizations.

[1]Sonoda (2003a) lists other advantages of shared services subsidiaries and Sonoda (2001a) lists disadvantages.

[2]Although this chapter shows three solutions to the ambivalence of responsibility centers, many shared services subsidiaries are still profit centers without selling services to companies outside their group. Pioneer Shared Services Japan is one of these companies. The reasons why Pioneer Shared Services Japan is a profit center is that: (1) it measures profits in order to motivate employees; and (2) it invests profits to promote shared services to group companies (Sonoda, 2004, p. 216).

	Independent	Consolidated	Solution
Present	P	C	—
Solution1	C	C	SSC in the Parent Company
Solution2	C	C	Shared Services Subsidiary as Cost Center
Solution3	P	P	Sell Services to Companies outside Groups

Fig. 27.1 Ambivalence of responsibility centers of shared services subsidiaries

Solution 2: Shared services subsidiaries are positioned as cost centers even though they are independent companies. They become the cost centers both of independent and consolidated organizations. This is the theme of this chapter.

Solution 3: Shared services subsidiaries sell their services to the companies outside their groups. Because they add profits to consolidated income statements, they become profit centers both of independent and consolidated organizations.

27.2.3 *Subsidiaries as cost centers*

Since shared services subsidiaries are independent corporations, they have both costs and revenues. They make income statements, so we can regard them as "profit centers without profits." But these companies decide their prices to cover costs and do not use profits as performance measures because they do not expect to make profits. They are cost centers since their accounting objectives are cost recovery and cost reduction.

27.3 Case of Teijin Creative Staff[3,4]

27.3.1 *Organization of Teijin Creative Staff*

Teijin Creative Staff (TCS) was established in 2001/3 and is a 100% subsidiary of Teijin Limited. TCS has three divisions: accounting and finance,

---

[3]Section 27.3 is based on interviews with TCS on 2003/3/12, 7/28, 2004/7/21 and a lecture by Shinya Yamamoto on 2003/3/6.

[4]Sonoda (2003c) describes the organization and activities of TCS in detail. After Sonoda (2003c), except for account payable and account receivable, TCS returned all activities, such as budgeting and closing process, to group companies (except for parent company).

human resources and general affairs, and purchasing and distribution. TCS has all the functions from strategic decisions to operations.

27.3.2 *Pricing and cost management*

TCS calculates costs of their activities to clarify their services prices. Before TCS was established, administrative activities costs were allocated to divisions by the number of heads or the capital employed. In 2003 (after TCS was established), TCS changed their allocation policy to use plural allocation bases.

1. direct charge: Costs that can be traceable to activities.
2. allocation to activities by cost drivers, such as sales, number of head, or labor hours.
3. contract amounts or unit price.

TCS is a cost center because TCS decides service prices to cover their costs. Prices for providing group companies with services are equivalent to service activities costs. Before budgeting, TCS and group companies contract services prices for one year. Though actual costs will not be equal to prices, TCS will not amend the variances between costs and prices.

TCS has some evaluation measures. One is cost reduction in TCS and another is cost reduction in Teijin group companies as the result of shared services received from TCS. For example, when TCS manages to reduce costs of company housing for employees of all the group companies successfully, it is conceived that TCS contributes to the Teijin group.

27.4 Case of Sumitomo Shoji Financial Management[5]

27.4.1 *Organization of Sumitomo Shoji Financial Management*

Sumitomo Shoji Financial Management (SFM) was established in 2001/4 after Sumisho Financial Management and Sumisho Accounting had integrated. SFM provides financing, accounting, foreign exchange services to the Sumitomo Corporation group companies. SFM provides not only routine operating activities but also consulting, for example, advice on accounting problems when the sales divisions develop new projects.

[5]Section 27.4 is based on interviews with SFM on 2004/5/12 and 7/28.

27.4.2 Pricing and cost management

SFM has almost finished concentrating financing, accounting, foreign exchange activities of Sumitomo Corporation and financing activities of group companies in Japan. As for accounting activities, keeping up with the consolidated tax and US accounting standards, and keeping accounting policies and compliances of subsidiaries on the same high level are very important for Sumitomo group. SFM is trying centralization of those activities of group companies.

SFM also decides services prices to cover their costs according to the number of heads who work for group companies. Before contracting with group companies, SFM examines their activities and calculates costs by the number of heads involved. SFM has the mission to provide shared services to Sumitomo group. If SFM adds margin on their prices, group companies may drop the contract with SFM. When group companies outsource their tasks to SFM, they can obtain high grade services at the same or lower costs. Sumitomo Corporation knows that SFM succeeded in reducing costs enough and serving high quality activities in time, and does not require further costs reduction to SFM.

27.5 Reasons for Making Subsidiaries as Cost Centers

There are three reasons why TCS and SFM are positioned as not profit centers but cost centers even though they are corporate organizations.

1. Some shared services subsidiaries sell their services to companies outside their group in order to gain profits. But TCS and SFM do not aim to sell services to outside group companies. Because their objectives are only to reduce costs and to improve quality of activities, cost centers suit them. Performance evaluation of TCS is not based on profits even though TCS is a subsidiary. Performance criteria of TCS are staff activities and support activities to the holding company (Teijin) and group companies, and accomplishment of cost down targets. SFM is also evaluated by not sales and profits but multiple targets such as year-on-year cost comparison and supports to the group companies.
2. Even though only operational activities are generally transferred to SSC, TCS and SFM have broader, strategic activities, too. TCS and SFM manage almost the same activities as parent companies did. One reason is that it is difficult to distinguish strategic from operational activities.

Moreover, if anyone who does not have experiences of operational activities makes strategic decisions, he/she will be theory-oriented and may not be able to solve actual problems. Even though TCS and SFM are independent corporations, they have close relationship with their parent companies and they function superbly as cost centers.

3. Sumisho Accounting which was one of the bases of SFM was a cost center. On the other hand, Sumisho Financial Management which was another base of SFM was a profit center because it raised funds (interest was X%) from Sumitomo Corporation, finance companies and group companies, and lent them to group companies (interest was $X + \alpha\%$). In this case, group companies might raise money below $X + \alpha\%$ interest from out of Sumitomo group. After SFM was established, for the group finance management, only Sumitomo Corporation raises funds from financial companies, and SFM changed its interest rates from $X + \alpha\%$ to X%[6] and positioned itself as cost center.

27.6 Reasons for Operating SSC as Subsidiaries

27.6.1 *Reasons for operating SSC as subsidiaries of cost center type*

Why TCS and SFM are not administrative departments in the head offices but shared services subsidiaries though they are costs centers? TCS offers two reasons: clarifying costs and improving activities quality. SFM offers following grounds: pursuing efficiency by concentration of activities and its salary system, providing high-quality services by experts, and providing continuously financing and accounting services to the group companies.

27.6.2 *Clarifying costs and improving activities quality*

When TCS was the administrative department in the head office, its costs were allocated to the divisions by the number of employees or capital employed in order to calculate costs of each division. Its objectives did not clarify costs structure and cost responsibility of administrative departments. Administrative departments' costs are underestimated because

---

[6]SFM charges group companies for actual costs of financing activities, but charges are small sum and do not have influence on decision making of group companies.

common costs are not taken into account. When TCS makes income statement, balance sheet and cash flow statement, those statements show its performance as an independent subsidiary.

Transactions have become externalized even though TCS is a group company. It requires TCS to implement activities as formally contracted. TCS motivates its employees strongly to improve activities and to reduce costs. As for enhancing activities, Teijin carried out reengineering and standardization of activities in the first and second structure reforms. The target of the first structure reform was Teijin itself, but the second structure reform expanded to the group companies. TCS as a subsidiary fitted in the organization that successfully achieved the second reform.

27.6.3 *Employment of experts and promotion of shared services*

In order to keep up with the consolidated management of the US standards and the globalization of accounting standards, SFM, rather than group companies, employs experts to achieve them more consistently and effectively. SFM can easily hire experts, such as certified public accountants and licensed tax accountants because of its flexible personnel system. SFM sets prices on financing and accounting services, which can be acceptable to group companies because of the hiring of employees under its salary system and the scale of economics by concentrating activities.

27.6.4 *Influence of organization change by a holding company*

In 2003/4, Teijin moved to a new group management system under a holding company. It generally becomes easy for the companies to establish the shared services subsidiaries to undertake group administrative activities. But Teijin did not consider this possibility when it decided to establish TCS.

27.7 Conclusion

Chapter 27 examined the cases of Teijin Creative Staff and Sumitomo Shoji Financial Management as shared services subsidiaries of the cost center type. The reasons why they are cost centers are: (1) consistency with objectives of shared services; (2) implementation of almost the same activities as in the head offices of parents companies; and (3) penetration of shared services to the group companies. The reasons why they are subsidiaries even though they are cost centers are: (1) clarifying costs and improving activities; and (2) employment of experts and promotion of shared services. In the future, reorganization by the holding companies would make some shared services subsidiaries as cost centers.

Shared services subsidiaries as cost centers can solve management problems of administrative function companies: profit center as an independent company, cost center as a part of a consolidated group. Moreover, pricing by cost base can eliminate adjustment costs in pricing negotiation with group companies. As long as shared services subsidiaries provide their services within the group companies, even if they will not make profits, it will have no effect on the consolidated performance. It means elimination of negotiation costs for pricing contributes to performance of the consolidated income statement.

Shared services subsidiaries as cost centers have not been a popular management styles yet, but it solves some problems of shared services subsidiaries. However, if group companies pay attention to only cost reduction, they will lower employees' morals. One of the solutions is using balanced scorecard in shared services subsidiaries.

References

Akamatu, K. (2002). A challenging reform of the organization and accounting department, *Business Research* 932, pp. 17–27. (in Japanese)

Arthur Andersen Business Consulting (1999). *Shared Services*, Toyo keizai Shinposha. (in Japanese)

Gunn, R., Cerberry, D., Frigo, R., and Behrens, S. (1993). Shared services, *Management Accounting* LXXV-5, pp. 22–28.

Hodo, C. and Kodaira, T. (1998). Restructuring the administrative departments by shared services, *DIAMONDO Harvard Business* 23-5, pp. 68–75. (in Japanese)

Hoshi, N. (2001). Effectiveness of outsourcing by consolidated management, in *Design and Performance Management of the Organization Structure*, edited by Monden, Y., Hamada, K., and I, K., Chuo Keizaisha, pp. 90–105. (in Japanese)

Ishikawa, Y. (2000). Strengthen core competence by enhancing support function, *Nikkei Business* 2000-2/7, pp. 45–48. (in Japanese)

Kigyo Kenkyukai (ed.). *Case Book of Shared Services*, Kigyo Kenkyukai. (in Japanese)

Makino, H. (2000). Integration of administrative departments beyond companies, *Nikkei Business* 2000-2/7, pp. 42–44. (in Japanese)

Matue, H. (2001). Shared services of group management(1)(2)(3), *Business Research* 925, pp. 38–45; 926, pp. 58–66; 927, pp. 80–88. (in Japanese)

Monden, Y. (1973). Decentralization system by transfer price — management accounting for the large organizations, Osaka Prefecture University. (in Japanese)

Schulman, D., Dunleavy, J., Harmer, M., and Lusk, J. (1999). *Shared Services*, New York: John Wiley & Sons.

Sonoda, T. (2001a). The management accounting problems of the shared service subsidiary, *Mita Business Review* 44-3, pp. 123–137. (in Japanese)

Sonoda, T. (2001b). Internal shared service department — managing as a cost center, *Mita Business Review* 44-5, pp. 129–141. (in Japanese)

Sonoda, T. (2003a). Performance evaluation of shared services subsidiaries, in *Organization Structure and Management Accounting*, edited by Monden, T., Zeimu Keiri Kyokai, pp. 175–190. (in Japanese)

Sonoda, T. (2003b). The basic concepts of shared services and performance evaluation of the administrative departments, in *Case Book of Shared Services*, edited by Kigyo Kenkyukai, pp. 3–18. (in Japanese)

Sonoda, T. (2003c). Managing shared services subsidiaries as cost centers — a type of shared services centers, Japan Accounting Association, Special Committee, Interim Report. (in Japanese)

Sonoda, T. (2003d). Shared services: centralization of several corporate groups' activities, Japan Accounting Association, Study Group, Final Report. (in Japanese)

Sonoda, T. (2004). Balanced scorecard for the administrative function subsidary, *Mita Business Review* 47-1, pp. 211–224. (in Japanese)

Takahashi, S. and Akamatu, K. (2003). *A Manual for Implementation of Shared Services*, Kigyo Kenkyukai. (in Japanese)

Triplett, A. and Scheumann, J. (2000). Managing shared services with ABM, *Strategic Finance* LXXXI-8, pp. 40–45.

Yamamoto, S. (2003). Activities reform and establishment of subsidiary of administrative department in Teijin, in *Case Book of Shared Services*, edited by Kigyo Kenkyukai, pp. 407–426. (in Japanese)

CHAPTER

28

Principles of Increased Productivity through Cell-Based Assembly*

Hiroshi Ozawa

Associate Professor, Graduate School of Economics and Management, Tohoku University

28.1 Introduction

In recent years, many corporate examples in Japan have reported of increased productivity due to cell-based assembly, which has also become the focus of several research initiatives.[1] Cell-based assembly's defining characteristic is that production processes are completed conclusively from start to finish by individuals or small groups, in contrast to the division of labor of assembly line production.

The division of labor provided the rationale behind productivity improvements gained by assembly line production, whereas the reasons why productivity may increase by integrating tasks during cell-based assembly have remained unclear. Consequently, the division of labor theory that forms the rationale for line production is opposed to reports of productivity improvements when tasks are integrated or conveyor belts removed for cell-based assembly.

Some attempts have been made to explain this dilemma in terms of improved worker motivation. It is known that higher worker motivation leads to higher productivity when operators perform whole, rather than fragmented tasks, or operate in an autonomous environment without work space limited by conveyor belts. This is probably due to the attempt to

*An early form of this chapter first appeared in *Organizational Science* Vol. 38 No. 3, 2005, Hakuto Shobo (Japanese).

[1]Kono (1999), Tsuru (2001), Ikoma (2002), Kanezawa (2002).

explain cell-based assembly using theories from the Volvo method, because cell-based assembly resembles the autonomous-group production line introduced at the Volvo Kalmar plant in Sweden.

Even so, different objectives and contexts gave rise to the Volvo method and cell-based assembly. The Volvo method was introduced during Swedish labor disputes in the 1960s and 70s in order to humanize labor by altering the working environment to address human needs.[2] By contrast, cell-based assembly was introduced to improve productivity under concerns that domestic manufacturing was shifting to China's cheaper labor market, aggravating deindustrialization in Japan. Because both cell-based assembly and the Volvo method were implemented with different purposes and circumstances, the two should not be equated simply because they appear similar. Moreover, one should not simply divide the rationales behind line production in terms of technical divisions of labor, or cell-based assembly in terms of psychological and motivation theories. Rather, both production methods should be explained using the same theoretical approach.

This paper seeks to explain how task integration, the reverse process of labor division, can be technically consistent with the division of labor, and explores relationships between task integration and productivity improvements.

28.2 Research Methods

Despite using the same name, cell-based assembly is conducted in many ways based on the ideas of different corporations, and comes in an infinite variety of styles. Arriving at a common definition of typical cell-based assembly is therefore difficult. This report discusses one form of cell-based assembly taught by an IE consulting firm, the PEC Industrial Education Center (PEC *sangyo kyoiku senta* Gifu City CEO: Yamada Hitoshi "PEC" below), as PEC has managed many cell-based assembly projects for major Japanese electronics manufacturers. Examples related to cell-based assembly in this report refer only to the PEC style of cell-based assembly.[3] Naturally, different explanations are possible for cell-based assembly

[2]See Akaoka (1989), Okubayashi (1991), Berggren (1992), and Tamura (2003) regarding the Volvo production system.

[3]PEC has managed cell-based assembly projects for major Japanese electronics manufacturers such as Sony, Sanyo Electric, Canon, NEC, etc. The term "cell-based assembly" was coined to describe the PEC style production techniques of Kon Tatsuyoshi (Sony Nakamura Laboratories) (adopted from a course by Kon Tatsuyoshi: The PEC Industrial Education Center 17th "Intensive Course

techniques conducted under different designs other than the PEC method presented in this paper.

Cell-based assembly implementation projects were observed during the actual consultation process allowing dynamic, rather than static, assessments of how each process was molded into its current form. Additionally, each process was looked at in terms of universal cell-based assembly principles without limiting the analysis to the conditions of one specific corporation.

In order to fully understand PEC style cell-based assembly, the author participated in improvement activities at five manufacturers[4] that were undergoing consultation with PEC. During this time, personal impressions were collected about the working environment and conditions from personnel that received PEC training on site. This information is used in this report to evaluate principles of productivity improvements based on the style of cell-based assembly created.

28.3 Relationships between Labor Division and Productivity

A central theme of this report is exploring the relationship between separating tasks and productivity. Preconditions of the argument are laid out in the first section. Factors are considered that increase or reduce costs when labor is divided based on these preconditions. This knowledge is then used to indicate how cell-based assembly can improve productivity by correcting excessively divided labor into the optimal amount of labor division.

28.3.1 *Preconditions*

Several assumptions need to be set up for lead time (L), the number of workstations (Ws), and cycle time (Cy) in order to simplify the model when looking for relationships between labor division and productivity.

on the TOYOTA Production System" February 15th, 2003). Currently, PEC style cell-based assembly is a highly controlled method and can be considered the prototype of cell-based assembly. While this report deals solely with PEC style cell-based assembly, this method is the most typical example of cell-based assembly activities.

[4]Five locations: Sony EMCS Corporation. Minokamo TEC (electronics), KANOU SHOUJUAN Inc. (traditional Japanese confectioner), Nagahama Canon, Inc. (electronics), Kashiwa Mokko CO., LTD (wood furniture), Asahi Organic Chemicals Industry CO., LTD. (construction materials).

First, lead time (L) in the following argument refers to the net amount of work time theoretically required during manufacturing. "Theoretically" in this case means that time fluctuations from coincidences and special circumstances that occur during actual production are ignored. Net work time means that time not directly related to production is ignored, such as time spent during part conveyance, parts bottle-necking, or operator wait time. Furthermore, since this report focuses on the costs and effects of labor division, reductions in lead time (L) caused by streamlining a production line are ignored. In other words, lead time (L) is assumed to remain constant.

Next, when labor on a process is divided it is considered to be done evenly. So the labor division process is represented in the number of workstations (Ws) created by the division, and the amount of cycle time (Cy) allocated to each work station. Stated differently, as labor is divided up on a process, the number of workstations (Ws) gets bigger while the amount of cycle time (Cy) gets smaller. Conversely, more task integration means fewer number of workstations (Ws) and higher cycle times (Cy). The relationship between lead time (L), number of workstations (Ws), and cycle time (Cy) is described as follows:

$$Ws = \frac{L}{Cy}, \quad 0 < Cy \leq L. \tag{28.1}$$

28.3.2 Factors that increase costs when dividing labor

The concept of cell-based assembly is an extension of the Kaizen activities known as "waste removal" (*Muda tori*).[5] By observing *waste removal* and seeing several types of waste, the author was able to classify three types of waste generated when dividing labor[6]: (1) waste from part pick-up and

[5]See Yamada (2002), pp. 17–28.

[6]Ono (1978) separates the motions of a line operator into *waste* and *work*. *Waste* is defined as motion performed during a job that is unnecessary, with *work* separated into *work with no value added*, and *net work that increases value added*. PEC uses a definition of waste that combines the *waste* and *work with no value added* defined by Ono. For instance, the motion from bringing down a hammer and hitting a work piece adds value, but the motion from raising a hammer merely prepares to lower the hammer, and is a wasteful motion with no value added. Kaizen activities aim to eliminate these seemingly trivial sources of waste, with the intention of using business resources (people, equipment, floor area, etc.) more effectively.

return; (2) waste from part conveyance; and (3) waste from bottle-necking or balance loss. These types of wastes increase costs when dividing labor.

1. Waste associated with part pick up and return occurs in the *pick up* and *return* motions when an operator picks up a work piece from a conveyor and places it on a workstation, and when the piece is returned to the conveyor after the job is performed.[7] These motions are standard for performing the job without adding any additional value.

   Part pick-up and return is performed by an operator once for each work piece, and increases proportionally with the number of workstations (Ws) when labor divisions are made. Figure 28.1 describes the cost caused from part pick-up and return to complete one piece (Tr).

$$Tr = t \cdot (Ws - 1) = t \cdot \left(\frac{L}{Cy} - 1\right). \tag{28.2}$$

   Where $t =$ the cost of 1 pick-up and return.
2. Part conveyance does not itself impart any additional value onto the work piece. Part conveyance can be considered in terms of the number of cycles and travel distance. The number of required conveyance

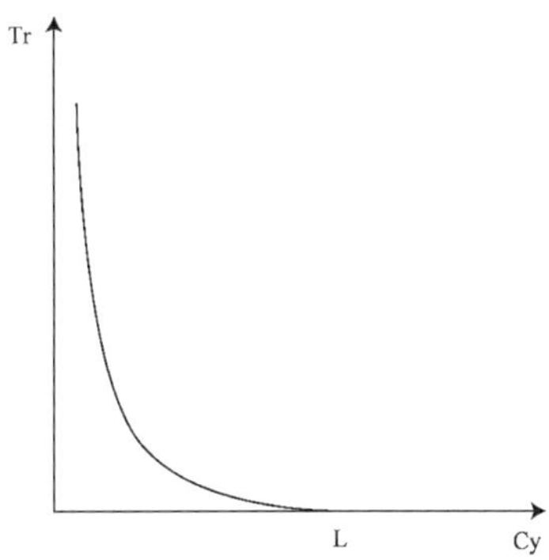

Fig. 28.1 Waste occurring from pick up and return

[7]Limited to fixed-work conveyor system models. Fixed-work conveyor system is a method in which an operator transfers a part from a conveyor to a work table to process it statically, whereas the Moving-work conveyor system describes when a part is processed while moving on a conveyor. Moving-work conveyor systems have no *pick-up and return waste.*

cycles increases with higher numbers of workstations (Ws). Process layout determines conveyance distance, and actual distances between workstations are not at equal intervals.[8] However, since conveyance distance is independent of the degree of labor division, conveyance distance is considered to be constant for the sake of simplification. Equation (28.3) below describes overall conveyance cost assuming h is the average conveyance cost of one cycle (Figure 28.2).

$$H = h \cdot (Ws - 1) = h \cdot \left(\frac{L}{Cy} - 1\right). \tag{28.3}$$

3. *Bottle-necking* describes when work pieces pile up and get stored between processes without being processed in any way.[9] *Balance loss* is the portion of time when operators or equipment lie idle. Bottle-necking and balance loss occur when workstation work loads are not evenly allocated, and there is a trade-off between the two. For example, if the work

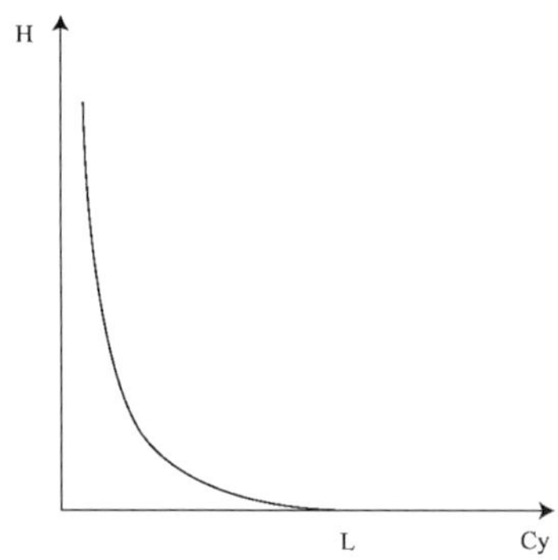

Fig. 28.2 Waste from conveyance

[8]While not related to labor division, waste removal activities seek to shorten the space between work stations to reduce conveyance distance. Doing so not only cuts back on conveyance man hours, but also floor area. Shortening the interval between work stations is called "gap shortening," cutting back on man-hours is called "personnel recovery," and cutting back on floor area is called "space recovery." These terms were invented by Kon Tatsuyoshi (Sony Nakamura Laboratories). These terms were translated from the original Japanese as closely as possibly. The original terms are "Majime: gap shortening," "Katsujin: personnel recovery," and "Katsu space: space recovery."

[9]An article by Sekine (1997) addresses the effect cell-based assembly has on balance loss reductions.

time on workstation 1 is shorter than that of workstation 2, then bottle-necking will occur between stations during push style production, and balance loss will occur on station 1 during pull style production.

In theory, bottle-necking and balance loss will not occur assuming a process is divided evenly and cycle times allocated to each workstation are equal. Assuming however that there is variation in work times for each workstation $Cy^* = \{Cy_1^*, Cy_2^*, \ldots, Cy_n^*\}$, then there is a maximum cycle time, $\max Cy^*$. Under these conditions, balance loss (B) is related to lead time (L) in the following manner:

$$B = 1 - \frac{L}{Ws \cdot \max Cy^*} = 1 - \frac{Cy}{\max Cy^*}. \qquad (28.4)^{10}$$

In order to estimate the connection between increasing cycle time (Cy) and the rate that balance loss (B) occurs, the difference in Cy and $\max Cy^*$ is assumed to be constant at p seconds regardless of short and long cycle times, rendering the following equation from Eq. (28.4).

$$B = \frac{p}{Cy + p}. \qquad (28.5)$$

Figure 28.3 shows a graph made from one side of a hyperbola, and demonstrates how a 1 second reduction in cycle time (Cy) can have a significant unbalancing effect. The relationship between balance loss (B) and cycle time (Cy) described by Wild (1975) follows a similar trend (Figure 28.4). Based on these findings, balance loss (B) falls at higher values of cycle time (Cy), so it is safe to assume that reductions in the

[10] Several preconditions were established in this report, so the following concept is provided to prevent confusion in terms definitions. Generally,

$$\text{Balance loss} = 1 - \text{organizational efficiency} \qquad \text{(a)}$$

$$\text{Organizational efficiency} = \text{Total (net) process time} \,/\, (\text{Number of work stations } x\text{'s cycle time}) \qquad \text{(b)}$$

This report defines lead time as equal to the number of work stations x's cycle time, but this definition of lead time uses net process time. Therefore, lead time (L) in this report matches the numerator of the above definition, Total (net) process time, and not the denominator. Next, Eq. (b) uses cycle time based on the newly introduced maximum process time, since it is the maximum process time that ultimately determines production line speed when there are various process times at each work station.

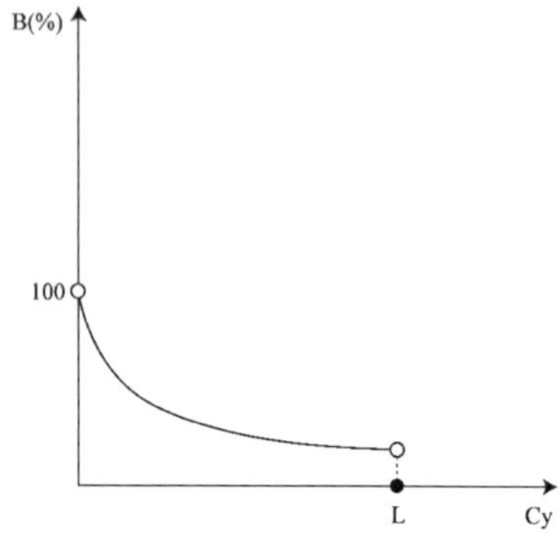

Fig. 28.3 Balance loss (1)

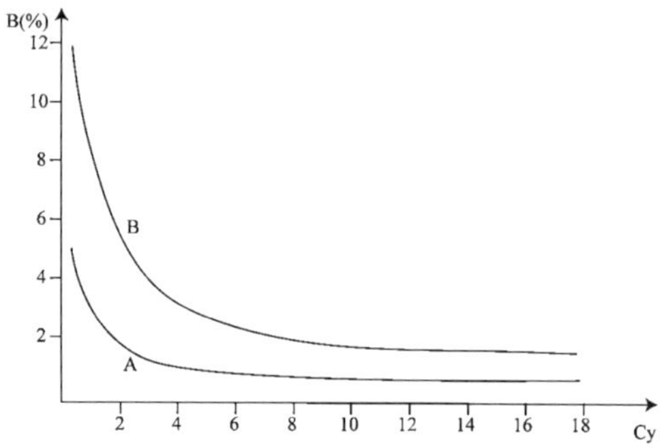

Fig. 28.4 Balance loss (2). Two curves are presented since in most situations the sophistication of the balancing procedure employed will influence the success of balance. (Wild, 1975)

rate of balance loss (ΔB) approach zero for every additional increase (ΔCy) in cycle time (Cy). Consequently, costs stemming from an unbalanced production line can be described in the following way.

$$U = u \cdot B. \tag{28.6}$$

Where $u =$ the cost of 1% balance loss.

28.3.3 *Factors that reduce costs when dividing labor*

Task integration was seen in several situations while observing the cell-based assembly implementation process, but labor division activities were not observed. Advantageous factors caused by task segmentation were indicated by Adam Smith, and include: (1) improved specialization (learning); and (2) the time (motion) required for moving on to another job. While no other incentives were observed that actively justified dividing labor, (3) equipment duplication was a factor that deterred task integration.[11]

1. Assessing learning requires making a distinction between learning and cumulative unit number, or learning and time. Generally in the IE field, learning is described in terms of the relationship between cumulative average performance time (Ac) and the cumulative unit number (x). Since the learning rate (n) for a certain job is fixed, cumulative average performance time (Ac) falls as cumulative unit number (x) increases. Reduction rates in per unit process time are not constant, but grow increasingly smaller or do not fall below a constant value. Patterns of process time reductions are shown in Figure 28.5.

$$Ac = \frac{t_1}{x^n}. \tag{28.7}$$

Where t_1 = per unit process time for first piece.

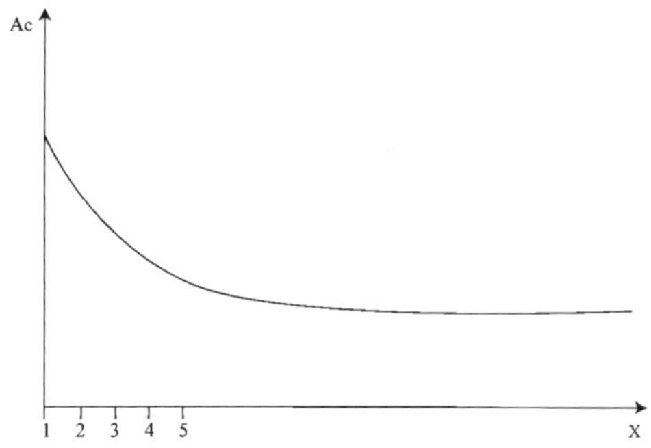

Fig. 28.5 Learning curve

[11]During observation, the author conducted a trial wherein 2 cells manufacturing the same part, A (4 operators, 7.5 second cycle time, 3,840 units produced daily) and B (3 operators, 9 second cycle time, 3,200 units produced daily) were modified into 3 cells (each with 2 operators and targets of 2,347 units daily production). Doing so could meet the daily production target and reduce one operator if cycle time could be set at 12.3 seconds. A 12.3 second cycle time was achieved, but the modification had to be abandoned since the 1 cell increase required adding another measuring device costing 4 million Yen.

In such circumstances, task division or integration has no effect on learning rates. For example, in a situation where one operator performs a job consisting of *install part, and attach seal*, or 2 operators perform the job so that 1 operator *installs part*, and the next operator *attaches seal*, the relationship between cumulative unit number and cumulative average performance time remains the same. Learning rates are calculated as equal to the combination of the individual learning rates of job elements when a job is divided, weighted according to how much total cycle time that element accounts for.[12] In other words, task division or integration plays no role when assessing the relationship between cumulative unit number and learning.

In contrast, many examples can be found where everyday intuition plays a role in assessing learning, and learning is assessed in terms of the amount of job time and per unit process time.[13] Equation (28.8) describes the cumulative unit number (x_T) after the start of a job and some discretionary point in time (T).

$$x_T = \frac{T}{Cy} \qquad (28.8)^{14}$$

Effectively, higher task integration and cycle times (Cy) result in lower cumulative unit number within a fix period of time (T). Using Eqs. (28.7) and (28.8) yields the following equation (Figure 28.6).

$$Ac = \frac{t_1}{T^n} \cdot Cy^n, \quad Cy \leq T. \qquad (28.9)$$

---

[12]Morooka (1969).

[13]For example, Masuda, Naito and Nakahama (1990) report a case where there are two groups A and B working on processes with no difference in difficulty level (B has 2.5 times as many parts, and 3 times the process time of A). Reaching skill on group A took 1 week, and 4 weeks on B. This example simply compares the relationship between time and learning, but the number of parts or longer process work time does not have a negative effect on the learning rate.

[14]In this instance, the effects shorter per unit process times (Ac) gained with skill have on shorter cycle times (Cy) or higher production totals in a fixed period of time (x) are ignored. This is because as long as the cycle times of upstream and downstream processes remain unchanged, the middle process can produce no more than $x = T/Cy$ units within a fixed period of time. Secondly, as stated in the preconditions, the effect of applying skill for line modifications in order to streamline the production line for shorter lead time (L) or cycle times (Cy) is ignored.

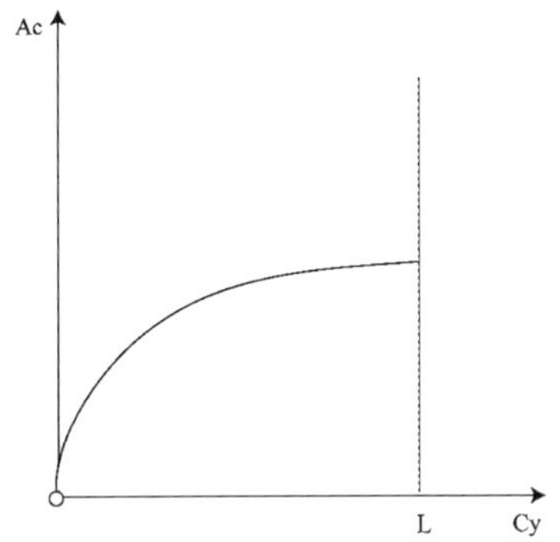

Fig. 28.6 Learning level at time T

This graph raises five points. The first is that the learning levels at time T falls at higher cycle times (Cy), and that as cycle time (Cy) increases, additional task integration (ΔCy) has diminishing effects on learning (ΔAc). In other words, extending for longer cycle times (Cy) has less and less of an impact on learning at time T, which stabilizes at a low threshold.

The second point is that at higher learning rates (n), additional task integration (ΔCy) has less of an effect on learning (ΔAc). This implies that integrating tasks that use easy-to-master techniques with high learning rates (n) will not compromise an effect on learning, but doing so when using difficult-to-master techniques with lower learning rates (n) can lower productivity. Experience suggests that cell-based assembly is easy to adopt on simple tasks like assembly, but not on highly difficult tasks like precision processing.

Third is that integrating tasks when production is conducted long term at higher values of T will not sacrifice learning, but learning cannot keep up when production volumes are high in a short time period. This can lower productivity. In effect, this refutes commonly held notions on cell-based assembly, and suggests paradoxically that cell-based assembly is not suitable for products with short lifecycles that constantly require new skill.[15]

[15]Switching to cell-based assembly is believed to typically reduce the amount of processing on products with short life cycles where cell-based assembly makes sense, but confirming this requires further research. This report does not address error regarding how cell-based assembly reduces processing work, and only describes how cell-based assembly may inadvertently affect learning.

Fourth is that hiring restrictions and using temporary part time labor inevitably cause shorter values of T. In such cases, personnel are replaced before acquiring enough skill, so learning can be sacrificed during cell-based assembly, possibly lowering productivity. This has been a widely indicated weakness of cell-based assembly.

Fifth is that learning rates (n) will naturally vary at each work station when each station is in charge of a different job. This can lead to variation in process times at each work station when learning levels fail to stabilize, leading to the balance loss previously cited.[16] Drawing again on the fourth point, learning levels will be difficult to stabilize and balance loss will occur more easily when using part time labor.

Two contrasting methods can be offered to prevent balance loss from occurring due to different skill levels (n). The first is to shorten cycle time (Cy) so that skill is acquired quickly, or essentially divide labor completely. The second method is to equate cycle time (Cy) with lead time (L), or essentially shift to single-operator production. Using Eq. (28.4), setting $Cy = L$, then $Ws = 1$, $\max Cy = Cy = L$, and balance loss $(B) = 0$. While this report is primarily concerned with analyzing situations where various production cells and production lines are arranged in series under different degrees of labor division, addressing the obvious problem of balance loss from different learning rates (n) means that intermittently running some units with labor completely divided and others with labor completely integrated is also an option.

If the cost caused by increasing cumulative average process time (Ac) by 1 second is a, then the cost (G_T) at time T from delayed learning can be expressed in the following equation:

$$G_T = a \cdot Ac. \tag{28.10}$$

Where $a =$ the cost per cumulative average process time.

2. The time (motion) required to move work to anther job and waste from part conveyance have a reciprocal relationship. An operator must switch tools and physically move when performing multiple tasks alone. Dividing tasks cuts down on time (and motion) because the same tool is used in the same location. On the other hand, dividing tasks generate more waste in conveyance, since the work piece is moving instead of the operator.

   Dividing labor does not have a clear cause and effect relationship on the final amount of tool switching or physical movement. Nonetheless,

[16] Nikkei Mechanical (1995) also addresses this problem with line production.

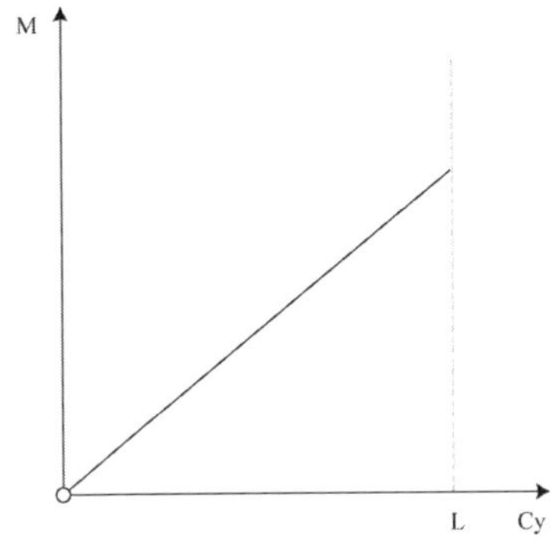

Fig. 28.7 Cost required to move work

the need for tool switching and physical movement is assumed to increase as more different tasks are integrated. Consequently, the total cost M occurring in tool change or physical motion can be expressed as follows (Figure 28.7).

$$M = m \cdot Cy. \tag{28.11}$$

Where $m =$ the average cost occurring during 1 tool change or physical motion.

3. Equipment duplication becomes an issue when tasks are integrated while trying to maintain a constant amount of production in a fixed period of time, or in other words, trying to maintain the same time interval (P) of product yield. Product yield time interval on a single line is equal to cycle time (Cy). The next equation describes time interval (P) for product yield on k number of lines.

$$P = \frac{Cy}{k}. \tag{28.12}$$

Consequently, shortening cycle time (Cy) while maintaining the same time interval (P) of product yield requires increasing the number of lines (k). Inevitably, increasing the number of lines (k) involves equipment investments. Equipment investment costs can be expressed in the following equation (Figure 28.8)

$$E = e \cdot k = \frac{e}{P} \cdot Cy. \tag{28.13}$$

Where $e =$ the average cost per equipment.

Then again, introducing cell-based assembly lowered the amount of equipment work loads through equipment modifications, self-producing

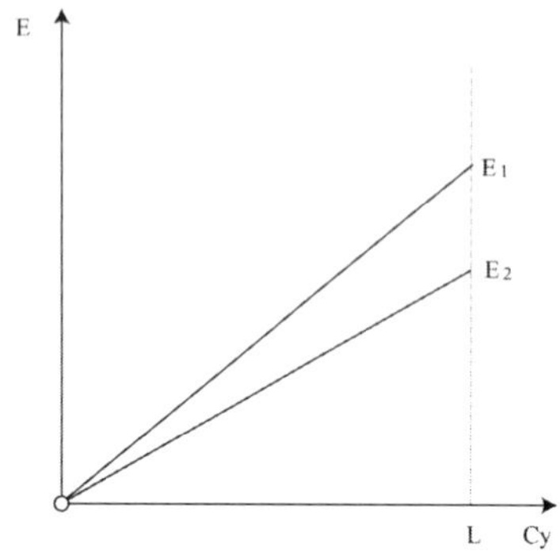

Fig. 28.8 Costs from additional equipment

equipment in-house, and lowered equipment costs. These situations were known as "*karakuri*" techniques (meaning "innovative techniques or procedures"). The *Karakuri* mechanisms to lower equipment loads are (1) *motion simplification* to remove wasteful motion on machines similar to *waste removal*; and (2) *specification downgrades*.

Based on the idea that "there are fundamentally two types of machine motion: rotational motion and back-and-forth motion," *motion simplification* aims to leverage these two types of motion into the simplest combination possible to complete the required task.[17]

Specification downgrades can be further divided into two types. The first reduces equipment costs when existing equipment has excessive and expensive capacity by self-producing in-house scaled down machines with only the bare essential functionality. The other method works to leverage the longer cycle times generated from task integration to lower machine processing speeds. Longer cycle times mean the machines do not have to work at the high speeds required by short cycle times. The need for maintaining high-precision, high-performance control, and high power output also decreases at lower operating speeds. As a result, comprehensive cuts can be made to equipment specifications.

Not as much energy is required as a result of *motion simplification* and *specification downgrades*. Machinery is typically powered using large amounts of electricity or air. However, small amounts of human power working together with machinery like a single motor can be used to ease

[17]Yamada (2002), pp. 33–37.

the cost of additional equipment investments by lowering costs, downsizing, saving energy, or allowing in-house machine fabrication.[18]

Assuming the reduction rate in equipment costs is r $(0<1)$, Eq. (28.13) can be expressed in the following new equation. Here, $E1$ in Figure 28.8 shifts to $E2$.

$$E = \frac{(1-r)e}{P} \cdot Cy. \tag{28.14}$$

28.3.4 Maximizing productivity with the optimal level of labor division and cell-based assembly

Previous sections presented factors reducing costs when labor is divided, and factors that increase costs when labor is divided. Consequently, finding the best production method is not merely choosing between dividing labor and task integration, but finding the optimal degree of labor division.

Figure 28.9 illustrates factors D that reduce costs when labor is divided (i.e., cycle time (Cy) is reduced), and factor I that increases costs when labor is divided. The cost occurring at a specific degree of task division, at some cycle time (Cy) is the total of both functions. This is expressed in the composite function C.

$$D = G_T + M + E. \tag{28.15}$$

$$I = Tr + H + U. \tag{28.16}$$

$$C = D + I. \tag{28.17}$$

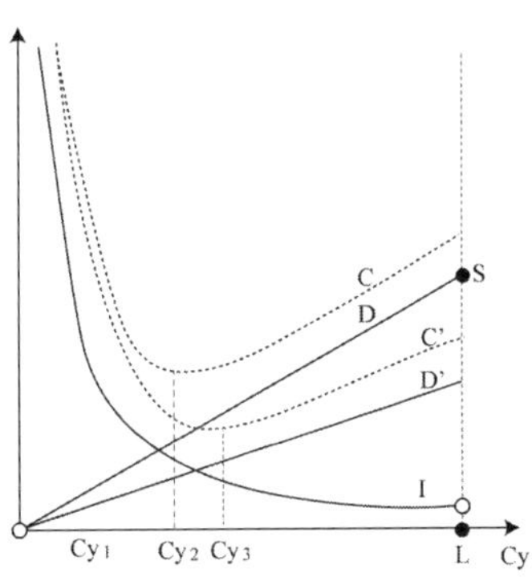

Fig. 28.9 Optimal degree of labor division

[18]Yamada (2002), pp. 32–33. This "karakuri" is also reported by Nikkei Mechanical (1996).

The cycle time (Cy) with the smallest value of C has the best labor division conditions. Based on this approach, cell-based assembly can increase productivity in situations exhibiting an excessive level of task division ($Cy = Cy_1$). By integrating tasks to correct the situation, it is possible to shift to a more optimal level of labor division ($Cy = Cy_2$). *Karakuri* techniques can then reduce equipment costs and shift D to D'. The composite function of these effects results in C', which shifts the cycle time (Cy) to the larger value of (Cy_3), and further integrates tasks to the optimal degree of task division.

Point S indicates a situation where one-operator production removes any balance loss and production units with labor integrated are run intermittently with units that are divided. Point S may be the optimal solution on processes where balance loss is an apparent problem.

28.4 Conclusion

This report described the technical aspects of how cell-based assembly can increase productivity through task integration, and looked to establish theoretical consistency with division of labor theory. Specifically, dividing labor is not necessarily a cost saving technique, yet can increase costs in some situations, in turn that suggesting there is a theoretically optimal situation that balances the cost reductions and cost increases of labor division. Consequently, cell-based assembly can be seen as way to correct production situations with excessive degrees of task divisions and increase productivity.

In addition, implementing cell-based assembly raises the following points regarding learning: (1) cell-based assembly is appropriate in situations with easy tasks and high learning rates; and (2) cell-based assembly can prevent the effects of learning and possibly lower productivity in situations without enough time for learning, such as when using short-term, part time employment.

Possibilities for lowering equipment costs by trying out *Karakuri* innovations were discussed, such as simplifying machine motion, reviewing machine function, and lowering operating speeds through task integration. *Karakuri* techniques demonstrate how the level of labor division is shifted further to higher degrees of task integration.

This report primarily explained the effects of different degrees of task division on production cells and production lines that are arranged in series. However, running completely divided, or completely integrated (one-operator production) units intermittently is also an option. Despite being opposite production scenarios, this may offer a solution when seeking to remove balance loss caused by different learning rates (n) on different processes. In contrast to the principle of organizing production around cells with small numbers of people, choosing one-operator production may increase productivity in some situations.

Acknowledgments

This work was supported by MEXT. Grant-in-Aid for Young Scientists (B)(15730202).

References

Akaoka, I. (1989). *New Theory on Reorganization of Work Organization*, Chikura. (in Japanese)

Berggren, C. (1992). *Alternatives to Lean Production: Work Organization in the Swedish Auto Industry*, Cornell University Press.

Ikoma, M. (2002). Problem in comparison between cell production and line production, *Communications of JIMA* 12-2, pp. 81–85. (in Japanese)

Kanazawa, T. (2002). 7 mysteries in cell production, *Communications of JIMA* 12-2, pp. 89–94. (in Japanese)

Kono, H. (1999). IE approach to cell production system, *IE Review* 40-4, pp. 9–14. (in Japanese)

Masuda, S., Naito, T., and Nakahama, T. (1999). A study of cell production system, *IE Review* 40-4, pp. 55–62. (in Japanese)

Morooka, K. (1969). *Learning Engineering*, Kenpakusha. (in Japanese)

Nikkei Mechanical (1995). Special issue: the impact by having removed conveyer: completing alone is enabled with cell production, *Nikkei Mechanical* 459, pp. 4–38. (in Japanese)

Nikkei Mechanical (1996). Special issue: recommendation of self-manufacturing of equipment, *Nikkei Mechanical* 486, pp. 20–35. (in Japanese)

Okubayashi, K. (1991). *Enlargement: Humanization of Work*, Yuhikaku. (in Japanese)

Ono, T. (1978). *Toyota Production System: Exceeding the Management of the Scale*, Diamond. (in Japanese)

Sekine, K. (1997). Efficiency of line balancing is 100% with single-operator production system, *Factory Mnagement* 43-4, pp. 19–22. (in Japanese)

Smith, A. (1950). *An Inquiry into the Nature and Causes of the Wealth of Nations*, 6th Edition Vol. 2, Edited by E. Cannan, London. (in Japanese)

Tsuru, Y. (ed.) (2001). *Innovation and Evolution of Production* System, Nippon Hyoronsha.

Tamura, Y. (2003). *Development and Conversion of Volvo Production System: From Ford to Uddevalla*, Taga Shuppan. (in Japanese)
Wild, R. (1975). On the selection of mass production systems, *International Journal of Production Research.* (in Japanese)
Yamada, H. (2002). *Waste Removal*, Gentosha. (in Japanese)

CHAPTER

29

The Influences of Competitive Environments on Process-Based Management in Japan

Masanobu Kosuga

Professor, School of Business Administration
Kwansei Gakuin University

Yoko Asakura

Associate Professor, Faculty of Management
and Information Sciences, Osaka International University

Takahisa Toyoda

Research Fellow, Graduate School
of Business Administration, Kwansei Gakuin University

With today's development of information technologies, business environments of Japanese companies have been changing drastically. Changing speed of the business environments is accelerated. As the result of these changes, the focus of management has changed from tangible assets to intangibles. In order to cope with such a situation, horizontal perspective for management is needed instead of vertical (bureaucratic) management (Monden and Lee, 2005), i.e., companies now need to adopt "process-based management." This chapter shows the result of a survey research conducted by the Committee of Strategic Process Management in Japanese Association of Management Accounting (JAMA).

29.1 The Importance of Process-based Management

Process-based management consists of a series of management activities towards all stages from inputs to outputs inside of the value chain (Lee, 2003). It deals with business processes, which are a series of company activities from inputs to outputs.

The importance of business processes already has been pointed out. For instance, from a point of customer relationship view, Borthick and Roth stated, "the most effective strategy for improving responsiveness is to eliminate noncontributing time by reengineering business processes" (Borthick and Roth, 1993). Carr said, "business process redesign is an approach for achieving radical, customer focused change" (Carr, 1993). To meet customers' demands, companies have to improve their business processes (Harrington, 1991). In response to an increasingly competitive business environment, companies are adopting such process-based management techniques as total quality management, benchmarking, and continuous quality improvement (Lawson, 1993).

Also, from an aspect of cost management, Ostrenga and Probst stated that "process value analysis is a methodology for reducing costs and improving processes by identifying resource consumption within a process and the underlying root causes of cost" (Ostrenga and Probst, 1992). In short, "process management is critical to cost management" (Dailey, 1998).

29.2 Design of the Survey

Process-based management is critical for Japanese companies to solve several problems of the functional base organization. But, unfortunately, it is still unclear what business processes in Japanese companies really are and how they are managed. Therefore, the Committee of Strategic Process Management, which was established as one of the research projects of JAMA, investigated into the actual state-of-the-art of business process management practices in Japanese manufacturing companies.

29.2.1 *Framework of the survey*

The theoretical framework to make a questionnaire of this survey is shown in Figure 29.1. This framework was built based on the literature survey with regards to business processes, business process reengineering, and process management.

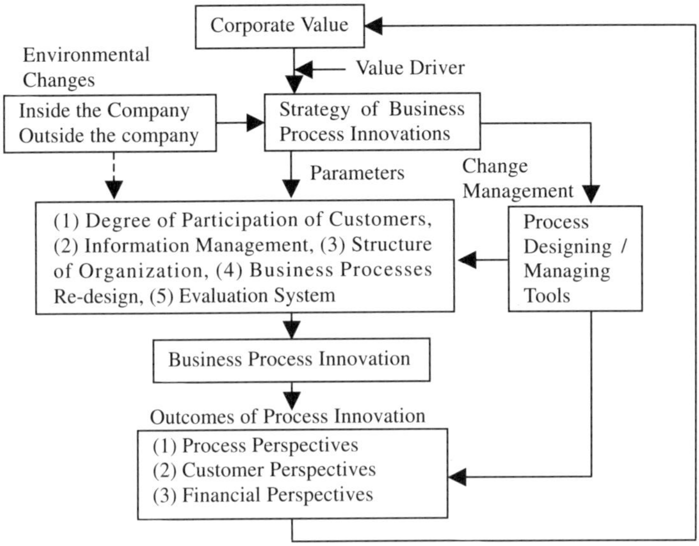

Fig. 29.1 Framework of the survey

Hypotheses of the survey are as follows: (1) Environmental changes (inside/outside of companies) trigger to develop some innovative strategy of business process; (2) This type of strategy makes business process innovation clear through some parameters: (i) degree of participation of internal/ external customers; (ii) information management adopting new information technology; (iii) structure of organization; (iv) business processes re-design; and (v) evaluation system; (3) It is possible to find the business process innovation strategy based on these parameters; (4) Process designing/ managing tools also affect these parameters; and (5) Outcomes from three points of view: (i) process; (ii) customer; and (iii) financial, connect business process innovation to corporate value. Therefore, it is important to clarify these outcomes to know several contributions of the innovation toward corporate value.

29.2.2 *Outline of the survey*

A questionnaire used in this survey consists of eight parts which are: (1) outline of company; (2) environment inside the company; (3) environment outside the company; (4) adopting new information technology; (5) customer relationships; (6) relation between business environment and organization; (7) business process strategy; and (8) globalization of business processes.

We sent the questionnaire to 1,282 Japanese manufacturers on March 1, 2004. Managers of management planning sections were selected as the intended subjects of the questionnaire. We asked them to return their responses by March 30, 2004.

198 companies responded (15.5% of 1,282 companies) and we rejected five defective answers; therefore 193 answers were finally accepted as valid answers (15.1% of 1,282 companies).

29.3 Outline of Responded Companies

The first part of the questionnaire is focused on the outline of the subject companies. We asked them some questions on the types of the business, number of the employees, etc.

In this section, we will show the outline of 193 companies, which responded to our questionnaires (in the below, we will say "responded companies" for these companies). The types of businesses of the responded companies are shown in Figure 29.2.

In this survey, we asked the number of employees (consolidated base) in order to know the scale of companies. Figure 29.3 shows the number of employees in 2002.

types of business	number of companies	%
foods and groceries	23	11.9%
textile fablics	7	3.6%
papers and pulp	4	2.1%
oil and rubbers	30	15.5%
medicaments	6	3.1%
steel, metal, metalloids	16	8.3%
equipments for transportation	11	5.7%
appliance and electrical equipments	35	18.1%
precision instruments	6	3.1%
petroleum and coals	2	1.0%
machines	22	11.4%
glasses	3	1.6%
others	18	9.3%
blank (no respond)	10	5.2%
total	193	100.0%

Fig. 29.2 Types of businesses of responded companies

number of employees	numbers of companies	%
1–100	13	6.7%
101–1,000	102	52.8%
1,001–3,000	29	15.0%
3,001–10,000	20	10.4%
10,001–50,000	18	9.3%
50,001–100,000	1	0.5%
100,001–300,000	4	2.1%
blank (no respond)	6	3.1%
total	193	100.0%

Fig. 29.3 The number of employees of responded companies (consolidated)

region	Production	sales	R&D
Asia	90(44.8%)	81(33.8%)	22(27.8%)
Europe	41(20.4%)	66(27.5%)	20(25.3%)
North America	56(27.9%)	74(30.8%)	32(40.5%)
Others	14(7.0%)	19(7.9%)	5(6.3%)

Fig. 29.4 The number of head offices

From Figure 29.3, it is clear that more than half of the responded companies employ less than 1,000 employees.

We also asked the degree of their globalization about production, sales, and R&D activities. Figure 29.4 shows the number of head offices of production, sales, and R&D in each region.

We can see that Asia has the largest number of the offices of production and sales, and North America has the largest number of head offices of R&D. In short Japanese companies have figured that Asia is an important region for production and sales.

29.4 Influences of Competitive Environments

In this section, we summarize the overview of our survey result, especially focus on four question items related to competitive environments, which are: (2) environment inside the company; (3) environment outside the company; (5) customer relationships; and (7) business process strategy. Details about the results on other items of the questionnaire are discussed in the next chapter.

29.4.1 Environment inside the company

Figure 29.5 shows the numbers of the companies answered the question: how the responded companies plan to produce their products (We eliminated three companies because of their defective answers).

Figure 29.6 shows the number of companies based on production forms and the number of employees (We eliminated 12 companies because of their defective answers).

Figure 29.7 also shows the number of companies answered the questions on production methods and the number of employees (We eliminated eight companies because of their defective answers).

29.4.2 Environment outside the company

The second item of the questions in our questionnaire is the environment outside the company. We asked the companies what the most vigorous part

number of employees	received orders	prospects	mixed	others
1–100	4	1	6	1
101–1,000	39	19	42	1
1,001–3,000	9	10	10	0
3,001–10,000	5	8	7	0
10,001–50,000	6	6	6	0
50,001–100,000	0	0	1	0
100,001–300,000	0	3	1	0
N.A.	1	4	0	0
total	64	51	73	2

Fig. 29.5 The planning style of production

number of employees	small	middle	large
1–100	4	5	2
101–1,000	43	37	17
1,001–3,000	4	9	14
3,001–10,000	4	4	11
10,001–50,000	4	4	10
50,001–100,000	0	1	0
100,001–300,000	1	0	3
N.A.	0	1	3
total	60	61	60

Fig. 29.6 The forms of production quantity

number of employees	manual	conveyer	cell	automation	others
1–100	8	3	2	4	1
101–1,000	41	22	19	44	5
1,001–3,000	7	6	9	20	0
3,001–10,000	2	7	6	13	1
10,001–50,000	1	6	4	11	1
50,001–100,000	0	0	1	0	0
100,001–300,000	0	2	2	1	0
total	59	46	43	93	8

Fig. 29.7 The methods of production

	last 5 years	next 5 years
price	129	102
quality	36	47
delivery time	2	1
new products release	16	27
after-sales service	1	2
ecology	0	3
product design	1	1

Fig. 29.8 The hardest part of competition

of competition was in the last five years and would be in the next five years. Figure 29.8 shows the result.

From Figure 29.8, we can see that: (1) The responded companies think price was the hardest part of competition in the last five years; (2) This trend will last in the next five years; (3) However, the number of companies for price has been decreased from 129 to 102; (4) On the other hand, the number of companies for quality and new products release has been increased; and (5) Companies are more and more interested in quality and/or new products instead of price.

Another question was asked with regard to their competitiveness of the responded companies based on 15 factors. We asked this question with five scale points, which are from 5: very good to 1: very poor. Figure 29.9 shows the result.

If we sum the numbers of the companies answered 5: very strong and 4: good, we can conclude that the responded companies think they have strong self-reliance in maintaining quality (131 companies: 67.9%), service

	5: very strong	4: strong	3: mean	2: poor	1: very poor
(1) service for customers	55 (28.5%)	74 (38.3%)	50 (25.9%)	8 (4.1%)	1 (0.5%)
(2) understanding customer needs	35 (18.1%)	66 (34.2%)	63 (32.6%)	23 (11.9%)	2 (1.0%)
(3) shortening deliver time	35 (18.1%)	58 (31.1%)	74 (38.3%)	20 (10.4%)	2 (1.0%)
(4) maintaining quality	61 (31.6%)	70 (36.3%)	52 (26.9%)	6 (3.1%)	0 (0.0%)
(5) new products release	37 (19.2%)	66 (34.2%)	44 (22.8%)	37 (19.2%)	3 (1.6%)
(6) cost	17 (8.8%)	54 (28.0%)	71 (36.8%)	44 (22.8%)	3 (1.6%)
(7) variety of products	48 (24.9%)	71 (36.8%)	53 (27.5%)	17 (8.8%)	0 (0.0%)
(8) production flexibility	33 (17.1%)	72 (37.3%)	64 (33.2%)	18 (9.3%)	2 (1.0%)
(9) reduction of inventory	10 (5.2%)	46 (23.8%)	84 (43.5%)	42 (21.8%)	5 (2.6%)
(10) high quality products	28 (14.5%)	82 (42.5%)	52 (26.9%)	24 (12.4%)	3 (1.6%)
(11) product design	35 (18.1%)	69 (35.8%)	64 (33.2%)	18 (9.3%)	1 (0.5%)
(12) information system	14 (7.3%)	54 (28.0%)	86 (44.6%)	31 (16.1%)	4 (2.1%)
(13) information share with partners	11 (5.7%)	44 (22.8%)	90 (46.6%)	34 (17.6%)	9 (4.7%)
(14) distribution system	8 (4.1%)	46 (23.8%)	104 (53.9%)	25 (13.0%)	2 (1.0%)
(15) ecology	20 (10.4%)	67 (34.7%)	83 (43.0%)	12 (6.2%)	4 (2.1%)

Fig. 29.9 Competitiveness on each factor

for customers (129 companies: 66.8%), and variety of products (119 companies: 61.7%). On the other hand, added up the numbers of the companies answered 2: poor and 1: very poor, it is clear that the companies think they do not have their confidence in cost (47 companies: 24.4%), reduction of inventory (47 companies: 24.4%), and sharing information with their partners (43 companies: 22.3%). And Figure 29.10 shows which factor the companies give first priority, second priority, and third priority to in order to get and/or sustain their competitiveness.

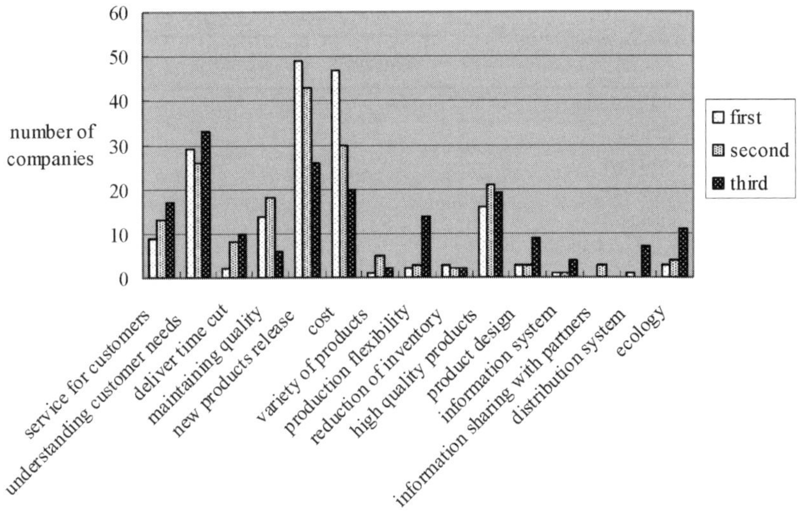

Fig. 29.10 The important factors for competitiveness

As Figure 29.10 shows, a lot of companies seem to think that improvement of their understanding customer needs, new products release, and cost are important factors to gain stronger competitiveness.

29.4.3 *Customer relationship*

The third item of the questions in our questionnaire is the customer relationship. The types of customers of the responded companies are shown in Figure 29.11 (three companies are eliminated because of their defective answers).

We also asked the question on the sales forms: (1) customers; (2) retailers; (3) dealers; (4) agencies; (5) companies; (6) wholesalers; and (7) others. The answer of this question is shown in Figure 29.12 (six companies are eliminated because of their defective answers).

From Figure 29.11, we can see that 75.3% of companies trade with companies, and 21.6% of companies trade with consumers. About the route of sales, it is clear that 46.5% of companies trade with customers directly, 19.2% through agencies, 11.8% through wholesalers (see Figure 29.12).

Besides types of customers and the route of sales, we asked the question about the relation with customers and business process innovation in the last five years and in the next five years. The answers of this question are

types of business	types of customers		
	companies	consumers	public institutions
foods and groceries	10	13	0
textile fablics	5	2	0
papers and pulp	4	0	0
oil and rubbers	23	7	0
medicaments	2	3	1
steel, metal, metalloids	14	1	0
equipments for transportation	9	2	0
appliance and electrical equipment	30	4	1
precision instruments	6	0	0
petroleum and coals	2	0	0
machines	20	1	0
glasses	2	0	1
others	8	7	2
blank (no respond)	8	1	1
total	143	41	6

Fig. 29.11 The types of customers

types of business	the route of sales						
	customers	retailers	dealers	agencies	companies	wholesalers	others
foods and groceries	7	3	1	1	2	7	1
textile fablics	0	1	0	4	1	0	0
papers and pulp	2	0	0	2	0	0	0
oil and rubbers	16	1	3	6	3	0	1
medicaments	0	1	0	1	1	3	0
steel, metal, metalloids	5	2	1	2	3	2	0
equipments for transportation	8	0	0	1	1	0	1
appliance and electrical	21	3	1	6	2	1	1
precision instruments	5	0	0	1	0	0	0
petroleum and coals	0	0	0	0	1	1	0
machines	15	1	0	5	0	0	0
glasses	1	0	0	1	0	0	0
others	4	0	1	5	1	4	2
blank (no respond)	3	0	0	2	1	4	0
total	87	12	7	37	16	22	6

Fig. 29.12 The route of sales

measured based on five point scales from 5: completely YES to 1: completely NO. The average of the answers is shown in Figure 29.13.

From all answers of the questions, the degree of the customers' participation increases from the past to the future. Moreover, customers'

	last 5 years	next 5 years
introduce customers demands into process	3.97	4.33
customers are concerned in process innovation	2.65	3.05
suppliers and partners are concerned in process innovation	2.81	3.10
several units in the company work in co-operation with in order to innovate processes	3.85	4.29
customers are concerned in developing new products	3.48	3.77
suppliers and partners are concerned in developing new products	3.02	3.38

Fig. 29.13 The degree of customers' participation of customers in process innovation (average)

participation depends on types of customers and the route of sales, that is, if a company trades with other companies, its customers are strongly concerned in new products development; if a company trades with customers directly, there is a tendency of cooperation between several units in the company to innovate processes.

29.4.4 *Business process strategy*

The fourth item of the questions in our questionnaire is the business process strategy. We identified two kinds of processes. The first is identified as: business to business (BtoB), business to customer (BtoC), and in house processes. The other is identified as: buy in, R&D, production, inventory manage, etc. the former is classified based on the type of the relationship with customers. The latter is classified based on the functions of the business.

Figure 29.14 shows the numbers of the companies answered the question about processes by the relationship with customers. We gave four points to company-wide reform, three points to partial reform, two points to improvement, and one point to remaining. From Figure 29.14, basic processes and support/management processes have been reformed or improved mainly in the last five years, and this situation will continue in the future. BtoC and BtoB processes would be reformed or improved more and more in the next five years. BtoC's average point has the sharpest growth, so we can conclude that a lot of Japanese companies need to improve customer relationship.

Figure 29.15 shows the numbers of the companies answered the question about processes by the functions of the business.

last 5 years	innovation		improve	remain	total	Ave.
	company-wide	partial				
BtoC	7(4%)	57(31%)	61(33%)	58(32%)	183(100%)	2.07
BtoB (inside the group)	10(5%)	51(28%)	56(31%)	66(36%)	183(100%)	2.03
BtoB (outside the group)	19(11%)	55(31%)	58(32%)	48(27%)	180(100%)	2.25
core process inside the company	30(16%)	79(42%)	58(31%)	19(10%)	186(100%)	2.65
support / management process	24(13%)	82(44%)	65(35%)	16(9%)	187(100%)	2.61

next 5 years	innovation		improve	remain	total	Ave.
	company-wide	partial				
BtoC	28(15%)	87(48%)	39(21%)	29(16%)	183(100%)	2.62
BtoB (inside the group)	21(12%)	79(44%)	56(31%)	25(14%)	181(100%)	2.53
BtoB (outside the group)	36(20%)	79(44%)	48(27%)	17(9%)	180(100%)	2.74
core process inside the company	56(30%)	88(47%)	35(19%)	7(4%)	186(100%)	3.04
support / management process	39(21%)	105(56%)	38(20%)	5(3%)	187(100%)	2.95

Fig. 29.14 The degree of process innovation (by the type of the relationship with customers)

last 5 years	innovation		improve	remain	Total	Ave.
	company-wide	partial				
buy in process	18(10%)	71(38%)	57(31%)	39(21%)	185(100%)	2.37
R&D process	10(6%)	67(37%)	57(31%)	47(26%)	181(100%)	2.22
production process	12(6%)	90(48%)	53(28%)	31(17%)	186(100%)	2.45
inventory management process	15(8%)	58(31%)	55(30%)	57(31%)	185(100%)	2.17
distribution process	22(12%)	56(30%)	59(32%)	49(26%)	186(100%)	2.27
after-sales service	3(2%)	38(21%)	61(34%)	80(44%)	182(100%)	1.80
management process	10(5%)	60(32%)	71(38%)	44(24%)	185(100%)	2.19
cooperation with abroad	6(3%)	44(25%)	48(28%)	75(43%)	173(100%)	1.89
recycle process	11(7%)	57(34%)	49(30%)	49(30%)	166(100%)	2.18

Fig. 29.15 The degree of process innovation (by the functions of the business)

From Figure 29.15, it seems that processes of after sales service and cooperation with abroad have been relatively less reformed or improved than other processes.

29.5 Conclusion

In this chapter, we summarized the results of the survey research on Japanese manufacturers conducted by the Committee of Strategic Process Management of JAMA on March, 2004. First, we reviewed the importance of business processes and explained the theoretical framework and research design of the survey.

About competitive environment outside the company, most responded companies focus on price (cost). They have strong confidence in maintaining quality, service for customers, and variety of products. On the other hand, most companies also think they have weakness in cost, reduction of inventory, and sharing information with partners. Moreover, the companies recognize that they need to improve especially understanding customer needs, new products release, and cost. It means that understanding what customers want as quickly as possible, and release better products faster with lower price are important. Therefore, Japanese companies need to become a customer-oriented organization more and more.

In the future, it seems that customers are more concerned in process innovation in each company. Customers are companies in most cases, but no matter customers are consumers or companies, it is truth that competitive environment requires every company to be customer-oriented.

Talking on business process strategy, most of responded companies focused on reform or improvement of core processes and support/management processes. However, companies keep them in try to reform BtoC and BtoB processes, too. Especially, BtoC processes are focused on more comparing with BtoB. In sum, we can conclude that being customer-oriented organization is most important matter for Japanese companies.

Of course, we must continue to work on this kind of survey not only in Japan but also in other countries to build a valid model of process management practices. Fortunately, our committee has already found some members who help our survey in Korea and Taiwan, so we will keep work on this survey and try to get some fruitful outcomes about business process management in the near future.

References

Borthick, A. F. and Roth, H. P. (1993). Accounting for time: reengineering business processes to improve responsiveness, *Journal of Cost Management* 7-3, pp. 4–14.

Carr, D. K. (1993). Managing for effective business process redesign, *Journal of Cost Management* 7-3, pp. 16–21.

Dailey, M. J. (1998). Pattern analysis for cost management: a case study and model, *Journal of Cost Management* 12-4, pp. 42–48.

Harrington, H. J. (1991). *Business Process Improvement*, McGraw-Hill, Inc.

Harrington, H. J. (1993). Process breakthrough: business process improvement, *Journal of Cost Management* 7-3, pp. 30–43.

Lee, G. (2003). Business process redesign and performance management, in *Organizational Structure and Management Accounting*, edited by Monden, Y., Zeimu Keiri Kyokai. (in Japanese)

Lawson, R. A. (1994). Beyond ABC: process-based costing, *Journal of Cost Management* 8-3, pp. 33–43.

Monden, Y. and Lee, G. (2005). Conceptual framework of process management and management accounting, *Accounting* 57-5, pp. 18–25. (in Japanese)

Ostrenga, M. R. and Probst, F. R. (1992). Process value analysis: the missing link in cost management, *Journal of Cost Management* 6-3, pp. 4–13.

CHAPTER

30

IT and Process Innovation in Japanese Enterprise

Yoshiyuki Nagasaka

Professor, Faculty of Business Administration, Konan University

Keisuke Sakate

Assistant Professor, Faculty of Business Administration
Osaka University of Commerce

Asako Kimura

Assistant Professor, Faculty of Commerce
Kyushu Sangyo University

30.1 Introduction

Companies must continue developing business while coping with external factors such as globalization, IT innovation and an increase of customer power. To meet these challenges, it is important to reform business processes in a timely, flexible and expedient manner, which means that companies must be increasingly agile. An agile requires broad change capabilities for business processes that are balanced across multiple dimensions. It was pointed out that "an enterprise to be agile must have a balanced response-to-change capability across the four change proficiency metrics: time, cost, robustness, and scope" (Devor, Graves and Mills, 1997). Here, process-based management plays a significant role. Process-based management deals with a series of company activities from input to output, which are called business processes (Monden and Lee, 2005).

In particular, the speed of IT innovation is intense. IT innovation has a big influence on business processes (Hammer and Champy, 1993). In the past, most Japanese companies conventionally divided their information systems by section, as part of efforts to achieve partial optimization. These days, information systems seem to be utilized cross-functionally for total optimization.

The Committee of Strategic Process Management in the Japanese Association of Management Accounting conducted a survey on business processes (see Chapter 29). This chapter will discuss the relationship between IT and business processes in Japanese companies based on the analyzed survey results.

30.2 Business Model, IT and Process-based Management

30.2.1 *Business model and process-based management*

Generally speaking, a business model is said to be a profit engine within business. Many varying definitions of business models have been discussed by many researchers. Also, the restructuring business models is repeated in accordance with a company's environmental changes. Business processes, which are part of the business model, are also forced to change by the restructuring.

Some researchers assume that a broad-sense business model consists of three business systems: (1) a business paradigm; (2) business processes; and (3) a domain of business architecture. On the other hand, it is said that a narrow-sense business model consists of: (1) business theory (or business concept); (2) a system model (a business process model that consists of a conceptual model, a theoretical model, and a practical model); and (3) business practice (or business method) (Ishikawa, 2001). In addition, it is said that the business model is not a strategy, a tactic, an action plan, an improvement plan, or an action style. This indicates that the business model is a system that creates a new value (Magretta, 2002).

On the other hand there have been reports that state that the business model can be concretely represented as a main characteristic of business (the architecture of business that consists of the incarnation of value in a product/service, the acquisition of customers and financial achievement within business affairs) (Teramoto and Iwasaki, 2000). These characteristics are the same at the point where a business model shows a frame that is the basis for a business design that creates customer value.

Figure 30.1 shows a schematic drawing of a business model. In this figure, the core value means customer value. The customer should be the main

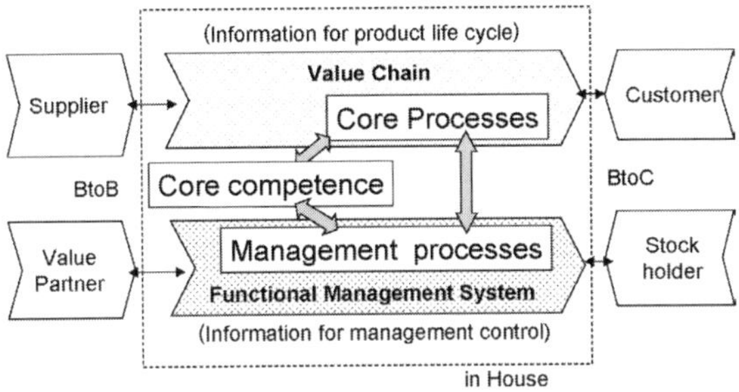

Fig. 30.1 Structure of business model

entity in all stake holders. Furthermore, the company must make clear in their business model what product or services they are offering for what kind of customer and with what kind of technology. Here, core competence, core processes, and value partners are very important. Core competence is the core power which makes it possible to transmit the company's particular value to customers. Management processes are necessary as mechanisms to support core competence. In other words, both core processes and management processes are important elements that support business models.

30.2.2 *IT and business process*

IT innovation should be emphasized over other environmental changes within a company. It is very important to make the relationship between IT and business processes clear.

In the later half of the 1980s, a tide of BPR (business process reengineering) was caused. BPR is a systematic approach for drastically redesigning using IT. Many companies have tried to introduce BPR. In 1998 in the U.S.A., there was a judgment that definitely accepted a business model patent. Many companies began to actively apply patents for new business models. Today, we are in the age of the ubiquitous. Ubiquitous comes from the Latin word meaning existence anywhere anytime. This word describes a network system that we can use in many kinds of terminals such as mobile phones, car navigation systems, and personal computers. These new ubiquitous systems will drastically change business processes.

IT influences all business processes either directly or indirectly. Business processes for redesign are categorized in three ways: (1) BtoC processes (business to customer); (2) BtoB processes (business to business); and (3) internal processes, as mentioned below.

1. BtoC process
   BTO (build to order) has become a popular method of direct trade on the internet. These new relations between enterprises and customers are strengthened by IT. This system is called CRM (customer relationship management). Individual customer management and needs collection have been enabled by interactive exchanges through the internet. This demand chain is very important for reflecting customer needs within core business processes.
2. BtoB process
   Relations between companies are improved by SCM (supply chain management). The accuracy of demand forecasting and manufacturing/physical distribution plans should be improved. The response should be returned to the customer quickly. Such efforts are very significant for synchronizing manufacturing and demand in the market. For this purpose, SCM software has been developed based on TOC (theory of constraint).

   ECM (engineering chain management) is very important for the collaboration of research and development, design and procurement. EDI (electronic data interchange) is used in most companies. E-market places for automobile parts and electricity have already been constructed and utilized. Digital mockups are useful for connecting engineering chains. IT alters business processes between suppliers and mother companies.
3. Internal process
   Core processes such as product plans, research, design, procurement, manufacturing, and quality inspection are managed internally within a company. They are very important and deeply influenced by IT. For example, three-dimensional CAD has changed design methods. CAE has made it possible to predict qualities before mass production. AGVs (auto guided vehicles) have been utilized in factories to drastically improve material handling. ERP (enterprise resource planning) has been implemented in many companies to pin-point their real time financial situation. Knowledge management systems are efficiently prepared to develop know-how and inherent knowledge within a company.

30.3 Brief Summary of Company Survey

Eight lead questionnaire items were set by a committee for company survey research about "strategic process management" (Lee, Kosuga and Nagasaka, 2004). These items were: (1) outline of the company;

(2) environment inside the company; (3) environment outside the company; (4) adopting new information technology; (5) customer relationships; (6) relationship between business environment and organization; (7) business process strategy; and (8) globalization of business processes.

We sent this questionnaire to 1,282 Japanese manufacturers on March 1, 2004. We chose managers of management planning sections as the intended subjects of the questionnaire. We asked them to return their responses by March 30, 2004.

198 companies responded (15.5% of 1,282 companies) and we rejected five defective answers; therefore 193 answers were accepted as valid answers (15.1% of 1,282 companies). Details about this survey are described in Chapter 29.

30.4 Trend of Informatization

30.4.1 *IT investment objectives*

In our mail survey, we asked about companies' IT investment objectives for previous five and the next five years to understand trend of informatization among respondents. Figures 30.2 and 30.3 summarize the results of the replies.

The results show that highest trend for both the last five years and the next five is "speed-up of operation." However, the ratio decreased from

Objective of IT investment	Last 5 years	Next 5 years
Reduction of inventory cost	51(9.6%)	57(10.5%)
Reduction of procurement cost	27(5.1%)	68(12.5%)
Reduction of personnel cost	61(11.5%)	38(7.0%)
Speed-up of operation	156(29.4%)	106(19.5%)
Improvement of Marketing and Sales force	81(15.3%)	78(14.3%)
Improvement of development capability of new product or service	30(5.6%)	21(3.9%)
Strengthening of relationships or Incrimination of business partners	20(3.8%)	23(4.2%)
Improvement of customer satisfaction	39(7.3%)	90(16.5%)
New entry into different business area	3(0.6%)	10(1.8%)
Organizational reformation	58(10.9%)	48(8.8%)
Etc	5(0.9%)	5(0.9%)

Fig. 30.2 Objectives of IT investment for the past 5 years

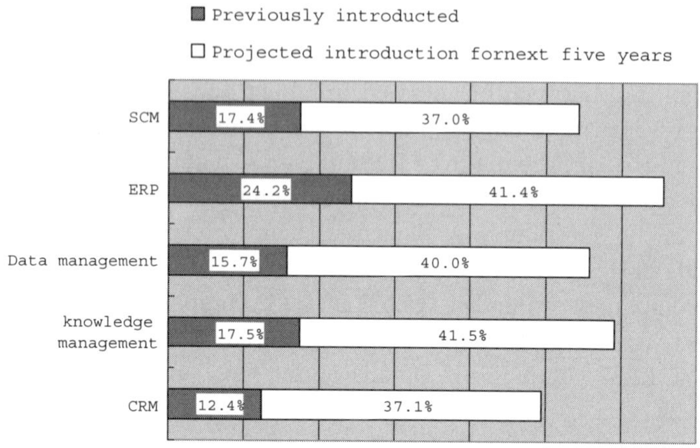

Fig. 30.3 Information sharing with IT

29.4% to 19.5%. It should also be noted that the ratio of the "improvement of customer satisfaction" which was less than 10% for last 5 years increased to 16.5% for next 5 years. The ratio of "Reduction of procurement cost" increased by 5.1% to 12.5%.

30.4.2 *Information sharing with IT*

Figure 30.3 summarizes trends in information sharing with IT. The results show that the number of companies that previously introduced each IT tool are much higher than those projected for the next five years.

Figure 30.3 shows that ERP is the most likely to accelerate introduction, followed by knowledge management.

30.4.3 *Information sharing with business partner using IT*

Figure 30.4 shows how much respondents currently use each IT tool to coordinate their business partners. In this case, over half the companies had previously introduced EDI. Furthermore, a little less than 80% of respondents had either introduced EDI or had plans to do so. Other than EDI, many companies had previously introduced or had plans to introduce data exchange using the Internet. Over the next five years, most companies planned to participate in a Portal site.

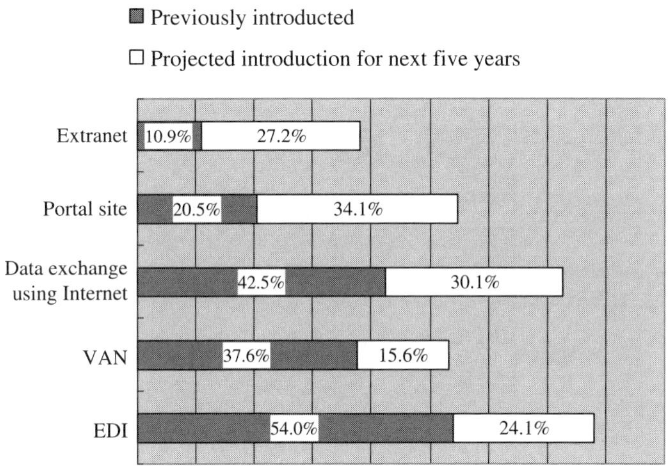

Fig. 30.4 Use of IT for business partners

30.4.4 *Information sharing with overseas divisions using IT*

We also asked respondents how often they use IT tools to coordinate with their overseas divisions. Their reply results (Figure 30.5) show that all tools are likely to accelerate introduction. Nonetheless, the levels of introduction of all tools in overseas divisions are lower than in the domestic divisions (Figure 30.3).

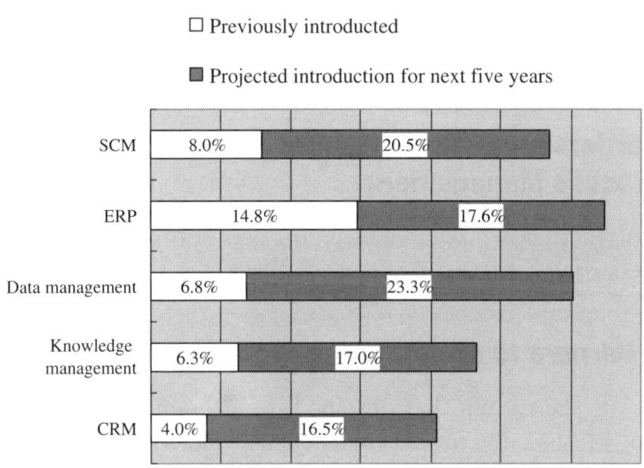

Fig. 30.5 Information sharing with overseas division using IT

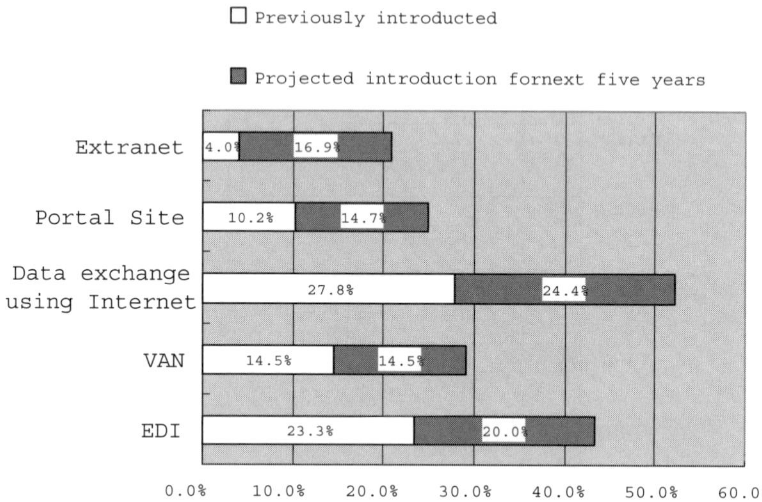

Fig. 30.6 Information sharing with overseas business partners

30.4.5 *Information sharing with overseas business partners*

Figure 30.6 shows how often respondents use each IT tool to share information with overseas business partners.

The highest ratio is "data exchange using Internet;" more than quarter of respondents had previously introduced data exchange using Internet or planned to do so in the next five years. Also, many companies had introduced or will do EDI. This tendency of Information sharing with oversea business partners is the same as with domestic ones.

30.5 Barriers and Pending Issues in Transforming Process Management

We must predict, clear up, or sidestep barriers and pending issues in transforming process strategies. It aims to clarify these points in this section.

30.5.1 *Barriers to transforming process strategy*

Figure 30.7 is the results that obtained from the questionnaire. There are barriers to transforming process management including a lack of consensus among process management practitioner (38.9%), deficiencies in organization, and a lack of human resources and money (26.3%). Each of these barriers aggravates existing situations as they affect one another. In other

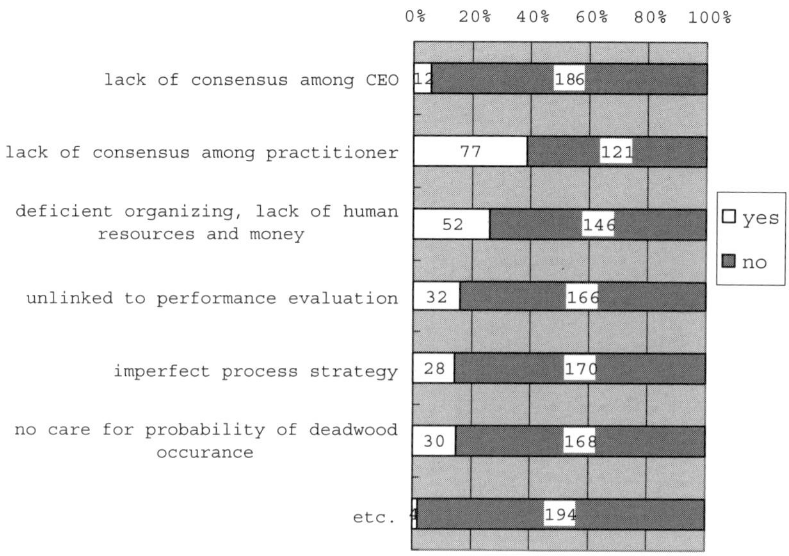

Fig. 30.7 Barriers to transforming process management

word, even though CEO made decisions for innovative change, most practitioners have not caught up enough to realize. As a consequence, failures may occur when organizing projects. Additionally, practitioners have not promoted incentive, because those transforming process management has not worked closely with performance evaluations.

30.5.2 *Pending issues with transforming process management*

According to the results of the questionnaire, "difficulty in maintaining quality (48.4%)," "technology or information leaks (37.6%)," and "decreases in one's technical capability and skill (31.2%)" are raised as a pending issues which companies must face at this time of change (Figure 30.9). Process management of this type is considered to give many companies "self dependence" (Figure 30.8). Figure 30.8 shows most companies can't turn quality maintenance over to other companies; they can't affiliate other companies to prevent leaks of technology and information. Outsourcing to another company reduces their capability and skill. In other word, they probably can't establish a relationship of trust including the company in a group of companies.

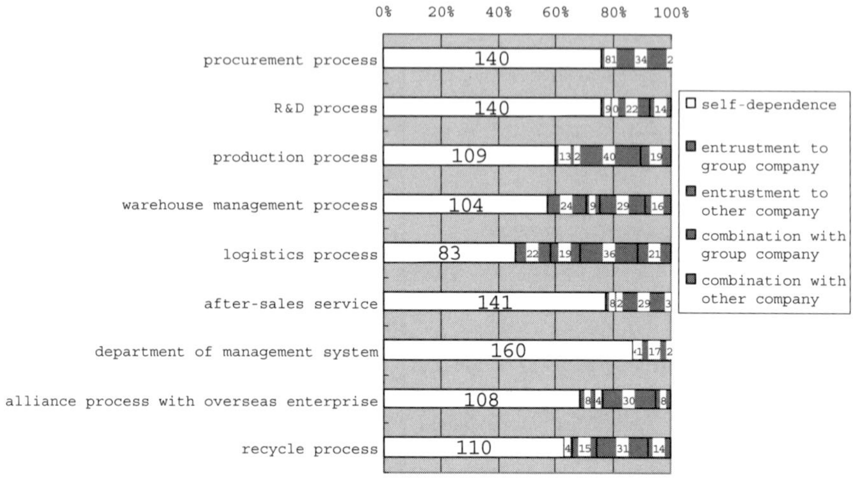

Fig. 30.8 Nucleus of process management

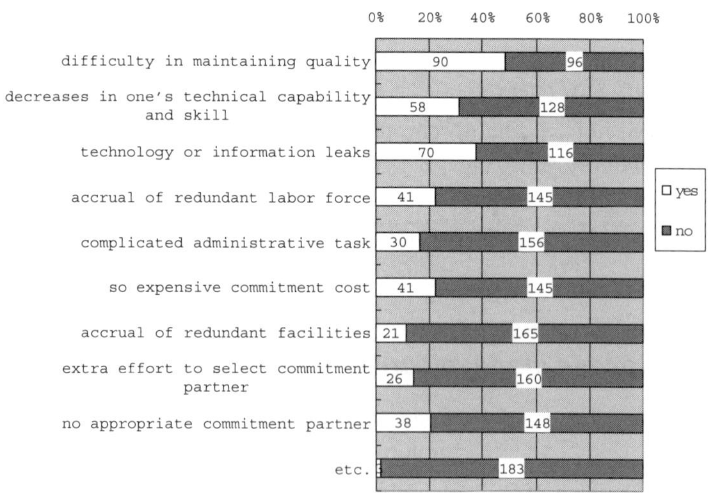

Fig. 30.9 Pending issues of entrustment

We must build a system that enables information sharing and that prevents information leaks. We should also strengthen confidential relations within a group of companies. In this way, individuals can also build trusting relations.

30.6 The Relationship between IT Investment and Process Innovation

30.6.1 *The relationship between Information sharing and process innovation*

We analyzed a cross with the degree of process innovation (see Figure 29.14 in Chapter 29) and the degree of information sharing with the IT tool which we discussed in a previous section. Figure 30.10 shows the number of the companies that indicated they had finished the introduction of each IT tool or plan introductions in the next five, still and companies that said they planned "whole or partial reform" in the next five years. Still as a result of having examined the chi-square after cross tabulation, the colored cell expresses some meaningful ("both side" significance probability <0.05) things.

Figure 30.10 shows that IT tools and process innovations are relevant. In other words, in companies making efforts to reform the BtoC process, the tendency to introduce CRM and SCM is strong, and, in companies making efforts to reform the BtoB process of the group "inside and outside," the tendency to introduce SCM is strong. In addition, in companies making efforts to reform the "inside basic process" and the inside support/management process, the tendency to introduce ERP is strong.

Process for Wholly and partial innovation	IT tool				
	CRM	Knowledge Management	Data Management	ERP	SCM
BtoC	66 58.9%	69 63.3%	67 60.9%	78 69.6%	72 65.5%
BtoB(Outside of group)	55 56.7%	56 62.8%	60 63.2%	67 68.4%	61 63.5%
BtoB(Inside of group)	58 52.3%	64 59.3%	65 59.6%	77 70.0%	67 61.5%
Internal Basic Process	72 51.4%	83 60.6%	80 58.0%	96 68.6%	80 58.0%
support/management process	73 52.1%	83 60.6%	76 55.1%	96 68.6%	79 57.2%

Fig. 30.10 Cross table with relationship between IT tools and process innovation

30.7 Result of Business Process Innovation

The outcomes of business process innovation have been examined based on the BSC framework (the Balanced Scorecard) (Kaplan and Norton, 1992). Figure 30.11 shows to what degree process innovation satisfied the

Group	Item	Satisfaction level 5	4	3	2	1	Average	Average of each group
Financial	Sales	8	41	69	35	26	2.83	3.00
	Cost effectiveness	5	35	97	34	11	2.94	
	Selling cost	2	39	92	40	10	2.91	
	General and administrative expenses	6	45	79	43	10	2.97	
	Production cost	11	92	43	26	12	**3.35**	
Customer	Customer satisfaction	5	67	86	19	6	**3.25**	3.07
	Market share	3	37	97	35	11	2.92	
	Customer fixing rate	0	38	119	18	6	**3.04**	
Internal process	Cycle time	5	64	74	29	8	**3.16**	3.02
	Return rate and claim	4	3	88	45	10	2.64	
	Ratio to keep appointed date of delivery	11	65	79	24	5	**3.29**	
	Quantity of inventory	10	65	57	39	11	**3.13**	
	Productivity of indirect section	4	39	73	49	11	2.86	
Learning and growth	Awareness of employees for changes	5	60	83	22	13	**3.12**	3.05
	Paradigm and climate	4	55	88	23	12	**3.09**	
	Employee satisfaction	1	31	116	31	5	2.96	

Satisfaction level = 5: satisfied very much, 4: satisfied a little, 3: fair, 2: not satisfied, 1: not satisfied at all.

Fig. 30.11 Satisfaction level after process innovation

companies expectations for each item. Gray-colored cells represent items with a satisfaction level of more than 3.0.

Many companies are satisfied with the awareness of their employees regarding changes and an improved paradigm. In addition, cycle time, ratios for maintaining the appointed date of delivery and inventory quantities have been improved. However, from a financial point-of-view, only a reduction in production cost has been achieved.

Categorical regression analysis was applied to investigate the causal relationship among the satisfied items of four groups such as financial, customer, inner process and learning & growth. We have analyzed which item has the biggest contribution ratio for satisfied items using the correlation coefficient. The analyzed result is shown in Figure 30.12. It was found that the relationship between financial and customer items is quite strong. However, the reduction of production costs is directly related to inner process items.

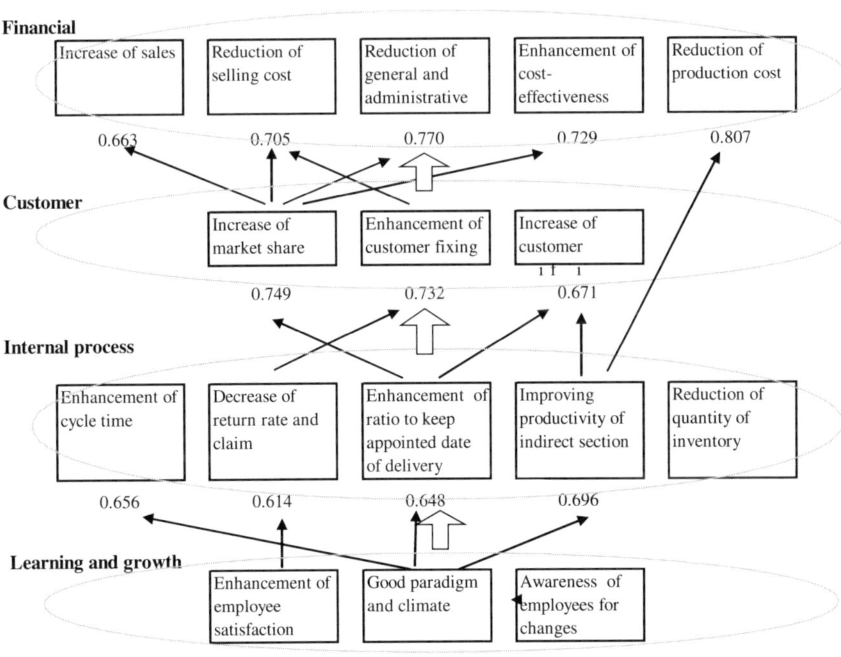

Fig. 30.12 A map of the causal relationship between satisfied items

30.8 Conclusion

Both core processes and management processes are important elements in supporting a business model. IT innovation has a big influence on business processes. Business processes for redesign are categorized into three parts: (1) BtoC processes (business to customer); (2) BtoB processes (business to business); and (3) internal processes. From our survey of Japanese companies, BtoB and BtoC process innovation are occurring as well as internal process innovation. The IT tools within the companies are related to specific business process innovations. The outocomes of business process innovation were examined based on the BSC framework. The causal relationship between satisfied items has been quantitatively established. Based on such the survey and analysis it may be possible to create clear and excellent business management models.

References

DeVor, R., Graves, R., and Mills, J. J. (1997). Agile manufacturing research: accomplishments and opportunities, *IIE Transactions* 29, pp. 813–823.

Hammer, M. and Champy, J. (1993). *Reengineering the Corporation: A Manifesto for Business Revolution*, New York, NY: Harper Business.

Magretta, J. (2002). Why business models matter, *Harvard Business Review* 80-5, May, pp. 86–92.

Kaplan, R. S. and Norton, D. P. (1992). The balanced scorecard: measures that drive performance, *Harvard Business Review* Jan–Feb, pp. 71–80.

Nagasaka, Y. and Sakate, K. (2005). Investigation of process management in Japanese companies, *Accounting* 57-5, pp. 33–41. (in Japanese)

Monden, Y. (2002). *The Introduction to Empirical Research of Accounting and Management, Analysis of Corporate Model by SPSS*, ChuoKeizai Co. (in Japanese)

Monden, Y. and Lee, G. (2005). Conceptual framework and management accounting of process management, *Accounting* 57-5, pp. 18–25. (in Japanese)

Teramoto, Y. and Iwasaki, N. (2000). *Business Model Revolution*, Japan Productivity Center. (in Japanese)

CHAPTER

31

Strategic Cost Management on IT Investment in Japan

Shuji Mizoguchi

Professor, Faculty of Business Administration
Yokohama National University

31.1 Introduction

Japanese investment in information system is about 4% of national GDP and 25% of the whole investment of plant and equipment. This figure was estimated around 19,700 billion yen (US$188 billion) based on various economic statistics and I/O investment data. If we breakdown this total investment, hardware investment was 12,100 billion yen and software (except inhouse software) investment was 7,600 billion yen respectively. The software investment ratio in comparison with total information system investment is increasing very rapidly in Japan. This figure was 10% in 1985, which increased very sharply in 1995 and 2001. According to Jyouhouka-Hakusho (2003, pp. 45–46), the investment in this area was around 25% and 39% of total information system investment in 1995 and 2001 respectively.

It is necessary for a manager to make an appropriate decision, which considers the profit and reasonable balance between cost and benefit should be maintained by rapid expansion of information system investments. Strategic construction of supply chain system from supplier to customer will be fruitful if proper information system can be developed in this globalized and diversified corporate management. Due to the economic stagnation caused by deflation in Japan, companies are seeking profit through merger which needs rebuilding of supply chain structure. Due to this, companies in Japan need to develop business model which will contribute value to the company. This new business model will pursue both short-term profitability in the information system investment and long-term growth potentiality of the company as a whole.

As a typical illustration of information system investments, electronic commerce is effective in business process reengineering (BPR) and this will reduce material supply cost between companies and groups. The market of Business to Business (B to B) electronic commerce was about 46,300 billion yen according to report of Ministry of Economy, Trade and Industry in 2002. E-market, which is also utilizing internet facility, secured 5,000 billion yen transaction in 2002. This figure was about 10.8% of B to B electronic commerce market. There is a prediction of Japanese Ministry of Economy, Trade and Industry that this ratio of e-market will increase from 7% to 18% in the year 2002 and 2007 respectively.

Investment for information infrastructure such as internet, intranet, extranet and other host system or network system will increase in future to deal with the electronic commerce. In my research, I explained information infrastructure investment, which is contributing to the entire company's communication, processing and accumulation not depending on specific application system. It is necessary to invest in the information system infrastructure, to develop and maintain large-scale new business model accompanied with electronic commerce concept. This investment will lead to improve productivity and management process innovation. There is a doubt whether investment in information infrastructure will lead to increase the productivity of the company or not. There would have productivity paradox which many not lead to ultimate competitive advantage due to lack of ultimate use of information system. For a proper measurement of information system, the managers need an appropriate information system which will be easy to use and should be equipped with evaluation technique based on qualitative judgement.

To evaluate a new technology based on quantitative measurement, net present value (NPV) technique is generally used. Shank claims, however, a very effective evaluation technique is not always available for information infrastructure investment especially for new information technology development (Shank and Govindarajan, 1992, pp. 39–40). In addition, there are many intangible advantages of using information system, which lead the evaluation process complicated if we consider time of investment. Furthermore, the evaluation process seemed to be very difficult when I evaluated the information technology of a new Supply Chain Management (SCM) and Customer Relationship Management (CRM) project.

Traditional evaluation technique is used when it evaluates feasibility of an information system investment project in the planning stage and it is difficult to perform a flexible decision in the situation of abandonment of investment project or to continue evaluation of IT. The company may be criticized in that case for not performing a flexible decision if the information system investment is not justified. According to Taudes's claim (2000, pp. 227–228), this kind of evaluation problem is still continuing in the business environment.

In my research, I have critically considered the above statement and try to find out a solution of IT. I have developed a model which examines information system investment classification in Section 2. In my paper, I have examined the traditional information system investment evaluation from the viewpoint of economic value analysis and discuss about it in Section 3.

31.2 General Structure of Information System Investment

31.2.1 *Information system investment classifications*

There are a lot of classification standards of an information system investment. I have divided an information system investment based on business strategy purpose into infrastructure investment, investment for market, investment for organizational innovation, investment for structural change. There are different measurements as an evaluation standard: scope of economies, profitability, response time and opportunity cost. I think that the evaluation techniques of information system investment are mainly dependent on the factors of business strategy, information system strategy, profitability and balance of short-time profitability and long-term growth. When I prescribe the attributes of information system investment based on business strategy purpose referring to Boynton, I can generally classify them in the following four types (Boynton, 1994, p. 307).

The first is investments for cost cut purpose. This reduces a cost of a business process and it is carried out to improve value creation and business achievements, which lead to increase the amount of sales. This investment is required in some specific situations to maintain competitive advantage. This method will lead to improve the efficiency of management within the organization and improve market competition by introducing point-of-sale terminal system and introduction of improved material distribution management system, which will be controlled by MIS.

The second is investment for management support purpose. It will help management through a design of a business process, a planning and control system and monitoring after the introduction for value creation, which can increase management efficiency. Information system construction for supply chain management will help to increase the efficiency and effectiveness of the management operations.

The third is investment for strategic planning purpose. This contributes to support of business strategy development and aims at matching with other information systems. This matching of information should be compliance with the mainframe, LAN, protocol or OS and hardware which is related to this standardized information infrastructure. This will help to develop future information system architecture. A design of system architecture such as SCM, CRM based on integrated information system such as ERP is equivalent to this.

The fourth is investment for the purpose of security of competitive advantage for specific services.

Achieving the competitive advantage in a market and preparing the business to overcome the future competitive advantage if needed is one of the most important aspects of business. This concept was proposed as SIS in the middle of 1980s, and the core idea is still effective.

The problem of information system investment is that it is not sorted according to the purpose and classification. For example, though the point-of-terminal was at first introduced to cost cut purpose, it contributes greatly from the management support to operational efficiency purpose. In addition to this use, it also helps in those competitive advantages related to customer. In the present distribution industry, point-of-sale system can be one of the bases for information infrastructure investment.

The basic stance of chief information officer (CIO) had in their mind for long term growth and continuation of the invested capital to the information system, and at the same time thought about short-term profitability of the company too. Profitability was expected from the individual project as short-term basis for the new business applications investment and after that growth was also considered for the entire organization from long-term perspective. However, Evans says that this way of thinking is changing its type in the e-business society. Now a day, companies are focusing on short-term basis (Evans and Wurster, 1997, pp. 71–82). Easy management of data and swiftness of database, change of the process of information services, security of networks and its maintenance, effective customer and vendor management, which are the current thinking a business.

31.2.2 Conceptual structure of information system

I can explain an information system conceptual structure from two dimensions. We can pay attention to short-term profitability with long-term growth characteristics from a strategic perspective of information system investment and we think that there is an attribute of information system investment in either domain. On the other hand, I can consider an attribute of an information system investment based on individual project and its application into entire company's information infrastructure investment based on availability of time and space. According to Ross, this is explained in Figure 31.1 (Ross and Beath, 1994, p. 53).

I have classified information system investments from the viewpoint of strategic purpose into "update," "conversion," "experiment" and "process improvement" in Figure 31.1.

I show that "conversion" domain foresees long-term growth and investment is carried out for an information infrastructure investment. If it is necessary to switch over from market environment to e-business environment rapidly, after the examination if it is understand that there is lack in the present information system, we need develop essential information system ability. If it is recognized that the application system development ability and the system solution adaptability are limited and it is necessary for growth of the corporate earnings, "conversion" investment is necessary

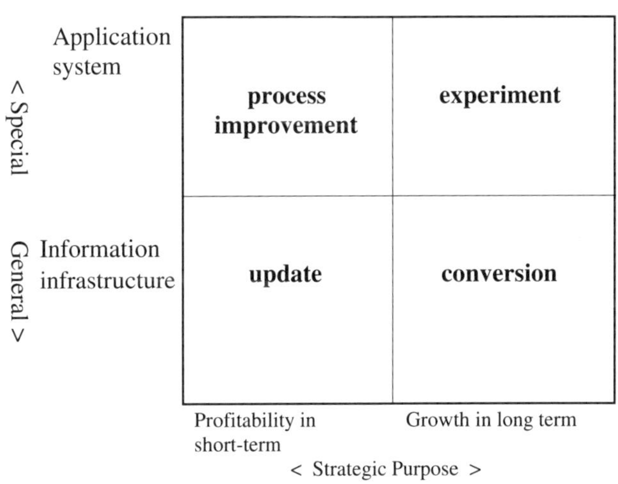

Fig. 31.1 Conceptual structure of information system

in that time. "conversion" investment strategy cannot evade a risk of an information infrastructure investment. That is why the company has to predict the long-term growth and rebuilding their information infrastructure and maintaining it to keep them in competitive advantage situation unless there is big risk to carry out this venture into entire company. As system of importance such as, construction of platform to realize a support system to introduce ERP, change of network environment, unification of customer data, construction of data warehouse, supply chain introduction and duties of part processing system, development of middleware for WEB environmental management, 24 hours operation, a "conversion" investment can be carried out as an introduction investment to improvement of security and a process of future growth characteristics. For example, when a company is driven into a crisis of competition due to the poor information infrastructure, it performs a large amount of "conversion" investment and rearranges a value chain and aims at security and maintenance of competitive advantage. When the information infrastructure which was first introduced became outdated, as a result of conversion investment, it is necessary to be updated into new information technology.

A company carries out an "update" to improve the information infrastructure and effective practical use of the system functions. This will lead to improve the information technology level and withdrawal from an obsolete technology or system. The advantage of an "update" investment promotes efficiency and ability to use the improvement of system conservatism, in addition this will reduce cost of information system support or education training and maintain system existence. Furthermore, due to the "update" investment, it also influence decisions such as termination of support from vendor for the old product. For example, many e-business systems have been offered on Windows based platform. However, companies in the limited conditions such as limited volume of business by Microsoft, increase the cost very high due to update investment or due to the stiffening characteristics of a system, may switch to other companies like UNIX platform or Linux platform to reduce administration cost during trouble time. A user of the new system can ask for discount while purchasing hardware or software and can bargain for the terms and conditions.

Clemons claims that the company with short-term profit motivation can improve business process information infrastructure by utilizing a "process improvement" investment (Clemons and Row, 1991, pp. 275–276). For example, reduction in cycle time can improve the customer service value by maintenance and promoting efficient customer service, reduction of document printing cost, mailing cost (billing and reporting cost) etc. The "process improvement" investment depends on specific project, and comparative future prediction is possible and risk is low. The "process improvement" is built on existing information infrastructure and improved based on future prediction of change. An updated "process improvement" promotes basic organization change and make the existing system simplified.

An "experiment" investment in case of information system and business process needs continuous learning of the present situation and should have ability to cope the information system with new technology. For example, a simulation of cost appraisal may limit the operative experiment, effects of change of new system and customer services. If the "experiment" investment succeeds, company will move to "process improvement" investment domain for their information infrastructure.

31.3 Value Creation by an Information Infrastructure Investment and the Evaluation

There are four types of the information system investment that I described in Section 2, which are distinguished conceptually, but clear division of them is substantially difficult. The conceptual structure particularly shows a stable state of information system at a certain point in time and it changes into other states from one state that is applicable dynamically. If the information system of an "experiment" domain achieves success in value creation process, this will shift to "conversion" domain from "experiment" domain on the basis of effectiveness of the success. Information system of "conversion" will adopt information infrastructure and will be "updated" in future. Specific operational application system is built on the "update" and "process improvement" is carried out and contributes to business performances of the individual division. The value creation process of an information system is modeled in Figure 31.2.

This process consists of four segments. These are value choice process of changing from "experiment" to "conversion," a value creation process of changing from "conversion" to "update," value realization process of changing from "update" to "process improvement" and the last one is value search process of changing from "process improvement" to "experiment."

Both "conversion" and "update" domain are information infrastructure investment domains.

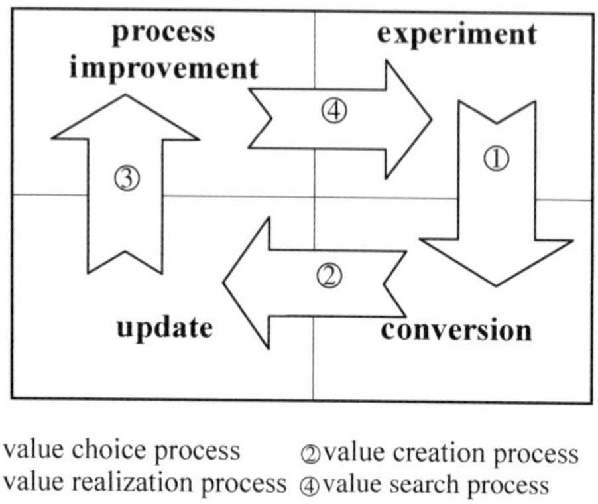

Fig. 31.2 Value creation process by information system

31.3.1 *A value choice process*

A characteristic of information system of an "experiment" domain is an examination of a business model for selective purposes, such as a practical use of new information system and software in the information system. For example, a competition related test among different sales channels of new data warehouse system, present condition of customer service evaluation, cost appraisal of IT implementation etc. Who is in charge of this investment at this stage? If IT investment is carried out in a certain division, division or SBU manager will be in charge of it. If it is done in the indirect department such as accounting or human affairs, CIO or the manager of the functional department will be in charge of it. When an investment effect of information system of "an experiment" domain is confirmed, the application scale is extended within the company and after that develops a new information infrastructure investment for an entire company. The "conversion" domain is the core information infrastructure for the entire company's business model. The cross functional data is necessary for this type of business model.

The characteristic of information system of "conversion" domain is core information infrastructure of an entire company's business model. This has necessity of joint data for each business. This requires an integrated information system and unified platform of information system and possible applicability for the entire company's information infrastructure. The common use of individual operation system improves the use of information system service in cost effective manner. In a "conversion" domain, top management involves in the fund allocation to information system section and after that CIO is mainly responsible for implementation and evaluation of information system for the entire company. The implementation of ERP in specific division is a concrete example of "experiment." There is a case of ERP introduction as an entire company's information infrastructure. In case of value choice process, "conversion" investment is chosen from "experiment" domain with a thinking of long-term growth of a company. However, it is not easy to measure creation of business value due to information infrastructure investment and business value creation will not come directly or immediately after the investment. "Conversion" of operational process by information system and a management process causes business value creation. In this case, it is necessary to invest the new information technology and information infrastructure by choosing value choice process from "experiment" domain to create future business value. Scarso (1996, pp. 41–42) claims if the evaluation of information technology and infrastructure investment is not possible in the "experiment" domain, real option analysis of EVA and ENPV can be applied to measure the quality of former pilot project of this domain, due to the uncertainty of cost-effectiveness.

31.3.2 *A value creation process*

A characteristic of information system of an "update" domain is quality improvement of an information service and examination of cost cut opportunity in a changing information environment due to the obsolescence of information technology and termination of vender support. In an "update" domain, it is common that information system department and CIO will take responsibility for entire company information system, "updating" of information infrastructure, perform evaluation and budget allocation for investment. The operative expense estimation and information system investment in a "conversion" domain is easier than "experiment" domain, but it is difficult to grasp cause and effect relationship with the effect of an information system investment.

The value creation process mentioned above, maintains the latest information infrastructure facilities from "conversion" domain to "update" domain and prepare for a base of value realization of each department. In practice, it is very difficult to make a line between "conversion" and "update" domain belonging to information infrastructure investment. "Conversion" domain plays a very important role of not only changing a future business model but also innovating the present business model and this revolutionizes company structure systematically and changes an earnings structure. On the other hand, "update" becomes new and stops old information infrastructure and it replaces information technology with cost effectiveness, accuracy and swiftness.

"Update" strategic value is not depending on changing the business model but creating total business value. Kaplan (1986, pp. 89–90) says that CIO is responsible for strategic realization and estimates cost efficiency of the investment. CIO is also responsible for fund distribution to "update" technology, information infrastructure and decision making.

31.3.3 *A value realization process*

A characteristic of information system of a "process improvement" domain is improvement of productivity by operational improvement and realization of business value. "Process improvement" domain will be connected directly with the customer, supplier and cross functional characteristics. Information system investment is generally strategic decision in this domain. In this domain, a specific department and SBU are in charge of cost-benefit evaluation of information system. In the value realization process, each department has clear idea about information technology and platform of information system. This process develops an individual application system for each department based on its own expenditure and realize business value for that department. A "process improvement" investment is different from information infrastructure investments such as "conversion" or "update" and this process can estimate business goal and expected profit from each investment accurately. According to Morton (1991, pp. 195–199), the evaluation of value realization and investment effect is done by financial analysis such as DCF.

31.3.4 *A value search process*

Among the information systems that the individual department implemented from the purpose of value realization in "process improvement" domain, a value search process is receiving a future information technological opportunity in advance and searches for information technology which can affect entire company's information system. CIO is mainly evaluating a future business trend and market trend in this domain. It is very important to search the future information technology in advance for long-term growth opportunity of the company. This kind of investment is unavoidable, considering the short-term profitability and long-term growth. When a company can differentiate the information infrastructure investment coming from "process improvement" investment to "conversion" or "update," it will realize the direction of value realization and factors of information infrastructure investment and can evaluate appropriate information infrastructure investment method.

31.4 Conclusion: An Evaluation of Information System Investment

As information system investment is depicted in Figure 31.2, the change of attributes in information system investment accords with the evaluation of IT from a viewpoint of four processes. Effective evaluation of information system investment is possible and the summary is showed for Figure 31.1 in this frame.

Most Japanese companies have their own information technology (IT), which manage their investments and help reduce information processing costs effectively and efficiently. In the recent past, IT has been one of the most valuable communication bases that are accelerating the speed of business process reengineering in Japan. Within the organization, IT is continually becoming more complex, and investments in this area are rapidly increasing in business areas such as production, sales and delivery.

In the 1970s, for IT and MIS, mainframe computers were primarily used. Today, however, personal computers and networks are replacing mainframes. The Information System Division (ISD) manages all activities related to information system (IS) and information technology (IT). Most information processing costs incurred within the organization are controlled by ISD because it is easy for ISD to appropriately collect, calculate and allocate these costs to the different user departments. This system is called the charge-back or charge-out system.

The information systems environment, however, has dramatically changed from the client-server system to the network system. Thus, the question arises as to whether the traditional IT investment evaluation method will work correctly or not in this complex, decentralized information systems environment. A kind of evaluation techniques depicted in Figure 31.3 should be used to manage information processing costs strategically. If not, some companies in Japan are no longer interested in managing these investments and are seriously considering outsourcing their IS.

	Value choice	Value creation	Value realization	Value search
Domain: from Domain: to	Experiment Conversion	Conversion Update	Update Process improvement	Process improvement Experiment
Attribute of IT investment	From Application to Infrastructure	Infrastructure	From Infrastructure to Application	Application
Subject of IT evaluation	IT Dept., CIO	IT Dept., CIO	Each Dept., SBU, Functional Dept.	Each Dept., SBU, Functional Dept.
Viewpoint of IT evaluation	Adaptability to new technology	Corporate value creation	Process improvement & value increase	Search for new technology & system
Objective of IT evaluation	Strategic value, System flexibility	Service quality up, CS	Process cost reduction, Value added	Trend of new technology
Purpose of IT evaluation	Choice of strategic value, Choice of KFS	Assist of corporate goal ,Achievement long-term profitability	Management assist in each Dept., Cost reduction	Application of new technology, Information strategy
Evaluation criteria	Response time to get competitive advantage, contribution to project achievement		Administrative criteria, financial criteria	IT technology criteria
Evaluation method	EVA, BSC, Real option theory		ABC, BSC, Cost driver analysis, Financial ratio	Financial ratio, Technology assessment

Fig. 31.3 Evaluation of information system investment

References

Boynton, A. C., Zmud, R. W., and Jacobs, G. C. (1994). The influence of IT management practice on IT use in large organization, *MIS Quarterly* 18-3, p. 307.

Clemons, E. K. and Row, M. C. (1991). Sustaining IT advantage: the role of structural differences, *MIS Quarterly* 15-3, pp. 275–276.

Evans, P. B. and Wurster, T. S. (1997). Strategy and the new economics of information, *Harvard Business Review* September–October, pp. 71–82.

Kaplan, R. S. (1986). Must CIM be justified by faith alone? *Harvard Business Review* 64-2, pp. 89–90.

Ministry of Economy, Trade and Industry, Densi-Shou-Torihiki Suisin-Kyougikai and Nomura Research Institute (2003). Heisei 14 Nendo Densi-Shou-Torihiki ni kansuru Sijyou-kibo and Jittai Chousa, April, p. 18. (in Japanese)

Morton, S. (1991). *The Corporation of the 1990s*, Oxford University Press.

Ross, J. W. and Beath, C. M. (1994). New approaches to IT investment, *MIT Sloan Management Review* 43-2, p. 63.

Scarso, E. (1996). Timing the adoption of a new technology: an option-based approach, *Management Decision* 34-3, pp. 41–42.

Shank, J. K. and Govindarajan, V. (1992). Strategic cost analysis of technological investments, *Sloan Management Review* 34-1, pp. 39–40.

Taudes, A., Feurstein, M., and Mild, A. (2000). Options analysis of software platform decisions: a case study, *MIS Quarterly* 24-2, pp. 227–228.

Zaidan-Houjin-Nihon-Jyouhou-Shori-KaihatuKyoukai (2003), *Jyouhouka-Hakusho*, Computer Age Inc. (in Japanese)

CHAPTER

32

The Tightness of Target Cost and Profit and the Achievement of Target Cost: The Japanese Evidence

Mahmuda Akter

Associate Professor, Faculty of Business Studies
University of Dhaka

32.1 Introduction

With the advent of lean manufacturing methods, target costing emerged as a system of not only profit planning but also cost management that is price led, customer focused, design centered, and cross functional (Ansari, Bell and CAM-I, 1997).[1] Since the late 1980s, target costing has become ever more closely connected with business strategy and considered as a strategic cost management tool for attaining target profit as well as for cost reduction (Sakurai and Scarbrough, 1997). To achieve this objective, it identifies the cost at which the product must be manufactured if it is to achieve its target profit margin when sold at its target-selling price. In the contemporary industrial environment that changes rapidly and plays by its own set of rules, prices are largely market driven and not controlled by management.[2] Target profit, on the other hand, is based on corporate profit

[1]For more researches on target costing, see also Hoque, Akter and Monden (2005), Hoque and Monden (2002), Monden and Hoque (2001), Hoque, Akter and Monden (2000), Hoque *et al.* (2000), and Monden and Hoque (1999).

[2]Our research assumes the environment where target sales price is established by market-based method. Usually, there are two methods of target sales price, cost-based and market-based. Although cost-based pricing is a very popular method of pricing used by many companies, it is unsuited for target costing environments. Because of the competitive nature of markets, prices lead costing in target costing

expectations, historical results and competitive analysis, and therefore is a decision variable.

If the target profit margin is very demanding, the resulting target cost will be difficult to achieve. However, the difficulty of implementing target cost methods depends not only on the tightness exercised in setting target profit, but also on the degree of tightness inherent in the target cost methods. The attainability of target profit influences the decision of using a target cost method. When a company decides to use a particular target profit method, it does not finalize the target profit figure immediately. Rather, a provisional target profit is determined first based on which allowable cost, the cost at which the product must be manufactured if it is to generate the desired profit margin, is determined. Subsequently, the attainability of allowable cost is checked. If this allowable cost is attainable, the management accepts provisional figure as the final profit and here target cost is determined by subtractive method. On the other hand, if management feels that the allowable cost objective is not possible to achieve, target cost is determined by adding-up or combination method. When either one of these two methods is used, the provisional target profit could not be attained because the target cost will be higher than the allowable cost. Thus, the target profit will be changed downward to derive the target costs. Therefore, the selection of a particular target cost method depends on the attainability of the allowable cost. Moreover, setting target profit margins in this manner makes the allowable cost reflect the relative competitive position of the firm. A highly efficient firm will set target profit margins higher and will have lower allowable cost (Cooper and Slagmulder, 1997, p. 102). Figures 32.1 and 32.2 depict this process.

The process of achieving the target profit and target cost often creates intense pressures on the product designers. The constant pressure to meet the target cost and target profit can cause management burnout and sometimes problems with the supplier, when the cost-reduction or profit-improvement demands are passed down to them (Kato, Boer and Chow, 1995). The decision to use different combinations of target profit and cost methods will create severity and/or motivation of different magnitudes. The target cost achievement of the product designers may vary according to the

---

situations. Use of cost-based pricing in competitive environments negates the entire rational for the use of target costing. In fact, being wedded to cost for product pricing is an impediment to the successful adoption of target costing (Ansari, Bell and CAM-I, 1997).

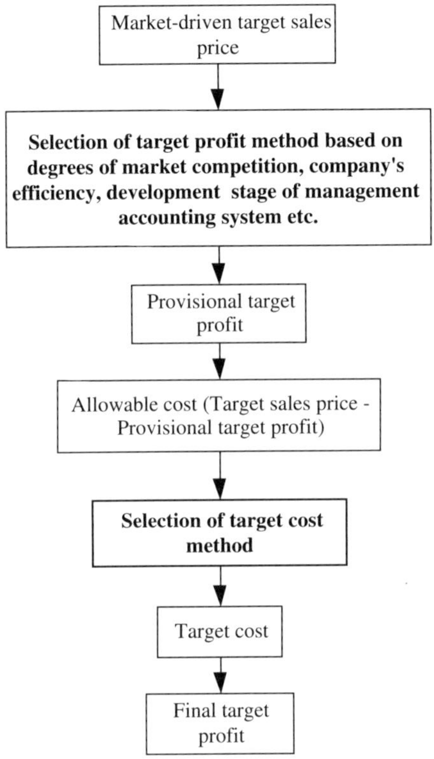

Fig. 32.1 Relationship between target profit and target cost

levels of tightness of different target profit and target cost methods since they will motivate them in different ways. However, there are hardly any previous studies to this effect. Therefore, the main objective of this study is to examine how the differences in the methods of target profit and target cost determination will influence the target cost achievement. More precisely, the paper aims to study how the tightness inherent in the target cost and target profit methods influences the target cost achievement level.

We chose for the study the companies that listed their stocks at the Tokyo Stock Exchange, Part I from four major manufacturing industries whose products require regular model changes having the features of discrete manufacturing process. Companies manufacturing machinery, electrical and electronics, transportation equipment and precision machinery were selected. Questionnaires were mailed to 518 companies on October 10, 1996.

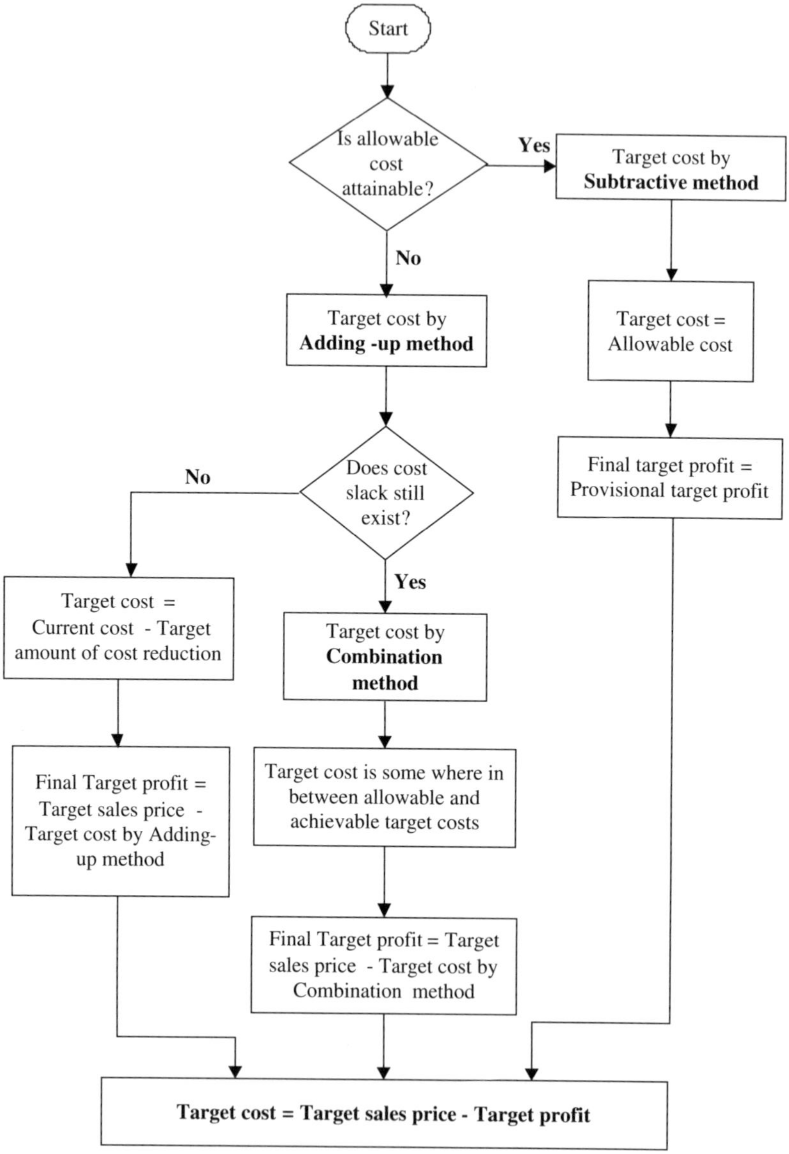

Fig. 32.2 Selection process of target cost

One hundred and forty six companies were responded by the deadline of November 10, 1996. The response rate is 28.1%. The structured questions used for the purpose of this study are included as the Appendix.

32.2 Different Methods of Target Profit and Target Cost

32.2.1 *Target profit (TP) methods*

The two considerations in setting target profit margins are to ensure that they are realistic and that the margin is sufficient to offset the life-cycle cost of the product (Cooper and Slagmulder, 1997, p. 100). Usually, there are three methods of calculating target profit by targeting: (1) return on sales ratio determined in the middle-range profit plan *(TP1)*; (2) reduction rate in the cost of the existing or similar product *(TP2)*; and (3) return on sales ratio based on past actual performance of the related product *(TP3)*. Among these, the first one is used for formulating macro plan and the would-be profit is termed as required profit, the third one is used at micro level and the profit to be materialized under the method is called planned profits, while the second one adjusts the gap between the first and third.

Target profit, if it is to be determined in the middle-range profit plan, reflects management's expectations that allow them at best to run the company smoothly or at worst to survive. This is somewhat unrealistic in that its attainability is presumed to be assured. On the other hand, when target profit is based on the past actual performance of the related product, the actual return-on-sales ratio for the current product is more achievable since the company has experiences in attaining this profit (Monden, 1995). Usually, there is a gap between management's profit expectations and actual profit.

Target profit determined at middle-range planning often begins at executive levels and follows top-down approach. It reflects the strategic profit needs of the organization for ensuring the survival and growth of the firm and its affiliates. By contrast, target profit based on past actual performance of the related products is usually determined at the product department level using a bottom-up approach. If there is gap between the profit decided at executive and departmental levels, the reconciliation process continues until there is no gap or both sides agree that it is not possible to close the gap. A company's prosperity depends on playing this kind of "catch" between top management and managers at the operational level (Sakurai and Scarbrough, 1997).

Simply by adhering to the target profit based on past actual performance of the related products the company is unlikely to reduce cost below the current level, which has already been achieved. When the profit expected in the middle-range profit plan exceed the actual one, the reconciliation process, or "catch" can proceed by calculating the target profit based on targeting reduction rate of cost of the existing or similar product. This method helps to identify the unachievable or unrealistic portion of target profit determined in the middle-range profit plan. In terms of earnings, this method stands in the middle of the desired and achievable earnings level.

32.2.2 *Target cost (TC) methods*

Target costing occurs in two phases that corresponds, roughly, to the first and second halves of the product development cycle, that is, the establishment phase, and the attainment phase (Ansari, Bell and CAM-I, 1997, p. 26). While establishment phase focuses on the allowable cost, the attainment phase focuses on how to make the allowable target cost achievable.

The allowable cost is calculated by subtracting the target profit from the target sales price. It is known as the "maximum permissible cost" that can be committed to a product in the product planning stage. It is the desired cost based only on market conditions, and is called "market-driven" cost. In competitive environment, firms that are highly efficient will have higher target profit margins and hence lower allowable costs than their less efficient competitor. Since the allowable cost is determined by market forces and does not take into account the internal design and production capabilities of the firm, there is a possibility that the allowable cost will not be achieved. In practice, however, it is not always possible for the designers to find ways to achieve the allowable cost and still satisfy the customers. (Cooper and Slagmulder, 1997).

Usually, allowable cost is the early estimate of the target cost. It is considered as the final target cost only when the product can be made for this amount. If this cost is adopted as the target of efforts, the requirement is very severe and not immediately attainable (Monden and Hamada, 1991). Target cost determined in this way is called "*subtractive method*" (*SUB*) or "*sales price-based method.*"[3] Subtractive method acts as a signal to all involved in the target costing process as to the magnitude of the

[3]Subtractive method calculates target cost as:

Target cost per unit = Target sales price per unit − Target profit per unit.

cost-reduction objective that inevitably must be achieved. From the management viewpoint, it is desirable to realize the largest possible profit and for this the target cost requirement by the subtractive method is likely to be demanding (Monden, 1986). The subtractive method will clearly have a strong linkage with firm's middle-range profit plan that incorporates projected profit figures to target costing.

When allowable cost is not achievable, to check its attainability the "drifting cost," which is the current estimated cost with no targets in mind, is calculated for each part. It is the preliminary estimate of a product, assuming the existing work structures, technology, and processes. The primary task in target costing is to perform the VE and continuous improvement activities to reduce the gap between drifting and allowable costs. The cost reduction target is continually refined until the "allowable" and "achievable" cost merge. If the allowable cost cannot be achieved, the process of attaining the target cost increases the allowable cost of the product to a level that can reasonably be expected to be achievable, given the capabilities of the firms and its extended enterprises, i.e. suppliers. Target cost determined in this way is called "*adding-up method*" (*ADD*) or "*estimated cost-based method.*"[4]

Under this method target cost is determined by examining every possible cost reduction opportunities, taking likely VE proposals, work structures, technology, and processes into considerations. In adding-up method, the target amount of cost reduction is deducted from the estimated or current cost of the product, where the target cost is set to an achievable level by considering the firm's and its suppliers' capabilities. This method is used when the designers are unable to achieve the allowable cost and signals that the firm is not as efficient as demanded by the competitive conditions. Usually, target cost requirement via the subtractive method is much harder to meet than that through the adding-up method because non-value-added cost slack still exist when adding-up method is applied (Tani and Kato, 1994).

When determining target cost by adding-up method, however, if there is any cost slack, the target cost figure is made lower and set somewhere in the middle of allowable and achievable costs. A hybrid of subtractive and

---

[4]According to adding-up method, target cost is computed as:

$$\begin{aligned}\text{Target cost per unit} &= \text{Estimated cost per unit}\\&\quad \times (1 - \text{Target reduction rate of cost})\\&= \text{Estimated cost per unit}\\&\quad - \text{Achievable target amount of cost reduction per unit.}\end{aligned}$$

adding-up methods, called the "*combination method*"[5] (*COM*) is used when target cost cannot be finalized either by subtractive or by adding-up method (Kato, 1993; Tanaka, 1992). It consolidates the operating focus on profitability and the technological focus on feasibility (Sakurai and Scarbrough, 1997). From the viewpoint of the tightness of target cost methods, combination method stands in the middle of the two extremes of subtractive and adding-up methods.

An organization establishes the targets for production efforts only when it is convinced that these are attainable. Therefore, determining the appropriate difficulty in attaining the targets is of particular interest. The targets would most likely be attainable when these are set quite low relative to the possible levels of attainment. On the other hand, the targets would be regarded as "impossible" if they were set quite high. Our definition of attainability excludes these two extremes. Moreover, irrespective of the methods of target cost and profit, the established targets get the product designers' acceptance in the process of checking their attainability by investigating alternative designs. Consequently, there would be no difference among these methods in terms of target acceptance.

32.3 Research Focus

The entire target costing process is ineffective if the methods of determining cost and profit targets are unrealistic. Deciding the appropriate level of attainability of target is of greatest importance for a meaningful target costing system. An effective way to determine the target cost rationally is to link cost reduction activity to profit planning, and to approach the target cost based on long-range profit planning (Makido, 1989).

Japanese companies follow that the cost-reduction or profit-improvement objectives must be challenging but achievable most of the time that can be achieved with considerable but not impossible effort (Coopers and Slagmulder, 1997). If the targets are continuously set too high, the design teams might give up trying to achieve these. Again, if the targets

---

[5] Combination method computes target cost as:

(a) Target sales price per unit − Target profit per unit = Allowable cost per unit.
(b) Target sales price per unit − Target cost per unit (as per adding-up method) = Revised target profit per unit.
(c) Target cost per unit = Somewhere between the allowable cost and the target cost determined by adding-up method.

are set quite low relative to possible levels of attainment, the firms will lose competitiveness because the new products will have excessively high target cost and the employees will be discouraged to strive for easy targets. To avoid these motivational problems, rational targets should be set where optimism is restrained in favor of realistic targets. It is important that the target assignments are not overly affected by the organizational power structure. Each target should be determined through consultation between manager and employees and each employee must tackle cost reduction positively. A company needs to devise methods that motivate employees to achieve their targets positively (Monden and Hamada, 1991). We test whether the differences in the levels of tightness in target profit and cost will have any impact on target cost achievement. Now, we formulate the hypothesis of this study,

Hypothesis: The tighter the target profit and cost methods employed the better the target cost achievement.

32.4 Variables

Target cost achievement level, the *TCAL*, a surrogate variable for the cost- reduction performance, is the response variable of the model and we measure how the target cost and profit methods influence the *TCAL*. Target profit methods (*TP1*, *TP2*, and *TP3*), and target cost methods (*SUB*, *COM*, and *ADD*) will be used as explanatory variables. In this research we assigned three levels of difficulty for three methods of target costs and profits, that is, tight, medium-tight, and loose.[6]

Three kinds of target profit methods have been considered as three independent variables and each of them along with the target cost method variable form the sets of explanatory variables. The reason why we consider three profit methods independently is that we intend to verify the effects of using a target cost method in a particular profit situation on the company's target cost achievement. The level of utilization of each profit method is further categorized into three groups, higher utilization, medium

[6]The tightness of a target cost method is different from that of a target profit method. The smaller the amount of target cost to be achieved, the tighter the target cost method, while the bigger the amount of target profit to be earned, the tighter the target profit method.

utilization and lower utilization. Here, "higher or wider utilization" means *the use of a particular profit method only for the company's entire product*. For example, the wider utilization of *TP1* means the use of only *TP1* for all the products of the company. "Lower utilization" means *the use of any other profit method, but not that particular one*. For example, the lower utilization of *TP1* means instead of *TP1* using *TP2* and/or *TP3* for entire products. "Medium utilization" means *the use of a particular profit along with any other profit method*. For example, medium utilization of *TP1* means using *TP1* for some products along with using *TP2* and/or *TP3* for other products.

Usually, the amount of profit by a tight or a medium-tight method (*TP1* or *TP2*) is bigger than that by loose method (*TP3*). The wider utilization of *TP1* and *TP2* results in earning bigger amount of profit at a greater extent than their medium or lower utilization. Therefore, for a tight or a medium-tight target profit, the higher utilization implies a more demanding environment than medium or lower utilization. Conversely, since the profit by a loose method (*TP3*) is smaller than that by a tight or medium-tight, its wider utilization means earning that smaller amount at a greater extent than its medium or lower utilization. Therefore, for a loose target profit, the higher utilization refers to a more lenient atmosphere than its medium or lower utilization level.

The lower utilization of *TP1* represents a less demanding environment. On the other hand, the lower utilization of *TP3* represents a more demanding environment. The lower utilization of *TP2* implies that instead of *TP2* using *TP1* and/or *TP3*. However, between *TP1* and *TP3*, the former provides more profit and the later provides less profit than *TP2*. Therefore, the lower utilization of *TP2* may represent either a more or a less demanding environment depending on whether the company is using *TP1* or *TP3* instead of *TP2*.

32.5 Analysis and Interpretation

32.5.1 *Findings*

When *TP1* is widely utilized we find that, the use of a tight (i.e., *SUB*) or medium-tight (i.e., *COM*) target cost method renders higher *TCAL*. This implies that performance improves more in a demanding situation than in an easy atmosphere, which reinforces our hypothesis.

In case of *TP2*, it is evident that when a company widely uses *TP2*, it would be able to achieve target cost at the highest level if it sets the target cost by *SUB* method. This also implies the superiority of fixing tight targets over loose targets and supports our theoretical proposition.

When *TP3* is used we notice that *TCAL* can be improved by not using *TP3* with *SUB* and *COM*. Since lower emphasis on a loose target profit necessarily represents a tight environment, the use of tight or medium-tight target cost method in that setting leads to higher *TCAL*. Thus, this evidence is congruent with our theoretical propositions.

32.5.2 *Analysis of the results*

Evaluating the regression results in three profits situations, we observe that when *TP1* is widely utilized, the use of both *SUB* and *COM* improve the *TCAL*. Similarly, when *TP2* is highly utilized, the use of *COM* improves *TCAL*. The effects of using *SUB* and *COM* along with *TP1* and *TP2* in improving the *TCAL* are supported by the findings in *TP3* profit situation. We observe that lower utilization of *TP3* along with *SUB* and *COM* improves the *TCAL*. In fact, lower utilization of *TP3* implies the use of *TP1* and/or *TP2* instead of *TP3*. Therefore, the findings observed in case of *TP1* and *TP2* are equivalent to that in case of *TP3*. The lower utilization of "loose" target profit is equivalent to the higher utilization of "tight" and/or "medium-tight" target profit and represents a demanding environment. Therefore, when a company decides to use "tight" or "medium-tight" profit method (*TP1* or *TP2*) but not the "loose" method (*TP3*), its *TCAL* will be improved if it adopts stricter methods (*SUB* and/or *COM*) for calculating target cost.

For improving *TCAL* the company should avoid using *TP3* with *SUB* and *COM*. Instead, it should use *TP1* and/or *TP2*. When a company decides to use *TP1*, it should employ both *SUB* and *COM* for better *TCAL*. Further, when a company decides to use *TP2* it should choose *SUB*. Irrespective of the profit methods, the company should avoid using adding-up method for calculating target cost.

Target profit set in the middle-range profit plan (*TP1*) is more suitable from managerial point of view, as they can set it according to their desire, they can make target cost determined by subtractive method tighter by making the target profit figure bigger. The entire target costing process is futile if the long-term profit objectives underlying it are unrealistic (Cooper and Slagmulder, 1997). Since the wider utilization of *TP1* improves *TCAL*, we can confirm that *TP1* is tight but realistic. The wider utilization of *TP2* also resembles the effect of tight and realistic target in improving *TCAL*. We observe that between the wider utilization of *TP1* and *TP2*, the former has more effect on *TCAL* than the later. Actually, *TP2* is based on target reduction rate of cost of the existing or similar product and gives a benchmark to which the present performance ought to be elevated. Probably the inherent characteristic of *TP2*, i.e., detecting how much cost improvement is possible by *TP2* over the actual realized figure (*TP3*) towards the desired one (*TP1*), would create continuous pressure on designers that would lead to its lower effect on *TCAL*.

TCAL in general improves with the tightness of target cost and profit. However, tightness in target cost and profit beyond a certain threshold cannot improve the performance as supported by the findings of Stedry's (1960) research on budget tightness. From the present findings, we observe that *TCAL* improves with the level of tightness in target profit and cost. Therefore, we can authenticate that the determined targets are tight, realistic, and attainable.

Finally, the ubiquitous presence of *SUB* with "tight" and "medium-tight" profit methods improves the *TCAL*. This is because the imposition of the fundamental rule of target costing, that is, "target cost must never be exceeded" is mainly possible by *SUB*, which facilitates the attainment of determined profit.

32.6 Conclusion

In this paper, we studied the effects of tightness of target cost and profit methods on target cost achievement. The theoretically formulated relationships among different methods of target profit and cost are mostly observed in the real-world situation in the Japanese manufacturing industries. We find that greater the tightness of the target profit and cost methods employed the better the target cost achievement. This is interesting in that in target costing, the adoption of a particular method of target cost and profit depends on company's ability in the periodical revision or continuous improvement of the target profit and cost. Therefore, the tighter the target profit and cost methods adopted, more efficient the firm is in improvement activities and hence better the target cost achievement. The superiority of subtractive method with "tight" and "medium-tight" profit and combination method with "tight" profit is prevalent which recommends their use in these situations. The company should avoid using adding-up method for calculating target cost in any profit situations. The judicious mixture of a tight target cost along with a tight and realistic target profit method is better choice for the companies to improve their target cost achievement level.

In a target-costing environment, identifying the appropriate degree of tightness of the targets for profit and cost is very crucial factor to take into account. In certain situations performance improves with the level of tightness while in the other circumstances, it deteriorates. The tight but attainable target should be established for high and persistent cost-reduction performance. In target costing, the overall accounting process consists of target cost determination and allocation processes. The effects of both of these processes on target cost achievement level may be interesting aspects to study in future.

Appendix: Questions Used in this Study

17. At what degree does your company consider the following factors in determining the target profit under target costing? Please put circle in the appropriate cell relating to each factor.

	Lower utilization	Medium utilization	Wider utilization
1. Target return on sales ratio determined in medium and long term profit planning.			
2. Target return on sales determined based on past actual return on sales ratio of the related product.			
3. Target reduction rate of cost of the existing and similar product.			

18. In your company, which formula is being used in determining target cost? Please put circle to the appropriate one.

    1. Target cost is determined by subtracting the target profit from target sales price.
    2. The difference between the target profit and target sales price is considered as allowable cost. This allowable cost is compared with

drifting cost (which is the estimated cost calculated at the present technological level) to determine the target cost.

3. Target cost is calculated by applying the (1 − target reduction rate of cost) to the drifting cost, which is predicted by the present technological level.

20. Presently at what degree does your company achieve target cost? Please put circle to the appropriate one.

    1. About 60% of target cost
    2. About 70% of target cost
    3. About 80% of target cost
    4. About 90% of target cost
    5. Almost 100% (or more) of target cost

References

Ansari, S. L., Bell, J. E., and CAM-I (1997). *Target Costing: The Next Frontier in Strategic Cost Management*, Irwin.

Cooper, R. (1995). *When Lean Enterprises Collide: Competing through Confrontation*, Boston, Massachusetts: Harvard Business School Press.

Cooper, R. and Slagmulder, R. (1997). *Target Costing and Value Engineering*, Portland: Productivity Press.

Hoque, M., Akter, M., and Monden, Y. (2005). Concurrent engineering: a compromising approach to develop a feasible and customer-pleasing product, *International Journal of Production Research* 43-8, pp. 1607–1624.

Hoque, M. and Monden, Y. (2002). An empirical study on simultaneous achievement of quality, cost and timing in product development, *International Journal of Manufacturing Technology and Management* 4-1/2, pp. 1–20.

Hoque, M., Akter, M., and Monden, Y. (2000). Effects of designers' participation and their evaluation measures on simultaneous achievement of quality and cost of product development teams, *International Journal of Innovation Management* 4-1, pp. 77–96.

Hoque, M., Akter, M., Yamada, S., and Monden, Y. (2000). How QFD and VE should be combined for achieving quality and cost in product development, in *Japanese Cost Management*, edited by Monden, Y., Imperial College Press, pp. 178–202.

Kato, Y., Boer, G., and Chow, C. W. (1995). Target costing: an integrative management process, *Cost Management* 9, pp. 39–51.

Makido, T. (1989). Recent trends in Japan's cost management practices, in *Japanese Management Accounting*, edited by Monden, Y. and Sakurai, M., Productivity Press, pp. 3–13.

Monden, Y. and Hamada, K. (1991). Target costing and kaizen costing in Japanese automobile companies, *Journal of Management Accounting Research* 3, pp. 16–34.

Monden, Y. (1995). *Cost Reduction Systems: Target Costing and Kaizen Costing*, Portland, Oregon: Productivity Press.

Monden, Y., Akter, M., and Kubo, N. (1997). Target costing performance based on alternative participation and evaluation methods: a laboratory experiment, *Managerial and Decision Economics* March, pp. 113–129.

Monden, Y. and Hoque, M. (2001). Simultaneous achievement system of quality and cost in product development: an empirical research by questionnaire, *Journal of Business Administration* 48-4, pp. 1–16. (in Japanese)

Monden, Y. and Hoque, M. (1999). Target costing based on QFD: a new approach for compromising customers' and designers' views, *Controlling* 11, pp. 525–534.

Sakurai, M. and Scarbrough, D. P. (1997). *Japanese Cost Management*, Crisp Publication.

Stedry, A. C. (1960). *Budget Control and Cost Behavior*, Englewood Cliffs, N. J.: Prentice-Hall.

Tani, T. and Kato, Y. (1994). Target costing in Japan, in *Neuere Entwicklungen im Kostenmahagement*, edited by Dellmann, K. and Franz, K. P., Bern: Verlag Paul Haupt.

CHAPTER

33

Effectiveness of Managerial Accounting Systems and Staffs' Participation in Product Development: An Empirical Study of Taiwan Industries

Chao-Hsiung Lee

Assistant Professor, Institute of Accounting and information Technology, National Chung Cheng University

33.1 Introduction

In order to win competitive edges in the market, enterprises have been devoted to advancing cost management and production rationalization. Aimed for more efficient operation and shorter production cycles, innovated production systems, such as Just-in-time production system (JIT system), Flexible management system (FMS), and Computer-integrated manufacturing system (CIM), have been adopted to achieve production rationalization. On the other hand, through cost management and conceptual revolution, the production cost is expected to be minimized while maintaining a certain quality.

The new approaches to cost management employed by enterprises include activity-based costing (ABC), target costing, Kaizen costing, benchmarking, reengineering, and Theory of Constraints (TOC). In particular, the first three cost management approaches are most broadly applied. In target costing systems, the structure of product development organization, collaboration from the suppliers and cross-functional teams in current engineering mechanism would affect the cost-reduction performance.

There are several studies on target costing systems in Taiwan. However, the production cost could not be calculated properly by the traditional quantity-based cost system. It would often overestimate the costs of the high-volume and simple-manufactured products; and would underestimate costs of the low-volume and complicated-manufactured products in the traditional costing system. The activity-based costing (ABC) is developed to solve this distortion of cost. Nowadays, the ABC system has been developed into one of the strategic decision-making tools, providing the management with prompt and efficient information for better pricing, investing, and budgeting.

Alnestig and Segerstedt (1996) pointed out the importance of ABC to the manufacturers in Sweden. In addition, the ABC or other advanced management accounting systems can highlight the importance of non-financial information and also make strategic decision-making. Cagwin and Bouman (2002) also mentioned that the ABC system can improve the financial performance. Establishing the advanced management accounting system depends on the overall transformation in internal organizations, such as structuring strict quality management, Just-in-time system implementation, the change of the organizational team culture, understanding, and performance, and the close cooperation from the upstream and downstream partners/assembly suppliers.

This study attempts to investigate through a questionnaire survey the potential and practical difficulties encountered when adopting management accounting systems for companies in Taiwan. The factors affecting efficient establishment of strategic cost management are also examined by analyzing the organizational characteristics, the implementation of management accounting system, and staff participation.

33.2 Effectiveness of Managerial Accounting Systems (MASs)

"Cost reduction" has always been the mission for companies. In order to meet the customers' needs, companies have to devote great effort to product innovation as well as cost control. However, because of intensive competition in the market and rapid innovation in production and technologies, management accounting systems (MASs) should be required to provide timely and accurate information to companies for cost control and productivity improvement. As a result, the managers could establish effectively the pricing policy and product development strategy with the assistance of the finest and reliable information from MASs.

Owing to organizations and productions, such as enlargement of organization, product diversification, and complexities of production procedure, companies have to accomplish the purposes of information exchange efficiency, cooperation between divisions, improvement of production efficiency, and rational evaluation on the staff performance by utilizing management accounting systems. Nowadays, MASs play an important role in cost planning and control, communication, and performance evaluation. The efficiency and effectiveness of MASs could deeply affect the competitive edge of a company.

To win the edge, a company needs to transform its organization from the pressures of the environment, strategy, culture, technology and scale. Under the interaction of these pressures, learning and efficiency of organization will grow. The so-called "learning organization" refers to the mutual communication, feedback, and cooperation between the organization and individuals. It could raise organizational productivity by utilizing human resources. An efficient organizational structure is characterized by frequent exchange of information and collaboration between members (or divisions or departments). In other words, the horizontal binding structure is a kind of cross-functional team. Under the empowering structure of organization, a company's competence could be enhanced through interactive learning and knowledge creation among members. It could be successful and efficient to achieve the cross-functional communication between the members under the highly-decentralized and lowly-hierarchical environments. This kind of organizational design could enhance the members' voluntary improvement in cost, time and quality.

On the other hand, strategic planning aims to achieve the organizational goals and is the key to continuous development. The implementation of organizational strategies would affect a company's mid/long-term plans, the extent of organizational operation, as well as the external and internal resources distribution. Obviously, a successful and efficient organizational strategy depends on the efficiency and effectiveness of MASs implementation. A company's MASs should be integrated and connected with management information system (MIS) and management control system (MCS). The MASs could provide the financial and non-financial information that a company needs for decision-making.

There are three organizational strategies for maintaining a company's competitiveness: differentiation, cost leadership, and focus strategy. No matter which strategy is adopted, different timely and integrated management accounting information will help the managers in decision-making. A company devoted to improving the efficiency of production requires both financial and non-financial management accounting information for the purpose of cost-reduction if the strategy of cost leadership is adopted.

The diversity and richness of MASs could help to control and monitor the business performance when a company faced the market with uncertainty. Because of the uncertainty of market environments, it may become complicated for managers and members in an organization to plan and execute the organizational goals. As a result, it is necessary that the members participate in decision-making and budgeting. The performance can be improved by members' participation in decision-making when the assignment is complicated or uncertain. Through organizational commitment, the staff participation in budgeting will directly or indirectly promote their performance. The process of budgeting-participation could help diminish the difficulties of works, lighten the stress, and improve the performance. Through the participation in budgeting, the managers established a communication mechanism with staff, which will reduce the occurrence of information asymmetries between them. It also gives the managers the opportunity to understand well the behaviors and attitudes of the staff, so the managers could be able to set a more precise and proper standard for performance evaluation of staff. If the staff in an organization participates in decision-making, they will be more concerned with the company's improvement and performance.

33.3 Survey of Effectiveness of MASs

A questionnaire survey on cost management in the current manufacturing environment was conducted. Not only did this research analyze the situation in implementing cost management in Taiwan, it also examined what kind of cost management system could be efficient in achieving cost-reduction performance. The result may provide a possible way for a company to maintain its competitive capabilities.

There are five topics in the questionnaire: (1) the profiles and organizational structures of the company for understanding its development, production and sales, as well as departments and structures; (2) the product development vs. cost management for studying the cost management, participants, and the implementation of accounting information during product development; (3) performance evaluation for looking into cost formulation and management performance; (4) the relations with the suppliers for investigating the suppliers' contribution to cost improvement as well as the shares of interests and risks; and (5) the external complication and uncertainty for finding out the changes and valuable factors encountered when the company is coping with external competition.

This survey is mainly targeted at the listed companies of industries in Taiwan, excluding trading, service, and financial industries. In November 2003, 665 companies were given the questionnaire, of which 121 were collected and three of them were incomplete. The response rate was around 18.2%.

33.4 Cost-reduction Performance in MASs

Based on the results of survey, most of the companies have achieved the criterion of cost target and the organizational structures tend to be centralized. It is shown that the updating information of MASs could not be provided timely. However, the companies still have high autonomy. Most of the companies would consider the factors of the long-term period, the profit performance of the past products, and the profit performance of his own products by comparing with other companies in the same industries. Companies tend not to follow-up when staff failed to achieve the cost-reduction performance established by the organizations. However, the unachievable cost-reduction performance could be the criterion for the next performance. The staff participation in product development is very common. Moreover, most of the companies have engaged in product development within three years; and the frequency of product development and the level of product customization are high. The similarity of business process in product development is also high. There is not much difference in marketing approaches of products and is not frequent in product development.

On the other hand, it is indicated that the staff at decentralized organizations could achieve higher cost-reduction performance than staff at non-decentralized organizations. In order to examine the operation of MASs, the factors of the timeliness of management accounting information, the autonomy of MASs implementation, the profit management of the product, and the evaluation on the cost performance are investigated to see how the cost-reduction performance could be affected by the diversification and richness of MASs. After the factors related to MASs was examined, it is proved that the timeliness of management accounting information could contribute to the cost-reduction performance. Regarding profit management, utilizing the profiting performance of the past products as the criterion will help attain cost reduction. Moreover, the cost-reduction performance could be somewhat affected by the profit management for the current or similar products. Additionally, the evaluation on cost performance such as attributable responsibility for cost-reduction performance, the unachieved criterion for continuous improvement, could also affect indirectly and positively the cost-reduction performance. Therefore, the diversification and richness of MASs could improve cost-reduction performance.

Examining the effect of staff participation on cost-reduction performance reveals that the cost-reduction performance by staff-involved decision-making. Obviously, staff involvement on cost decision-making could improve the cost-reduction performance.

It shows that the cost-reduction performance could be improved when it took four years and more for product development. Generally, cost management becomes more difficult when the product development gets too long or is too short. This survey reveals that most of the companies take about four years for product development, and hence, it is useless to improve the cost-reduction performance if the period of product development is too short or too long. The proper duration of product development will help achieve efficiency and accuracy of cost management.

In addition, it is not easy to achieve the cost-reduction performance when there is product diversification in a company. The more diversified the services/products are, that harder it is to achieve cost reduction. Observing the factor of customization, it shows that it would be easy to achieve cost-reduction performance under customized manufacturing environments.

The complexity of manufacturing process will affect the achievement of cost-reduction performance. The cost-reduction performance may be achieved easily if the manufacturing process is similar or identical. Therefore, the cost-reduction performance could be achieved easily in highly similar process environment. The diversity of marketing methods may not be one of the factors that affect cost-reduction performance. Generally, the leading launch of a new product will boost the market share, and the cost of product development can be recovered quickly. Therefore, frequent product development can help meet the target cost-reduction performance assigned by the organization.

33.5 Conclusions

This study examined the impacts of organizational decentralization, management accounting systems and staff participation in product development on cost-reduction performance. The following conclusions can be drawn from the findings.

1. Cost-reduction performance can be more efficiently achieved under decentralized environments because it is easy to implement cost-reduction activities in decentralized organizations.
2. The cost-reduction performance could also be affected by the diversity and richness of MASs. In particular, it could be affected by the timeliness of management accounting information and profit management according to past profiting performance.
3. Staff participation in cost decision-making could help achieve cost-reduction performance.

Past studies simply examined the organizational performance in association with decentralization, MASs, and staff participation in cost decision-making. In this research, the relationship between the three factors and cost-reduction performance was examined. The empirical results revealed some approaches to implementing cost-reduction activities for companies.

It is found in this research that these factors are related to cost-reduction performance, but the approaches to cost-reduction implementation are not described in detail. Moreover, some issues that may affect cost-reduction performance have not been discussed in this research, such as the goal congruence of organization, human capital issues, and business process. This research involves empirical analysis of the surveys submitted by the listed manufacturers in Taiwan, so it could not be proved whether the managers distorted the meanings of surveys and provided false responses when they answered the questions. On the other hand, only the manufacturing industries in Taiwan are studied, thus the results cannot be generalized to other industries, which is also a limitation of this research.

Numerical data of this questionnaire survey is seen in Lee, C. H. (2005).

Appendix: Survey of Cost Management

Q1. How much is the cost reduction performance in your company?

1. Less 20%
2. Within 21%~40%
3. Over 41%

Q2. What is the kind of organizational structure in your company?

1. Decentralization
2. Centralization
3. Others

Q3. What level is there the timeliness of managerial accounting information in your company?

1. High
2. Low

Q4. What level of autonomy in MASs implementation is there in your company (MASs implementation would not be controlled by Mother Company)?

1. High
2. Low

Q5. What reasons will be considered when your company executes the profit planning?

		Yes	No
1.	Using the estimated profit rate by mid/long-term profit planning	1	2
2.	Setting the profit rate by the past profit rate of the product	1	2
3.	Setting the profit rate by the prices of the current product or the outstanding product by other companies.	1	2
4.	Others (------------------------------)		

Q6. What actions will be carried out in your company when estimated cost (or target cost) is not attained?

		Yes	No
1.	Attributable responsibility	1	2
2.	As a criterion for the next cost management	1	2
3.	As a criterion for continuous improvement	1	2
4.	Others (------------------------------)		

Q7. Do the staffs participate in cost decision-making and product development in your company?

1. Participation
2. Non-participation

Q8. How long does the new product launch in your company?

1. Over 4 years
2. within 3 years

Q9. What is the level of product (or service) diversification in your company?

1. High
2. Low

Q10. What is the level of product (or service) customization in your company?

1. High
2. Low

Q11. What is the level of complexity in selling approaches in your company?

1. High
2. Low

Q12. How is the frequency of R & D in your company?

1. High
2. Low

References

Alnestig, P. and Segerstedt, A. (1996). Product costing in ten Swedish manufacturing companies, *International Journal of Production Economics* 46-47, pp. 441–457.

Amburgey, T. L. and Dacin, T. (1994). As the left foot follows the right? The dynamics of strategic and structural change, *Academy of Management Journal* 37-6, pp. 427–452.

Anderson, S. W., Hesford, J. W., and Young, S. M. (2002). Factors influencing the performance of activity based costing teams: a field study of ABC model development time in the automobile industry, *Accounting, Organizations and Society* 27, pp. 195–211.

Armstrong, P. (2002). The costs of activity-based management, *Accounting, Organizations and Society* 27, pp. 99–120.

Arnold, V. and Sutton, S. G. (1997). *Behavioral Accounting Research: Foundations and Frontiers*, FL: AAA.

Besterfield, D. H., Besterfield-Michna, C., Besterfield, G. H., and Besterfield-Sacre, M. (1999). *Total Quality Management*, Prentice Hall, Inc.

Blanchard, K., Carlos, J. P., and Randolph, A. (1996). *Empowerment Takes More Than a Minute*, Harvard Management Service, Inc.

Bonner, S. E. and Sprinkle, G. B. (2002). The effects of monetary incentives on effort and task performance: theories, evidence, and a framework for research, *Accounting, Organizations and Society* 27, pp. 303–345.

Busch, T. (1998). Attitudes towards management by objectives: an empirical investigation of self-efficacy and goal commitment, *Scandivan Journal of Management* 14-3, pp. 289–299.

Cagwin, D. and Bouwman, M. J. (2002). The association between activity-based costing and improvement in financial performance, *Management Accounting Research* 13, pp. 1–29.

Campbell, D. T. and Gingrich, K. F. (1986). The interactive effects of task complexity and participation on task performance: A field experiment, *Organizational Behavior and Human Decision Process* October, pp. 162–180.

Chenhall, R. H. (1997). Reliance on manufacturing performance measures, total quality management and organizational performance, *Management Accounting Research* 8, pp. 187–206.

Chenhall, A. D. and Landfield-Smith, K. (1998). The relationship between strategic priorities, management techniques and management accounting: an empirical investigation using a systems approach, *Accounting, Organizations and Society* 23-3, pp. 243–264.

Chenhall, R. H. and Morris, D. (1986). The impact of structure, environment, and interdependence on the perceived usefulness of management accounting system, *The Accounting Review* 61, pp. 16–35.

Child, J. (1984). *Organization*, New York: Harper & Row.

Choe, J. M. (1998). The effects of user participation on the design of accounting information systems, *Information & Management* 34, pp. 185–198.

Chopra, S. and Meindl, P. (2001). *Supply Chain Management: Strategy, Planning, and Operation*, Prentice Hall, Inc.

Daniel, S. J., Reitsperger, W. D., and Gregson, T. (1995). Quality consciousness in Japanese and U.S. electronics manufacturers, *Management Accounting Research* 6, pp. 367–382.

Euske, K. J., Lebas, M. J., and Mcnair, C. J. (1993). Performance measurement in an international setting, *Management Accounting Research* 4, pp. 275–300.

Fullerton, R. R. and McWatters, C. S. (2002). The role of performance measures and incentive systems in relation to the degree of JIT implementation, *Accounting, Organizations and Society* 27, pp. 711–735.

Gul, F. A. (1991). The effects of managerial accounting systems and environmental uncertainty on small business manager's performance, *Accounting and Business Research* 22, pp. 57–61.

Jermias, J. and Gani, L. (2004). Integrating business strategy, organizational configurations and management accounting systems with business unit effectiveness: a fitness landscape approach, *Management Accounting Research* 15, pp. 179–200.

Johnson, G. (1987). *Strategic Change and the Management Process*, Basil Blackwell.

Lau, C. M., Low, L. C., and Eggleton, I. R. C. (1995). The impact of reliance on accounting performance measures on job-related tension and managerial performance: additional evidence. *Accounting, Organizations and Society* 20-5, pp. 359–381.

Lawler, E. E. III (1996). *From the Ground up — Six Principles for Building the New Logic Corporation*, Jossey-Bass.

Lee, C. H. (2004). Interdepartmental interaction effects on cost reduction performance in product development organizations: empirical research in Japanese industries, *Journal of Management* 21-4, pp. 515–530.

Lee, C. H., Lee, J. Y., and Monden, Y. (2005). Early evidence on the interactive effects involving product development organizations and target cost management, *Advances in Management Accounting* 14, pp. 193–214.

Lee, C. H. (2005). Cost reduction performance affected by organizations, managerial accounting information systems and staffs' participation — An empirical study of Taiwan industries, *Journal of Performance Strategy Research* 2-1, pp. 19–37 (in Chinese). (The unpublished English version of this paper is also available.)

Lee, C. W. (1999). Strategic cost management and target costing, *Accounting Nowadays* 75, pp. 2–9. (in Chinese)

Lin, W. H. (1997). Target costing, *Managerial Accounting* 41, pp. 1–9. (in Chinese)

Mauldin, E. G. and Ruchala, L. V. (1999). Towards a meta-theory of accounting information systems, *Accounting, Organizations and Society* 24-4, pp. 317–331.

Mia, L. (1993). The role of MAS information in organizations: an empirical study, *British Accounting Review* 25, pp. 269–285.

Mia, L. and Clarke, B. (1999). Market competition, management accounting systems and business unit performance, *Management Accounting Research* 10, pp. 137–158.

Mia, L. and Chenhall, R. H. (1994). The usefulness of management accounting systems, functional differentiation and managerial effectiveness, *Accounting, Organizations and Society* 19-1, pp. 1–13.

Miles, R. E. and Creed, W. E. D. (1995). Organizational forms and managerial philosophies: a descriptive and analytical review, *Research in Organizational Behavior* 17, pp. 333–372.

Nouri, H. and Parker, R. J. (1998). The relationship between budget participation and job performance: the roles of budget adequacy and organizational commitment, *Accounting, Organizations and Society* 23-5–6, pp. 467–483.
Porter, M. E. (1985). *Competitive Advantage*, New York: Free Press.
Ranson, S., Hinings, B., and Greenwood, R. (1980). The structuring of organizational structures, *Administrative Science Quarterly* 25, pp. 1–17.
Renn, R. W. (1998). Participation effect on task performance: mediating roles of goal acceptance and procedural justice, *Journal of Business Research* 41, pp. 115–125.
Salafatinos, C. (1996). Modelling resource supply and demand: expanding the utility of ABC, *International Journal of Production Economics* 43-1, pp. 47–57.
Scott, T. W. and Tiessen, P. (1999). Performance measurement and managerial teams, *Accounting, Organizations and Society* 24, pp. 263–285.
Subramaniam, N. and Mia, L. (2003). A note on work-related values, budget emphasis and managers' organisational commitment, *Management Accounting Research* 14-4, pp. 389–408.
Stashevsky, S. and Elizur, D. (2000). The effect of quality management and participation decision-making on individual performance, *Journal of Quality Management* 5, pp. 53–65.
Wilkinson, J. W. (1989). *Accounting Information Systems: Essential Concepts and Applications*, John Wiley & Sons, Inc.
Yang, C. W. (2002). VA/VE application in target costing, *Quality Monthly* 38-7, pp. 98–106. (in Chinese)
Yang, C. S. and Liao, E. S. (1999). Empirical study in target costing implementation and innovative approaches, *Managerial Accounting* 50, pp. 16–37. (in Chinese)

PART 5

BASIC THEORY ON THE NATURE OF ACCOUNTING FOR ORGANIZATION MANAGEMENT

CHAPTER

34

The Basic Idea of French Analytical and Management Accounting: A Comparative Analysis of Management Accounting in France, the US and Japan*

Johei Oshita
Professor, Faculty of Economics
Kyushu University

34.1 Introduction

After the "relevance lost" dispute in North America, French management accounting (in the wide sense) research has attracted increasing world interest. French analytical accounting, traditionally emphasizing technology, is now reinforcing its organizational aspect. Once it made a relative retreat from the economic calculation function that was its main attribute, it became known as management accounting. And now, a new type of French management accounting has emerged, characterized by a signal function with cause-and-effect relevancy as one of its important internal attributes. This strengthens the connection with management control systems. We are witnessing the birth of a new French management accounting style.

*In this text, the term "management accounting" is used in the narrow sense, in the wide sense, and generally. Management accounting in the narrow sense refers to the French management accounting style shaped in the 1990's and onward along the lines of the manager's information demand, that is, after the "relevance lost" dispute. Management accounting in the wide sense includes management accounting in the narrow sense and the French industrial and analytic accounting style developed after the 19th century. "Management accounting" is used generally, without further connotations, unless otherwise specified.

This chapter is built on two axes of analysis. The first is the axis of the economic calculation function and the signal function, which are obtained through a historical analysis of analytical and management accounting in France (see Bouquin, 1997). The second is the axis of technological emphasis and organizational emphasis. This chapter discusses the subject of management accounting, in particular its methodology and characteristics, based on these two axes. My intention is to proceed by examining the specifics of French cases as one way to gain a broader perspective on the more general issues of management accounting research.

This chapter adopts a comparative research method that contrasts the specifically French management accounting model and its circumstances with the North American management accounting model. As far as it is necessary for the comparison, the Japanese management accounting model will also be considered. Furthermore, both the structural aspect (the cost model design) and the functional aspect (its application in management control) will be examined, in view of determining the effects of management accounting techniques to be homogenized across a globalized economy on management accounting theories and practices.

First, this chapter discusses two accounting techniques: activity-based costing (ABC) and *la méthode des sections homogènes* (MSH) (concerning MSH, see CEGOS, 1928). In Section 34.2, we focus on why the appearance of ABC has represented a good opportunity to draw attention to the importance of structural problems in French management accounting. Then, it is shown that ABC can be called a structural approach to accounting, based on a rediscovery of the "homogeneity principle," which is a basic concept of French analytical accounting.

Further, in Section 34.3, we discuss the Balanced Scorecard (BSC) and *Tableau de Bord* (TDB), which are considered to be management techniques from the functional viewpoint, in the context of the development of links between management accounting and management control systems. As management accounting begins to incorporate the two management techniques just mentioned, it becomes more able to integrate itself into management control systems than ever before.

In Section 34.4, we examine the development of management accounting. The importance of the problem becomes clearer as management and accounting techniques become globalized and homogenized, along with the globalization of the economy and finance.

When management accounting is called on to intensify its signal function and to move from the stage where, based on the technological emphasis, the logic of economic calculation is assumed to be fundamental, to the stage where the logic of complex organization prevails, it is openly put in the paradoxical situation inherent to management. In order to ascertain the direction in which management accounting and management control will develop from now on, this chapter clarifies the relationship between the management paradox and management accounting.

Finally, the results of the analysis will be presented in the conclusion.

34.2 Comparison between MSH and ABC: Cost-flow Modeling

In this section, in order to draw out the specific features of French analytical and management accounting, MSH and ABC are compared from the perspective of cost-flow modeling. This analytical perspective is peculiar to France.

Let us refer first to MSH. This method is the foundation of current French analytical accounting, which was invented in the first half of the 20th century. Although the gradual institutionalization of accounting standards in the post-war era experienced many twists and turns, the *principle of homogeneity* has consistently formed the backbone of French analytical accounting. The management post in French companies is traditionally occupied by an engineer, and this peculiarity has led to the birth of MSH in analytical accounting. The well-known initiator of MSH, Rimailho, was a military engineer (Rimailho, 1947). Sweeping reforms were introduced by Napoléon during the French Revolution, and it is necessary to pay attention to the role played by military engineers in the formation of French economy in general, not only accounting. It is the engineers who have written the majority of texts in the management accounting field (in the wide sense).

Now, what is the "homogenous section method"? It is a method of apportioning overheads based on the idea that each section (or department) of a production facility contributes to the finished product in the same proportion; this means that the work unit (unité d'oeuvre) in a work entity (entité), which corresponds to the cost driver of the ABC, can be defined. It has been thought in France that the cost homogeneity principle can be used to model the cost flow. The homogeneous cost is the part of the cost generated in the same ratio for all activities involved; this means that the homogeneous cost enables the synchronized accumulation and mutual supplementation of resources, which is a very important feature.

So, a homogeneous cost does not have to be contingent on the same kind of resource. For the first time, it becomes possible to model the cost flow by totaling the homogeneous costs, all of which constitute the same proportion of the full cost. In France, it has become traditional to think that any principle of cost modeling must be based on the concept of homogeneity.

Next, it should be noted that the attribute of homogeneity is strongly influenced by technology. In a word, the technology determines the level of homogeneity, and the proportion of the homogeneous cost is usually the result of the technology involved in the production. If a technical process which consumes cost is stable, the cost itself is stable. Therefore, it is possible to consider MSH and ABC as special accounting techniques determined by specific manufacturing circumstances. This understanding is also peculiar to France. The relationship between the technology and the level of homogeneity has to be determined, based on the relationship between the cost-flow modeling technique and the technology. As Bouquin shows, the homogeneity level is determined somewhere between the *task stage* and the *customer stage* according to the processing technology used, and in turn an appropriate accounting method is selected according to the relevant homogeneity level (Bouquin, 2003, p. 89). Process costing and job order costing are the two poles between which MSH and ABC are located.

On the other hand, the accounting method determined by the processing technology at a different level of homogeneity is metaphorically called an "accounting factory." The method of processing the information coming from the "factory" is decided according to the management demands (Figure 34.1).

Product / Accounting factory	Full cost	Direct cost	Rational imputation	Predetermined cost
Homogeneous section method Process costing GP-UVA ABC	All factories can carry out all types of calculation			

Source: Bouquin (2003), pp. 230. A part of Fig. 34.1 is corrected and quoted.

Fig. 34.1 Management accounting information and data processing techniques corresponding to the manufacturing environment

For instance, even when the cost flow is modeled under ABC, it is rearranged into full costs, direct costs and other costs. The mechanism is planned in such a way that the information produced by the selected accounting method is further processed according to the management goals. This is just an aspect of basic idea of French analytical accounting and management accounting.

In addition, Bouquin elaborates his framework of management accounting (in the narrow sense) based on the accounting idea just described (Bouquin, 2003). First of all, he lets the method structure and model the cost flow (the generation of a company map), with the method as the basic theory of management accounting. And, espousing the principle "different costs for different purposes," he begins to construct his framework of control with the aim of judiciously placing and using these cost concepts. For instance, at the strategic control level, the strategic full cost, which is different from the full cost in the traditional calculation of results, and the quality cost and value chains based on the systemic approach, are assumed to be typical "costs as method." At the management control level, which is related to short-term decision making, various "costs as method," such as the direct cost, the predetermined (standard) cost and the rational imputation method, etc. are dealt with. In a word, the ideal way of handling various costs as a result of the cost-flow modeling are grasped in the form of "costs as method." This perspective is shared by many managers and accountants in France.

Let us return to Figure 34.1, the basic framework of management accounting. There is a clear difference between MSH and ABC, although it is widely thought that they merely operate on different homogenous levels, as already described. According to Bouquin, the cost driver in ABC is characterized by the logic of causal relationships, while the work unit in MSH only reflects the logic of correlation (Bouquin, 1997, p. 74). ABC's logic penetrates to the true cause of the cost, and surpasses the multi-step cost allocation system of MSH, aiming at a more accurate cost and a more exact representation of the cost flow. In addition, the closer estimation of the true cause of the cost, as exemplified by the shift from ABC to activity-based management (ABM), means that management is entering a phase in which it is necessary to recognize the real connection between the activity and the performance of the company.

The shift from the logic of costing to the logic of cost management is only apparent. Therefore, it is necessary to propose a measurement index of activity performance, exceeding only the traditional costing. As shown by the strategic theory of Michael E. Porter of the Harvard Business School, this shift in logic leads to the search for a law of cost advantages and disadvantages governing all ABC activities.

The tendency of the causes of cost to recur raises a serious organizational problem. Bouquin analyzes the development process of MSH and clarifies the historical significance of MSH and the management idea of Rimailho. His analysis leads to some striking insights into Japanese cooperative organizations, particularly regarding the target costing system.

At any rate, the proposal of a measurement index of activity performance leads to an idea of the BSC. In France, the logic of the traditional accounting method is being shaped by the current discussion on MSH and ABC. In North America, on the other hand, the logic of ABC persists, veering toward the cause-modeling of performance, as embodied by the BSC. The difference between North America and France is precisely here. Incidentally, there is hardly any discussion on general cost principles in Japan. MSH leads to the assumption that, while French analytical accounting demands a substantive rationality, Japanese cost management requires procedural rationality. If so, is Japanese cost management similar to that of the United States in this respect?

In the next paragraph, we will discuss the structure and meaning of the BSC, paying attention to the influence exerted by the modeling of the performance causes on management accounting. As far as it is necessary for the analysis, the TDB will also be referred to.

34.3 Result of the Extensive Development of Management Accounting: The BSC and the TDB

The BSC proposed by Kaplan and Norton represents an endeavor to solve the problem of modeling the causes of performance, based on a measurement index of activity performance, which exceeding the traditional costing system.

Recent TDB theory has been strongly influenced by the appearance of the BSC. In this section, we will outline the current state of the extensive development of management accounting, using the BSC as the focal point of the discussion, and assess the outcome of this development.

According to Kaplan and Norton (1996), the BSC provides executives with a comprehensive framework that translates a company's vision and strategy into a coherent set of performance measures. As is well known, the

BSC translates the mission and strategy of a company into performance evaluation measures based on four perspectives (the financial perspective, the customer's perspective, the internal business process perspective, and the learning and growth perspective). Suppose a company is not performing well, even though the manager formulates powerful slogans and a clear corporate mission to inspire and inform the employees. In such a case, the BSC can be used as a means of converting the manager's vision into a vision which can be understood and shared by all of the company's employees.

Needless to say, *strategy* is the core concept of the BSC, which is based on the infiltration of information into the lower employee strata and the learning and growth activities that it enables and requires. The management of strategy implementation (strategy → consensus → improvement → strategy) is the main purpose of the BSC. The function of the BSC is to translate a strategy, that is, a set of hypotheses regarding causes and effects, into a message which all employees are able to relate to, and which entrains both financial and non-financial performance measures from the four perspectives mentioned above.

Therefore, it is necessary to forge a firm link between strategy and performance evaluation to utilize the BSC effectively. Kaplan and Norton present three principles governing that link: (1) the cause-and-effect relationships between strategy and performance; (2) the relationships between outcomes and performance drivers; and (3) the connection with financials. These three principles are the keys to the success of the BSC.

The financial perspective is the most important and definitive of the four perspectives on which the BSC is based. Therefore, it is clear that the BSC is deeply related to the problems of stockholder-value-based management now coming up. However, the BSC is distinct from traditional responsibility accounting, not only because of its four-perspective framework, but also because of the performance evaluation measures set for each perspective. The BSC is constructed in such a way that the process through which the desired outcome is achieved is of utmost interest, whereas responsibility accounting pays less attention to the process and more to the result. In order to utilize the BSC successfully, top management must inform all employees beforehand as to the courses of action which must be implemented to achieve specific goals, by combining lag indicators with lead indicators. This means that the plan becomes a strategy. The vision of top management is shared with all employees, and so the real power of the BSC consists in its ability to prefigure a process where strategy is implemented downward according to the financial and non-financial performance measures.

The BSC incorporates the information route starting at the summit of the company's organizational hierarchy and ending at the lowest employee level, as a process of strategy implementation. In this sense, it is easy to see why Malo considers the modern TDB as a BSC and characterizes it as a total management technique (Malo, 2000). If the TDB is thought of as a framework of measures, then various tendencies to influence the system, within the range consistent with the attributes of various functions of the technical system under a manager's voluntary control, can be clarified. Therefore, thinking of the modern TDB as a BSC has given us the possibility to formulate a new use for the TDB. As such, it seems obvious that the big problem of both the BSC and the modern TDB is how the participant's motivation to serve the company's objectives can be improved. Now, the specific features of the BSC can be elucidated by comparing it with the TDB, as in Figure 34.2.

Let us define the TDB before explaining Figure 34.2. The definition differs depending on the viewpoint adopted, and Bouquin's is as follows (Bouquin, 2004, p. 441): the TDB is a means of supporting decision making and forecasting, and is the totality of measures (5–10) designed to help the manager recognize the current state and the development process of the system under his or her control, and to clarify various tendencies to influence the system within the range consistent with the attributes of various functions of the technical system. In short, Bouquin regards the TDB as a tool used in decision making and forecasting in view of system control.

Figure 34.2 clearly shows that the TDB is interested in system control as the business activity unfolds, whereas the BSC emphasizes strategy decision before any action is taken. In addition, the BSC focuses on strategy

	BSC	TDB
Point of control	Planning stage before action	Steering stage during action
Relationship to the budget	Design of the scenario before budgeting	Supplementing the budget during the course of its implementation
Kind of decision	Mainly, short-term to long-term	Mainly, Short-term
Method of control	Comparison between future measures	Comparison between future measures and actual measures
Character as management control technique	Build the paradox inherent to management (long-term or short-term, internal or external, financial or non-financial, etc.) into one management system	Management control in response to environmental changes
Kind of information used	Financial and non-financial (Organization-oriented)	Financial and non-financial (Technology-oriented)

Fig. 34.2 Comparison between the BSC and the TDB

translation and implementation and the designing of a scenario (strategy) for the achievement of the company's objectives before the budget is set, whereas the TDB supplements the budget as it is being consumed, evolving side by side with the budget. Moreover, it is obvious that both devices use financial and non-financial measures.

However, the BSC is a device that builds the paradox of management (long-term or short-term planning, financial or non-financial measures, etc.) into the management system itself, while the TDB is a management control device that responds to the changes in the management conditions.

The conclusions up to this point can be expressed in a diagram, as Figure 34.3 shows. The BSC is supported by the cause-and-effect cost model inherent in ABC. It is crucial that the BSC and ABC were designed by the same authors. The BSC would not have been invented without the ABC's principle of cost allocation and the ABM, which uses ABC data. The cause-and-effect principle on which the BSC is based proves exactly this point.

The BSC further activates the outward extension of management accounting by modeling the cause of the performance. This is shown in the BSC's use of performance drivers, while ABC uses cost drivers. In addition, the idea of performance drivers clearly implies the importance of quality control and organizational learning, neither of which were evaluated in the TDB.

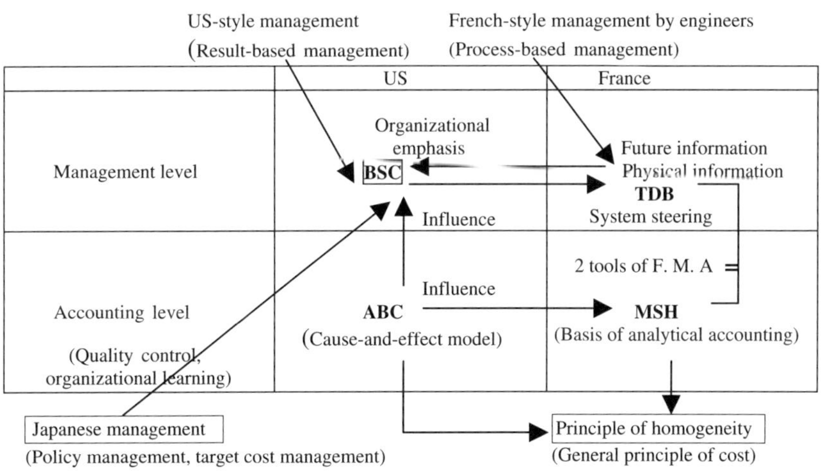

Note: M. Lebas understands the TDB and MSH as two original tools of French management accounting (F. M.A.). See Lebas (1996).

Fig. 34.3 Convergence of accounting and management techniques

However, the TDB has become strongly influenced by the BSC recently. The two techniques have in common the logic of achievement through communication. The difference between the two is that, while the TDB is a system of measures used to control a technical system for which the engineer/manager is entirely responsible, thereby excluding the customer's perspective, the BSC is an expression of the company's objective laid out as causes and effects (strategy) which infiltrates all levels of the employment hierarchy of the company through a system of measures, because it is driven by the logic of corporate value maximization inevitably derived from the recent corporate governance style of the United States. In this sense, the BSC is part of a top-down management style.

Of course, although the BSC is schematized in Figure 34.3 as a point of convergence of different management techniques, this might be the result of the globalization and homogenization of management techniques in general.

It was mentioned above that the homogeneity principle is a general cost principle extracted from MSH and influenced by ABC; Figure 34.3 shows, though, that the homogeneity principle issues from MSH downward. In addition, it was already stated that all cost-flow modeling is based on this principle, and that the setting of the total cost and the rearrangement of cost is conducted according to a variety of information demands. The globalization and homogenization of accounting techniques has led, as seen here, to the formulation of a universal principle of cost modeling at the confluence of MSH and ABC, which has not been given much attention so far. From the perspective of this universal principle, MSH and ABC are merely two accounting techniques with different levels of homogeneity.

But the confluence of MSH and ABC represents an opportunity to transform management accounting from a means of confirming facts by following the cost flow to a means of modeling the cause of costs and, further, the cause of performance, as exemplified by the BSC. This development is transforming the TDB radically.

In France, this shift to a cause-and-effect analysis raises the question of how to overcome the organizational problem that supports target cost management; one solution would be the adoption of Japanese-style labor organization. However, the organizational climate in French companies would have to make too many sacrifices to adopt Japanese-type labor organization (Lorino, 1994).

Is the extensive development of management techniques, as exemplified by the BSC, a real development of management accounting? In the next paragraph, we will examine further the basic idea of French analytical and management accounting, by analyzing the relationship between management paradox and management accounting.

34.4 Management Paradox and Management Accounting

The direction in which management accounting and management control seems to be evolving can be expressed in a diagram based on our analysis, as shown in Figure 34.4. Though Figure 34.4 is a correction of Figure 34.3, the elements involved are the same.

Figure 34.4 consists of both the axis of the economic calculation function and the signal function and the axis of technological emphasis and organizational emphasis. With the appearance of ABC, a new management control theory has come to be discussed, although French management control has been composed of the techniques of the TDB, the budget, the ratio, the cost, etc., as shown in Figure 34.4 (see Meyer, 1983). It is a new management control theory explicitly constructed with the potential elements of past management control theory: organization, strategy, and technology, etc.

There have been many opportunities for management accounting to transform itself from a means of confirming facts by following the cost flow to a means of modeling the cause of cost and, further, the cause of performance, as exemplified by the BSC. In Figure 34.4, this change

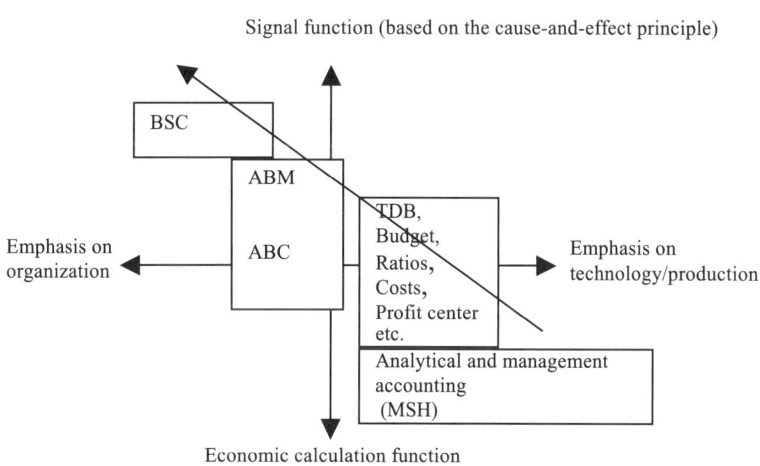

Fig. 34.4 Direction of the apparent evolution of management accounting and management control

is expressed by the arrow drawn from the fourth quadrant to the second quadrant through the first quadrant.

However, it is unclear whether this extensive development of management accounting represents a real development. Presently, the direction taken by management control, as indicated by the arrow in Figure 34.4, is new in France; on the other hand, French management accounting is still thought to incorporate the economic calculation function by modeling the cost flow, even if it is strongly influenced by this new style of management control. In France, management accounting is planned not at the level of complex organization but at the level of economic calculation focused on technology. On the other hand, French management control is currently developing in a direction where the signal function, which involves cause-and-effect relationships, is further strengthened, resulting in the paradoxical situation inherent in organizational management.

A change in the given management conditions, such as organization, strategy, technology, etc., is required in order to implement a new form of management control, since the importance of the strategic control level is steadily rising. In addition, the paradox of management will be amplified when the management capabilities of an organization are overwhelmed and inter-organizational management and positive market connotation are set as the goal.

Now, let us examine the "balance" in the BSC from the perspective of the management paradox (Bouquin, 2004).

There are those who are uncomfortable with using the term "paradox" when discussing management control and management accounting. But a theoretical framework based on this concept can be very suggestive, especially when considering the relationship between strategic management and management accounting.

We can determine the nature of management control and management accounting by means of the concept of paradox.

As typically shown by the BSC, in the United States, management is based on concepts such as *balance* and *integration* rather than that *paradox*. The reason why balance and integration are preferred is clear. A balance between various decision-making and performance-evaluation measures has become imperative, because it has gradually become clear that if a balance between such measures is not secured, the competitiveness of the company and the continuous increase in stockholder value cannot be established and maintained (Bouquin, 2004, p. 26). As the management process becomes more complex, it is necessary to provide order and integration by balancing the measures that constitute the management process. It can be said that the BSC embodies this paradoxical situation, as well as the drive toward its resolution.

Long-term strategic control and short-term management control/operational control form a typical paradox. Although it is often said that the manager must act with the long-term consequences in mind, his performance is always evaluated based on short-term results. This discrepancy is the typical expression of the management paradox. Tools such as the profit plan, the budget, the center of responsibility, etc. reflect this paradox as well. Although profit planning enables the forecasting of management results, it transforms a company into a bureaucracy, delaying flexible and prompt correspondence between plans and outcomes. Moreover, an exclusive focus on the budget inclines the manager to adopt a short-term view, and, according to circumstances, may plunge him into mere formalism, even though it enables him to wield short-term power (Bouquin, 2004).

However, as seen in the functions of various management control techniques, it is impossible to have short-term empowerment and profit forecasting without bureaucracy, or to judge a manager's performance without falling into business localism. Recognizing the contradiction between the two tendencies, Bouquin established the concept of paradox as the main axis of his management control theory.

On the other hand, although a technique requires its own type of rationality, it easily becomes irrational if applied to domains to which it is not suited. In short, it is impossible to create a management control technique suited to all situations. This means that a combination of various management control techniques must be devised, and a balance between long-term strategic control and short-term management control/operational control must be struck.

It is necessary to find the way to decrease the paradox. As mentioned above, the BSC seems to embody the management paradox with a view to establishing a balance, as reflected by the four perspectives. There are methods other than the BSC which try to achieve a balance by combining the techniques of the control systems at each level of responsibility, in the hope of overcoming the management paradox. But such techniques do not bring about any essential change to themselves (the same can be said of management accounting; see Piget and Cha, 2003) The techniques only have to achieve a balance so that rationality can be maintained as a whole.

At the level of the profit plan, the budget, etc., it might be possible to overcome the paradox partially by strengthening the top manager's immediate participation and control, in accordance with the existing hierarchy.

Although bureaucracy has often been looked upon with disdain, it really constitutes the foundation of management. Without bureaucracy, attributes which are highly valued, such as flexibility, creativity, etc. are almost unattainable (Numagami, 2003). The bureaucracy is supported by the various devices and tools of management control, and it is evident that management cannot take a move without it. The bureaucracy and the management control devices are mutually supportive. Also, management accounting offers cost information to various management control devices, supporting the bureaucracy together with them. In this sense, management accounting is an important part of the foundation of management in any company.

Management accounting offers cost information to various management control devices and contributes to the self-analysis of the company precisely through "cost as method," reinforcing the foundation of management. On the other hand, the company should obviously have enough marketing strategy to enable an accurate analysis of market positioning, in addition to the self-analysis.

34.5 Conclusion

Here is a summary of French analytical and management accounting, based on the analysis presented in this chapter.

First, management control can be thought of as a systematic methodology whose purpose is to overcome the management paradox. A process that combines management control techniques, such as the profit plan, the budget, the center of responsibility, etc., is necessary, depending on the real situation of the enterprise. Within that process, each level of decision making and control will require appropriate cost concepts; these concepts are provided by the cost analysis of the company's management accounting. Nevertheless, there is no essential change in the idea of "cost as method," even in such a situation.

Second, it is thought that the homogeneity principle of MSH can be applied universally, and is a general principle of cost that supports the concept of "cost as method" in France. In this context, the principle underlying ABC is likely to be highly valued as a homogeneity principle. Therefore, the development of analytical and management accounting in France must be thought of as selecting the organizational modeling styles incorporated in MSH and ABC.

Third, the operative range of the TDB, whose main duty is to enable the engineer to maintain control over technical systems, is limited. On the other hand, as is often the case with the BSC, the paradox will become more apparent in time, and it will have to be overcome by combining various economically rational techniques, according to the demands of the manager.

An important lesson can be learned from the French experience: management control needs to use the "cost as method" issued by the cost network of the company's management accounting. Both the self-analysis of the company and the analysis of other companies are necessary, along with the implementation of various management control techniques in a way which minimizes the management paradox.

References

Bouquin, H. (2004). *Le Contrôle de gestion*, 6e éd., Paris: PUF.

Bouquin, H. (2003). *Comptabilité de gestion*, 2e éd., Paris: Economica.

Bouquin, H. (1997). *Comptabilité de gestion*, Paris: PUF.

CEGOS (Commission Générale d'Organisation Scientifique du Travail) (1928). *Etablissement des prix de revient*, rapport du lieutenant-colonel Rimailho, Paris.

Kaplan, R. S. and Norton, D. P. (1996). *The Balanced Scorecard, Translating Strategy into Action*, HBS Press.

Lebas, M. (1996). Management accounting practice in France, *Management Accounting: European Perspectives*, edited by Bhimani, A., Oxford University Press.

Malo, J. L. (2000). Tableaux de bord, in *Encyclopédie de Comptabilité, Contrôle de Gestion et Audit*, edited by Colasse, B., Paris: Economica.

Meyer, J. (1983). *Le Contrôle de Gestion*, Paris: PUF.

Lorino, P. (1994). Target costing ou gestion par coût-cible, *Revue Française de Comptabilité* 255; 256.

Numagami, S. (2003). *Idea of Organizational Strategy — For the Health of Enterprise Management*, Chikuma Shobo. (in Japanese)

Piget, P. and Cha, G. (2003). *Comptabilité Analytique*, 4e éd., Paris: Economica.

Rimailho, H.(1947). *Chacun sa part*, Paris: Delmas.

CHAPTER

35

The Nature of Accounting in Respect of the Relationship between Financial and Managerial Accounting

Tsuneto Miyosawa

Professor, College of Business Administration
Ritsumeikan University

35.1 Introduction

Accounting is an act of human beings or human groups. A human act forms a process. Thus, the accounting act could be called an "accounting process" and this act could also involve a social process. Such an accounting process in business involves not only business accounting, but also managing accounting. However, it could be said that what is basic among these accounting fields is business accounting.

As is generally known, accounting, that is, the accounting process is divided into financial accounting and managerial accounting. These two fields are both a part of business accounting as a whole, at least on a theoretical basis. Therefore, when we consider the basic characteristics of accounting, it is important to consider both of these fields, and try to come to an understanding of accounting as a whole.

However, previously in accounting science,[1] business accounting has not been examined from this point of view, at least in Japan. Accounting has been considered as if it were synonymous with financial accounting; and the

[1]Needless to say, the science of accounting is usually called accounting. The word "accounting" means not only the science of accounting, but also accounting practice. In this paper, the science of accounting will be distinguished from accounting practice, and called "accounting science."

basic characteristics of accounting have been examined in conformity with the characteristics of financial accounting, ignoring the aspects of managerial accounting. Since financial accounting and managerial accounting are both part of accounting in general, it could be said that there can be no financial accounting apart from managerial accounting, even though both are separable.

The managerial characteristics/function of accounting have become submerged in the overall characteristics of accounting, and, as a result, it is difficult to explain these characteristics/function of the accounting concept. In this respect, there is a problem with the above-mentioned method of examining the characteristics of accounting, when dealing with them on a theoretical basis.

In this paper, the basic characteristics and in particular the nature of accounting in general, taking into account both financial accounting and managerial accounting, will be discussed. In particular, the basic processes of each type of accounting will be explained.

35.2 The Bookkeeping Process and Managerial Accounting

Previously in accounting science, the basic characteristics of accounting have been explained using the characteristics of bookkeeping, and indeed bookkeeping has been considered the technical basis of financial accounting. One reason that accounting has been considered as if it were synonymous with financial accounting is probably because of this relationship between bookkeeping and financial accounting.

Needless to say, the central task of financial accounting is considered to be the preparation/calculation of financial statements for external purposes and reporting/communicating of financial information. This aspect/process is generally called reporting (external reporting). Thus, financial accounting is referred to as accounting for external reporting. The preparation/calculation of financial statements is executed through closing accounts in bookkeeping. Financial accounting is therefore sometimes considered to be the same thing as closing accounts or closing accounting. Moreover, since bookkeeping, especially closing accounts, is considered to be a method of *ex post facto* calculation or the past calculation, and closing accounts in particular is seen as a method for examining and summing up the actual results of business activities, financial accounting has been given the characteristics of an *ex post facto* calculation or past calculation in accounting science.

However, in these methods of understanding the characteristics of financial accounting, the following three points must be mentioned:

1. The summing up of the actual results of business activities is not only a process in financial accounting, but is also an indispensable process in managerial accounting. Yet managerial accounting is generally regarded as if this were not the case. It is questionable as to whether or not accounting can be divided into financial accounting and managerial accounting, if that division is based upon the assumption that the summing up of actual results is not an indispensable process of managerial accounting.
2. Although closing accounts are generally explained as the procedure of executing the summing up of actual results, it appears that in actuality financial accounting, especially the calculation of financial statements for external reporting, is not the mere calculation of actual results of business activities. Since the summing up of actual results is also an indispensable process in managerial accounting, it is necessary to define the characteristics of the calculation of financial statements for external reporting (the so-called financial accounting) as opposed to the characteristics of the calculation of actual results.
3. Since daily entry/calculation of the actual results in bookkeeping is executed not only for external reporting, but also for managing business activities, it also means managerial accounting. Thus, when financial accounting is considered as if it were synonymous with bookkeeping, financial accounting becomes the same thing as managerial accounting so far as daily entry/calculation is concerned. Therefore, the same question as found in 1 should be mentioned.

Since bookkeeping is not only a process in financial accounting, but also an important process in managerial accounting, the system of bookkeeping in financial accounting should be considered to be a different one from the system for managerial accounting, if financial accounting and managerial accounting are thought of as being different.

In this section, the problem of the relationship between bookkeeping and managerial accounting in regard to above-mentioned questions of 1 and 3 will be discussed.

Needless to say, managerial accounting is an accounting field, which is concerned with the administration/management of business activities. To begin with, in managerial accounting, it is important to make the most profitable business plans for a firm based upon certain conditions. These plans become concrete in the form of a budget, which is then carried out.

This planning process in managerial accounting will be called "planning accounting" or "planning process," in response to its function. It could be said that the function of planning accounting is the organizing of the most favorable structure of business activities for the firm.

The process of carrying out the budget (plan) is a process that adapts actual results of plans in order to achieve goals according to those plans. Therefore, in managerial accounting, it is necessary for management to pursue/grasp the actual results and actual situation of business activities in detail, as well as being able to grasp them as precisely as possible. Of course, regarding the sphere and degree of detail and preciseness, there will not only be variation from firm to firm but also variation in the objects of calculation.

The shortest term for the summing up and examining of the actual results is the daily calculation. The actual results are also summed up and then examined periodically. Of course, this summing up and examining of the actual results in managerial accounting go hand-in-hand. The examination includes analysis of the actual results. At the same time, it includes analysis of differences between budgets (plans) and actual results (analysis of budget variances, analysis of cost variances).

The analysis of differences between plans and the actual results includes the following processes: (1) the comparison of budget (plans) with results; (2) the examination of the reasons for differences (between budgets and results); (3) the examination of the place where the responsibility lies and of the persons who are responsible; (4) the examination/evaluation of the profitability of performance, business activities and all other kinds of activities; and finally, (5) the examination of the various sources for improvement of actual results and so forth. The results of the periodical summing up and examination of the actual results are used to make plans for the next business year as well as for the future.

In the above-mentioned processes, that which pursues actual results and actual situations, and adapts those actual results for plans to conform to budgets is called controlling. Thus, this controlling process in managerial accounting could be called "control accounting" or "controlling process," in response to its function in managerial accounting. The process of the periodical summing up of the actual results, particularly at the end of the business year, is called closing (closing accounts).

Therefore, it is obvious that the two function/processes not only of financial accounting but also of managerial accounting are firstly the daily grasping or calculation of the actual results in bookkeeping and secondly the periodical summing up of the actual results — that is the preparation/calculation of financial statements with regard to the actual results. That is what both financial accounting and managerial accounting have in common — the process of the daily grasping and the periodical summing up of the actual results. The controlling function should thus be considered to be the function not only of managerial accounting, but also of financial accounting.

It could be said that both of these processes are the two basic processes in accounting as a whole. The daily grasping process of actual results in accounting will be called "control accounting" or "controlling process," in response to its function in accounting. The periodical summing up process of actual results at the end of the planned business year will be called "closing accounting" or the "closing process." Moreover, it will be possible to include the function of examining and appraisal in both of these two processes, because the grasping of actual results is not limited to the calculation, and it usually brings about the examination and appraisal of the actual results.

In short, so far as the daily grasping and summing up of the actual results of business activities in bookkeeping are concerned, it must be understood that they not only form the process of financial accounting but also the process of managerial accounting. That is, they are the processes that both financial accounting and managerial accounting have in common.

35.3 The Characteristics of the Calculation of Financial Statements for External Reporting

35.3.1 *The methods of the calculation of financial conditions for external reporting*

Since the periodical summing up of the actual results of business activities is also the process of managerial accounting, the division of accounting into financial accounting and managerial accounting would have no significance if the task of calculation of financial statements for external reporting were only in the periodcal summing up of the actual results.

However, as mentioned, it appears that in actuality the calculation of financial statements for external reporting does not have the characteristics of the periodical summing up of actual results of business activities. In this section, these actualities and characteristics of the calculation of financial statements for external reporting (that is, the above-mentioned question 2) will be discussed.

It is a matter of common knowledge that financial statements prepared for external reporting, are manipulated by a firm. Although what is called window dressing is, of course, an illegal type of manipulation, it is a well-known fact that even financial statements prepared legally are manipulated. In Japan, the reported income of big business is generally calculated as a smaller amount than the actual results. This way of calculation and/or reporting of financial statements is called "inverse window dressing" in Japan. In this paper, this legally executed accounting will be examined.

When looking at the above-mentioned aspects of accounting, it appears that there is deception in the accounting process. That is to say, it appears that accounting means misrepresentation of the financial conditions of a firm. Yet, accounting which operates within the boundaries of the law, rules, and accounting standards is considered to be proper accounting. It could be said that one of the reasons for which accounting appears to be misrepresented is as follows:

The preparation/calculation process of financial statements for external reporting is called closing accounts. Closing accounts means the calculation of the actual results of business activities, particularly the income of a firm for a certain period of time, and the financial conditions of a firm on the closing day. However, these financial statements are always manipulated, and so they do not show the actual results of business activities.

Particularly in the calculation of income on financial statements for external reporting, some basic methods of manipulation employed by a large number of firms are as follows:

Since firms must keep public trust, they always try to maintain or raise the stock price relative to the stock prices of other companies or to the movement of the stock market as a whole. Therefore, when they calculate the firm's income on financial statements, they base it on the calculation of dividends that decisively affect the stock price. It is important that there be a calculation of the amount of income needed to pay these dividends. Of course, the firms also must pay taxes from their income, and they have to keep some of the income as reserve. The income on financial statements that are prepared by firms for external reporting is decided according to these factors.

Moreover, since investors prefer steady dividends, the amount of dividends are stabilized, and the reported income is also stabilized. The stabilization of reported income is also called the "smoothing policy of reported income." With this policy, income on financial statements is, in general, reduced.

Therefore, it could be said that the most favorable/advantageous income for firms is first calculated in the calculation of financial statements for external reporting. Needless to say, these methods of income calculation are similar to those methods of profit planning in managerial accounting in which target profit (profit goal) is calculated.

Revenue and expenses on the financial statements, especially expenses, are calculated based on this, so to speak, optimum income. Assuming that revenue is a given amount, expenses are generally reported as larger than they actually are. The income reported on financial statements for external reporting is not decided as the difference/balance of revenue minus expenses. Rather, the reported income is calculated backward (from the above-mentioned factors). Needless to say, this method of income calculation is called the "calculation of profits in inverse order." Based on these income calculations, the content of the balance sheet indicating assets, liabilities and equity of a firm is also calculated. The amount of assets, in particular, are reported as a smaller amount than their current value or actual results. In addition, various kinds of allowances are used.

35.3.2 *The aim of the calculation of financial conditions for external reporting*

The financial statements of a firm do not indicate the actual results of operating activities in a certain period. It could be said that the calculation of financial statements for external reporting does not aim at reporting the actual results of business activities to external interest groups. In actuality factors such as the stabilization and restraint of dividends, reporting of a smaller income than the actual results, the smoothing of reported income, the use of an allowance system and so on, all mean, in general, the retaining of profits, that is, the accumulation of capital. The firm reserves a certain amount of the profits from the reported income on financial statements as earned surplus, and also retains a certain amount of the profits using the above-mentioned manipulation. This part of the retained profits is deducted from revenue prior to figuring out the reported income on the financial statements.

Of course, these calculations have to be calculations which have taken into account the methods of evaluation of a firm in the securities market, and that provide the most favorable financial conditions for a firm in order to raise capital as much as is planned. Thus, the calculation of financial statements for external reporting always aims at the raising of capital, that is, the accumulation of capital. For this aim, as has been outlined, financial statements for external reporting are executed deliberately and intentionally.

The basic objective of these calculations in a firm is, in actuality, the organizing of the most favorable structure of financial conditions that the firm can realize, and that will be useful in order to raise capital in the future. Moreover, the content of financial statements is "decided" through the procedure of approval by the board of directors or in the general meeting of stockholders. Needless to say, these characteristics of the calculation of financial statements for external reporting are the same as the calculation for business planning (planning accounting) in managerial accounting. This is true even though there are some differences in their direct tasks and in their methods of calculations. It is obvious that the task of the calculation of financial statements for external reporting does not mean the calculation of actual results of business activities in a certain period, that is, the previously so-called closing accounts. Of course, it is obvious that the above-mentioned calculation of financial statements for external reporting would not be able to be executed nor have any significance if it were not for the periodical summing up of the actual results.

Therefore, the calculation of financial statements for external reporting should be distinguished from the periodical summing up of the actual results (closing accounts), at least on a theoretical level. In this paper, the function or process of the calculation of financial statements for external reporting will be called "planning accounting" based on the above-mentioned characteristics. These characteristics are basically the same as for planning accounting in managerial accounting, and are distinguished from the function/process of closing accounting. Thus, what both managerial accounting and financial accounting have in common is the function/process of planning accounting.

Therefore, it could be said that planning accounting is the basic function/process of accounting as a whole. Planning accounting will also be referred to as "planning process" in accounting.

35.3.3 *The characteristics of external reporting*

As has already been mentioned, in accounting science, the preparation/calculation of financial statements is also called reporting. However, in the case where this concept concerns external reports, it could be said that the relationship between the calculation process of financial statements and reporting (external reporting) becomes unclear. External reporting as distinguished from the calculation of financial statements in and of itself includes the followng aspects: (1) providing financial statements to interest groups; (2) making the financial conditions public through the securities report and in newspaper; and (3) an oral explanation of the financial conditions.

It is apparent that the content of financial statements and the explanation of financial conditions, whether large or small, influence the decision-making process of external interest groups. Moreover, as already mentioned, financial statements for external reporting are calculated while taking into account the effects of disclosure in order to keep public trust and raise capital as much as is planned. That is to say, financial statements for external reporting are specifically prepared and used as a means to lead and regulate the behavior of external interest groups. This will help the firm to move in a direction which will result in its achieving its goals, in regard to plans for raising capital, that is to say, the firm's profit planning.

Therefore, external financial reports, that is, the disclosure of financial conditions, are not mere reporting. It could be said that one way a firm creates certain new relationships with external interest groups is through the external reporting of financial conditions. In these processes, the firm aims to manage these external interest groups in order to successfully achieve the objectives of the firm. In actuality, the function/process of external reporting through the above-mentioned financial statements could be called controlling. Thus, the function/process of external reporting in accounting will be called "control accounting" which is a basic function/process of accounting as a whole.

35.4 The Basic Characteristics of Accounting as a Whole

35.4.1 *The basic process of accounting as a whole*

As mentioned, what both financial accounting and management accounting have in common are the functions/processes of "closing accounting," "control accounting" and "planning accounting." These three processes are the basic functions/processes of accounting as a whole. The reciprocal relationship of these three processes will now be examined.

Needless to say, closing accounting aims at the summing up and the examination of actual results and actual situations of planned business activities over a certain period. Moreover, the results of closing accounting are used in the planning process concerning the business activities of the succeeding period. It also could thus be said that closing accounting is executed for new planning. The closing accounting process is a process which follows planning accounting and control accounting, and connects with the new planning accounting process concerning the business activities of the following period. The closing process is the final process in a cyclical process, which is repeated over and over.

Controlling is the function in the process which executes the plans and adapts the actual results or plans to conform to the plans (budgets). Thus, control accounting will follow planning accounting, and planning accounting is the starting point in a cyclical process. The results of control accounting during a certain period are summed up and examined in closing accounting. Thus, it could be said that the closing accounting process follows the controlling process.

Therefore, in the basic process of accounting as a whole, the three basic accounting processes of planning, controlling and closing — each process being accompanied by the recording and reporting/communicating function — are connected to one another by this sequence, and they form one cyclical process as a whole. Accounting repeats this cycle, and moves continuously from one process to the next. Moreover, it could be said that, in a spiraling effect, accounting develops through repeating this cyclical process, adding information/data which contributes to an accumulation of data, which in turn is made use of as the process continues.

35.4.2 *The meaning of distinction between financial accounting and managerial accounting*

It could be said that the function of accounting as a whole, that is, planning, controlling and closing, are the function of management. Needless to say, this function of management is what both financial accounting and managerial accounting have in common. Thus, financial accounting cannot discard the management function, even though financial accounting is distinguished from managerial accounting. Therefore, the relationship between financial accounting and managerial accounting must be examined.

When, as at present, accounting is divided into financial accounting and managerial accounting, financial accounting is generally referred to as accounting for external reporting as opposed to managerial accounting which is called accounting for internal reporting and/or "internal accounting."[2] However, it has been also mentioned that financial accounting provides information to the management. Moreover, it could be said that in actuality the management is responsible for financial accounting. Thus, accounting for external reporting (financial accounting) is contained within the accounting for internal reporting or internal accounting. Needless to say, the information that is reported externally is part of the information in internal accounting. It is obvious that externally reported information is made a division of the internal information.

Therefore, it could be said that the distinction made between financial accounting and managerial accounting is, in fact, based on a distinction between the information reported externally and the information which is not reported outside. Moreover, both types of information are for internal use. Thus, the division between financial accounting and managerial accounting is a distinction made for the purpose of limiting the sphere of the information which is reported externally. Although, as mentioned, the characteristics of accounting have been explained as if accounting were synonymous with financial accounting, ignoring the aspects of management accounting, it might also be said that this tendency in accounting science is not irrelevant to the need for limiting the accounting information to that which is reported outside of a firm.

Moreover, it seems that the perimeters given to the information reported outside are decided based on the interests of the predominant class of firms which have the greatest influence on the formation of accounting institutions. Thus, it could be said that the division between financial accounting and managerial accounting is a reflection in theory of the interests of these firms. Further, this division is only based on the differences in the objective of the direct task in the superficial level of accounting as a whole, even though this division is very important for these firms.

35.4.3 *Nature of accounting*

As above-mentioned, the three basic accounting processes of planning, controlling and closing — each process being accompanied by the recording and reporting/communicating function — are connected to one another, and they form one entire cyclical process. However, each of the tasks in

[2]Anthony (1964), p. 272.

these processes is different. Therefore, at least on a theoretical basis, it is necessary to make clear what is essential among the three basic processes. The essential process is that which characterizes accounting and is the most predominant process among the three basic processes. It has a direct relationship to the essential purpose of a firm, namely, gaining profit and accumulating capital.

Needless to say, controlling is the function in the process which executes the plans and adapts the actual results for plans to conform to the plans (budgets). Thus, the controlling process will follow the planning process, which is the starting point in the cyclical process. The results of the controlling process during a certain period are summed up and examined in the closing process. Thus, it could be said that the closing process follows the controlling and planning processes. Moreover, the closing process involves making plans for the next business year as well as for the future.

Therefore, it would seem that the planning process is the most predominant process among the three basic processes. Moreover, the planning process is autonomous in that even if the controlling and closing processes have not been completed, the planning process can be executed at any time. This is because the planning process is basically concerned with future business activities, and it is always driven to do so by the purpose of a firm. The planning process connects directly with the essential purpose of a firm, and executes the tasks, that is to say, the organizing of the most favorable/advantageous structure of a firm that the firm will have to realize. Thus, accounting is characterized by the planning process, and in addition, the planning process is the essential process of accounting. Furthermore, it could be said that accounting involves repeating the cyclical process of planning.

Then, it would seem that the essential meaning of accounting is understood by the content/task of the planning function. Thus, the essential meaning of accounting is the organizing of the most favorable/advantageous structure of a firm. Moreover, the essential purpose of something is understood by its essential meaning. Therefore, it must be that the organizing of the most favorable or advantageous structure of a firm is also the essential purpose of accounting.

It could indeed be said that the essential purpose of a firm is to protect the fundamental interests of a firm, and the plans or goals of a firm are fundamental to these interests. Accounting, especially planning accounting forms concrete interests based on those fundamental interests. Moreover, the fundamental interests of a firm, that is, the purpose of a firm is also established based on planning accounting. Thus, accounting, especially planning accounting, calculates and organizes the interests of a firm. This function of calculating interests in accounting could be called "interests calculation." The above-mentioned function of planning accounting, that is, the organizing of the most favorable/advantageous structure of a firm is obviously the function of interests calculation. Fundamentally interests calculation means value judgment. Value judgment in planning accounting always needs evaluation of profit and loss, or, cost-benefit. This function means decision-making. Therefore, the function of accounting is compared to the work of the head or brain on a human body. It could be said that accounting carries the destiny of the firm on the shoulders.

35.5 Conclusion

In this paper, some basic characteristics of accounting as a whole were examined. In particular, the paper focused on the process of accounting as a whole. Previously, in accounting science, the idea of accounting as a whole has not been explained sufficiently, although financial accounting and managerial accounting are, in actuality, both part of accounting. There is a need to explain the characteristics of accounting as a whole, at least on a theoretical basis.

In this paper, the basic process of accounting is understood to be the cyclical process of the three processes/functions: planning, controlling and closing. Needless to say, these processes/functions are those which both financial accounting and managerial accounting have in common, and the function as a whole means management. Therefore, the management function cannot be kept separate from financial accounting, even though financial accounting is distinguished from managerial accounting. This is also because managerial accounting cannot help but include the problem/field of so-called financial accounting.

Moreover, the essential process among the three basic processes of accounting as a whole is understood to be the planning process. This is because the planning process is the most predominant process among the three basic processes, and can be independent of the others. The planning process is also essential because it has a direct relationship to the essential purpose of a firm. Therefore, the essential meaning of accounting is understood by the content of the planning function. Thus, the essential meaning of accounting is the organizing of the most favorable/advantageous structure of a firm. It is clear that this is also the essential purpose of accounting.

References

American Accounting Association (1966). A statement of basic accounting theory, Committee to Prepare A Statement of Basic Accounting Theory.

Anthony, R. N. (1964). *Management Accounting*, 3rd ed., R.D. Irwin, Inc.

Anthony, R. N. and Reece, J. S. (1975). *Management Accounting: Text and Cases*, 5th ed., R.D. Irwin, Inc.

Davidson, S., Stickney, C., and Weil, R. (1988). *Financial Accounting, An Introduction to Concepts, Methods, and Uses*, 5th ed., The Dryden Press.

Goldberg, L. (1965). *An Inquiry Into The Natue of Accounting*, American Accounting Association Monograph No.7.

Gordon, N. J. and Shillinglaw, G. (1974). *Accounting: A Management Approach*, 5th ed., R.D. Irwin.

Gray, J. and Johnston, K. S. (1977). *Accounting and Management Action*, 2nd ed., McGraw-Hill Book Company, Inc.

Horngren, C. T., Harrison Jr, W. T., and Bamber, L. S. (2002). *Accounting*, 5th ed., Prentice Hall International, Inc.

May, G. O. (1943). *Financial Accounting: A Distillation of Experience*, The Macmillan Company, New York.

Miyagami, K. (1969). *Fundamentals of Business Accounting*, Moriyamashoten.

Miyosawa, T. (2004). *Accounting*, Hosodaigaku Kyoikushinkoukai.

Miyosawa, T. (2005). *Accounting Process*, Chuokeizaisya.

Monden, Y. (2001). *Management Accounting*, Zeimukeirikyoukai.

Smith, A. C. and Ashburne, J. G. (1960). *Financial and Administrative Accounting*, McGraw-Hill Book Company, Inc.

CHAPTER

36

Japanese Divestiture Accounting in View of Business Reorganization

Nozomi Moue

Research Associate, Faculty of Business Administration
Mejiro University

36.1 Introduction

With the publication of the "Accounting Standard for Business Combinations" by the Business Accounting Council (of Japan) on October 31, 2003 as a momentum, research on business combination accounting in corporate reorganizations is gaining force. The main corporate reorganization techniques are divestiture and business combination. Properly speaking, the merger, acquisition, transfer of business and the exchange/transfer of stocks, all of which are means of combining businesses, and investment in kind, transfer of business and divestiture, all of which are means of divesting businesses, should be dealt with in a comprehensive manner, and the accounting procedures related thereto should conform to a uniform accounting standard.

In Europe and the United States, there is an accounting procedure for business combinations, but there is no accounting standard for divestitures. However, a divestiture is in fact a type of business combination from the standpoint of the newly established joint venture or the acquiring company. An accounting standard for divestitures has been established recently in Japan, and this should be used as the accounting standard for business combinations from the standpoint of the newly established joint venture or the acquiring company. Accordingly, in this paper, I would like to look into the concept of uniform accounting for business combinations, including divestitures, by examining the Japanese standard for divestiture accounting.

In discussing this topic, I will refer to the following documents which have been published by various organizations engaged in setting Japanese accounting standards:

1. Research report #7: "Accounting procedure for divestitures" (hereinafter referred to as "Research Report #7,") prepared by the Accounting System Commission and made public by the Japanese Institute of Certified Public Accountants (JICPA).
2. Exposure draft #5 on the business accounting standard: "Accounting standard (draft) for business separations" (hereinafter referred to as the "Draft Accounting Standard.")
3. Exposure draft #8 on the guideline for the application of the business accounting standard: the "Guideline (draft) for the application of the accounting standards for business combinations, business separations, etc." (hereinafter referred to as the "Draft Guideline.")

36.2 Business Combinations and Divestitures

36.2.1 *The relationship between business combinations and divestitures*

There are various corporate reorganization techniques, depending on the purpose of the reorganization. Research Report #7, made public by JICPA in 2001, has classified them systematically. The report lists the following as the main corporate reorganization techniques: (1) business combinations (integration type): merger, acquisition, transfers of business and exchange/transfer of stocks; and (2) business separations (disintegration type).

A review of the large literature on accounting shows that, of the two types (integration and disintegration) of techniques, the integration-type techniques are generally considered to be the object of business combination accounting, and considerably detailed standards are set therefore in the US and Japan as well as by the International Accounting Standards Board (IASB). On the other hand, the disintegration-type accounting techniques are not frequently mentioned in the US or by the IASB, although in Japan research reports and summaries thereon have been published.

Now, simply put, the various types of divestiture fall into the category of business combination, because, from the standpoint of the acquiring company (the existing company which takes over the separated business), two or more companies merge into one business entity, i.e., it is a disintegration of an organization from the standpoint of the dividing company, whereas it is a merger with another organization from the standpoint of the company taking over the separated business.

Tanaka (1999) has described this relationship, using the concept of "offsetting possibility based on a fundamental converse relation;"[1] he has resolved the basic structure of accounting into more fundamental systems, explaining that each accounting entity records its own side of the transaction, and that the two parties to the transaction form a complementary pair.[2] This "fundamental converse relation" theory proposed by Tanaka (1999) can provide the background for the theme of this paper, which is the concept of uniform accounting for business combinations, including divestitures, because a divestiture is also a business combination from the standpoint of the newly established joint venture or the acquiring company.

From this viewpoint, it can be said that the accounting procedures for company integrations (business combinations) and company disintegrations (divestitures) should be based on a uniform standard.

36.2.2 *Types of divestiture*

Divestiture is the process in which a company (the dividing company) separates off a specific division by detaching it from itself and transferring it to an exiting or a new company. There are various ways of detaching a division, including the transfer of business and investment in kind by a specific division stated above.

In the United States, divestiture means the disposal of the controlling interest in a division or a subsidiary company, and is classified into various types: (1) the transfer of business, in which the stock in the subsidiary company or the assets of the detached division are exchanged with other assets, such as cash, or used for the payment of debt; (2) spin-off, in which the stock in the subsidiary company is distributed to the parent company's own shareholders as dividend in kind; (3) split-off, in which the stock in the subsidiary company is distributed to the parent company's shareholders in exchange for the stock in the parent company; and (4) split-up, in which the

[1] Tanaka (1999), p. 14.

[2] Tanaka (1999), pp. 14–15. This view may contradict common belief. Therefore, further examination of this structural theory is necessary. However, I find such an idea attractive.

parent company is liquidated after the stocks in its subsidiary companies are distributed to the parent company's shareholders in exchange for the parent company's own stock.[3]

If this separation of business is referred to as "divestiture in a broad sense," it can be classified into "spin-out" and "divestiture in the narrow sense," depending on the way in which the stocks of the companies which are separated and transferred are handled.

The spin-out applies to the case where the dividing company surviving after the divestiture holds the stocks of the divided companies. In this case, the relationship between the dividing company and the divided companies is the relationship between a parent company and its subsidiary companies. The spin-out comprises two factors: the establishment of a subsidiary company and the transfer of a division thereto. On the other hand, the start of a new business through the establishment of a mere subsidiary company without the transfer of any division or the mere transfer of a division to an existing subsidiary company is sometimes called spin-out. Anyway, the spin-out means only the physical division of a company without the division of its shareholders, so it is sometimes called "physical division," "spin-out-type division" or "*de facto* division."[4]

On the other hand, divestiture in the narrow sense refers to cases in which the shareholders of the dividing company acquire the stock in the divided company. There are no capital ties between the dividing company and the divided company in the case where the dividing company survives, and between the two or more divided companies in the case where the dividing company disappears, and all of the stocks of these companies will be held by the shareholders of the dividing company. Accordingly, with divestiture in the narrow sense, the spin-out includes an element of distribution of the stock in the divided company to the shareholders of the dividing company. As just described, divestiture in the narrow sense comprises the division of the shareholders, or human division, as well as physical division through the spin-out. Therefore, it is also referred to as "human divestiture" or "divisional-type divestiture." The above-stated spin-off, split-off and split-up, as practiced in the United States, belong to this category.

[3]Cumming and Mallie (1999).
[4]Divestiture Workshop (1997).

36.2.3 *Types of divestiture and accounting procedure, as per Research Report #7 of the Accounting System Commission*

There are various types of divestiture, such as absorption-type division[5] and common incorporation-type division.[6] It can be said that, from the standpoint of the divided company, divestiture has the same features as business combination. Therefore, the accounting procedure for divestiture should be consistent with that for business combination.

If divestiture is a form of business combination, the applicable accounting procedure would depend on the type of transaction involved, that is, on the combination of interests or on the acquisition to which it corresponds. Regarding the accounting procedure for divestiture, Research Report #7, compiled by the Japanese Institute of Certified Public Accountants, argues that the "transaction processing method" or the "book-value takeover method" should be used.

The "transaction processing method" is an accounting method in which the assets and liabilities transferred as a result of a divestiture are considered to have been sold, and is applicable to cases in which the divestiture has been determined to be an acquisition for the acquiring company. In this method, as a rule the divided company evaluates the assets and liabilities taken over as of the date of division as per the cost of investment (sum total of the price and cost of the acquisition), and the book values of the assets and liabilities which were owned by the divided company before the division shall remain the same even after the division.

The "book-value takeover method" combines the book-value assets and liabilities held by each company, because the control exerted by each of the parties to the combination continues. Therefore, the transfer value becomes the book value of the assets and liabilities constituting the business transferred as a result of the divestiture.

Example 1: Business B of company X was transferred to company Y in exchange for the stock in company Y. The control exerted by company X (or its shareholders) over company Y continues because the scale of the capital stock of company Y before the transfer was smaller than that of business B which was taken over.

---

[5]A type of divestiture carried out through the transfer of the operation of an existing company.

[6]A type of divestiture in which two or more companies establish a new company by investing in kind and the operation is transferred thereto.

Balance sheet of company X

Assets of business A	340	Liabilities of business A	100
Assets of business B	140	Liabilities of business B	80
		Capital stock	160
		Capital reserve	30
		Profit reserve	10
		Surplus	100
	480		480

The book-value takeover method is applicable to this case, because the control exerted by the dividing company continues.

Company X (spin-out type)

(Debit) Liabilities of business B	80	(Credit) Assets of business B	140
Stock in company Y:	60		

Company Y (spin-out type)

(Debit) Assets of business B	140	(Credit) Liabilities of business B	80
		Capital stock	30
		Capital reserve	30

Company X (divisional type)

(Debit) Liabilities of business B	80	(Credit) Assets of business B	140
Capital stock	32		
Capital reserve	6		
Profit reserve	2		
Surplus	20		

Company Y (divisional type)

(Debit) Assets of Business B	140	(Credit) Liabilities of business B	80
		Capital stock	32
		Capital reserve	6
		Profit reserve	2
		Surplus	20

Example 2: In the above divestiture, if company X (or its shareholders) loses its control over company Y, which took over business B, the accounting procedure is as shown below because the scale of the capital stock of company Y before the transfer was far greater than that of business B which was taken over. However, the fair evaluation value of the stock in company Y received by company X in compensation therefore is 160, reflecting the market value, 240, of the assets of business B.

The transaction processing method is applicable to this case because the control over the divided company exerted by the dividing company is lost.

Company X (spin-out type)

(Debit)	Liabilities of business B	80	(Credit)	Assets of business B	140
	Stock in company Y	160		Transfer profit or loss	100

Company Y (spin-out type)

(Debit)	Assets of Business B	240	(Credit)	Liabilities of business B	80
				Capital stock	80
				Capital reserve	80

Company X (divisional type)

(Debit)	Liabilities of business B	80	(Credit)	Assets of business B	140
	Capital stock	48		Transfer profit or loss	100
	Capital reserve	9			
	Profit reserve:	3			
	Surplus	100			

Company Y (divisional type)

(Debit)	Assets of Business B	240	(Credit)	Liabilities of business B	80
				Capital stock	80
				Capital reserve	80

36.3 Accounting Procedure for Divestiture, with Emphasis on the "Accounting Standard (Draft) for Business Separations, etc." and the "Guideline (Draft) for the Application of the Accounting Standards for Business Combinations, Business Separations, etc."

36.3.1 *Background of the publication and the necessity of the accounting procedure for business separations, etc.*

The "Accounting Standard for Business Combinations" made public by the Business Accounting Council in October 2003 provides the background behind the publication of the draft standard, etc. According to the Accounting Standard for Business Combinations, the Accounting Standards Board of Japan (ASBJ) must ensure the application of concrete guidelines to daily business affairs. Regarding corporate reorganization, it stipulates that accounting methods such as the purchase method and pooling-of-interests method should be adopted by all parties to a business combination. However, in corporate reorganization, an accounting standard for business separations, etc. becomes necessary, because the accounting procedure on the part of the separating company (on the recognition of the transfer profit or loss) and the accounting procedure on the part of the shareholders of the combining companies (on the recognition of the exchange profit or loss) must be examined. Below, I will mainly analyze the accounting procedure on the part of the separating company.

36.3.2 Accounting procedure on the part of the separating company

It is not from the standpoint of the separating company but of the acquiring company that a divestiture is regarded as a business combination. But on what sort of theory should the accounting procedure on the part of the separating company rely in terms of the accounting for business combinations? I would like to examine this point further.

The Draft Accounting Standard uses an accounting procedure based on the Accounting Standard for Business Combinations. In ordinary accounting procedures, account processing takes place when goods are exchanged between a company and an outsider. However, in business combinations, since companies are dealt in instead of goods, it becomes necessary to determine whether the investment by shareholders as a whole is going on. Therefore, the Accounting Standard for Business Combinations deems that, from the standpoint of all shareholders involved in a given business combination, the party whose continuation of interest is interrupted liquidates the investment once and invests in the relevant assets and liabilities again, and the party whose interest continues is continuing its investment as before. As just described, the Accounting Standard for Business Combinations stipulates that, considering that the business combination has two economic factors, that is, the acquisition and the combination of interests, the purchase method is applicable to the former and the pooling-of-interests method is applicable to the latter, based on the concept of the continuation/non-continuation of interest.

Figure 36.1 illustrates this decision flow, which is original and unique to Japanese companies.

Now, depending on whether the investment is considered to continue or not, the transfer profit or loss may or may not be recognized on the side of the dividing company. The criterion of the Draft Accounting Standard

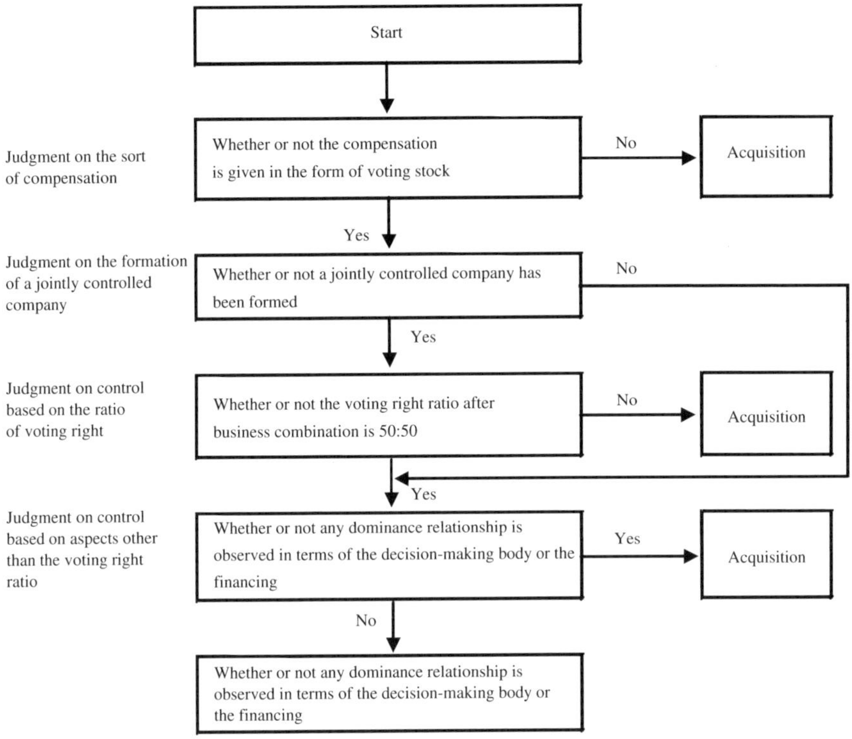

Fig. 36.1 A judgment of the acquisition or combination of interests

is whether the type of compensation differs from the character of the transferred business, based on the accounting procedure used in general trading and exchange. Furthermore, since the Accounting Standard for Business Combinations stipulates that the accounting procedure for transactions under common control be applied, the Draft Accounting Standard stipulates, for the sake of consistency, that the accounting procedure for the dividing company be based on the case in which the separated-business succeeding company falls under its subsidiary company. Therefore, the Draft Accounting Standard first classified the received compensation into the following three cases: (1) only property, such as cash; (2) only the stocks of the separated companies; and (3) property, such as cash, and the stocks of the separated companies. Then, it stipulated the accounting procedures, further classifying each of the three cases into the following three sub-cases: (1) the separated companies are subsidiary companies of the

Classification of separated-business succeeding company	Treatment in individual financial statements	Treatment in the consolidated financial statements
(1) Subsidiary company	Transfer profit or loss is not recognized.	The goodwill of the separated-business succeeding company acquired and the amount of change in interest of the transferred business are recognized.
(2) Associated company	Idem	Idem
(3) Others	Transfer profit or loss is recognized.	N/A

Fig. 36.2 Accounting method of the dividing company in the case where the received compensation comprises only the stock of the separated-business succeeding company

dividing company; (2) the separated companies are associated companies of the dividing company; and (3) the separated companies are neither (1) nor (2).

The main thing here is the compensation provided in the form of voting stock. In this case, if the separating company continues to own the separated-business succeeding company (or divided company) as a subsidiary company, the pooling-of-interests method applies, and thus no transfer profit or loss is recognized. (In consolidated accounting, however, it is natural that the goodwill and the difference in the fluctuation of interest are recorded on the consolidated balance sheet upon the assessment of the assets and liabilities of the separated-business succeeding company at the actual market values.)

Fig. 36.2 illustrates accounting method of the dividing company in the case where the received compensation comprises only the stock of the separated-business succeeding company.

36.4 Conclusion

As mentioned in the Introduction, in Europe and the United States, there is an accounting procedure for business combinations, but there is no accounting standard for divestitures. However, a divestiture is in fact a type of business combination from the standpoint of the newly established joint venture or the acquiring company. An accounting standard for divestitures has been established recently in Japan, and this should be used as the accounting standard for business combinations from the standpoint of the newly established joint venture or the acquiring company. Accordingly, in this paper, I looked into the concept of uniform accounting for business combinations, including divestitures, by examining the Japanese standard for divestiture accounting.

In the conclusion, the matters elucidated hereinbefore will be summarized and then the details of the originality of the Japanese accounting standards for business combinations, etc., will be made clear.

First, the "fundamental converse relation" theory proposed by Tanaka (1999) can provide the background for the theme of this paper, which is the concept of uniform accounting for business combinations, including divestitures, because a divestiture is also a business combination from the standpoint of the newly established joint venture or the acquiring company.

However, there are cases where a company within a consolidated entity establishes a subsidiary company through the separation of a business. Also, the integration of similar businesses engaged in a group of companies into a subsidiary company with the aim of pursuing the economy of scale of the relevant businesses is frequently observed. The technique of divestiture is used here as well. However, regarding such business separation within a consolidated entity, the transferred business should be evaluated by the pooling-of-interests method, because the parent company continues to control, in terms of capital stock, the company taking over the relevant business. The continuation of control is the basic principle involved in the evaluation of the business at the book value. In this case, no transfer profit or loss due to the business transfer is generated in the dividing company.

Next, as I mentioned, in a divestiture in which another company takes over a separated business through a merger or more than one company establishes a joint venture, the divestiture is a business combination from the standpoint of these companies taking over the business or businesses. In this case, if the dividing company or its shareholders have no control in terms of capital stock or no *de facto* control over the acquiring company (that is, the control is not continuous), the relevant transferred business can be regarded as acquired from the standpoint of the acquiring company. Accordingly, it is appropriate to evaluate the transferred business at a fair acquisition value (market value); this means that it should be evaluated using the purchase method. In the transaction, the transfer profit or loss is recognized on the part of the dividing company.

Also, in the very rare case where none of the dividing companies established by the above-mentioned new joint venture has control in terms of capital stock or *de facto* control over that joint venture, it can be said that the dividing companies jointly own their respective interests therein, join their respective interests together or continue owning their respective interests therein. If this is the case, no transfer profit or loss is recognized on the part of the dividing companies because the transferred business is evaluated using the pooling-of-interests method.

Furthermore, by way of a supplement, in the case where any property other than the stock (e.g., cash) is used as compensation for the transferred business, the company which took over the business evaluates it using the purchase method, deeming that the company acquired the business in a normal transfer of business which is considered to be the same as an ordinary sales transaction of goods between companies. As a matter of course, the transfer profit or loss is recognized on the part of the dividing company, as in the case of a sales transaction of goods.

Even in this case, if the separating company continues to hold the separated-business succeeding company (or divided company, or acquiring company) as a subsidiary company, no transfer profit or loss is recognized in the pooling-of-interests method. (In consolidated accounting, however, it is natural that the goodwill and the difference in the fluctuation of interest are recorded on the consolidated balance sheet upon the assessment of the assets and liabilities of the separated-business succeeding company at the actual market values.)

In the above description, the concepts of "acquisition" and "joining together of the respective interests" are converted into the two assessment methods, the purchase method and the pooling-of-interests method, respectively. The two concepts and the corresponding two assessment methods which are used in their respective proper ways were originally adopted in APB Opinion No. 16 of "Business Combinations" published by the APB in 1970 in the United States, and these have been used for nearly 30 years since then. However, in the international accounting standard and the US accounting standard, business combinations which essentially correspond to acquisitions were frequently categorized, in practice, under the concept of "joining together of the respective interests," and thus the pooling-of-interests method began to be misused. Therefore, the pooling-of-interests method was prohibited and the policy of using the purchase method without exception was adopted, instead of judging which method is in accordance with the reality of each business combination. The reason for this misuse of the pooling-of-interests method is that, from the viewpoint of improving the profitability of companies, in general the profit on the profit-and-loss statement becomes smaller with the purchase method, in which the assets and liabilities of the acquired companies are taken over at the actual market values, than with the pooling-of-interests method, in which they are taken over at the book values, due to (1) the increase in depreciation costs; and (2) the additional burden of goodwill amortization, etc.

The important aspect is the joining together of the respective interests of the parties. In real transactions, cases where the continuation of interests of both shareholder sides (both parties to the business combination) is observed cannot be said to be extreme or very rare; one can even say that such cases are frequently observed. These are the cases in which the pooling-of-interests method is misused. However, even if the pooling-of-interests method is prohibited in order to prevent its misuse, and only the purchase method is allowed, contrivances on the part of management are possible. That is, management may yield to the temptation of arbitrarily designating the side which carries the greater effect as a result of the reevaluation at the market value as the acquired company; that is, the so-called "reverse acquisition" state may be arbitrarily induced.

In order to prevent management from yielding to this temptation, the Japanese accounting standards for business combinations, etc., have their own criteria to clearly determine whether the stockholder equity of each party to the business combination continues (without control) or the shareholders of one of the parties establish control. The originality of the Japanese accounting standards for business combinations, etc., lies in this. However, it should be remarked that even under the Japanese standards, the purchase method still applies to most business combinations and divestitures.

References

Accounting Standards Board of Japan (2005). Accounting standard for business separation, etc., draft. (in Japanese)

Accounting Standards Board of Japan (2005). The guideline for the application of the accounting standards for business combinations, business separations, etc., draft. (in Japanese)

Accounting System Commission, Japanese Institute of Certified Public Accountants (2001). Research report #7: Accounting procedure for divestitures. (in Japanese)

Business Accounting Council (2003). *Accounting Standard for Business Combinations.* (in Japanese)

Cumming, J. and Mallie, T. Y. (1999). Accounting for divestitures: a comparison of sell-offs, split-offs and split-ups, *Issues in Accounting Education* 14-1. http://www.asb.or.jp/

Daigo, S. (1980). Basic structure of the accounting for divestitures, *Industrial Accounting* 40-7. (in Japanese).

Daigo, S. (2003). *Close-up Today's Accounting 1: Accounting for Business Reorganizations*, Tokyo-keizaijoho-shuppan. (in Japanese)

Kurokawa, Y. (2001). Accounting for business combinations and divestitures, *Business Accounting* 53-8. (in Japanese)

Ogawa, K. (2001). Profit recognition in divestitures, *Business Accounting* 53-8. (in Japanese)

Tanaka, S. (1999). *Deep-structure Theory of Accounting*, Chuo University Publishing Dep. (in Japanese)

Workshop on Business Finance System (1999). *Points at Issue on Business Combination Accounting; Separate-volume Data.* (in Japanese)

Workshop on Divestitures (1997). Legal study of divestitures, *Financial Study* 16-1. (in Japanese)

Index

About the Volume Editors

Yasuhiro Monden

Professor and Dean of Faculty of Business Administration, Mejiro University, Tokyo, Japan
Professor-Emeritus of Tsukuba University, Tsukuba-shi, Japan
President, Monden Institute of Management (http://mondeninst.hp.infoseek. co.jp/)
Majoring in Operations Management, Managerial Accounting, and Corporate Finance
BA from Kwansei Gakuin University, MBA from Kobe University, Ph.D. from Tsukuba University

Main publications

Toyota Production System, 1st edition. Industrial Engineering and Management Press 1983 (awarded Nikkei Prize in 1984).
Toyota Production System, 3rd edition. Industrial Engineering and Management Press 1998.
Japanese Management Accounting, Productivity Press 1989.
Cost Reduction System: Target Costing and Kaizen Costing, Productivity Press 1996.
Japanese Cost Management, Imperial College Press 2000.

Kanji Miyamoto

Professor of Faculty of Corporate Intelligence, Osaka Gakuin University, Osaka, Japan
Majoring in International Management Accounting

BA from Kwansei Gakuin University, MBA from Kwansei Gakuin University, MBA from Michigan State University, Ph.D. from Kwansei Gakuin University

Main publications

Fundamentals of International Managerial Accounting, Chuoukeizai-sha, Inc. 1983 (in Japanese).
Managerial Accounting in Multinational Enterprises, Chuoukeizai-sha, Inc. 1989 (in Japanese).
Managerial Accounting in Global Enterprises, Chuoukeizai-sha, Inc. 2003 (in Japanese).

Kazuki Hamada

Professor of Department of Commerce, Seinan Gakuin University, Fukuoka, Japan
Majoring in Managerial Accounting, Operations Research, and Financial Statement Analysis
BA from Kwansei Gakuin University, MBA from Kwansei Gakuin University, Ph.D. from Tsukuba University

Main publications

"Profit Management at Kyocera Corporation: The Amoeba System," Chap. 12 in Monden, Y. & Sakurai, M., eds., *Japanese Management Accounting*, Productivity Press 1989.
"Target Costing and Kaizen Costing in the Japanese Automobile Companies," *Journal of Management Accounting Research*, Vol. 3, 1992, 16–34, (co-authored with Monden, Y.).
Evolution of Management Accounting Method, Chuoukeizai-sha 1998 (in Japanese).
"A Method for Simultaneously Achieving Cost Reduction and Quality Improvement," "A Management System for the Simultaneous Attainment of Customer Satisfaction and Employee Satisfaction," Chap. 7 and Chap. 19 in Monden, Y., ed., *Japanese Cost Management*, Imperial College Press 2000.

Gunyung Lee

Professor of Faculty of Economics, Niigata University, Niigata-city, Japan
Majoring in Managerial Accounting
BA from Sogang University, Korea, Ph.D. from Tsukuba University

Main publications

Strategic Process Management (Research Project Series No. 4), Japanese Association of Management Accounting 2006 (in Japanese).
"Japanese Management Style in Achieving the Cost Reduction Targets," Chap. 18, in Monden, Y., ed., *Japanese Cost Management*, Imperial College Press 2000, 397–415.
Cost Management in Korea, Honmunsa 1995 (in Korean).

Takayuki Asada

Professor of Graduate School of Economics, Osaka University, Osaka, Japan
Majoring in Management Accounting
BA from Osaka University, MBA from Kobe University, Dr. of Business Administration from Kobe University
Paper Award of IMA in 2002 (Institute of Management Accountants, USA)
Association Award of JAA in 1994 (Japan Accounting Association)

Main publications

Inter-Firms Management Accounting, Donbunkan Publisher 2005 (in Japanese).
Project Balanced Score-card, Seisan-sei Publisher 2004 (in Japanese).
"A Study on Strategic Management Control as a Driver of Environmental New Product Development," *The Journal of Management Accounting, Japan*, Vol. 14, No. 1, 2005 (in Japanese).
"The Relationship between Financial Centralization and Management Accounting: A Questionnaire Survey of Japan-Based Multinational Enterprises," *Asian Pacific Management Review*, Vol. 7, No. 1, 2002.